Systems of Logic

SYSTEMS OF LOGIC

Norman M. Martin

Department of Philosophy
University of Texas at Austin

The right of the University of Cambridge to print and sell all manner of books was granted by Henry VIII in 1534. The University has printed and published continuously since 1584.

CAMBRIDGE UNIVERSITY PRESS

Cambridge
New York Port Chester Melbourne Sydney

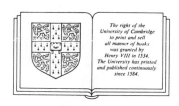

Published by the Press Syndicate of the University of Cambridge
The Pitt Building, Trumpington Street, Cambridge CB2 1RP
40 West 20th Street, New York, NY 10011, USA
10 Stamford Road, Oakleigh, Melbourne 3166, Australia

First published 1989

Printed in the United States of America

Library of Congress Cataloging-in-Publication Data

Martin, Norman M.
Systems of logic / Norman M. Martin.
p. cm.
Bibliography: p.
ISBN 0–521–36589–9. ISBN 0–521–36770–0 (pbk.)
1. Logic, Symbolic and mathematical. I. Title.
BC135.M325 1989
160–dc19 88–7893
CIP

British Library Cataloguing in Publication Data

Martin, Norman M.
Systems of logic
1. Logic
I. Title
160

ISBN 0–521–36589–9 hard covers
ISBN 0–521–36770–0 paperback

In memory of

Michael John Edward Martin (1963 –1981)

Contents

Preface

This book is a textbook on logic. It does, however, differ in a number of respects from the greater number of its sister textbooks with which the reader may be familiar, including, very probably, the one used in the reader's first course in logic. In the first place, it is not entitled "introduction to" or any of its total or partial synonyms, such as "elements," "fundamentals," or the like. While there are several reasons for this, the most important one is that it is not an introduction, but is written primarily with an eye to students who have already been introduced to the subject, presumably in the form of a college course in modern, or symbolic, logic (there is a sense in which it is nevertheless an introduction, but that would be hair-splitting). By and large, the main (and important) purpose of such courses, and consequently of texts appropriate to them, is to teach students how to use a certain technique, modern formal logic, in the evaluation of arguments and, while doing so, to introduce some of the concepts and theory of modern logic. In consequence, most of these books rightly devote a considerable portion of their material to, for instance, the problem of translating arguments from colloquial language into the formal system or systems used (in some cases, where the course or book is intended primarily for mathematicians, common mathematical language, which is often indeed more closely related to the formal systems, is the main object of comparison, instead of "natural" language). In contradistinction to this, our main interest will be the characteristics of systems which are generally similar to those which form the basis of such an elementary course or its textbook.

Accordingly, one might say that this is a book about, rather than of, logic. Since the twenties it has been more or less customary to call a language (or part of one) used to characterize another language, a **metalanguage** and the language or system thus characterized the **object language**; and in general, to use the prefix **meta-** to characterize studies with such second-order purposes ("metaphysics", being a much older term, is of course an exception). Using this terminology, this book is thus deliberately metalogical. It has also (since the forties) come to be customary to divide what might be called metalogic into three divisions, called, following Charles W. Morris, "pragmatics", "semantics" and "syntax" (or "syntactics"). While I have no objection to this division as indicative of one or another variety of emphasis of the particular study, I am somewhat less inclined than some to absolutize it. Presumably, syntax refers to those features which can be handled in abstraction from both the meaning of the signs and the uses to which they are put, semantics to those that include meaning considerations but abstract from use, and pragmatics to the remainder. If we allow for the fact that there are areas of interest which, depending on our emphasis, could be considered as on either side of the boundaries thus demarcated, which unlike old-fashioned European national boundaries do not have neat customs houses and striped barriers clearly marking the passage from one to another, we can, I think, accept the division for the present. In these terms, our treatment can be said to be primarily syntactical in character, although we will from time to time introduce some notions that are arguably semantic (or less frequently, even pragmatic). In most cases we shall characterize these notions so that they are capable of being considered primarily syntactical; that is, we will examine relations between two formal systems, one of which has a "natural" interpretation as a semantic system, but the characteristics actually used for that system are described in formal terms and hence it could alternatively be viewed as simply another formal system. In such cases, the real interest in the system may come from its semantic possibilities, but by virtue of the formulation, these become extraneous to the proofs, which hold even if such a system is considered to have an interpretation other than the most natural one. The main reason for this type of procedure, which may well strike the reader as peculiar (in a sense it is like playing roulette with chips without saying whether or not they will be cashed), is that it allows us to get on with the game while retaining a greater degree of neutrality with regard to the semantical and pragmatical issues which underlie many of the disputes in the philosophy of logic. It is not our contention that these issues are not worthy of consideration, but rather that by and large, we are not interested in considering them in this book. With regard to a few of them, there will be some discussion (perhaps more out of human weakness than expository necessity) primarily in chapter 15 below. On the whole, however, we shall preserve an attitude of relative neutrality, so that the results rest on a minimum of philosophical presumptions.

For those using this as a textbook in the narrower sense, or are otherwise relatively less experienced, it is desirable to note that the terms are introduced in, so to speak, their logically, rather than psychologically, natural order. In this connection, it is likely to be useful to read chapter 4 and perhaps chapter 5 and 6, before studying the first three chapters in full detail. Many of the concepts found in these early chapters have good "natural" examples in the systems we examine but in order to be able to introduce these concepts in the very general framework we desire, it would be very inconvenient to introduce the examples at that time.

Before starting the text it is fitting that I express my general indebtedness to the many people, colleagues and students who have helped and encouraged me during the many years that this work has been in preparation, but especially the sources and inspiration of so much of my thought: Rudolf Carnap, Stephen C. Kleene, Evert W. Beth, Alonzo Church, and Alfred Tarski. In addition I should like to thank Prof. Ignazio Angellelli for reviewing a significant part of the work; I am also indebted to four of my students, Al Carruth, M. Richard Diaz, Bernhard von Stengel, and Hardy Tichenor, for countless hours spent discussing and reviewing portions of the text. In addition, I would like to express my appreciation to Emilia R. Martin, both for typing the earlier drafts of this book and for helping edit this version of it, as well as for providing me the encouragement without which this book would never have come to be.

1
Formal Systems and Structure Theory

An essential characteristic of the systems which we are going to introduce is the fact that they are finite sequences of sets satisfying a certain principle of composition. The reader will note in the following that, usually, the particular nature of the sets which form the sequences is not essential. Specifically, we will define a **zero-order system** as an infinite family of decidable sets S_i ($i = 0,1,2,\cdots$). We will term the union of the S_i (i.e., the set of those elements that are elements of an S_i), S and we can formally define:

$$S = \cup S_i \; (i \in \mathbf{N})$$

To qualify as a zero-order system, two further conditions must be satisfied:

c1. If $i \neq j$, $S_i \cap S_j = \varnothing$ (i.e., nothing is in more than one S_i)

c2. If x, $y \in S$, $x \neq y$ and y is a sequence, then x is not an initial segment of y.

Depending on the details of the theory of classes we assume, c2 may be dispensable. Its function is to ensure that every finite sequence of elements of S is uniquely decomposable. If A, AB, BC and C were all elements of S, ABC could presumably be decomposed as AB followed by C or as A followed by BC. In some ways of interpreting classes, these sequences could be interpreted so that they are distinct; in such a case, c2 would presumably be redundant. However, in order to make our definition independent of the fine detail of our set theory, we adopt c2 nonetheless.

Let S' be the sequence $S_0, S_1, S_2, \cdots$. (More formally, S' is a set of ordered pairs whose first elements are sets and whose second are natural numbers such that if $< A,i > \in S'$ and $< B,i > \in S'$, then $A = B$ and distinct first elements satisfy c1 and c2.) We can now define $\sigma_{S\cap}$, the set of finite sequences of elements of S. We will say that a set T has property $\mathcal{T}_{S\cap}$ if and only if (iff) it satisfies the following conditions:

1. The null sequence, $\varnothing$, is an element of T ($\varnothing \in T$)
2. If there exists an i such that $x \in S_i$, then $x \in T$.
3. If $y \in T$ and $x \in S_i$, for some i, then there is a $z \in T$ such that $z =$

$x^\frown y$ (which we will normally write xy).

Then we can define $\sigma_{S\frown}$ (the set of finite sequences of elements of S or **formulae**) as:

$\sigma_{S\frown} = \bigcap T$ (T has the property $\mathcal{T}_{S\frown}$).

Strictly speaking, $\sigma_{S\frown}$ is a function of S and of the meaning assigned to "follows" ($^\frown$); but only if $^\frown$ satisfies the following conditions for all values:

F1. $\varnothing^\frown A = A^\frown\varnothing = A$

F2. If $A \neq B$, $A \neq \varnothing$, $B \neq \varnothing$, then $A^\frown B \neq B^\frown A$, for all A and B in S.

F3. $A^\frown(B^\frown C) = (A^\frown B)^\frown C$

F4. $A^\frown B^\frown C = A^\frown D^\frown C$, iff $B = D$

F5. If $A \subset S$, $B \subset S$ and $A \neq B$, then $A^\frown D \neq B^\frown C$.

The reader will note that many relations between many kinds of elements will satisfy F1-F5, but in our later text we will not specify which of these relations we use. Also that when, later on, we have occasion to speak of "sequence of sequences", "sequence of sequences of sequences", it is neither affirmed nor denied that the notion of "following" which is then used is in each case the same, but only that in each case F1-F5 are satisfied. We shall, in our examples, use linear (left to right) order of certain marks for first level sequences, a vertical ordering down the page for second order sequences, and additional columns at sufficient distance for third level ones, but these specific choices are only for the sake of convenience.

We now define a property C applicable to elements of $\sigma_{S\frown}$.

1. If $x \in S_0$, then x has property C.
2. If $f \in S_k$ $(k > 0)$ and $x_1,\cdots,x_k$ have property C, then $fx_1\cdots x_k$ has property C.

We then define W_S to be the intersection of all sets of elements of $\sigma_{S\frown}$ which have property C.

Following the terminology applied in the most familiar type of zero-order system, we will in the future call elements of S **symbols** and elements of W_S **well-formed formulae** (**wffs** for short). The reader should be warned that we have not used any of the properties of symbols in the ordinary sense (except that they can be members of certain sets), nor shall we, so that "symbol" and "wff" are being used in a very abstract, perhaps peculiarly denatured sense.

In this connection, it is worth remarking that much of the customary terminology of modern logic is strongly affected by the linguistic views of some of the most prominent contributors to the field, such as Frege, Russell, and Carnap. In this book, we will not try either to defend these views or to subject them to thorough criticism. Nonetheless, the formulations of this book neither presuppose these views nor require that they be rejected. This happy situation (which we believe to be of some philosophical significance) is due largely to the somewhat abstract standpoint adopted. It does, however, have some unpleasant terminological consequences. Since the terminology commonly used is influenced by these linguistic views, we frequently have to choose between inventing new terms with the risk of being incomprehensible, or else using the customary terms with the risk of, at least, being misleading, and, at worst, reinforcing the Fregean-Logical Positivist family of views (by, so to speak, "brainwashing"). Since we regard these views as debatable rather than established, we would consider this to be unfortunate.

Faced with this choice, we have, as the reader will see, temporized. Where an alternative usage is available which is free of these philosophical implications, we have chosen it. Therefore, we will generally refer to "structure theory" and "proof theory" rather than "syntax", and also "model theory" rather than "semantics" (following Kleene). Similarly, we have chosen to use the term "first-order" instead of "lower predicate" or its variants with regard to calculi and logics and even, by analogy, "zero-order" instead of "propositional" or "sentential," to refer to those calculi whose only variables have wffs as substituends. (This characterization is used for identification; our formal definitions will come later.) On the other hand, we have preserved the common terms "symbol", "formula", "predicate," "variable," and the like, despite the fact that our definitions do not imply, as the terms themselves suggest, that they are linguistic or that they are symbolic in the Peirce-Mead sense of referring to something else. This philosophic semantic reticence should not be taken as insisting that one **cannot** so interpret them, but only that one need not do so. The reader should be careful when understanding our concepts -- and using them -- not to smuggle into them features suggested by the more usual meanings of the terms employed. We shall endeavor to give explicit warnings when this seems appropriate.

In the succeeding text, we shall be interested in characterizing in very general terms the elements or building blocks which go into the construction of a logical system (**structure theory**), the notions of derivation and proof and the comparative relations between systems (**proof theory**), the notions of interpretation and satisfaction and the resulting notions of implication (or entailment) and equivalence (**model theory**), and the interrelations of the three. In addition, we will apply the resulting concepts in our examination of a number of logical systems, guided in our choice by several kinds of pragmatic motivations, which should be clear as we go along. Considerations of space and simplicity prevent our exploring more than a few possibilities. In our treatment, we shall be more thorough with regard to zero-order systems (and among them, the non-modal ones), although we shall include a partial treatment of some other systems as well. Unless specifically stated otherwise, omissions are dictated by space, convenience, and to a degree, our judgment as to what is easier to learn first and do not suggest that systems and topics not covered are unimportant.

Somewhat similar considerations of convenience have influenced us in our decision to omit first and higher order concepts from our initial presentation of structure and proof theory and to limit our first treatment of model theory to extensional methods. When in our later discussions the earlier presentations are used, we will say so.

For our presentation we will need several concepts from elementary mathematics. Suppose there is a property P of natural numbers such that:

α. 0 has property $\mathcal{P}$

β. For any number n, if n has property $\mathcal{P}$, then so does n+1; under these conditions, a form of reasoning which is termed **mathematical induction** (or, more specifically, **weak induction**) allows us to conclude

Every number has property $\mathcal{P}$.

We shall not attempt to prove this form of reasoning, but simply adopt it without further ado. For those who are not familiar with it and possibly worried by its adoption, it may be helpful to point out that each particular case subsumed under the general conclusion asserts that $\mathcal{P}$ holds for some particular finite number k. Premise α asserts $\mathcal{P}$ of 0. Then by β, $\mathcal{P}$ holds of 1. By the same argument, also of 2, and of 3, and of 4, and so on. But no matter how large k may be, if it is (as we have stated) a finite number, we can eventually count up to it, so that the argument will eventually get us to assert that k has property $\mathcal{P}$ (without specific use of induction).

An alternative form, frequently called **strong induction**, and equivalent to the preceding for finite numbers, consists of the premise:

For every finite number k, if n has property $\mathcal{P}$ for all numbers n ($0 \leq n < k$), then k has property $\mathcal{P}$;

and the conclusion:

Every number has property $\mathcal{P}$.

We will, where convenient, use this form as well. We can of course present the same kind of argument as before. Drawing then a figurative deep breath, we return to the consideration of zero-order systems:

We now define a function on $\sigma_{S\frown}$, whose values are natural numbers and which may be informally considered the **length of** or the **number of symbols in** an element of $\sigma_{S\frown}$. The function $\ell(x)$ with the domain $\sigma_{S\frown}$ is defined, as follows:

1. $\ell(\varnothing) = 0$
2. $\ell(xy) = 1 + \ell(y)$, provided $x \in S$

It follows trivially that $\ell(x) = 0$ if and only if $x = \varnothing$ and as a result, $\ell(x) = 1$ if and only if $x \in S$. Hence if neither x nor y is the empty sequence $\varnothing$, $\ell(xy) > \ell(x)$ and $\ell(xy) > \ell(y)$. Given sequences x and y, we say that x is an **initial segment** of y provided there exists a sequence z in $\sigma_{S\frown}$ such that $y = xz$.

We will now prove a number of basic theorems:

Theorem 1-1. If x and y are in $\sigma_{S\frown}$ then xy is in $\sigma_{S\frown}$.

Proof: By induction on $\ell(x)$:

(α) $\ell(x) = 0$. Then $x = \varnothing$ by the definition of ℓ. Hence $xy = \varnothing y = y$, by F1. Since $xy = y$ and $y \in \sigma_{S\frown}$, $xy \in \sigma_{S\frown}$.

(β) Assume the theorem is true for all z with $z \in \sigma_{S\frown}$ and $\ell(z) < k$. Suppose $\ell(x) = k > 0$. Then there exist v and w such that $v \in S$, $w \in \sigma_{S\frown}$ and $x = vw$. Then $xy = (vw)y = v(wy)$, by F3 . Then $\ell(wy) = k-1$ and hence $wy \in \sigma_{S\frown}$ and therefore $xy \in \sigma_{S\frown}$.

Theorem 1-2. If $x_1,\cdots,x_k \in \sigma_{S\frown}$, then so is $x_1\cdots x_k$.

Proof: By induction on k:

(α) For $k = 1$, there is nothing to prove

(β) Assume the theorem is true for $k = n$. We will prove it for

$k = n+1$. By the hypothesis of induction, $x_1 \cdots x_n \in \sigma_{S\cap}$. Hence, by theorem 1-1, $x_1 \cdots x_n x_{n+1} \in \sigma_{S\cap}$.

Theorem 1-3. Let x, y, z, w be elements of $\sigma_{S\cap}$ and $xz = yw$. Then either x is an initial segment of y or y of x.

Proof: By induction on $\ell(x)$:

(α) If $\ell(x) = 0$, then $x = \varnothing$ and hence $y = \varnothing y = xy$.

(β) Assume the theorem holds for all v with $\ell(v) < k$. Prove that it holds for x with $\ell(x) = k$. Since x and y are elements of $\sigma_{S\cap}$, there must exist $t \in S$ and $u \in \sigma_{S\cap}$ such that $x = tu$, and also $q \in S$ and $r \in \sigma_{S\cap}$ such that $y = qr$. Thus $(tu)z = (qr)w$. Hence by F3, $t(uz) = q(rw)$. By F5, it follows that $t = q$ and hence by F4, $uz = rw$. Since $\ell(u) < \ell(x)$, the induction hypothesis implies u is an initial segment of r, or r of u. Consequently tu is an initial segment of tr or vice versa and since $x = tu$ and $y = q\,r = t\,r$, x is an initial segment of y, or vice versa.

Theorem 1-4. If S is a zero-order system, $x \in W_S$ and $xy \in W_S$, then $y = \varnothing$.

Proof: By induction on $\ell(x)$:

(α) If $\ell(xy) > \ell(x)$ and $x \in W_S$, $\ell(x) \geq 1$. Let $\ell(x) = 1$. Then $x \in S_0$. If $xy \in S_0$, $xy = fz_1 \cdots z_k$ and $f \in S_k$. But then by c2, $x = f$, so that $k = 0$ and $y = \varnothing$. If, however, $xy \in S_0$, $\ell(xy) = 1$. Since $\ell(xy) = 1 + \ell(y)$, $\ell(y) = 0$. Thus $y = \varnothing$.

(β) Suppose the theorem is true for $\ell(x) < k^*$. We prove it for x' and y' such that $\ell(x') = k^* > 1$. Then $\ell(x'y') \geq \ell(x') > 1$. Hence $x' = fz_1 \cdots z_k$ with $f \in S_k$, $z_1, \cdots, z_k \in W_S$ and $x'y' = gy_1 \cdots y_j$ with $g \in S_j$ and $y_1, \cdots, y_j \in W_S$, then $x'y' = gy_1 \cdots y_j = fz_1 \cdots z_k y'$ and by c2, $f = g$ and hence $j = k$. Let i be the first index (if any) such that $z_i + y_i$. Then $z_i \cdots z_k y' = y_i \cdots y_k$. Since $\ell(z_i) < \ell(x') = k^*$ and by the hypothesis of induction z_i cannot be an initial segment of y_i. Since, however, z_i is an initial segment of $y_i \cdots y_k$ then y_i is an initial segment of z_i by theorem 1-3, but then $\ell(y_i) = \ell(z_i) < k^*$ and as above y_i cannot be an initial segment of z_i. Hence $x' = fz_1 \cdots z_k = gy_1 \cdots y_k = x'y'$. Since $x'\varnothing\varnothing = x'y'\varnothing$, we have $y' = \varnothing$ by F4.

These results lead to the following rather far-reaching theorem:

Theorem 1-5.(**Unique Decomposition Theorem for Well-Formed Formulae**) Let $x_1, \cdots, x_j, y_1, \cdots, y_k \in W_S$, $f \in S_j$, $g \in S_k$, and $fx_1 \cdots x_j = gy_1 \cdots y_k$. Then $j = k$, $f = g$ and $x_i = y_i$ for $i = 1, \cdots, j$.

Proof: By induction on $\ell(fx_1 \cdots x_j)$:

(α) $\ell(fx_1 \cdots x_j) = 1$. Then $fx_1 \cdots x_j \in S_0$, $gy_1 \cdots y_k \in S_0$ and hence $j = k = 0$ and $f = g$.

(β) Assume the theorem is true for all x' such that $x' \in W_S$ and $\ell(x') < k^*$. Let $\ell(fx_1 \cdots x_j) = k^*$. By F5, $f = g$ and hence $j = k$ by C1. Let i be the least natural number such that $x_i \neq y_i$. If i exists, let $x_{i+1} \cdots x_k$ be X and $y_{i+1} \cdots y_k$ be Y. Then $x_i X = y_i Y$ by F4 and hence by theorem 1-3, either x_i is an initial segment of y_i or vice versa. By theorem 1-4, neither can be the case. If i doesn't exist, there is nothing more to prove.

The Unique Decomposition Theorem guarantees the uniqueness of the way any wff can be decomposed into partial wffs. One consequence of it that will be useful is:

Theorem 1-6. Let $x, v \in W_S$, $y, z, w \in \sigma_{S\cap}$ and $xy = zvw$. Then either zv is an initial segment of x or x is an initial segment of z.

Proof: By theorem 1-3, either zv is an initial segment of x or x of zv. Let us assume that the former fails and hence the latter holds. Then we show that x is an initial segment of z. By induction on $\ell(x)$:

(α) Assume $\ell(x) = 1$. Suppose $z \neq \varnothing$. Hence there is a t and a u such that $t \in S$ and $u \in \sigma_{S\cap}$ and $z = tu$. Thus $xy = tuvw$ and $x = t$, and x is an initial segment of z. If $z = \varnothing$, $xy = vw$ and since by assumption v (which is zv) is not an initial segment of x, x is an initial segment of v by theorem 1-3. Hence there is a t in $\sigma_{S\cap}$ such that $v = xt$ and $t = \varnothing$ by theorem 1-4, so that $zv\varnothing = zv = v = x$ and

zv is, contrary to assumption, an initial segment of x.
(β) Assume the theorem holds for all $x' \in W_S$ such that $\ell(x') < k^*$. Assume $\ell(x) = k^* > 1$. Then there exist k, f and $x_1,\cdots,x_k$ such that $f \in Sk$ and $x_1,\cdots,x_k \in W_S$ and $x = fx_1\cdots x_k$ by theorem 1-5. Since x is an initial segment of zw there exists a t in $\sigma_{S\cap}$ such that $fx_1\cdots x_k t$ = zv. Hence by theorem 1-3, $fx_1\cdots x_k$ is an initial segment of z (in which case the proof is done) or z is an initial segment of $fx_1\cdots x_k$. Assume the latter. If $z = \emptyset$, x is an initial segment of v and hence by theorem 1-4, x = v = zv and therefore zv is an initial segment of x contrary to assumption. If $z \neq \emptyset$, there exist u and p such that $u \in S$, $p \in \sigma_{S\cap}$ and z = up. Then $fx_1\cdots x_k t = upv$ and hence f = u and $x_1\cdots x_k t = pv$. Let j be the least natural number such that $x_1\cdots x_j$ is not an initial segment of p. If j doesn't exist, then x is an initial segment of fp = up = z and the proof is done. Assume that j exists. Then $x_1\cdots x_{j-1}$ is an initial segment of p (when j = 0, $x_1\cdots x_{j-1}$ is taken to be $\emptyset$). Therefore, there is a $q \in \sigma_{S\cap}$ such that $x_1\cdots x_{j-1}q = p$. Hence, $x_1\cdots x_{j-1}\ x_j\cdots x_k t = x_1\cdots x_{j-1}qv$ and by F4, $x_j\cdots x_k t = qv$. It follows by theorem 1-3 that q is an initial segment of x_j. Since, however, $\ell(xj) < k^*$, and $qv = qv\emptyset$ and $xj \in W_S$ and $v \in W_S$, by the hypothesis of induction, qv is an initial segment of x, contrary to assumption, or xj is an initial segment of q contrary to assumption. It follows that no such j could exist and hence x is an initial segment of z.

We will now define an operator on W_S which is intended to produce the result of uniformly substituting one wff for another in a wff. It will be denoted $\mathbf{S}^{A}_{B}C$ (to be read **the result of substituting B for A uniformly in C**) and is defined as follows:

1. $\mathbf{S}^{A}_{B}A = B$
2. If $f \in S_k$, $k > 0$ and $x_1,\cdots,x_k \in W_S$, and $A \neq fx_1\cdots x_k$, then $\mathbf{S}^{A}_{B}fx_1\cdots x_k = f\mathbf{S}^{A}_{B}x_1\cdots \mathbf{S}^{A}_{B}x_k$.
3. If $A \neq C$ and either $C \in S_0$ or $C \notin W_S$, then $\mathbf{S}^{A}_{B}C = C$.

Theorem 1-7. If A, B and $C \in W_S$, $\mathbf{S}^{A}_{B}C \in W_S$.

Proof: By induction on $\ell(C)$:

(α) If $\ell(C) = 1$, then $C \in S_0$. Hence either $A = C$ and $\mathbf{S}^A_B C = B$, or $A \neq C$ and $\mathbf{S}^A_B C = C$. Hence $\mathbf{S}^A_B C \in W_S$.

(β) Suppose the theorem true for all D such that $\ell(D) < k$ and assume that $\ell(C) = k > 1$. Since $C \in W_S$, there exist n, f and $x_1 \cdots x_n$ such that $C = fx_1 \cdots x_n$, $f \in S_n$ and $x_1 \cdots x_n \in W_S$. Hence $\mathbf{S}^A_B C = f\mathbf{S}^A_B x_1 \cdots \mathbf{S}^A_B x_n$. By the definition of ℓ, $\ell(x_i) < k$, for each i ($1 \leq i \leq n$). By the hypothesis of induction, $\mathbf{S}^A_B x_i \in W_S$, and so is $\mathbf{S}^A_B C$.

To extend the notion of substitution to several wffs, we first define a **sequential substitution**:

$$\mathcal{S}^{A_1}_{B_1} C = \mathbf{S}^{A_1}_{B_1} C$$

$$\mathcal{S}^{A_1}_{B_1} \cdots ^{A_{n+1}}_{B_{n+1}} C = \mathbf{S}^{A_{n+1}}_{B_{n+1}} \mathcal{S}^{A_1}_{B_1} \cdots ^{A_n}_{B_n} C$$

We can then define **simultaneous substitution** as:

$$\mathbf{S}^{A_1}_{B_1} \cdots ^{A_n}_{B_n} C = \mathcal{S}^{v_1}_{B_1} \cdots ^{v_n}_{B_n} \mathcal{S}^{A_1}_{v_1} \cdots ^{A_n}_{v_n} C$$

where $v_1, \cdots, v_n$ are distinct elements of S_0 that do not occur in any of $A_1, \cdots, A_n, B_1, \cdots, B_n$ or C.

Note that no insurmountable difficulty results even if a formal system $\mathfrak{S}$ has only a finite number of elements in S_0 and hence that the conditions on $v_1, \cdots, v_n$ may turn out to be unsatisfiable. This is true because we can, in that case, introduce a system $\mathfrak{S}'$ which differs from $\mathfrak{S}$ only by having an infinite set of additional elements of S_0, $\{w_1, w_2, \cdots\}$ that are not in the alphabet of $\mathfrak{S}$, and then define our simultaneous and sequential substitution operators in $\mathfrak{S}'$. Since no w_i will occur in $\mathbf{S}^{A_1}_{B_1} \cdots ^{A_n}_{B_n} C$, the resulting operator always generates an element of W_S. (The reader who now worries about the existence of non-elements of S would have to be reminded that this language is recursive so that standard diagonalization arguments, unfortunately beyond the scope of this work, will guarantee their existence.) We can use the $\mathbf{S}$-operator to define a notion of occurrence for wffs as follows: **A S-occurs in B** iff A and B are wffs andeither:

1. If W_S contains at least two elements, there exists a $C \in W_S$

such that $\mathbf{S}^A{}_C B \neq B$, or

2. W_S has only one element

Theorem 1-8. If $B = fx_1 \cdots x_k \in W_S$, then A S-occurs in B, if and only if, either $A = B$ or for some i ($1 \leq i \leq k$), A S-occurs in x_i.

Proof: We assume A S-occurs in B. If A = B, there is nothing to prove, so we assume $A \neq B$. By the definition of S-occurs there is a $C \in W_S$ such that $\mathbf{S}^A{}_C B \neq B$. Since $\mathbf{S}^A{}_C B = f\mathbf{S}^A{}_C x_1 \cdots \mathbf{S}^A{}_C x_n$, there must be an i such that $\mathbf{S}^A{}_C x_i \neq x_i$. Hence A S-occurs in x_i. We now prove the implication in the other direction. For our first case, we assume A = B. If A is the only element of W_S, then A S-occurs in B by definition. Otherwise, there is a $C \in W_S$ such that $C \neq A$. Therefore, $\mathbf{S}^A{}_C B = \mathbf{S}^A{}_C A = C \neq A$ and we again have A S-occurs in B. Next we assume there exists an i ($1 \leq i \leq k$) such that A S-occurs in x_i. Then there exists a C with $\mathbf{S}^A{}_C x_i \neq x_i$. By theorem 1-5, $B \neq f\mathbf{S}^A{}_C x_1 \cdots \mathbf{S}^A{}_C x_n = \mathbf{S}^A{}_C B$. This implies that A S-occurs in B.

Theorem 1-9. If A S-occurs in $\mathbf{S}^A{}_B C$, $A \in S_0$, $B \in W_S$ and $C \in W_S$, then A S-occurs in B.

Proof: By induction on $\ell(C)$:

(α) Assume $\ell(C) = 1$. Then $C \in S_0$. If $C = A$, $\mathbf{S}^A{}_B C = B$ and hence A S-occurs in $\mathbf{S}^A{}_B C$ iff A S-occurs in B. If $C \neq A$, then $\mathbf{S}^A{}_B C = C$. Hence we also have that for every $D \in W_S$, $\mathbf{S}^A{}_B C = C$ and therefore $\mathbf{S}^A{}_D \mathbf{S}^A{}_B C = \mathbf{S}^A{}_D C = C$, contrary to the assumption that A S-occurs in $\mathbf{S}^A{}_B C$.

(β) Assume the theorem holds provided $\ell(C) < j$. We will prove it for $\ell(C) = j$. Since $C \in W_S$, there exist k, f and $x_1, \cdots, x_k$ with $f \in S_k$ and with the $x_i \in W_S$ such that $C = fx_1 \cdots x_k$. Then $\mathbf{S}^A{}_B C = f\mathbf{S}^A{}_B x_1 \cdots \mathbf{S}^A{}_B x_n$. If A S-occurs in $\mathbf{S}^A{}_B C$, either $A = \mathbf{S}^A{}_B C$ or there is an i ($1 \leq i \leq k$) such that A S-occurs in $\mathbf{S}^A{}_B x_i$ by theorem 1-8. If the former, A = f and hence $f \in S_0$ so that $\ell(C) = 1$, contrary to assumption. Thus A must

S-occur in $\mathbf{S}^{A}{}_{B}x_i$. Since $\ell(x_i) < \ell(C) = j$, A S-occurs in B by the hypothesis of induction.

Theorem 1-10. If $A, B \in W_S$, then A S-occurs in B iff there exist $C, D \in \sigma_{S\cap}$ such that $B = CAD$.

Proof: If W_S has only one element, $A, B \in W_S$ implies $A = B$, A S-occurs in B and $B = \varnothing B \varnothing$. Otherwise, by induction on $\ell(B)$:

(α) $\ell(B) = 1$. Then $B \in S_0$. Then A S-occurs in B, $\mathbf{S}^{A}{}_{C}B = B$, which can only be the case if $A = B$ and hence also $\varnothing A \varnothing$. If, on the other hand, $B = CAD$, $\ell(CAD) = 1$ and $CAD \in S_0$. But since $B \in W_S$, this can only be true if $C = D = \varnothing$ and hence $B = \varnothing A \varnothing = A$.

(β) $\ell(B) = k > 1$ and the theorem holds for all E such that $\ell(E) < k$. Let A S-occur in B. Since $k > 1$, then there is a $j > 0$ and wffs $x_1,\cdots,x_j$ and $f \in S_j$, such that $B = fx_1\cdots x_j$. Then by theorem 1-8, either $A = B$ in which case $B = \varnothing A \varnothing$ and the result follows, or for some i, A S-occurs in x_i. But then by the hypothesis of induction, $x_i = C_iAD_i$. Therefore, if $C = fx_1\cdots x_{i-1}C_i$ and $D = D_ix_{i+1}\cdots x_j$, $B = CAD$. For the converse, suppose $B = CAD$. Hence by theorem 1-6, since $B = B\varnothing$, either B is an initial segment of C or C of B. Therefore, if $C = \varnothing$, A is an initial segment of B and by theorem 1-4, $A = B$ and $\mathbf{S}^{A}{}_{F}B = F$ for every F and A S-occurs in B. If, however, $C \neq \varnothing$, there is an $F \in S$ and $G \in \sigma_{S\cap}$ such that $C = FG$. Hence $B = fx_1\cdots x_j = FGAD$ and, by F5, $x_1\cdots x_j = GAD$. Since $A \in W_S$ and hence $A \neq \varnothing$, $x_1\cdots x_j$ is not an initial segment of G. Let p be the first i such that x1$\cdots$xj is not an initial segment of G. Then $x_1\cdots x_{p-1}H = G$ and, since GA is not an initial segment of $x_1\cdots x_p$, $x_1\cdots x_{p-1}x_p = GAI = x_1\cdots x_{p-1}HAI$. Hence $x_{p-1} = HAI$. Since $\ell(xp) < k$, $A \in W_S$ and $x_p \in W_S$, A S-occurs in x_p by the hypothesis of induction, and by theorem 1-8, A S-occurs in B.

Before moving on, it is worthwhile to repeat that although the notation we have been using for our theorems (viz., the one for which "follows" is taken literally in a left to right sense) is the so-called Polish notation, that notation is by no means the only one that satisfies F1-5 and which therefore satisfies our theory. Obviously linear order right to left would do as well. There is another, even better known variety, which is less immediately obvious, namely, the one first introduced by Peano and used, in several variations, in the majority of systems. We will illustrate this with a very simple example. The alphabet consists of variables $x_1, x_2, \cdots$, one one-place connective (~) and one two-place connective (⊃) and left and right parentheses [(,)]. A formulation for wff might be: all variables are wffs; if A is a wff, so is ~A; and if A and B are wffs so is (A ⊃ B). In our terms, S_0 consists of the set $\{x_1, x_2, \cdots\}$, S_1 has ~ as its only member, S_2 has ⊃ as its only member and all other S_i are empty. We then consider the parentheses as devices which help define "follows." A suitable algorithm for calculating the order is:

1. If X starts with a (and contains a ⊃, the first element is ⊃ and the remainder sequence is X, eliminating: (1) the initial (, then (2) the first ⊃ with as many) as (to its left, and (3) the final) – provided that this is the last sign.

2. If X starts with (and contains no ⊃, eliminate the initial (and final) – if any – and recalculate.

3. If X does not start with (or) , the first element of X is the leftmost sign of X; the remainder sequence is X with the first sign eliminated.

4. If X starts with) , eliminate it and recalculate.

For example, consider $(\sim(x_1 \supset x_2) \supset x_3)$

Remainder	First element
$(\sim(x_1 \supset x_2) \supset x_3)$	⊃
$\sim(x_1 \supset x_2)\ x_3$	~
$(x_1 \supset x_2)\ x_3$	⊃
$x_1 x_2) x_3$	x_1
$x_2) x_3$	x_2
$) x_3$	
x_3	x_3

So that the order is: $\supset \sim \supset x_1 x_2 x_3$

A second case: $(\sim x_1 \supset (x_2 \supset x_3))$

Remainder	First element
$(\sim x_1 \supset (x_2 \supset x_3))$	⊃
$\sim x_1 (x_2 \supset x_3)$	~
$x_1 (x_2 \supset x_3)$	x_1

$(x_2 \supset x_3)$	$\supset$
x_2x_3	x_2
x_3	x_3

and the order is: $\supset \sim x_1 \supset x_2 x_3$

And a third example: $\sim(x_1 \supset (x_2 \supset x_3))$

Remainder	First element
$\sim(x_1 \supset (x_2 \supset x_3))$	$\sim$
$(x_1 \supset (x_2 \supset x_3))$	$\supset$
$x_1 (x_2 \supset x_3)$	x_1
$(x_2 \supset x_3)$	$\supset$
x_2x_3	x_2
x_3	x_3

and the order is: $\sim \supset x_1 \supset x_2\ x_3$

Note that F1-F5 are satisfied (and indeed, any two distinct wffs determine distinct orderings).

An additional substitution concept will have a certain bearing in the formulation of those theorems we shall term **"equivalence theorems."** The intended condition is that two wffs C and D are related in such a way that C differs from D at most by containing an occurrence of a wff A at one place in C where D contains an occurrence of the wff B. Clearly, this can be reduced to the concept of a variable not occurring more than once in a wff by means of the following definition:

For wffs A,B,C and D, C **differs from** D **at most by having an occurrence of** A **at one place where** D **has** B provided there is a wff E and a variable v which occurs at most once in E such that $\mathbf{S}^{v}_{A}E = C$ and $\mathbf{S}^{v}_{B}E = D$. (For our treatment of variables, refer to p.23.)

We will define the operator $\mathbf{S}^{*v}_{B}C$ (to be read as **the result of substituting** B **for** v **the first time it appears in** C) as follows:

1. $\mathbf{S}^{*v}_{B}v = B$
2. If C is not v, then:

   (α) If $C \in S_0$, $\mathbf{S}^{*v}_{B}C = C$

   (β) If C is $fA_1 \cdots A_n$ where $f \in S_n$ $(n > 0)$ and $A_1, \cdots, A_n \in W_S$:

i) $\mathbf{S}_0{}^{*v}{}_B C = C$

ii) $\mathbf{S}_{k+1}{}^{*v}{}_B C = f\mathbf{S}_k{}^{*v}{}_B A_1 \cdots \mathbf{S}_k{}^{*v}{}_B A_k \mathbf{S}^{*v}{}_B A_{k+1} A_{k+2} \cdots A_n$,

provided $f\mathbf{S}_k{}^{*v}{}_B A_1 \cdots \mathbf{S}_k{}^{*v}{}_B A_k\ \mathbf{S}^{*v}{}_B A_k A_{k+1} \cdots A_n = C$

iii) $\mathbf{S}_{k+1}{}^{*v}{}_B C = \mathbf{S}_k{}^{*v}{}_B C$, otherwise

iv) $\mathbf{S}^{*v}{}_B C = \mathbf{S}_n{}^{*v}{}_B C$

We can now define $\mathbf{S}_n{}^{v}{}_B C$ (to be read as **the result of substituting** B **for the variable** v **the first k times it occurs in** C) as follows:

1. $\mathbf{S}_0{}^{v}{}_B C = C$
2. $\mathbf{S}_{k+1}{}^{v}{}_B C = \mathbf{S}^{*v}{}_B \mathbf{S}_k{}^{v}{}_B C$.

It is easy to see that by induction, since $\mathbf{S}_{k+1}{}^{v}{}_B C$ is as defined, then $\mathbf{S}_{i+j}{}^{v}{}_B C = \mathbf{S}_i{}^{v}{}_B \mathbf{S}_j{}^{v}{}_B C$. We can now define v **occurs at most n times in** C as: if v does not occur in B, v does not occur in $\mathbf{S}_n{}^{v}{}_B C$. Similarly, we can define v **occurs at least n times in C as**: v does not occur at most n-1 times in C. We can then, if we desire, define **v occurs n times in C** as: v occurs at least and at most n times in C.

It now follows readily by induction that if v does not occur in B and v occurs n times in C, v does not occur in $\mathbf{S}_n{}^{v}{}_B C$. By an equally trivial induction we can also establish that if S_0 has more than one element for every element x of S_0 there is a $B \in W_S$ in which x does not occur.

Exercises
Chapter I

1. Show that theorem 1 - 9 is not true if we substitute "$A \in W_S$" for "$A \in S_0$".

2. Let ω be the set of natural numbers. Show that if every subset of ω has a least element (i.e. if $A \subset \omega$ there is a $k \in A$ such that k is less than or equal to each element of A), then weak induction holds.

3. If $x,y \in \sigma_{S\cap}$, is $\ell(xy) = \ell(x) + \ell(y)$? If so, prove it; if not, give a counterexample.

4. If S is such that $S_0 = \{0,1\}$, $S_2 = \{+, \cdot\}$, and $S_i = \emptyset$ for i = 1,3,4,···, what are some elements of $\sigma_{S\cap}$ and W_S?

5. We will write $F \leq G$ if F is an initial segment of G. Prove that

$F \leq F$

$F \leq G$ iff $EF \leq EG$ for any E

($E \leq F$ and $F \leq G$) implies $E \leq G$

Is it true that $F \leq G$ implies $FE \leq GE$?

6. We say that a function **f** is an **order isomorphism** (or **order-preserving**) iff $A \leq B$ implies $\mathbf{f}(A) \leq \mathbf{f}(B)$. If $x,y \in \sigma_{S\cap}$ and $\mathbf{f}: \sigma_{S\cap} \to \sigma_{S\cap}$ is defined as $\mathbf{f}(x) = \mathbf{S}^B{}_A x$, show that **f** is an order isomorphism (with the ordering defined in exercise 5.)

7. If $x,y,z \in \sigma_{S\cap}$, then $\ell(y) \leq \ell(z)$ iff $\ell(yx) \leq \ell(zx)$.

8. If $S \neq \emptyset$, then the range of ℓ as defined on $\sigma_{S\cap}$ is ω, the natural numbers.

9. If A is an initial segment of B and $A = a_1,\cdots,a_n$ and $B = b_1,\cdots,b_k$, $a_i,b_i \in S$, then $n \leq k$ and $a_1 = b_1,\cdots, a_n = b_n$.

10. Show that the uniform substitution operator is well-defined (i.e. A = B implies $\mathbf{S}^D{}_C A = \mathbf{S}^D{}_C B$ for any wff C and D). Is it true that $\mathbf{S}^D{}_C A = \mathbf{S}^D{}_C B$ implies A = B?

2
Zero-Order Logic: Proof Theory

Our next task is to formulate exactly the notion of a derivation of a wff A from a set of wffs α (in a calculus). The basic notion is that of a string or sequence of wffs each of which is an element of α or follows from earlier wffs by application of a rule of the calculus and whose last element is A. For suitable calculi, a minor revision of this condition would suffice to define derivation. But because we also want to allow systems that use subordinate derivations (sometimes called "natural deduction" systems), we will have to take a more complicated path. Perhaps the paradigm of the kind of rule we have to accommodate is "conditionalization," which asserts that if we can derive B from a set of premises a together with an additional premise A, we can derive "if A, then B" from the premise set a. Intuitively, we have a sequence of derivations in the first sense, except that the rules must allow reference to earlier "derivations" in the sequence. Here the matter is complicated by the fact that, normally at least, it is not the details of the subordinate derivation, but what conclusion follows from what premises, which is the relevant information. However, the fact that the principal derivation has certain premises and conclusions unfortunately does not specify what wffs are allowed to be premises and conclusions in the subordinate derivations. In order to avoid this difficulty while keeping the ability to check step-by-step whether a derivation is valid, we are forced to introduce the concept of derivation couple, to serve as surrogate for the notion of derivable. In order to serve our purpose, a derivation couple must have two properties. First, given a putative subordinate derivation we must be able to tell whether or not a given couple is a derivation couple of that sequence with the information limited to (a) the sequence itself, (b) earlier sequences (since these may be subordinate to it) and (c) the rules of the calculus. Second, given a sequence of sequences $S_1,\cdots,S_n$, if the couple α, A is a derivation couple of S_i ($1 \leq i \leq n$), $S_1,\cdots,S_i$ should be a derivation of A from α (with S_i as the main derivation).

Accordingly, we can give derivation couple (α, A) these properties (1) by requiring α to be the last wff in S_i, (2) by restricting α so that every element of α occurs in S_i and (3) by allowing α to be any of the possible sets of premises of A which are relevant to the problem. As you will see from the definition, if S_i consists of n wffs, it will have at least one and at most 2^n derivation couples.

With the help of the "derivation couple" notion we then have no difficulty in defining an intuitively satisfactory concept of derivation, namely, $S_1,\cdots,S_n$ is a derivation of A from a iff for some $\alpha' \subset \alpha$, (α', A) is a derivation couple of S_i in $S_1,\cdots,S_n$ (and this holds as well for every initial segment).

Let $\mathbf{S}$ be the set of non-empty finite sequences of non-empty finite sequences (fsfs) of elements of W_S. A **derivation rule** is a recursive (i.e. decidable) function $\mathbf{R}: \mathbf{S} \times W_S \rightarrow \{0,1\}$. That is, given any fsfs F of W_S, and any wff B, $\mathbf{R}$(F,B) is 0 or 1 and it is determinable in a finite number of steps whether it equals 0 or 1. A **zero-order calculus** is a system with:

1. An alphabet (i.e. a defined recursive family of sets S_i), including a defined recursive criterion of "sameness"
2. A defined recursive criterion for linear order ("follows") and for sequential order of wffs (both satisfying F1-5 of chapter 1)
3. A finite set of derivation rules

As we have seen in chapter 1, conditions 1 and 2 specify a set of wffs and a recursive criterion for sameness of wffs.

Let $\mathcal{L}$ be a zero-order calculus and S the corresponding set of fsfs. Let $F \in S$ and $F_1,\cdots,F_n$ be the elements of F. Then (α,A) is a **derivation couple** of F_i (in F) provided:

1. $a \in F_i$
2. A is the last element of F_i
3. For every wff B, if (1) $B \in F_i$, (2) F_B is the fsfs consisting of $F_1,\cdots,F_{i-1},F_i^B$, where F_i^B is the initial segment of F_i preceding B and (3) $\mathbf{R}(F_B,B) = 0$ for every derivation rule $\mathbf{R}$ of $\mathcal{L}$, then $B \in \alpha$.

A **logical derivation rule** is a derivation rule such that the value of $\mathbf{R}$(S,B) is solely dependent on what the derivation couples of $F_1,\cdots,F_{n-1}$ and what the elements of F_n are, where $S = F_1,\cdots,F_n$. A **zero-order logical calculus** is a zero-order calculus and all of the derivation rules are logical derivation rules. A **derivation of A from α in** L is a fsfs $F_1,\cdots,F_n$ such that

1. If A_i is the ith element of F_n and F^i is $F_1,\cdots,F_{n-1},F'$ where F' is the sequence $A_1,\cdots,A_{i-1}$ and, for every rule $\mathbf{R}$ of $\mathcal{L}$ if $\mathbf{R}(F^i, A_i) = 0$, then $A_i \in \alpha$.

2. A is the last element of F_n.

A is derivable from α in $\mathcal{L}$ or $\alpha \vdash_{\mathcal{L}} A$ (also read as **α yields A in $\mathcal{L}$**) provided there is a derivation of A from α in $\mathcal{L}$.

Note that if a is recursive, "derivation from a" is also, but that even then "derivable" may not be.

For those who hold a classical view of mathematics (and, when "derivable" is recursive, for intuitionists as well), " $\alpha \vdash_{\mathcal{L}} A$ " (which we will term a Y-statement) is not an arbitrary sequence of signs (as wffs may be) but is a statement which is true or false.

It follows easily from the definition of "derivation couple" that if α is finite, $\alpha \vdash_{\mathcal{L}} A$ if and only if (α, A) is a derivation couple of a subsequence of a fsfs in $\mathcal{L}$. From this it follows for logical calculi that for each rule, its instances could be expressed in the form:

$$\alpha_1 \vdash A_1, \cdots, \alpha_n \vdash A_n, \alpha \vdash B_1, \cdots, \alpha \vdash B_n \Rightarrow \alpha \vdash A,$$

where $\alpha_1, \cdots, \alpha_n$ and α are finite sets. This has the effect of permitting the added assertion $\alpha \vdash A$ whenever the appropriate n+m Y-statements are already given.

It is also significant to note that a derivation thus defined has the following two important properties provided L is a logical calculus.

Theorem 2-1. (The finite derivation property) A is derivable from a set of wffs α in $\mathcal{L}$ iff there exists a finite subset α' of α, such that A is derivable from α' in $\mathcal{L}$.

Proof: Right to left: This is a trivial consequence of the definition since if A is derivable from a finite subset of α, α', there exists a subset of α', α'', such that (α'', A) is a derivation couple of the last subsequence of a derivation of A from a in $\mathcal{L}$. But then $\alpha'' \subset \alpha'$ and A is derivable from α.

Left to right: Assume A is derivable from α. Then there is a derivation of A from a in $\mathcal{L}$ whose last subsequence has a derivation couple for a finite subset α' of α. But then A is derivable from α'.

Theorem 2-2. (The closure property) (1) Given any two sets of wffs α and β, then every wff in α is derivable from β iff every wff derivable from α is derivable from β and (2) Every wff is derivable from the set of all wffs.

Proof: Since the fsfs consisting of a single subsequence whose sole member is A is a derivation of A from any α, if A ϵ α, A is derivable from α. As a result, (2) follows immediately, but also (1) in the right to left direction follows as well, since the elements of α are derivable from α.

(1) left to right: Let $S_1,\cdots,S_n$ be a derivation of a wff A from α. Then there is a finite subset $\alpha' = \{A_1,\cdots,A_m\}$ of α, such that (α',A) is a derivation couple of S_n. Let $S_{j\,1},\cdots, S_{j\,m_m}$ (j = 1,2,$\cdots$,m) be a derivation of A_j from β. Then the fsfs: $S_1,\cdots,S_{n1},S_{11},\cdots,S_{1(m_1 1)},\cdots, S_{m1},\cdots,S_{m(m_m-1)},S^*$, where S^* is the sequence: S_{1m_1}, followed by S_{2m_2}, followed by $\cdots$ followed by S_{m,m_m}, followed by S_n, is a derivation of A from β, since it is true that for every A_i which appears in α', A_i will be the last wff of S_{im_i}. Hence by definition, A_i will follow from wffs earlier in the final sequence together with derivation couples of earlier sequences.

The closure property embodies in a particularly strong form what is sometimes called the "transitivity" of the derivability relation.

A convenient consequence of these facts allows us to represent the derivability situation in terms of what we shall call Y-derivations ("Y" is of course intended to suggest "yields").

A **Y-derivation of A from α in $\mathcal{L}$** is a sequence $\alpha_1 \vdash A_1,\cdots,\alpha_n \vdash A_n$ of Y-statements such that α_n is α and A_n is A, and for each i ($1 \leq i \leq n$), either:

1. $A_i \in \alpha_i$
2. There is a $j < i$ such that A_i is A_j and $\alpha_j \subset \alpha_i$
3. There is a rule **R** in $\mathcal{L}$ such that one of its instances is $\beta_1 \vdash B_1, \cdots, \beta_k \vdash B_k \Rightarrow \alpha_i \vdash A_i$ and for every i ($1 \leq i \leq k$) there is an r ($1 \leq r \leq i$) such that β_j is α_r and B_j is A_r.

Theorem 2-3. If $\mathcal{L}$ is a logical calculus, $\alpha \vdash_{\mathcal{L}} A$ iff there is a Y-derivation of $\alpha \vdash A$ in $\mathcal{L}$.

Proof: Suppose $\alpha \vdash_{\mathcal{L}} A$. Then there is a fsfs $S = S_1, \cdots, S_m = A_{11}, \cdots, A_{1n_1}, A_{21}, \cdots, A_{2n_2}, \cdots, A_{m1}, \cdots, A_{mn_m}$. For each j ($1 \leq j \leq m$)

there is a least α_j such that (α_j, A_{jn_j}) is a derivation couple of S_j in S (viz., the set of elements of S_j which precede A_{jn_j} and which do not follow by a rule). Construct the Y-derivation as follows:

(1) A_{11} either follows from the null set of wffs by the rules of $\mathcal{L}$ or it does not. If it does, let the first step be $\vdash A_{11}$, justified by the rule in question, and the second step be $\alpha_1 \vdash A_{11}$ which follows by condition 2, since $\emptyset \subset \alpha_1$.

(2) Suppose we have among the earlier steps of the Y-derivation:

$\alpha_1 \vdash A_{11}, \cdots, \alpha_1 \vdash A_{1n_1} \cdots, \alpha_{i-1} \vdash A_{i-1,1}, \cdots, \alpha_{i-1} \vdash A_{i-1,n_{i-1}}, \cdots, \alpha_i \vdash A_{i1}, \cdots, \alpha_i \vdash A_{ij-1}$.

Let $F_{i,j-i}$ be: $A_{11}, \cdots, A_{1n_1}, \cdots, A_{i1,1}, \cdots, A_{i1,n_{i1}}, A_{i1}, \cdots, A_{i,j1}$. Then either $\Sigma^q_{p=1} R_p(F_{i,j-i}, A_{ij}) > 0$ or $\Sigma^q_{p=1} R_p(F_{i,j-i}, A_{ij}) = 0$, where $R_1, \cdots, R_q$ are all of the rules of $\mathcal{L}$. If the former, (1) there is a p such that $R_p(F_{i,j-i}, A_{ij}) = 1$ and hence one can derive a statement of the form:

$\beta_1 \vdash B_1, \cdots, \beta_s \vdash B_s, \alpha_i \vdash A_1, \cdots, \alpha_i \vdash A_{i-1} \Rightarrow \alpha_i \vdash A_i$ where for each x $(1 \leq x \leq s)$ there is a y $(1 \leq y \leq i)$ such that (1) (β_x, B_x) is a derivation couple of the yth subsequence of the derivation, or (2) there is a y $(1 \leq y \leq j)$ such that (β_x, B_x) is a derivation couple of the ith subsequence of the derivation and thus B_x is A_{ij}. If (1), $\alpha_y \vdash B_x$ is an earlier step of the Y-derivation and we may assert $\beta_x \vdash B_x$ by condition 2 in the definition of Y-derivation; if (2), $\alpha_i \vdash B_x$ is an earlier step and we may likewise insert $\beta_x \vdash B_x$ in the same manner. We may then insert $\alpha_i \vdash A_{ij}$ by conditions 2 and 3. If on the other hand, $\Sigma^q_{p=1} R_p(F_{i,j-i}, A_{ij}) = 0$, A_{ij} does not follow from earlier steps and hence by condition 3 of the definition of derivation couple, $A_{ij} \in \alpha_i$ and we may insert $\alpha_1 \vdash A_{ij}$ by condition 1. Hence, we can eventually obtain the step $\alpha_n \vdash A$. Since however $\alpha_n \subset \alpha$, we can add $\alpha \vdash A$, by condition 2. Assume on the other hand, we have a Y-derivation of $\alpha \vdash A$ in $\mathcal{L}$, $\alpha_1 \vdash A_1, \cdots, \alpha_n \vdash A_n$. We shall show by induction on the number of steps i that $\alpha \vdash A$.

(α) i = 1. Either there is a rule R_p in $\mathcal{L}$ such that $\alpha_1 \vdash A_1$ follows from the null set of derivation pairs or there is not. If the former, we have $\alpha_1 \vdash A_1$ by the derivation $B_1, \cdots, B_m, A_1$, where $\alpha_1 = \{B_1, \cdots, B_m\}$. If not, since condition 2 and 3 of Y-derivation do not apply, condition 1 must and $A_1 \in \alpha_1$ and hence there is a j such that A_1 is B_1, and $B_1,\cdots,B_{j-1},B_{j+1},\cdots,B_m,A_1$ is a derivation of A_1 from α_1 where α_1 is defined in the same way.

(β) Suppose it is true for $i < k$. Then $\alpha_k \vdash A_k$ must follow by one of the conditions on Y-derivation. By the hypothesis of induction, we have $\alpha_1 \vdash_{\mathcal{L}} A_1, \cdots, \alpha_{k-1} \vdash_{\mathcal{L}} A_{k-1}$.

Case 1: $A_k \in \alpha_k$. Then $\alpha_k = \{B_1,\cdots,B_j,A_k\}$ and $B_1,\cdots,B_j,A_k$ is a derivation of A_1 from α_1.

Case 2: There is a $j < i$ such that A_i is A_j and $\alpha_j \subset \alpha_i$. By the hypothesis of induction there is a derivation D of A_j (i.e.A_i) from α_j. But then D is also a derivation of A_i from α_i.

Case 3: There is a rule $\mathcal{R}$ in $\mathcal{L}$ such that one of its instances is $\beta_1 \vdash B_1, \cdots, \beta_q \vdash B_q \Rightarrow \alpha_k \vdash A_k$ and for every j ($1 \leq j \leq q$) there is an r ($1 \leq r \leq k$) such that β_j is α_r and B_j is A_r. Then the sequence of sequences which consists of the derivations (in order) of A_1 from α_1, A_2 from $\alpha_2, \cdots, A_{k-1}$ from α_{k-i}, followed by the elements of α_k and then A_k include sequences with derivation couples $(\beta_1,B_1), \cdots, (\beta_q,B_q)$ and hence the resulting sequence is a derivation of A_k from α_k in $\mathcal{L}$.

It should be noted that the derivations and Y-derivations obtained from this theorem are not necessarily the shortest ones. Nevertheless, the theorem allows us to use Y-derivations to establish the existence of derivations.

The advantage of this should be clear if we consider that derivations are (in general) sequences of sequences, while Y-derivations are simple sequences, so that proofs by induction in the former case generally involve inductions on inductions, while in the latter, single inductions suffice.

We will now further specialize our notion of logical calculus in the direction of familiar logical systems.

We will call $\mathcal{L}$ a **(zero-order) logical calculus with variables** provided $\mathcal{L}$ is a logical calculus whose alphabet is $S_0,S_1,\cdots$ and there is a non-empty recursive subset V of S_0. We will call the elements of V variables. We will call a logical calculus with variables **normal** if V is (denumerably) infinite and $S - V$ is finite but not null. In general we shall be concerned with normal logical calculi. We shall call a zero-order logical calculus with variables a zero-order logic provided that $v \in V$, $\alpha \subset W_S$, $A,B \in W_S$ and $\alpha \vdash_{\mathcal{L}} A$ imply $\mathbf{S}^{v}_{B}\alpha \vdash \mathbf{S}^{v}_{B}A$, where $\mathbf{S}^{v}_{B}\alpha$ is defined as the set of wffs D such that $D = \mathbf{S}^{v}_{B}C$ for some $C \in \alpha$. This property is sometimes expressed by saying that derivability classes are closed under uniform substitution for variables. Of course, this condition is not an arbitrary one, since it amounts to insisting that the elements we term "variables" behave like variables – indeed, but for some very minor technical disadvantages in doing so, it would not be unreasonable to define variable by this property (in addition to being an element of S_0).

One type of zero-order logic of special interest to us is the **deductive zero-order system** (abbreviated **DZOS**). We shall define a (logical) derivation rule as a **substitution-instance rule** if it satisfies the following:

Assuming $\alpha_1,\cdots,\alpha_k$ and $\beta_1,\cdots,\beta_m$ are specific sets of wffs and $A_1,\cdots,A_k$, $B_1,\cdots,B_m$, $C_1,\cdots,C_n$ are specific wffs, if (1) $\alpha \subset W_S$ and for some substitution instance $\mathbf{S}$ (i.e. some finite number of substitutions of wffs for variables), each of $(\alpha\cup\mathbf{S}(\alpha_1), \mathbf{S}(A_1)), \cdots, (\alpha\cup\mathbf{S}(\alpha_k), \mathbf{S}(A_k))$, $(\mathbf{S}(\beta_1), \mathbf{S}(B_1)),\cdots,(\mathbf{S}(\beta_m),\mathbf{S}(B_m))$ are derivation couples F_i in $F_1\cdots F_p$ for some i $(1 \le i \le p-1)$ and (2) $\mathbf{S}(C_1),\cdots,\mathbf{S}(C_n)$ are elements of F_p and there is a set $\beta \subset \alpha$ which is the first element of a derivation couple of F_p in $F_1\cdots F_p$. Then $\mathbf{R}(F_1\cdots F_p, \mathbf{S}(A)) = 1$. It should of course be understood that k, m or n or even all three of these may be 0, or in other words that any of the three conditions may be absent.

A **deductive zero-order system** (**DZOS**) is then a logic (i.e. a sufficiently well-behaved logical calculus) all of whose rules are substitution instance rules.

This type of system is of special interest, since within them, derivability steps depend only on what is usually called their form (and hence they are paradigms of **formal** logic).

One special case of substitution instance rule which deserves mention is that kind in which in the definition of $\mathbf{R}$ $k = n = m = 0$, or in other words, one which drops the requirement that certain derivation couples and certain wffs are already present. As a consequence, any substitution instance of A may be placed at any point of any derivation without any effect on the premise set. In this event, A is termed an **axiom schema** and its instances **axioms**. (In a somewhat analogous usage we call wffs that are deducible from the null set **theorems**.)

Normally, a DZOS is called **axiomatic** if it has axioms (especially if it has few and relatively simple rules other than those specifying axiom schemata) and a DZOS without any rules specifying axioms is frequently called a **natural deduction system** (although of course substitution-instance derivation rules which are not axiom schemata can be very complex or otherwise "unnatural"). Both because of the potentially misleading implications of this terminology and the fact that this distinction will not be of great importance to us, we will not place substantial emphasis on this classification.

Systems of the kind we are discussing can be compared in many ways. Of special interest to us are those relations which allow us to deduce properties of one system from those of another. One interesting relation of this kind arises when one system can be characterized by starting with another system and adding items to the description of the latter. Perhaps the most important cases are those which arise by adding additional rules. If we have two zero-order systems $\mathbf{S}$ and $\mathbf{S}'$ and $\mathbf{S}'$ differs from $\mathbf{S}$ (in its description) at most in its rules and furthermore every rule of $\mathbf{S}$ is either a rule or a derived rule of $\mathbf{S}'$, we call $\mathbf{S}'$ an **R-extension of S**, or equivalently, we say that **S' R-includes S**. When this is the case, every particular Y-statement of $\mathbf{S}$ also holds in $\mathbf{S}'$. This stems from the fact that if $\mathbf{S}'$ is an R-extension of $\mathbf{S}$ and every rule of $\mathbf{S}'$ which is not a rule of $\mathbf{S}$ is a derived rule of $\mathbf{S}$ [in other words, $\mathbf{S}'$ can be obtained by adding as (primitive) rules of $\mathbf{S}'$ some of the derived rules of $\mathbf{S}$] the set of true Y-statements of $\mathbf{S}$ and $\mathbf{S}'$ correspond. Oddly enough, this is not necessarily true about derived rules in general, since these represent general properties we are able to demonstrate.

It is convenient to develop a little terminology here.

Let us say that $\mathbf{S}$ **simply deductively includes** $\mathbf{S}'$ if $W_S = W_{S'}$ and if for every $\alpha \subset W_S$ and $A \in W_S$, $\alpha \vdash_{S'} A$ implies $\alpha \vdash_S A$. Let us call $\mathbf{S}$ and $\mathbf{S}'$ **simply deductively equivalent** if they simply deductively include each other. We can then assert:

1. If $W_S = W_{S'}$ and $\mathbf{S}$ R-includes $\mathbf{S}'$, $\mathbf{S}$ simply deductively = includes $\mathbf{S}'$.

2. If $W_S = W_{S'}$ and every rule of $\mathbf{S}$ is a rule or derived rule of $\mathbf{S}'$, $\mathbf{S}'$ simply deductively includes $\mathbf{S}$.

3. If $W_S = W_{S'}$, S' R-includes S and every rule of S' which is not a rule of S is a derived rule of S, S and S' are simply deductively equivalent.

It is easy to see that if S and S' are simply deductively equivalent and S'' simply deductively includes S, it simply deductively includes S'. However, if S and S' are simply deductively equivalent and M and M' are the result of adding the same rule to S and S' respectively, it is not necessarily the case that M and M' are simply deductively equivalent.

To appreciate how this can occur (this is not quite a proof), consider the case in which S' consists of S with an additional rule, R_1, which is a derived rule of S. Hence, by 3 above, S and S' are simply deductively equivalent. Now assume that the rule added to form M, R_2, is not a derived rule of S. It follows that both M and M' deductively include both S and S'. However since there are derivations in M which are not derivations of S (they involve explicit use of R_2), it is possible that R_1 may not be a derived rule of M. If it is not, M' will simply deductively include M, but not vice versa.

When S includes S' but not vice versa, we say that it **strictly includes** it. Suppose S simply deductively includes S' and S' simply deductively includes S''. Obviously S simply deductively includes S''. Suppose further that not-[$\alpha \vdash_{S'} A$] and $\alpha \vdash_S A$. It follows that not-[$\alpha \vdash_{S''} A$] and hence that S strictly includes S''.

Of course, when the proof of a derived rule of S does not depend on the rules used in the proof being limited to those of S, it applies also to every R-extension of S. By and large, metatheorems establishing derived rules are of one of three types:

1. Those which obtain their generality as a consequence of closure with respect to substitution.
2. Those which achieve generality by induction on the structure of the formulae concerned (most usually, the length of the formulae)
3. Those which achieve generality by induction on the number of steps in the derivation.

Only in the third case does the argument sometimes depend on previous steps having been established by the rules of S **and no others** and hence only the third type (among these three) generates cases where a derived rule may not hold in a **R**-extension. When a theorem holds in **S** and all its **R**-extensions, we will say that it holds **R extendibly** in **S** and we will sometimes indicate this either explicitly or by adding **RE** in parentheses after the statement of the theorem.

In addition to extending a system by adding rules, one might extend a system by adding new elements to the alphabet S. If **S'** differs from **S** only in having additional elements in its set of connectives S - V, we will call it an **F-extension** of **S**; derived rules of **S** will similarly hold in **S'** provided their proof is not dependent on the particular connectives of **S**. When a theorem thus holds in S and every **F**-extension of it, we will say it is an **F-extendible** theorem of **S**. Generally speaking, among the type of theorems mentioned above, types 1 and 3 are **F**-extendible, but type 2 frequently is not. If **S'** is both an **R**- and an **F**- extension of **S**, we can only be certain that a theorem of **S** holds in **S'** (without a separate proof) if the theorem is both **R**- and **F**- extendible; usually, this means that it is a theorem of the first kind. A significant relation between systems is one that holds when each rule of one is a rule of the other (a special case of this was, as you may recall, **R**-extension).

In order to make this more precise, we define a **translation** of a zero-order system $\mathcal{L}$ into another $\mathcal{L}'$ as a function $\mathbf{f}: W_{\mathcal{L}} \rightarrow W_{\mathcal{L}'}$, such that

1. If v is a variable of $\mathcal{L}$, $\mathbf{f}(v)$ is a variable of $\mathcal{L}'$
2. For every n-place connective C in $\mathcal{L}$, there exists a wff of $\mathcal{L}'$, A and variables $v_1, \cdots, v_n$ of $\mathcal{L}$ such that $\mathbf{f}(Cv_1 \cdots v_n) = A$ and for every n-tuple of wffs of $\mathcal{L}$ $A_1, \cdots, A_n$, $\mathbf{f}(CA_1 \cdots A_n) =$
$\mathsf{S}^{\mathbf{f}(v_1)}_{\mathbf{f}(A_1)} \cdots {}^{\mathbf{f}(v_n)}_{\mathbf{f}(A_n)} A$.

We can now say that $\mathcal{L}'$ deductively includes $\mathcal{L}$ under the translation $\mathbf{f}$ provided $\alpha \vdash_{\mathcal{L}} A$ implies $\mathbf{f}(\alpha) \vdash_{\mathcal{L}'} \mathbf{f}(A)$ where $\mathbf{f}(\alpha)$ is the set of wffs $\mathbf{f}(B)$ with $B \in W_{\mathcal{L}'}$.

Where $\mathcal{L}$ and $\mathcal{L}'$ are deductive zero-order systems, it is sufficient that the above condition hold for each of the rules of $\mathcal{L}$, since by virtue of the closure property it will then hold without restriction. Where $\mathbf{f}$ is the identity transformation, or the intended translation is otherwise unambiguous, we will eliminate special mention of the translation $\mathbf{f}$.

Where $\mathbf{f}$ is a one-one transformation and $\mathcal{L}'$ **R**-includes $\mathcal{L}$ under $\mathbf{f}$, while $\mathcal{L}$ **R**-includes $\mathcal{L}'$ under its converse $\mathbf{f}^{-1}$, we say that $\mathcal{L}$ and $\mathcal{L}'$

are **R-equivalent** (or, where there is no danger of misunderstanding, **equivalent**) under **f**. Again where **f** is the identity transformation, we suppress reference to **f**.

When the number of connectives remains constant and **f** is the identity transformation, the force of adding additional primitive rules to a DZOS is to ensure deductive inclusion. Notice that when connectives are added, a derived rule which previously held, may fail.

Given a logic (and specifically a zero-order logic), the definition of derivable allows us to characterize sets of wffs by their derivability properties.

When $\mathcal{L}$ is a logic and α is a set of wffs of $\mathcal{L}$, we call the set of those wffs A in $\mathcal{L}$ such that $\alpha \vdash A$ the **derivability set** of α in $\mathcal{L}$. It is easy to see that:

1. For every set of wffs α, α is included in its derivability set (since $\alpha \vdash A$ holds if $A \in \alpha$).
2. If α is included in the derivability set of β, so is its derivability set (by the closure property).

We call a set **deductively inconsistent** if its derivability set is the set of all wffs. A set is **deductively complete** if every set β (with the exception of α itself) such that $\alpha \subset \beta$ is deductively inconsistent.

A logic $\mathcal{L}$ is **deductively inconsistent** if the null set is deductively inconsistent in $\mathcal{L}$. A logic $\mathcal{L}$ is called **virtually deductively inconsistent** provided every non-null set of wffs is deductively inconsistent in $\mathcal{L}$.

A logic $\mathcal{L}$ is **deductively complete** if for every set α of wffs and every wff A, either $\alpha \vdash_{\mathcal{L}} A$ or any logic $\mathcal{L}'$ with the alphabet of $\mathcal{L}$ which R-includes $\mathcal{L}$ and which satisfies $\alpha \vdash_{\mathcal{L}'} A$, is deductively inconsistent. Similarly, a logic $\mathcal{L}$ is **virtually deductively complete** provided that for every non-empty set α of wffs and every A, either $\alpha \vdash_{\mathcal{L}} A$ or any logic $\mathcal{L}'$ which R-includes $\mathcal{L}$ and which satisfies $\alpha \vdash_{\mathcal{L}'} A$, is virtually deductively inconsistent.

For each of these properties, a set (or logic) is **consistent** provided it is not inconsistent, and is **incomplete** provided it is not complete.

A few elementary properties are worth noting:

Theorem 2-4. A deductively inconsistent set is deductively complete.

Theorem 2-5. A deductively inconsistent logic is deductively complete.

Theorem 2-6. A virtually deductively inconsistent logic is virtually deductively complete.

Theorem 2-7. A virtually deductively inconsistent logic $\mathcal{L}$ is deductively inconsistent if and only if there exists a wff A such that $\vdash_{\mathcal{L}} A$.

Proof: Obviously if $\mathcal{L}$ is inconsistent $\vdash_{\mathcal{L}} A$. Suppose $\mathcal{L}$ is virtually deductively inconsistent and there is a wff A such that $\vdash_{\mathcal{L}} A$. Let B be any wff. Then $A \vdash_{\mathcal{L}} B$. Hence $\vdash_{\mathcal{L}} B$ and for every set α of wffs, $\alpha \vdash_{\mathcal{L}} B$.

Theorem 2-8. Let $\mathcal{L}$ be a virtually deductively complete logic such that for some wff A, $\vdash_{\mathcal{L}} A$. Then $\mathcal{L}$ is deductively complete.

Proof. Suppose $\vdash$ B does not hold in $\mathcal{L}$, and $\mathcal{L}'$ is an $\mathbf{R}$-extension of $\mathcal{L}$ such that $\vdash_{\mathcal{L}'} B$. Then since $\mathcal{L}$ is virtually deductively complete, $\mathcal{L}'$ is virtually inconsistent. Since $\mathcal{L}'$ $\mathbf{R}$-includes $\mathcal{L}$, $\vdash_{\mathcal{L}'} A$. Thus by Theorem 2-7, $\mathcal{L}'$ is deductively inconsistent. Hence $\mathcal{L}$ is deductively complete.

Consistency and completeness can also be defined in one system relative to another. Here the simplest case occurs, as usual, where the wffs of the two systems are the same. Specifically, if $W_{\mathcal{L}} = W_{\mathcal{L}'}$, $\mathcal{L}$ **is complete relative to** $\mathcal{L}'$ provided $\alpha \vdash_{\mathcal{L}'} A$ implies $\alpha \vdash_{\mathcal{L}} A$. Similarly, $\mathcal{L}$ **is consistent relative to** $\mathcal{L}'$ provided $\alpha \vdash_{\mathcal{L}} A$ implies $\mathbf{S}^{v_1}_{A_1}\cdots{}^{v_n}_{A_n}\alpha \vdash_{\mathcal{L}'} \mathbf{S}^{v_1}_{A_1}\cdots{}^{v_n}_{A_n}A$ for some variables $v_1,\cdots,v_n$ and wffs $A_1,\cdots,A_n$.

These definitions have the following features:

1. Every logic is both complete and consistent relative to itself.
2. If $\mathcal{L}$ is an $\mathbf{R}$-extension of $\mathcal{L}'$, $\mathcal{L}$ is complete relative to $\mathcal{L}'$.
3. If $\mathcal{L}$ is an $\mathbf{R}$-extension of $\mathcal{L}'$, $\mathcal{L}'$ is consistent relative to $\mathcal{L}$.

4. If $\mathcal{L}$ is deductively inconsistent and $\mathcal{L}'$ is deductively consistent, $\mathcal{L}$ is inconsistent relative to $\mathcal{L}'$.

Deductive inclusion provides the basis for two further equivalence concepts. The more restricted one of the two we shall call **simple deductive equivalence** and the more general one, **deductive equivalence**. Specifically, we will call $\mathcal{L}$ and $\mathcal{L}'$ **simply deductively equivalent under the translation f** provided **f** is a one-one function, $\mathcal{L}'$ simply deductively includes $\mathcal{L}$ under a (one-one) translation **g** and for every $x \in W_{\mathcal{L}}$, $g(f(x)) = x$. We shall call $\mathcal{L}$ and $\mathcal{L}'$ **simply deductively equivalent** if they are so under some translation.

This condition is sufficient for the equivalence of systems which differ only notationally, and for which the translation could be expressed as a transformation on the alphabets (as opposed to merely the wffs). A more intuitive and general equivalence notion would demand only that the transformation can be expressed in terms of the equivalence classes of wffs generated by interderivability. Specifically, $\mathcal{L}$ and $\mathcal{L}'$ are **deductively equivalent under the translations f and g** respectively provided (1) $\mathcal{L}'$ deductively includes $\mathcal{L}$ under **f**, (2) $\mathcal{L}$ deductively includes $\mathcal{L}'$ under **g**, (3) for every $x \in W_{\mathcal{L}}$, $g(f(x)) \vdash_{\mathcal{L}'} x$ and $x \vdash g(f(x))$, (4) for every $y \in \mathcal{L}'$, $f(g(y)) \vdash_{\mathcal{L}} y$ and $y \vdash_{\mathcal{L}} f(g(y))$, (5) if x is a variable of $\mathcal{L}$, $f(x)$ is a variable of $\mathcal{L}'$, and (6) if y is a variable of $\mathcal{L}'$, $g(y)$ is a variable of $\mathcal{L}$.

Note that when two logics are deductively equivalent, their derivation sets correspond relative to the translations, so that the respective translations f and g induce transformations on the derivation sets which are inverses of each other. As a result, to whatever extent each derivation set can be identified with a certain meaning, deductively equivalent logics express the same meanings. What the nature of these meanings is, however, may be a matter of dispute.

Further proof theoretic considerations involve the notion of a wff-function. In the way they are normally used, connectives are one example of such functions. Specifically, an **n-place wff-function** (over a logic $\mathcal{L}$) is defined as a function $f: (W_{\mathcal{L}})^n \rightarrow W_{\mathcal{L}}$. For any logic $\mathcal{L}$ and any wff in $W_{\mathcal{L}}$, we will call the **logical equivalence class of A (in $\mathcal{L}$)** the set of wffs of $\mathcal{L}$ which are deductively equivalent to A (i.e. $\{x : \mathrm{Equiv}_{\mathcal{L}}(A,x)\}$, where $\mathrm{Equiv}_{\mathcal{L}}(x,y)$ holds iff $x \vdash_{\mathcal{L}} y$ and $y \vdash_{\mathcal{L}} x$). We will denote this set by $\mathbf{E}_{\mathcal{L}}(A)$. We will denote the set of all such equivalence classes $(\{x:(\exists y)(y \in W_{\mathcal{L}} \text{ and } x = \mathbf{E}_{\mathcal{L}}(y),\})$, by $\mathfrak{E}_{\mathcal{L}}$. A particularly interesting case arises when the wff functions are invariant with respect to equivalence. An n-place wff function in $\mathcal{L}$ will be called a **logical operation** in $\mathcal{L}$ iff $\mathbf{Equiv}_{\mathcal{L}}((A_i,B_i), (1 \leq i \leq n)) \Rightarrow \mathbf{Equiv}_{\mathcal{L}}(\mathbf{f}(A_1,\cdots, A_n\rangle, \mathbf{f}(B_1,\cdots,B_n))$.

Related to the notion of logical operation is a function defined on the equivalence classes of a logic instead of on the wffs of the logic. An n-place abstract logical operation is a function $\mathbf{g}:(\mathfrak{E}_{\mathcal{L}})^n \rightarrow \mathfrak{E}_{\mathcal{L}}$. It is associated with the logical operation $\mathbf{f}$ when $\mathbf{g}(\mathbf{y}_1, \cdots, \mathbf{y}_n) = \{x:(\exists x_1,\cdots,x_n)[x_i \in \mathbf{y}_i \text{ and } \mathbf{Equiv}_{\mathcal{L}}(x, \mathbf{f}(x_1,\cdots,x_n))]\}$ for $1 \leq i \leq n$. We will call a wff function ,$\mathbf{f}$, **structure preserving** provided:

1. If v is a variable then v occurs in $\mathbf{f}(A_1,\cdots,A_n)$, iff for some i, v occurs in A_i.
2. $\mathbf{S}^{v}_{A}\mathbf{f}(A_1,\cdots,A_n) = \mathbf{f}(\mathbf{S}^{v}_{A}A_1, \cdots,\mathbf{S}^{v}_{A}A_n)$

Note that if f is an n-place connective, the function $\mathbf{g}(A_1,\cdots,A_n) = fA_1\cdots A_n$ is a structure preserving wff function. Indeed, structure preserving logical operations correspond to what are frequently called definable connectives.

Theorem 2-9. For any logical operation $\mathbf{f}$, there exists a unique abstract logical operation associated with $\mathbf{f}$.

Proof: Let f be a logical operation. Suppose $z_1,\cdots,z_n,z'_1,\cdots,z'_n \in W_S$. Let $\mathbf{Equiv}_{\mathcal{L}}(z_1,z'_1),\cdots,\mathbf{Equiv}_{\mathcal{L}}(z_n,z'_n)$. Then by the definition of logical operation, we have $\mathbf{Equiv}_{\mathcal{L}}(\mathbf{f}(z_1,\cdots,z_n),\mathbf{f}(z'_1,\cdots,z'_n))$. Let $\mathbf{g}(y_1,\cdots,y_n) = \{x:(\exists x_1,\cdots,\exists x_n)\,(x_i \in y_i)\,[1 \leq i \leq n]\}$ and $\mathbf{Equiv}_{\mathcal{L}}(x,\mathbf{f}(x_1,\cdots,x_n))\}$. Let $z_i = \{x:\mathbf{Equiv}_{\mathcal{L}}(z_i,x)\}$. Then $\mathbf{g}(z_1,\cdots,z_n) = \mathbf{g}(z'_1,\cdots,z'_n)$. Uniqueness follows trivially.

If f is an n-place connective, $\mathbf{g}(x_1,\cdots,x_n) = fx_1\cdots x_n$ is obviously a wff function but may not be a logical operation. The following theorem gives the necessary and sufficient conditions for the connectives of a logic to be logical operations. In passing, we note that the most widely familiar systems do indeed satisfy those conditions.

Theorem 2-10. Let $f_1,\cdots,f_n$ be connectives of a logic $\mathcal{L}$. Then each of their corresponding wff functions are logical operations iff $\mathbf{Equiv}_{\mathcal{L}}(A,B)$ implies $\mathbf{Equiv}_{\mathcal{L}}(\mathbf{S}^{v}_{A}C, \mathbf{S}^{v}_{B}C)$ for every variable v and wffs A, B and C where C has no well formed parts which start with any symbol other than either a variable or one of the connectives $f_1, \cdots, f_n$.

Proof: (Left-right): Suppose $\mathbf{Equiv}_{\mathcal{L}}(A,B)$. We argue by induction on $\ell(C)$:

(α) $\ell(C) = 1$. then $C \in S_0$.

Case 1. $C = v$. Then $\mathbf{S}^{v}_{A}C = \mathbf{S}^{v}_{A}v = A$ and $\mathbf{S}^{v}_{B}C = \mathbf{S}^{v}_{B}v = B$ and hence $\mathbf{Equiv}_{\mathcal{L}}(\mathbf{S}^{v}_{A}C,\mathbf{S}^{v}_{B}C)$ trivially.

Case 2. $C \neq v$. Hence $\mathbf{S}^{v}_{A}C=C = \mathbf{S}^{v}_{B}C$ and $\mathbf{Equiv}_{\mathcal{L}}(\mathbf{S}^{v}_{A}C,\mathbf{S}^{v}_{B}C)$ trivially.

(β) Assume the assertion holds for any wff D whose initial symbol is a variable or one of the $f_1,\cdots,f_n$ and $\ell(D) < k$. Let $\ell(C) = k$. Then there is an m-place connective f_i $(1 \leq i \leq n)$ and wffs $A_1,\cdots,A_m$ such that $C = f_iA_1\cdots A_m$. Hence $\mathbf{S}^{v}_{A}C = \mathbf{S}^{v}_{A}f_iA_1\cdots A_m = f_i\mathbf{S}^{v}_{A}A_1\cdots\mathbf{S}^{v}_{A}A_m$ and $\mathbf{S}^{v}_{B}C = \mathbf{S}^{v}_{B}f_iA_1\cdots A_m = f_i\mathbf{S}^{v}_{B}A_1\cdots \mathbf{S}^{v}_{B}A_m$. Now let $D_0 = \mathbf{S}^{v}_{A}C$ and $D_i = f_i\mathbf{S}^{v}_{B}A_1\cdots\mathbf{S}^{v}_{B}A_i\mathbf{S}^{v}_{A}A_{1+1}\cdots\mathbf{S}^{v}_{A}A_m$, so that $D_m = \mathbf{S}^{v}_{B}C$. For each j $(1 \leq j \leq m)$, $\ell(A_j) < \ell(C) = k$. Hence by the hypothesis of induction, $\mathbf{Equiv}_{\mathcal{L}}(\mathbf{S}^{v}_{A}A_j,\mathbf{S}^{v}_{B}A_j)$, since A_j is a well-formed part of C. Let v' be a variable not in A, B or C and different from v. Let $E^{i}_{i'} = \mathbf{S}^{v}_{A}A_i$ for $i < i'$, $E^{i}_{i'} = \mathbf{S}^{v}_{B}A_i$ for $i > i'$ and let $E^{i'}_{i'} = v'$. Let $H(i') = \mathbf{S}^{v}_{A}A_{i'}$ and $H'(i') = \mathbf{S}^{v}_{B}A_{i'}$. Then $D_{i'} = \mathbf{S}^{v'}_{H(i')}f_iE^1_{i'}\cdots E^m_{i'} = f_i\mathbf{S}^{v}_{B}A_1\cdots\mathbf{S}^{v}_{B}A_{i'}\mathbf{S}^{v}_{A}A_{i'+1}\cdots\mathbf{S}^{v}_{A}A_m$ and $\mathbf{S}^{v'}_{H(i')}f_iE^1_{i'}\cdots E^m_{i'} = f_i\mathbf{S}^{v}_{B}A_1\cdots\mathbf{S}^{v}_{B}A_{i'-1}\mathbf{S}^{v}_{A}A_{i'}\cdots\mathbf{S}^{v}_{A}A_m = D_{i'+1}$. Hence $\mathbf{Equiv}_{\mathcal{L}}(D_i,D_{i+1})$. Therefore $\mathbf{Equiv}_{\mathcal{L}}(\mathbf{S}^{v}_{A}C,\mathbf{S}^{v}_{B}C)$.

(Right-left): Assume $\mathbf{Equiv}_{\mathcal{L}}(A,B)$ implies $\mathbf{Equiv}_{\mathcal{L}}(\mathbf{S}^{v}_{A}C,\mathbf{S}^{v}_{B}C)$

for all A,B and C such that no wff has an initial element other than a variable or one of the f_i. Let f_j $(1 \le j \le m)$ be a k-place connective and let $A_1,\cdots,A_k,B_1,\cdots,B_k$ be wffs such that $\mathbf{Equiv}_{\mathcal{L}}(A_i,B_i)$ for $i=1,\cdots,k$. Let $C_i = f_jA_1\cdots A_iB_{i+1}\cdots B_k$ for $i = 1,\cdots,k$.

Then if v does not occur in any A_i or B_i, $\mathbf{S}^{v}_{A_{i+1}}(f_jA_1\cdots A_ivB_{i+2}\cdots B_k)$ $= f_jA_1\cdots A_i\mathbf{S}^{v}_{A_{i+1}}vB_{i+2}\cdots B_k = f_jA_1\cdots A_{i+1}B_{i+2}\cdots B_k = C_{i+1}$ while $\mathbf{S}^{v}_{B_{i+1}}(f_jA_1\cdots A_ivB_{i+2}\cdots B_k) = f_jA_1\cdots A_i\mathbf{S}^{v}_{B_{i+1}}vB_{i+2}\cdots B_k = f_jA_1\cdots A_iB_{i+1}\cdots B_k = C_i$. Hence $\mathbf{Equiv}_{\mathcal{L}}(C_i,C_{i+1})$. Therefore $\mathbf{Equiv}_{\mathcal{L}}(C_0,C_k)$ - i.e. $\mathbf{Equiv}_{\mathcal{L}}(f_jA_1\cdots A_k,f_jB_1\cdots B_k)$. Consequently, the wff function associated with f_j is a logical operation.

We noted above that structure preserving logical operations behave in many ways like connectives. It is therefore not surprising that we get a rather analogous result for structure preserving logical operations.

Theorem 2-11. Let $\mathbf{O} = \{\mathbf{f}^i{}_j\}$ be a set of structure preserving logical operations. Let $W_{\mathbf{O}}$ be the intersection of all subsets $\mathcal{A}$ of $W_{\mathcal{L}}$ such that:

1. $V_{\mathcal{L}} \subset \mathcal{A}$ (where $V_{\mathcal{L}}$ is the set of variables of $\mathcal{L}$)
2. If $\mathbf{f}^i{}_j \in \mathbf{O}$, and $A_1,\cdots, A_i \in \mathcal{A}$, then $\mathbf{f}^i{}_j(A_1,\cdots,A_i) \in \mathcal{A}$.

If $(C \in W_{\mathbf{O}},\ A, B \in W_{\mathcal{L}}$ and $\mathbf{Equiv}_{\mathcal{L}}(A, B))$, then $\mathbf{Equiv}_{\mathcal{L}}(\mathbf{S}^{v}_{A}C, \mathbf{S}^{v}_{B}C)$.

Proof: Let $A \in W_{\mathbf{O}}$. Then n is a quasi-order of A provided:

1. If A is a variable, 0 is a quasi-order of A
2. If $A = \mathbf{f}(A_1,\cdots,A_i)$, $\mathbf{f} \in \mathbf{O}$, $a_1,\cdots,a_i$ are quasi-orders of $A_1,\cdots,A_i$ respectively, then $\max(a_1,\cdots,a_i)+1$ is a quasi-order of A.

Then let the order of A be its least quasi-order. By induction on the order of C:

(α) $n = 0$. Then C is a variable and either C is v and $\mathbf{S}^{v}_{A}C = A$ and $\mathbf{S}^{v}_{B}C = B$, or C is not v and $\mathbf{S}^{v}_{A}C = \mathbf{S}^{v}_{B}C = C$. In either case, the result follows.

(β) Suppose the theorem holds for all $D \in W_0$ such that the order of D is n or less. We prove that it is true when the order of C is n+1. By the hypothesis of induction, $C = \mathbf{f}(A_1,\cdots,A_i)$, when the order of A_j $(1 \le j \le i)$ is less than or equal to n. Then

$\mathbf{Equiv}_{\mathcal{L}}(\mathbf{S}^{v}_{A}C, \mathbf{f}(\mathbf{S}^{v}_{A}A_1,\cdots\mathbf{S}^{v}_{A}A_i))$ and

$\mathbf{Equiv}_{\mathcal{L}}(\mathbf{S}^{v}_{B}C, \mathbf{f}(\mathbf{S}^{v}_{B}A_1,\cdots,\mathbf{S}^{v}_{B}A_i))$. Therefore by the hypothesis,

$\mathbf{Equiv}_{\mathcal{L}}(\mathbf{S}^{v}_{A}A_j,\mathbf{S}^{v}_{B}A_j)$, for all j $(1 \le j \le i)$. Hence,

$\mathbf{Equiv}_{\mathcal{L}}(\mathbf{f}(\mathbf{S}^{v}_{A}A_1,\cdots,\mathbf{S}^{v}_{A}A_i),\mathbf{f}\mathbf{S}^{v}_{B}A_1,\cdots,\mathbf{S}^{v}_{B}A_i))$. Since $\mathbf{Equiv}_{\mathcal{L}}$ is an equivalence relation and $\mathbf{f}$ is a logical operation, we have

$\mathbf{Equiv}_{\mathcal{L}}(\mathbf{S}^{v}_{A}C,\mathbf{S}^{v}_{B}C)$.

The feature: $\mathbf{Equiv}_{\mathcal{L}}(A,B) \Rightarrow \mathbf{Equiv}_{\mathcal{L}}(\mathbf{S}^{v}_{A}C, \mathbf{S}^{v}_{B}C)$, for all variables v and **all** wffs A,B and C, is common to most well known logics. We will call logics for which this feature holds, **E-Logics**.

Certain logical operations have customary names. In particular, a logical operation f satisfying:

1. $A, \mathbf{f}(A,B) \vdash B$
2. $\alpha, A \vdash B \Rightarrow \alpha \vdash \mathbf{f}(A,B)$

is called a **positive implication**.

A logical operation **f** satisfying:

1. $A \vdash \mathbf{f}(A,B)$
2. $B \vdash \mathbf{f}(A,B)$
3. $(\alpha,A \vdash C$ and $\alpha,B \vdash C) \Rightarrow \alpha, \mathbf{f}(A,B) \vdash C$

is called a **normal disjunction**.

A logical operation satisfying:

1. $\mathbf{f}(A,B) \vdash A$
2. $\mathbf{f}(A,B) \vdash B$
3. $A,B \vdash \mathbf{f}(A,B)$

is called a **normal conjunction**.

A logical operation satisfying:

1. $\mathbf{f}(A,B), A \vdash B$
2. $\mathbf{f}(A,B), B \vdash A$
3. $(\alpha, A \vdash B$ and $\alpha, B \vdash A) \Rightarrow \alpha \vdash \mathbf{f}(A,B)$

is called a **positive equivalence**.

A logical operation satisfying:

1. α,A$\vdash$ **f**(B) $\Rightarrow$ α,B$\vdash$ **f**(A)

1a. α, A$\vdash$ **f**(A) $\Rightarrow$ $\alpha\vdash$ **f**(A)

is called a **minimal negation.**

A minimal negation satisfying:

2. A, **f**(A)$\vdash$ B

is called a **rejective negation.**

A rejective negation satisfying:

3. (α,A $\vdash$ B and α,**f**(A) $\vdash$ B) $\Rightarrow$ $\alpha\vdash$ B

is called a **classical negation.**

Theorem 2-12. In any logic, any two positive implications are equivalent. Consequently, in any logic there is at most one abstract positive implication.

Proof: Suppose **f** and **g** are positive implications. Then **f**(A,B), A$\vdash$ B. Hence **f**(A,B)$\vdash$**g**(A,B). By the same argument (reversing **f** and **g**), **g**(A,B)$\vdash$**f**(A,B). Then $\mathbf{Equiv}_{\mathcal{L}}$[**f**(A,B),**g**(A,B)]. Therefore, [$\mathbf{Equiv}_{\mathcal{L}}$(A,B) and $\mathbf{Equiv}_{\mathcal{L}}$(C,D)] imply $\mathbf{Equiv}_{\mathcal{L}}$(**f**(A,C), **g**(B,D)), and **f** and **g** determine the same abstract logical operation.

Theorem 2-13. In any logic, any two normal disjunctions are equivalent. Consequently, in any logic there is at most one abstract normal disjunction.

Proof: Suppose **f** and **g** are normal disjunctions. Then A$\vdash$ **g**(A,B) and B$\vdash$**g**(A,B). Then **f**(A,B)$\vdash$**g**(A,B). By the same argument (reversing **f** and **g**), **g**(A,B)$\vdash$**f**(A,B). Hence $\mathbf{Equiv}_{\mathcal{L}}$[**f**(A,B),**g**(A,B)]. Therefore, [$\mathbf{Equiv}_{\mathcal{L}}$(A,B) and $\mathbf{Equiv}_{\mathcal{L}}$(C,D)] imply $\mathbf{Equiv}_{\mathcal{L}}$(**f**(A,C), **g**(B,D)), and **f** and **g** determine the same abstract logical operation.

Theorem 2-14. In any logic, any two normal conjunctions are equivalent. Consequently, in any logic there is at most one abstract normal conjunction.

Proof: Let **f** and **g** be normal conjunctions. Then **f**(A,B)$\vdash$ A and

$\mathbf{f}(A,B) \vdash B$. Hence $\mathbf{f}(A,B) \vdash \mathbf{g}(A,B)$. By the same argument (reversing **f** and **g**), $\mathbf{g}(A,B) \vdash \mathbf{f}(A,B)$. Then $\mathbf{Equiv}_{\mathcal{L}}[\mathbf{f}(A,B),\mathbf{g}(A,B)]$. Therefore, $[\mathbf{Equiv}_{\mathcal{L}}(A,B)$ and $\mathbf{Equiv}_{\mathcal{L}}(C,D)]$ imply $\mathbf{Equiv}_{\mathcal{L}}(\mathbf{f}(A,C), \mathbf{g}(B,D))$, and **f** and **g** determine the same abstract logical operation.

Theorem 2-15. In any logic, any two positive equivalences are equivalent. Consequently, in any logic there is at most one abstract positive equivalence.

Proof: Suppose **f** and **g** are positive equivalences. Then $\mathbf{f}(A,B), A \vdash B$ and $\mathbf{f}(A,B), B \vdash A$. Hence $\mathbf{f}(A,B) \vdash \mathbf{g}(A,B)$. By the same argument (reversing **f** and **g**), $\mathbf{g}(A,B) \vdash \mathbf{f}(A,B)$. Then $\mathbf{Equiv}[\mathbf{f}(A,B),\mathbf{g}(A,B)]$. Therefore $[\mathbf{Equiv}_{\mathcal{L}}(A,B)$ and $\mathbf{Equiv}_{\mathcal{L}}(C,D)]$ implies $\mathbf{Equiv}_{\mathcal{L}}(\mathbf{f}(A,C),\mathbf{g}(B,D))$, and **f** and **g** determine the same abstract logical operation.

Theorem 2-16. In any logic, any two rejective negations are equivalent. Consequently, in any logic there is at most one abstract rejective negation.

Proof: Suppose **f** and **g** are rejective negations. Then $\mathbf{f}(A), A \vdash \mathbf{g}(\mathbf{f}(A))$. Hence $\mathbf{f}(A), \mathbf{f}(A) \vdash \mathbf{g}(A)$, i.e $\mathbf{f}(A) \vdash \mathbf{g}(A)$. By the same argument (reversing **f** and **g**), $\mathbf{g}(A) \vdash \mathbf{f}(A)$. Then $\mathbf{Equiv}_{\mathcal{L}}[\mathbf{f}(A),\mathbf{g}(A)]$. Therefore, $\mathbf{Equiv}_{\mathcal{L}}(A,B)$ implies $\mathbf{Equiv}_{\mathcal{L}}(\mathbf{f}(A),\mathbf{g}(B))$, and **f** and **g** determine the same abstract logical operation.

Note that despite their simplicity, theorems 2-12 to 2-16 have some interesting and perhaps surprising consequences. For instance, since both intuitionistic and classical implication are positive, they could not both occur (as logical operations) in the same logic. Similarly, no logic could have both intuitionistic and classical negation, since both are rejective. However, not every connective leads to this type of result. For instance, it is well known that many modal systems, for instance, those of C.I. Lewis, have both a modal and a non-modal conditional. Nevertheless, both may be logical operations, since in these cases the modal conditional is not a positive implication.

Theorem 2-17. Let $\{f_k\}$ be the set of all elements of S_i, then: for every k and j ($1 \le j \le n(k)$), [$\mathbf{Equiv}_{\mathcal{L}}(A,B) \Rightarrow \mathbf{Equiv}_{\mathcal{L}}(f_k v_1 \cdots v_{j-1} A v_{j+1} \cdots v_{n(k)}, f_k v_1 \cdots v_{j-1} B v_{j+1} \cdots v_{n(k)})$] implies $\mathcal{L}$ is an E-logic.

Proof: We will prove that for all wffs C, D and E and variable v, $\mathbf{Equiv}_{\mathcal{L}}(D,E)$ implies $\mathbf{Equiv}_{\mathcal{L}}(\mathbf{S}^v_D C, \mathbf{S}^v_E C)$. If v does not occur in C, $\mathbf{S}^v_D C = C = \mathbf{S}^v_E C$ and the result is obvious. We will now assume that v occurs in C. By induction on $\ell(C)$:

(α) $\ell(C) = 1$. Then $C \in S_0$, and since v occurs in C, $v = C$. Hence $\mathbf{S}^v_D C = \mathbf{S}^v_D v = D$ and $\mathbf{S}^v_E C = \mathbf{S}^v_E v = E$ and $\mathbf{Equiv}_{\mathcal{L}}(\mathbf{S}^v_D C, \mathbf{S}^v_E C)$ in a trivial way.

(β) Assume the theorem is true for all wffs G such that $\ell(G) < m$. We assume $\ell(C) = m > 1$. Then $C = f_k w_1 \cdots w_{n(k)}$ where $w_j \in W_S$ ($1 \le j \le n(k)$). Then $\mathbf{S}^v_D C = f_k \mathbf{S}^v_D w_1 \cdots \mathbf{S}^v_D w_{n(k)}$ and $\mathbf{S}^v_E C = f_k \mathbf{S}^v_E w_1 \cdots \mathbf{S}^v_E w_{n(k)}$. Let $C_j = f_k \mathbf{S}^v_E w_1 \cdots \mathbf{S}^v_E w_j \mathbf{S}^v_D w_{j+1} \cdots \mathbf{S}^v_D w_{n(k)}$. Then $C_0 = \mathbf{S}^v_D C$ and $C_{n(k)} = \mathbf{S}^v_E C$. Let $D_i = \mathbf{S}^v_D w_i$ and $E_i = \mathbf{S}^v_E w_i$. Then $C_j = \mathbf{S}^{v_i}_{E_1} \cdots {}^{v_j}_{E_j} {}^{v_{j+1}}_{E_{j+1}} \cdots {}^{v_{n(k)}}_{E_{n(k)}} f v_1 \cdots v_{n(k)}$ where $v_1, \cdots, v_{n(k)}$ are variables which do not occur in D, E or $w_1, \cdots, w_{n(k)}$. Let $f_j = f_k v_1 \cdots v_{j-1} D v_{j+1} \cdots v_{n(k)}$. Let $f'_j = f_k v_1 \cdots v_{j-1} E v_{j+1} \cdots v_{n(k)}$. Now assume $\mathbf{Equiv}_{\mathcal{L}}(D,E)$. By the hypothesis of induction, since $\ell(w_i) < m$, $\mathbf{Equiv}_{\mathcal{L}}(D_j, E_j)$. Hence, by assumption, $\mathbf{Equiv}_{\mathcal{L}}(F_j, F'_j)$. By closure under substitution, $\mathbf{Equiv}_{\mathcal{L}}(C_{j+1}, C_j)$. Since $\mathbf{Equiv}_{\mathcal{L}}$ is an equivalence relation, $\mathbf{Equiv}_{\mathcal{L}}(C_{n(k)}, C_0)$ and $\mathbf{Equiv}_{\mathcal{L}}(\mathbf{S}^v_D C, \mathbf{S}^v_E C)$.

Exercises Chapter 2

1. Let $S_0 = \{0\}$ (We will write t_0 for 0), $S_1 = \{1\}$ (We will write t_1 for 1), $S_2 = \{t_2\}, \cdots, S_n = \{t_n\}, \cdots$

Rules:

1. $\vdash t_0$
2. $t_n x_1 \cdots x_n \vdash t_{n+1} x_1 \cdots x_n t_1$ for $x_1, \cdots, x_n \in W_S$

a. Prove that in the above described logic all theorems are of the form:
t_n followed by t_0 followed by n-1 t_1's.

b. Are there wffs which are provable?

2. Let S be a zero- order structure. We define the property $\mathbf{f}$ to hold of x and L iff:
$x = g x_1 \cdots x_n$
$g \in S_n$
and $x_1, x_2, \cdots, x_n \in L$ and write $\mathbf{f}_{\mathcal{L}}(x)$.

We now define a sequence of sets relative to S:

$\mathcal{L}_0 = S_0$
$\mathcal{L}_{n+1} = \{x : x \in \mathcal{L}_n \text{ or } f_{\mathcal{L}_n}(x)\}$
$\mathcal{L}_\omega = \bigcup_{i \in Z} \mathcal{L}_i$

Prove that if m > n then $\mathcal{L}_n \subset \mathcal{L}_m$. Prove $\mathcal{L}_\omega = W_S$.

3. Prove that in theorems 2-12 through 2-16, the assumption that the positive implication, normal disjunction, normal disjunction, positive equivalence or rejective negation is a logical operation is dispensable. (In other words, any wff function satisfying the indicated condition must be a logical operation).

3
Zero-Order Model Theory

In this chapter, we will present an alternative way of characterizing zero-order logics. In some of its instances, this new way will be familiar to the reader with experience in elementary symbolic logic as "truth functional" logic. As we shall see, our characterization will be somewhat more general than the usual presentation. It is, however, in an important sense not as general as it might be. The overall methodology, as we shall see, consists of defining a class of mathematical structures which, when they are playing this role, are called **model structures**. One then defines a relation, analogous in some sense to "truth," between wffs and model structures; this relation is usually called **satisfaction**. Substantial parts of the theory then are not specific to the particular version of satisfaction we will introduce in this chapter but are relative to whatever structures and "satisfaction" are used. We will indeed introduce a few of these alternatives in chapter 11. In this chapter (and in chapter 12), we will be addressing perhaps the mathematically simplest of these: those which have the variables ranging over arbitrary sets and which copy the functional structure of the logics over which they are defined. When necessary we will refer to this family of model theory as "**extensional model theory**."

Let us first consider a mathematical concept called a zero-order structure. A **zero-order structure** $\mathbf{S}$ is an ordered triple $(\mathbf{U},\mathbf{D},\mathbf{K})$ whose first element $\mathbf{U}$ is a set of at least two distinct elements (referred to as the **values** of $\mathbf{S}$), whose second element $\mathbf{D}$ is a non-empty proper subset of $\mathbf{U}$ (whose elements are called **designated values**), and whose third element $\mathbf{K}$ is a non-empty set of functions $\mathbf{f}: \mathbf{U}^n \to \mathbf{U}$. These functions are many-one relations between the n-tuples of elements of $\mathbf{U}$ and the elements of $\mathbf{U}$ itself such that for every n-tuple of the domain there is a member of $\mathbf{U}$ to which it corresponds – that member of $\mathbf{U}$ is called the value of the function for the n-tuple in question. Since the function values are themselves elements of $\mathbf{U}$, this allows us to speak meaningfully of functions of functions, i.e. if $\mathbf{f}$ is an n-place function and an element of $\mathbf{K}$, and $\mathbf{g}_1,\cdots,\mathbf{g}_n$ are elements of $\mathbf{K}$ and $x_1,\cdots,x_n$ are finite sequences of variables on elements of $\mathbf{U}$ such that $\mathbf{g}_1(x_1),\cdots,\mathbf{g}_n(x_n)$ are defined, then $\mathbf{f}(\mathbf{g}_1(x_1),\cdots,\mathbf{g}_n(x_n))$ is a function from the m-tuple of distinct variables on $\mathbf{U}$ in $x_1,\cdots,x_n$ to $\mathbf{U}$. We shall call a set of functions $\{\mathbf{f}_n\}$ on $\mathbf{U}$ **closed**, if $\mathbf{f},\mathbf{g}_1(x_1),\cdots,\mathbf{g}_n(x_n) \in \{\mathbf{f}_n\}$ implies $\mathbf{f}(\mathbf{g}_1(x_1),\cdots,\mathbf{g}_n(x_n)) \in \{\mathbf{f}_n\}$. If X is a set of functions, we shall call the intersection of all closed sets of functions containing X **the closure of** X (we shall symbolize it as clos(X)).

We shall term two zero-order structures $(\mathbf{U},\mathbf{D},\mathbf{K})$ and $(\mathbf{U}',\mathbf{D}',\mathbf{K}')$ **equivalent** if $\mathbf{U} = \mathbf{U}'$, $\mathbf{D} = \mathbf{D}'$ and clos($\mathbf{K}$) = clos ($\mathbf{K}'$).

We shall now define a **realization** $(\mathbf{S},\mathbf{g})$ of a zero-order system $\mathcal{L}$ to be an ordered couple of a zero-order structure $\mathbf{S} = (\mathbf{U},\mathbf{D},\mathbf{K})$ and a function $\mathbf{g}$ on the elements of $S_{\mathcal{L}}$, the alphabet of $\mathcal{L}$, and for every $x \in S_i$, $\mathbf{g}(x)$ is an i-place function which is an element of $\mathbf{K}$.

Intuitively, the significance of these definitions is that a zero-order structure is a class of elements construed as values, some of which are regarded as "acceptable" (the elements of $\mathbf{D}$) -- the analogue, in effect, of "true. " Notice that this makes the value, and hence the "acceptability", of well-formed formulae a function of the value of their parts, and ultimately, of the value of their variables. As a result, all that is necessary to determine which wffs are "acceptable" is contained in the specification of a realization. Note that it is not a part of our development that all, or any part, of language is of this character (as, for example, Frege claimed). If some of language is, suitable parts of our theory become interesting to linguists and philosophers of language. But that is a matter extrinsic to what we are doing here.

Theorem 3-1. (The unique valuation theorem) Let $\mathbf{r} = (\mathbf{S},\mathbf{g})$ be a realization of a zero-order system $\mathcal{L}$. Then there is a unique function $\mathbf{g}'_{\mathbf{r}}: W_{\mathcal{L}} \to \mathbf{U}$ such that :

1. If $A \in S_0$, $\mathbf{g}'_{\mathbf{r}}(A)$ is the constant value of the function $\mathbf{g}(A)$.
2. If $f \in S_n$ $(n > 0)$ and $x_1,\cdots,x_n$ are elements of $W_{\mathcal{L}}$ (wffs), then $\mathbf{g}'_{\mathbf{r}}(fx_1\cdots x_n) = (\mathbf{g}(f))(\mathbf{g}'_{\mathbf{r}}(x_1),\cdots,\mathbf{g}'_{\mathbf{r}}(x_n))$.

Proof: Let A be a wff. By induction on $\ell(A)$:

(α) $\ell(A) = 1$. Then $A \in S_0$. Hence $\mathbf{g}'_{\mathbf{r}}(A) = \mathbf{g}(A)$. Suppose $\mathbf{g}'_{\mathbf{r}}$ and $\mathbf{g}''_{\mathbf{r}}$ both satisfy condition 1. Then $\mathbf{g}''_{\mathbf{r}}(A) = \mathbf{g}(A)$. Hence $\mathbf{g}''_{\mathbf{r}}(A) = \mathbf{g}(A) = \mathbf{g}'_{\mathbf{r}}(A)$.

(β) Suppose the theorem is true for all wffs B such that $\ell(B) < k$. Let $\ell(A) = k > 1$. Then $A = fx_1\cdots x_n$ for some $n > 0$,

$f \in S_n$, and n wffs $x_1,\cdots,x_n$. Then $\mathbf{g}'_{\mathbf{r}}(A) = (\mathbf{g}(\mathbf{f}))(\mathbf{g}'_{\mathbf{r}}(x_1),\cdots,\mathbf{g}'_{\mathbf{r}}(x_n))$, since $\mathbf{g}(\mathbf{f})$ exists and is an n-place function from $\mathbf{U}^n$ to $\mathbf{U}$ and since for $1 \le i \le n$, $\ell(x_i) < k$, we have, by the hypothesis of induction, $\mathbf{g}'_{\mathbf{r}}(x_i) \in \mathbf{U}$; therefore, $\mathbf{g}'_{\mathbf{r}}(A) \in \mathbf{U}$. Let $\mathbf{g}'_{\mathbf{r}}$ and $\mathbf{g}''_{\mathbf{r}}$ satisfy conditions 1 and 2. Then $\mathbf{g}'_{\mathbf{r}}(A) = (\mathbf{g}(\mathbf{f}))(\mathbf{g}'_{\mathbf{r}}(x_1),\cdots,\mathbf{g}'_{\mathbf{r}}(x_n))$ and since, by the hypothesis of induction, $\mathbf{g}'_{\mathbf{r}}(x_i)=\mathbf{g}''_{\mathbf{r}}(x_i)$, for $1 \le i \le n$, $\mathbf{g}'_{\mathbf{r}}(A) = (\mathbf{g}(\mathbf{f}))(\mathbf{g}''_{\mathbf{r}}(x_1),\cdots,\mathbf{g}''_{\mathbf{r}}(x_n)) = \mathbf{g}''_{\mathbf{r}}(A)$.

We term the function $\mathbf{g}'_{\mathbf{r}}$ **the valuation function on $W_{\mathcal{L}}$ generated by r**, and for $A \in W_{\mathcal{L}}$, $\mathbf{g}'_{\mathbf{r}}(A)$ **the value of A in r**.

If $A \in W_{\mathcal{L}}$ and $\mathbf{g}'_{\mathbf{r}}(A) \in \mathbf{D}$, we say that r **is a model of** A (symbolically, $\mathbf{r} \Vdash A$). Similarly if α is a set of wffs and for every $A \in \alpha$, $\mathbf{g}'_{\mathbf{r}}(A) \in \mathbf{D}$, we say that **r** is a model of α ($\mathbf{r} \Vdash \alpha$).

Let **R** be a set of realizations of a zero-order system $\mathcal{L}$ such that, if $(\mathbf{S},\mathbf{g})$ and $(\mathbf{T},\mathbf{h})$ are both elements of **R**, then $\mathbf{S} = \mathbf{T}$ and for any $x \in S_i$ and x not a variable, $\mathbf{g}(x) = \mathbf{h}(x)$. Then we will term **R** a **realization family.** We will term a set α of wffs of $\mathcal{L}$ **(model-theoretically) consistent** relative to **R**, provided **R** is a realization family whose elements are realizations of $\mathcal{L}$, and there is a realization $\mathbf{r} \in \mathbf{R}$ which is a model of α. If the elements of **R** are realizations of $\mathcal{L}$ and α is not consistent relative to **R**, it is **(model-theoretically) inconsistent** relative to **R**. If A is a wff and every member of the realization family **R** is a model of A, we term A **valid relative to R**.

If α is a set of wffs and A is a wff and every model of α in **R** is a model of A, we say that α **entails** A **relative to R** or that A is a **consequence of α relative to R** (symbolically, $\alpha \vDash_{\mathbf{R}} A$). Obviously, A is valid relative to **R** if and only if $\varnothing \vDash_{\mathbf{R}} A$.

It is equally obvious that the entailment relation satisfies the closure property. To show that substitution behaves naturally, we need the help of a further theorem.

Theorem 3-2. Let **R** be a realization family and $B \in W_{\mathcal{L}}$, $\mathbf{r} \in \mathbf{R}$, and v a variable of $\mathcal{L}$. Then there is a realization **r'** such that $\mathbf{r}' \in \mathbf{R}$ and for every wff A, $\mathbf{g}'_{\mathbf{r}'}(A) = \mathbf{g}'_{\mathbf{r}}(\mathbf{S}^{v}_{B}A)$.

Proof: Let **r'** be the realization such that $\mathbf{g}_{\mathbf{r}'}(v) = \mathbf{g}'_{\mathbf{r}}(B)$, and for $x \in S_i$

and $x \neq v$, $\mathbf{g}_{\mathbf{r}'}(x) = \mathbf{g}_{\mathbf{r}}(x)$. Then $\mathbf{r}' \in \mathbf{R}$. We will prove the desired result by induction on $\ell(A)$.

(α) $\ell(A) = 1$. Then $A \in S_0$.

Case 1. $A = v$. Then $\mathbf{g}'_{\mathbf{r}'}(A) = \mathbf{g}_{\mathbf{r}'}(v) = \mathbf{g}'_{\mathbf{r}}(B) = \mathbf{g}'_{\mathbf{r}}(\mathbf{S}^{v}_{B}A)$.

Case 2. $A \neq v$. Then $\mathbf{g}'_{\mathbf{r}'}(A) = \mathbf{g}_{\mathbf{r}'}(A) = \mathbf{g}'_{\mathbf{r}}(A) = \mathbf{g}'_{\mathbf{r}}(\mathbf{S}^{v}_{B}A)$.

(β) Assume true for all wffs C such that $\ell(C) < k$. Let $\ell(A) = k$. Then $A = fx_1 \cdots x_n$ where $f \in S_n$ and $x_1, \cdots, x_n$ are wffs for some $n > 1$. Then, $\mathbf{g}'_{\mathbf{r}'}(A) = \mathbf{g}'_{\mathbf{r}'}(fx_1 \cdots x_n) = (\mathbf{g}_{\mathbf{r}'}(f))(\mathbf{g}'_{\mathbf{r}'}(x_1), \cdots, \mathbf{g}'_{\mathbf{r}'}(x_n)) = (\mathbf{g}_{\mathbf{r}}(f))(\mathbf{g}'_{\mathbf{r}'}(x_1), \cdots, \mathbf{g}'_{\mathbf{r}'}(x_n))$. By the hypothesis of induction, since we have for each i ($1 \leq i \leq n$), $\ell(x_i) < k$, then $\mathbf{g}'_{\mathbf{r}'}(x_i) = \mathbf{g}'_{\mathbf{r}}(\mathbf{S}^{v}_{B}x_i)$.

Hence, $\mathbf{g}'_{\mathbf{r}'}(A) = (\mathbf{g}_{\mathbf{r}}(f))(\mathbf{g}'_{\mathbf{r}}(\mathbf{S}^{v}_{B}x_1), \cdots, \mathbf{g}'_{\mathbf{r}}(\mathbf{S}^{v}_{B}x_n)) = \mathbf{g}'_{\mathbf{r}}(f\mathbf{S}^{v}_{B}x_1 \cdots \mathbf{S}^{v}_{B}x_n) = \mathbf{g}'_{\mathbf{r}}(\mathbf{S}^{v}_{B}(fx_1 \cdots x_n)) = \mathbf{g}'_{\mathbf{r}}(\mathbf{S}^{v}_{B}A)$.

With the help of theorem 3-2, we can easily show that entailment satisfies the substitution property.

Theorem 3-3. If $\alpha \models_{\mathbf{R}} A$, v is a variable and B is a wff, then $\mathbf{S}^{v}_{B}\alpha \models_{\mathbf{R}} \mathbf{S}^{v}_{B}A$.

Proof: Let $\mathbf{r}$ be a model of $\mathbf{S}^{v}_{B}\alpha$. Then if $\mathbf{r}'$ is the realization described in theorem 3-2, $\mathbf{r}'$is a model of α. Hence, since $\mathbf{r}' \in \mathbf{R}$ and $\alpha \models_{\mathbf{R}} A$, $\mathbf{r}'$ is also a model of A and $\mathbf{r}$ is a model of $\mathbf{S}^{v}_{B}\alpha$.

Hence, if there is a decision procedure for $\alpha \models_{\mathbf{R}} A$ when α is finite and implication satisfies the finite implication property, we have a zero order logic with "$\alpha \models_{\mathbf{R}} A$ (α finite) $\Rightarrow \alpha \vdash A$" as its only rule. Let us call $(\mathcal{L}, \mathbf{R})$ a **finite-valued realization system**, if $\mathcal{L}$ is a zero-order system with a finite number of elements as connectives (i.e. elements of US_i that are not variables) and $\mathbf{R}$ a realization family with a finite number of values (i.e. elements of $\mathbf{U}$).

Theorem 3-4. For any realization family **R**, if **r** $\in$ **R**, A a wff and x a variable which does not occur in A, then $\mathbf{g'_r}(A)$ is independent of $\mathbf{g_r}(x)$.

Proof: (α) $\ell(A) = 1$. Then $A \in S_0$ and $A \neq x$. Since x is a variable, $\mathbf{g_r}(x)$ is independent of $\mathbf{g_r}(y)$ for every $y \in S_0$ except if y=x. Then the result follows since $\mathbf{g'_r}(A) = \mathbf{g_r}(A)$.

(β) $\ell(A) = k$. Assume the theorem is true for all wffs C, such that x does not occur in C and $\ell(C) < k$. Then $A = fx_1\cdots x_n$, where $f \in S^n$ for some $n > 0$ and $x_1,\cdots,x_n$ are wffs. Then $\mathbf{g'_r}(A) = \mathbf{g'_r}(fx_1\cdots x_n) = (\mathbf{g_r}(f))(\mathbf{g'_r}(x_1),\cdots,\mathbf{g'_r}(x_n))$. $\mathbf{g_r}(f)$ is independent of $\mathbf{g_r}(x)$ by the definition of realization family and $\mathbf{g'_r}(x_i)$ for $1 \leq i \leq n$ is independent of $\mathbf{g_r}(x)$ by the hypothesis of induction since by theorem 1-8, x does not occur in x_i. Hence $\mathbf{g'_r}(x)$ is independent of $\mathbf{g_r}(x)$.

It follows immediately from theorem 3-4 that in a finite valued realization system, the values of wffs of a finite set α are dependent only on the finite number of variables occurring in α. Suppose $x_1,\cdots,x_n$ are the variables in α, m is the number of elements of **V**, and $\mathbf{r}_1,\cdots,\mathbf{r}_{m^n}$ are the elements of the realization family **R** which satisfies the condition, if $i \neq j$ ($i \leq m^n$, $j \leq m^n$), then there is a k such that $\mathbf{g_{r_i}}(x_k) \neq \mathbf{g_{r_j}}(x_k)$. Then, for every **r** $\in$ **R**, there is an i ($1 \leq i \leq m^n$) such that $\mathbf{g'}(A) = \mathbf{g'_{r_i}}(A)$ for every $A \in \alpha$. It follows from this that to determine whether $\alpha \vDash_{\mathbf{R}} A$ holds, we only need to consider a finite number of realizations (at most m^n).

Theorem 3-5. Let $(\mathcal{L},\mathbf{R})$ be a finite-valued realization scheme and $\alpha \subset W_{\mathcal{L}}$. Then α has a model in **R** if and only if every finite subset of α has a model in **R**.

Proof: Let $v_1,v_2,\cdots$ be an enumeration of all of the variables. We will prove that there exists a sequence of elements of **V**, $w_1,w_2,\cdots$ where each finite subset of α has a model $\mathbf{r}(\alpha)$ such that $\mathbf{g_{r(\alpha)}}(v_i) = w_i$ for each i. By induction on i:

(α) i = 1. Let us suppose that for every value w except w_1, it is false that every finite subset of α has a model $\mathbf{r}(\alpha)$ such that $\mathbf{g_r}(\alpha) = w$. Hence for every value w except w_1 there is an α_w such that α_w is a finite subset of α and α_w has no models $\mathbf{r}$ such that $g_{\mathbf{r}}(v_1) = w$. But since there are only a finite number of values, $\cup\alpha_w$ ($w \neq w_1$) is a finite set. Then there is an $\mathbf{r}$ such that $\mathbf{r}$ is a model of $\cup\alpha_w(w \neq w_1)$, $g_{\mathbf{r}}(v_1) = w_1$, since for every $w \neq w_1$, $g_{\mathbf{r}}(v_1) \neq w$.

(β) Suppose the assertion is true for $v_1,\cdots,v_k$. Assume that the property fails for the m-1 values $w \neq w_{k+1}$ (of course, if this were not the case, we would simply choose w_k to be the value for which the property holds). Then by the same argument as above there are m-1 finite subsets α_w of α such that each α_w ($w \neq w_{k+1}$) has a model $\mathbf{r}_w$ where $g_{\mathbf{r}_w}(v_i) = w_i$ for $i \leq k$, but no models $\mathbf{r}'$ such that $g_{\mathbf{r}'}(v_i) = w_i$ and $g_{\mathbf{r}'}(v_{k+1}) = w$. Their union is a finite subset of α and hence has a model $\mathbf{r}$ with $g_{\mathbf{r}}(v_i) = w_i$ for $i \leq k$. Consequently, $\mathbf{r}$ is a model of each of the α_w and hence $g_{\mathbf{r}}(v_{k+1}) \neq w$. Consider the realization $\mathbf{r}$ such that $g_{\mathbf{r}}(v_i) = w_i$ for each i and $\mathbf{r} \in \mathbf{R}$. If $A \in \alpha$, $\{A\}$ is a finite subset of α and as a result, $\mathbf{r}$ is a model of every element of α, and therefore a model of α.

We would like to mention a few points in connection with theorem 3-5. First, the proof goes through by the same steps, even with the added restriction to realizations that are not models of a particular wff A (we will refer to this modified form as **Theorem 3-5a**). When there exists a connective h with $g_{\mathbf{r}}(h) = \mathbf{f}$, where $\mathbf{f}$ is a function such that $\mathbf{f}(x) \notin \mathbf{D}$ implies $x \in \mathbf{D}$, 3-5a is a consequence of 3-5. This leads immediately to an alternative way of proving 3-5a. We can extend the alphabet by adding a new connective h and having its value be a truth function satisfying $\mathbf{f}(x) \notin \mathbf{D}$ implies $x \in \mathbf{D}$, and therefore able to function as a negation. Theorem 3-5 is then applied to $\alpha \cup \{hA\}$. It should be noted, incidentally, that while our assumptions concerning calculi allow us the enumerability of the variables, our proof of theorem 3-5 uses only the weaker assumption of the well-ordering of the variables (i.e. that the set of variables can be ordered in such a way that each subset has a least member). If the set of variables were not denumerable, we would need a stronger variant of induction called "transfinite induction". As it is, ordinary induction is sufficient.

Theorem 3-5 is ordinarily called the **Compactness Theorem** and leads immediately to the model theoretic equivalent of the finite deduction property.

Theorem 3-6. Let $\alpha \models_{\mathbf{R}} A$, where $\mathbf{R}$ is a finite valued realization scheme. Then there exists a finite set α' such that $\alpha' \subset \alpha$ and $\alpha' \models_{\mathbf{R}} A$.

Proof: Suppose there is no finite set $\alpha' \subset \alpha$ such that $\alpha' \models_{\mathbf{R}} A$. Then every finite subset α' of α has a model which is not a model of A, and α has a model which is not a model of A and hence not-$(\alpha \models_{\mathbf{R}} A)$.

The notion of relative completeness defined in chapter 2 has an interesting correlate in m-valued logic. We will define a logic $\mathcal{L}$ to be **model theoretically complete relative to a realization family R** provided that for every $A \in W_{\mathcal{L}}$ and every $\alpha \subset W_{\mathcal{L}}$: if (1) $\mathbf{r} \in \mathbf{R}$, and (2) for each $x \in \alpha$, $\mathbf{g}'_{\mathbf{r}}(x) \in \mathbf{D}$ implies $\mathbf{g}'_{\mathbf{r}}(A) \in \mathbf{D}$, then $\alpha \vdash_{\mathcal{L}} A$.

One trivial case of model theoretic completeness relative to a realization family $\mathbf{R}$ occurs when "$\alpha \models A \Rightarrow \alpha \vdash A$" is regarded as the only rule of the logic. The resulting logic is called the **m-valued logic (over $W_{\mathcal{L}}$) defined by R**.

Let us now turn briefly to the arithmetics (or, if you prefer, the algebras) connected with the third element $\mathbf{K}$ of zero-order structures, i.e. the sets of functions $\mathbf{f}: \mathbf{V}^n \to \mathbf{V}$ (where $n \geq 0$ and $\mathbf{V}$ is the set of values and is finite). In considering sets of functions. $\mathbf{V}$ will be kept constant. In addition we will define equality among functions to hold whenever their function values are the same for all values of their variables; more precisely: let $\mathbf{f}(x_1,\cdots,x_{n_1})$ and $\mathbf{g}(y_1,\cdots,y_{n_2})$ be n_1 and n_2 -place functions respectively (note that no assumptions are made here concerning distinctness). Then: $\mathbf{f}(x_1,\cdots,x_{n_1}) = \mathbf{g}(y_1,\cdots,y_{n_2})$ if and only if for every $n_1 + n_2$- tuple of elements of $\mathbf{K}$, $(a_1,\cdots,a_{n_1},b_1,\cdots,b_{n_2})$ such that (1) x_i is x_j implies $a_i = a_j$, (2) y_i is y_j implies $b_i = b_j$, and (3) x_i is y_j implies $a_i = b_j$, then $\mathbf{f}(x_1,\cdots,x_{n_1})$ and $\mathbf{g}(y_1,\cdots,y_{n_2})$ are the same element of $\mathbf{V}$. This is of course what is normally meant by asserting that they represent the same assignment rule. Consequently, if $\mathbf{f}(x,y)$ is x for all values of x and y and $g(z)$ is z for all values of z, $\mathbf{f}(x,y) = g(x)$.

If there are m values and a set $\mathfrak{K}$ of functions, the question naturally arises as to which functions can be generated by a finite number of applications of elements of $\mathfrak{K}$ [e.g., if $\mathbf{f}(x) = m + 1 - x$ and $\mathbf{g}(x,y) = \max(x,y)$, $\mathbf{f}(\mathbf{g}(\mathbf{f}(x),\mathbf{f}(y))) = \min(x,y)$]. Of special interest is the case in which a set of functions $\mathfrak{K}$ of an m-valued arithmetic has the property that any function of those m values can be generated by such a finite number of applications of elements of $\mathfrak{K}$. Such a set is called **functionally complete**. We will prove the existence of such a set for m = 2. Although two-valued arithmetic (and logic) is best known in connection with an interpretation in which the values are "true" and "false," we will nevertheless use the values 0 and 1. For some purposes 1 will behave like some concepts of "truth" (for instance **D** will be {1}). This correlation of "true" with 1 and "false" with 0 will have nothing to do with the correctness of our theorems.

Theorem 3-7. Let $\mathfrak{K}$ be a set of functions $\{\mathbf{f}_1(x,y), \mathbf{f}_2(x,y), \mathbf{f}_3(x)\}$ of two-valued arithmetic such that $\mathbf{f}_1(x,y) = 0$ if and only if $x = y = 0$, $\mathbf{f}_2(x,y) = 1$ if and only if $x = y = 1$, and $\mathbf{f}_3(x) \neq x$ for all x. Then $\mathfrak{K}$ is functionally complete. (The careful reader will have noted that the functions are the ones customarily called "disjunction," "conjunction," and "negation.")

Proof: Let $\mathbf{f}(x_1,\cdots,x_n)$ be an arbitrary function of two-valued logic. By induction on n, we obtain:

(α) n = 0. Then f is one of the two constant functions (i.e either the function that is identically 0 or the one identically 1). But $\mathbf{f}_1(0,\mathbf{f}_3(0)) = \mathbf{f}_1(0,1) = 1 = \mathbf{f}_1(1,0)$ and $\mathbf{f}_1(1,\mathbf{f}_3(1)) = 1$. Hence $\mathbf{f}_1(x,\mathbf{f}_3(x))$ is identically 1. Similarly $\mathbf{f}_2(0,\mathbf{f}_3(0)) = \mathbf{f}_2(0,1) = 0 = \mathbf{f}_2(1,0) = \mathbf{f}_2(1, \mathbf{f}_3(1))$ and $\mathbf{f}_2(x,\mathbf{f}_3(x))$ is identically 0.

(β) Suppose any function can be generated provided n = k. We shall prove that this holds if n = k+1. Let $\mathbf{f}(x_1,\cdots,x_k,x_{k+1})$ be a function of two-valued arithmetic (of k+1 variables). Let $\mathbf{g}_1(x_1,\cdots,x_k) = \mathbf{f}(x_1,\cdots,x_k,1)$ and $\mathbf{g}_0(x_1,\cdots,x_k) = \mathbf{f}(x_1,\cdots,x_k,0)$. By the hypothesis of induction since $\mathbf{g}_1$ and $\mathbf{g}_2$ are k place functions they can be generated by a finite number, say q_1 and q_2, of applications of functions of $\mathfrak{K}$. Let $\mathbf{g}(x_1, \cdots, x_k, x_{k+1}) = \mathbf{f}_1(\mathbf{f}_2(x_{k+1},\mathbf{g}_1(x_1,\cdots, x_k)),\mathbf{f}_2(\mathbf{f}(x_{k+1}),\mathbf{g}_0(x_1,\cdots, x_k)))$.

Let $(v_1,\cdots,v_k,v_{k+1})$ be a k+1-tuple of values. Obviously $\mathbf{g}$ can be generated in (at most) $q_1 + q_2 + 4$ applications.

Case 1. $v_{k+1} = 1$. Then $\mathbf{g}(v_1,\cdots,v_k,v_{k+1}) =$
$\mathbf{f}_1(\mathbf{f}_2(v_{k+1},\mathbf{g}_1(v_1,\cdots,v_k)),\mathbf{f}_2(\mathbf{f}_3(v_{k+1},\mathbf{g}_0(v_1,\cdots,v_k))) =$
$\mathbf{f}_1(\mathbf{f}_2(1, \mathbf{g}_1(v_1\cdots,v_k)), \mathbf{f}_2(\mathbf{f}_3(1), \mathbf{g}_0(v_1,\cdots,v_k))) =$
$\mathbf{f}_1(\mathbf{g}_1(v_1\cdots,v_k)),\mathbf{f}_2(0,\mathbf{g}_0(v_1,\cdots,v_k))) = \mathbf{f}_1(\mathbf{g}_1(v_1\cdots,v_k),0) =$
$\mathbf{g}_1(v_1,\cdots,v_k) = \mathbf{f}(v_1,\cdots,v_k,1) = \mathbf{f}(v_1,\cdots,v_k,v_{k+1})$

Case 2. $v_{k+1} = 0$. Then $\mathbf{g}(v_1,\cdots,v_k,v_{k+1}) =$
$\mathbf{f}_1(\mathbf{f}_2(v_{k+1},\mathbf{g}_1(v_1,\cdots,v_k)),\mathbf{f}_2(\mathbf{f}_3(v_{k+1}),\mathbf{g}_0(v_1,\cdots,v_k)))) =$
$\mathbf{f}_1(\mathbf{f}_2(0,\mathbf{g}_1(v_1,\cdots,v_k)),\mathbf{f}_2(\mathbf{f}_3(0),\mathbf{g}_0(v_1,\cdots,v_k))) =$
$\mathbf{f}_1(0,\mathbf{f}_2(1,\mathbf{g}_0(v_1,\cdots,v_k)) = \mathbf{f}_1(0,\mathbf{f}_2(1, \mathbf{g}_0(v_1,\cdots,v_k)) =$
$\mathbf{f}_1(0,\mathbf{g}_0(v_1,\cdots,v_k)) = \mathbf{g}_0(v_1,\cdots,v_k) = \mathbf{f}(v_1,\cdots,v_k,0) = \mathbf{f}(v_1,\cdots,v_k,v_{k+1})$.

Consequently, $\mathbf{f}(v_1,\cdots,v_k,v_{k+1}) = \mathbf{g}(v_1,\cdots,v_k,v_{k+1})$ and hence can be generated from elements of $\mathbf{K}$ in a finite number of steps.

There are naturally many sets which are functionally complete, and using theorem 3-7 we can establish this by showing that we can generate $\mathbf{f}_1$, $\mathbf{f}_2$ and $\mathbf{f}_3$ (i.e., "or," "and," and "not"). For example, that the set $\{\mathbf{f}_2(p,q), \mathbf{f}_3(p)\}$ is functionally complete can be seen from the identity $\mathbf{f}_1(p,q) = \mathbf{f}_2(\mathbf{f}_3(p),\mathbf{f}_3(q))$ which, except for the change in notation, is the well-known DeMorgan law: $(p \vee q) \equiv \sim(\sim p \wedge \sim q)$.

To show that a set of truth functions is **not** functionally complete is a trifle more complicated, since we must show that there is at least one function that cannot be generated, no matter how long the expression. Fortunately, it is possible to express the situation in a form that is not excessively complex, because of a theorem first proved (in a slightly different form) by E. L. Post.

In approaching this theorem, it is useful to introduce a few concepts. Given two sets of functions α and β, if $\alpha \subset \beta$, every function that can be expressed in terms of functions of α can obviously be expressed in terms of functions of β. Some sets of functions furthermore have the property of being **closed**, i.e., every function that can be expressed in terms of elements of that set is itself a member of that set. Some examples are the sets $\{\mathbf{g}_1(x)\}$ and $\{\mathbf{g}_1(x),\mathbf{f}_3(x)\}$ where $\mathbf{f}_3$ is defined as in theorem 3-7 and $\mathbf{g}_1(x) = x$, for all values of x. If β is closed and not identical to the set of all functions and $\alpha \subset \beta$, it follows immediately that α is not functionally complete. Our basic strategy will be to define five sets, each of which we shall show to be closed and not functionally complete. We shall then show that any set of functions contained in none of the five is functionally complete. Since, as shall be seen, the defining characteristic is in each case fairly easily checked, our result constitutes a complete (and practical) solution to the problem of which sets of functions of two-valued arithmetic are functionally complete.

We will say of a function **f** that it can be **immediately generated** by functions of a set β, provided **f** is the identity function, $\mathbf{f} \in \beta$ or **f** can be expressed as the result of applying a function which is an element of β to functions, each of which is the identity function or an element of β.

We will call a function $\mathbf{f}(v_1,\cdots,v_n)$ **0-preserving** provided $\mathbf{f}(0,\cdots,0)= 0$. Similarly, we will call a function $\mathbf{f}(v_1,\cdots,v_n)$ **1-preserving** provided $\mathbf{f}(1,\cdots,1) = 1$. We will call the set of all 0-preserving functions $\mathcal{P}_0$ and the set of all 1-preserving functions $\mathcal{P}_1$.

Theorem 3-8. $\mathcal{P}_0$ is closed.

Proof: Let $\mathbf{f}(x_1,\cdots,x_m)$ be a function that can be immediately generated by elements of $\mathcal{P}_0$. Hence there are functions $\mathbf{g}(x_1,\cdots,x_m)$, $\mathbf{g}_1(x_1,\cdots,x_m)$, $\cdots$,$\mathbf{g}_n(x_1,\cdots,x_m)$) such that $\mathbf{f}(x_1,\cdots,x_m) = \mathbf{g}(\mathbf{g}_1(x_1,\cdots,x_m),\cdots, \mathbf{g}_n(x_1,\cdots,x_m)$ and $\mathbf{g}$ and $\mathbf{g}_1$ through $\mathbf{g}_n$ are elements of $\mathcal{P}_0$. Note that no generality is lost by having each of the $\mathbf{g}_i$ be functions of all m variables, since we do not exclude the case that some (or indeed, all) of the variables be "dummy" (i.e., that the value of the function is independent of the variable). Since $\mathbf{g}_1$ through $\mathbf{g}_n$ are elements of $\mathcal{P}_0$, $\mathbf{g}_i(0,\cdots,0) = 0$ and hence $\mathbf{g}(\mathbf{g}_1(0,\cdots,0),\cdots, \mathbf{g}_n(0,\cdots,0) = \mathbf{g}(0,\cdots,0) = 0$, since $\mathbf{g} \in \mathcal{P}_0$. Hence $\mathbf{f} \in \mathcal{P}_0$. Since all functions immediately generated from $\mathcal{P}_0$ are in $\mathcal{P}_0$, $\mathcal{P}_0$ is closed.

Theorem 3-9. $\mathcal{P}_0$ is not functionally complete.

Proof: $\mathbf{f}_3(p)$ of theorem 3-7 is not 0-preserving and hence is not an element of $\mathcal{P}_0$. Since $\mathcal{P}_0$ is closed, $\mathbf{f}_3$ cannot be expressed in terms of elements of $\mathcal{P}_0$.

Theorem 3-10. $\mathcal{P}_1$ is closed and not functionally complete.

Proof: By an argument analogous to theorem 3-8, $\mathcal{P}_1$ is closed and since f_3 is not an element of $\mathcal{P}_1$ either, $\mathcal{P}_1$ is not functionally complete.

Let us call $(v_1,\cdots,v_n)$ an **n-tuple assignment** provided for every i, $(1 \leq i \leq n)$, v_i is either 0 or 1. We shall call an n-place function $f(v_1,\cdots,v_n)$ **self-dual** provided for every n-tuple assignment $(v_1,\cdots,v_n)$, $f_3(f(v_1,\cdots,v_n)) = f(f_3(v_1),\cdots,f_3(v_n))$ where f_3 is defined as in theorem 3-7. Let $\mathcal{SD}$ be the set of all self-dual functions.

Theorem 3-11. $\mathcal{SD}$ is closed.

Proof: Let $f(x_1,\cdots,x_m)$ be a function that can be immediately generated by elements of $\mathcal{SD}$. Hence there is a $g(x_1,\cdots,x_n)$ and $g_1(x_1,\cdots,x_m)$, $\cdots$, $g_n(x_1,\cdots,x_m)$ such that g and g_1, $\cdots$, g_n are elements of $\mathcal{SD}$ and $f(x_1,\cdots,x_m) = g(g_1(x_1,\cdots,x_m),\cdots,g_n(x_1,\cdots,x_m)$. Let $(a_1,\cdots,a_m)$ be an arbitrary m-tuple assignment. Then $g_i(f_3(a_1),\cdots,f_3(a_m)) = f_3(g_i(a_1,\cdots,a_m))$ for $1 \leq i \leq n$. Hence
$f(f_3(a_1),\cdots,f_3(a_m)) =$
$g(g_1(f_3(a_1),\cdots,f_3(a_m)),\cdots,g_n(f_3(a_1),\cdots,f_3(a_m))) =$
$g(f_3(g_1(a_1,\cdots,a_m),\cdots,f_3(g_n(a_1,\cdots,a_m)) =$
$f_3(g(g_1(a_1,\cdots,a_m),\cdots,g_n(a_1,\cdots,a_m)) = f_3(f(a_1,\cdots,a_m))$
and f is an element of $\mathcal{SD}$. Therefore, $\mathcal{SD}$ is closed.

Theorem 3-12. $\mathcal{SD}$ is not functionally complete.

Proof: Since $f_3(f_2(1,0)) = f_3(0) = 1$ and $f_2(f_3(1),f_3(0)) = f_2(0,1) = 0$, f_2 of theorem 3-7 is not self-dual. Since $\mathcal{SD}$ is closed f_2 cannot be expressed in terms of elements of $\mathcal{SD}$.

Let us call a function $f(x_1,\cdots,x_m)$ **linear** provided there exists an m+1-tuple $(c_0,c_1,\cdots,c_m)$ of elements of $\{0,1\}$ such that $f(x_1,\cdots,x_m) = c_0 \oplus c_1 x_1 \oplus \cdots \oplus c_m x_m$ for all values of the variables $x_1,\cdots,x_m$ where $1 \oplus 1 = 0 \oplus 0 = 0$ and $0 \oplus 1 = 1 \oplus 0 = 1$. Note that in a linear function, for any argument position, say the ith, either $c_i = 0$ and the ith variable is a dummy variable, or $c_i = 1$ and a change in the value of the ith variable (all others remaining unchanged) will always produce a change in the function value. Let $\mathcal{Ln}$ be the set of all linear functions.

Theorem 3-13. $\mathcal{Ln}$ is closed.

Proof: Let $f(x_1,\cdots,x_m)$ be a function that can be immediately generated by elements of $\mathcal{Ln}$. Hence there is a $g(x_1,\cdots,x_n)$ and $g_1(x_1,\cdots,x_m), \cdots, g_n(x_1,\cdots,x_m)$ such that g and $g_1, \cdots, g_n$ are elements of $\mathcal{Ln}$ and $f(x_1,\cdots,x_m) =$ $g(g_1(x_1,\cdots,x_m), \cdots, g_n(x_1,\cdots,x_m))$. Let $g(x_1,\cdots,x_n) =$ $c_{00} \oplus c_{01}x_1 \oplus \cdots \oplus c_{0n}x_n$ and $g_i(x_1,\cdots,x_m) =$ $c_{i0} \oplus c_{i1}x_1 \oplus \cdots \oplus c_{im}x_m$. Then $f(x_1,\cdots,x_m) =$

$$g(g_1(x_1,\cdots,x_m),\cdots,g_n(x_1,\cdots,x_m)) =$$

$$c_{00} \oplus c_{01}g_1(x_1,\cdots,x_m) \oplus \cdots \oplus c_{0n}g_n(x_1,\cdots,x_m) =$$

$$c_{00} \oplus c_{01}(c_{10} \oplus c_{11}x_1 \oplus \cdots \oplus c_{1m}x_m) \oplus \cdots$$

$$\oplus c_{0n}(c_{n0} \oplus c_{n1}x_1 \oplus \cdots \oplus c_{nm}x_m) =$$

$$(c_{00} \oplus c_{01}c_{10} \oplus \cdots \oplus c_{0n}c_{n0}) \oplus$$

$$(c_{01}c_{11} \oplus \cdots \oplus c_{0n}c_{n1})x_1 \oplus \cdots \oplus \cdots$$

$$\oplus \ (c_{01}c_{1m} \oplus \cdots \oplus c_{0n}c_{nm})x_m ,$$ which is linear.

Theorem 3-14. $\mathcal{Ln}$ is not functionally complete.

Proof: Consider the function f_2 of theorem 3-7. $f_2(1,1) \neq f_2(1,0)$ but $f_2(0,1) = f_2(0,0)$. Therefore, f_2 could not be linear and hence $\mathcal{Ln}$ cannot be functionally complete, since it is closed.

Let us define a partial ordering $\leq$ on the m-tuple assignments as: $(\upsilon_1,\cdots,\upsilon_m) \leq (\upsilon'_1,\cdots,\upsilon'_m) \Leftrightarrow$ (for every i $[1 \leq i \leq m]$, $\upsilon_i \leq \upsilon'_i$). We then call a function $f(x_1,\cdots,x_m)$ **monotonic**, provided $(\upsilon_1,\cdots,\upsilon_m)$ $(\upsilon'_1,\cdots,\upsilon'_m)$ implies $f(\upsilon_1,\cdots,\upsilon_m) \leq f(\upsilon'_1,\cdots,\upsilon'_m)$. Let us call the set of all monotonic functions $\mathcal{M}$.

Theorem 3-15. $\mathcal{M}$ is closed.

Proof: Let $f(x_1,\cdots,x_m)$ be a function that can be immediately generated by elements of $\mathcal{M}$. Hence there is a $g(x_1,\cdots,x_n)$ and $g_1(x_1,\cdots,x_m),\cdots,g_n(x_1,\cdots,x_m)$ such that g and $g_1,\cdots,g_n$ are elements of $\mathcal{M}$ and $f(x_1,\cdots,x_m) = g(g_1(x_1,\cdots,x_m),\cdots,g_n(x_1,\cdots,x_m))$. Let $(v_1,\cdots,v_m)$ and $(v'_1,\cdots,v'_m)$ be m-tuple assignments and $(v_1,\cdots,v_m) \leq (v'_1,\cdots,v'_m)$. Then for every i $(1 \leq i \leq n)$, $g_i(v_1,\cdots,v_m) \leq g_i(v'_1,\cdots,v'_m)$. Hence,
$g(g_1(v_1,\cdots,v_m),\cdots,g_n(v_1,\cdots,v_m)) \leq$
$g(g_1(v'_1,\cdots,v'_m),\cdots,g_n(v'_1,\cdots,v'_m))$. Hence $f(v_1,\cdots,v_m) \leq$ $f(v_1,\cdots,v_m)$ and f is monotonic and therefore $\mathcal{M}$ is closed.

Theorem 3-16: $\mathcal{M}$ is not functionally complete.

Proof: Since for f_3 of theorem 3-7, $f_3(0) = 1$ and $f_3(1) = 0$, f_3 is not monotonic. Since $\mathcal{M}$ is closed, it is not functionally complete.

Theorem 3-17. Let α be a set of functions such that none of the following holds: $\alpha \subset \mathcal{P}_0$, $\alpha \subset \mathcal{P}_1$, $\alpha \subset \mathcal{SD}$ and $\alpha \subset \mathcal{M}$. Then α will generate every one-place function of two-valued arithmetic.

Proof: Since α is not a subset of $\mathcal{P}_0$, there is a function $f_0(x_1,\cdots,x_m)$ which is not 0-preserving and a function $f_1(x_1,\cdots,x_m)$ which is not 1-preserving. Then let $g_0(x) = f_0(x,\cdots,x)$ and $g_1(x) = f_1(x,\cdots,x)$. Then either $g_0(x) = 1$, in which case g_0 is the constant function 1, or $g_0(x) = 0$ in which case g_0 is negation. Similarly g_1 is either the constant 0 or negation. Since the negation of either constant is the other constant, we can conclude that we can either generate negation or else both constants (or both, in which case we can generate all one-place functions).

Case 1: Negation has been generated. Since $\alpha \subset \mathcal{SD}$ does not hold, there exists a function $f_{\mathcal{SD}}(x_1,\cdots,x_m)$ in α which is not self-dual. Since $f_{\mathcal{SD}}$ is not self-dual, there exists an m-tuple assignment $(v_1,\cdots,v_m)$ such that $f_{\mathcal{SD}}(v_1,\cdots,v_m) = f_{\mathcal{SD}}(f_3(v_1),\cdots,f_3(v_m))$. We now define for each i, $x^*_i = x$ if $v_i = 1$ and $x^*_i = f_3(x)$ if $v_i = 0$. Now let $g_{\mathcal{SD}}(x)$ be $f_{\mathcal{SD}}(x^*_1,\cdots,x^*_m)$. Then $g_{\mathcal{SD}}(1) =$

$f_{SD}(v_1,\cdots,v_m) = f_{SD}(f_3(v_1),\cdots,f_3(v_m)) = g_{SD}(0)$ and g_{SD} is a constant, so that all one-place functions can be generated.

Case 2. Both constants can be generated. Since $\alpha \subset \mathcal{M}$ does not hold, there exists a function $f_{\mathcal{M}}(x_1,\cdots,x_m)$ which is not monotonic. Hence there exist m-tuple assignments $(v_1,\cdots,v_m)$ and $(w_1,\cdots,w_m)$ such that $f_{\mathcal{M}}(v_1,\cdots,v_m) = 1$ and $f_{\mathcal{M}}(w_1,\cdots,w_m) = 0$ and $v_i \leq w_i$, for every i. Define x^*_i to be the constant function 0 if $v_i = w_i = 0$, or the constant function 1 if $v_i = w_i = 1$, and otherwise the variable x. We define $g_{\mathcal{M}}(x)$ to be $f_{\mathcal{M}}(x^*_1,\cdots,x^*_m)$. Then $g_{\mathcal{M}}(0) = f_{\mathcal{M}}(v_1,\cdots,v_m) = 1$ and $g_{\mathcal{M}}(1) = f_{\mathcal{M}}(w_1,\cdots,w_m) = 0$. Hence $g_{\mathcal{M}}$ is negation and all one-place functions have been generated.

Theorem 3-18. If α can generate all one-place functions and at least one two-place function f which takes the value 1 for an odd number of the four cases: $f(0,0)$, $f(0,1)$, $f(1,0)$ and $f(1,1)$, then α is functionally complete.

Proof: Suppose f takes the value 1 for exactly one of the four cases. Then the same will be true of all of $f(p,q)$, $f(p,f_3(q))$, $f(f_3(p),q)$, and $f(f_3(p),f_3(q))$. But then each will take the value 1 in a different case and hence represent all four of the functions that take 1 in exactly one case; consequently, one of the four must be f_2 of theorem 3-7 ("conjunction"). Similarly, the same argument holds for f_1 if f takes 0 in exactly one case. In either case, f_3 and either f_1 or f_2 can be generated and the other one is $f_3(f(f_3(p),f_3(q)))$. Hence by theorem 3-7, α is functionally complete.

Theorem 3-19. α is functionally complete, if and only if, none of: $\alpha \subset \mathcal{P}_0$, $\alpha \subset \mathcal{P}_1$, $\alpha \subset \mathcal{SD}$, $\alpha \subset \mathcal{M}$, $\alpha \subset \mathcal{L}n$ hold. (**Post's Functional Completeness Theorem**)

Proof: By theorems 3-9, 3-10, 3-12, 3-14 and 3-16, if α is functionally complete none of the indicated inclusions hold. Now assume none of the inclusions hold. Then by theorem 3-17, all one place functions can be generated. Then there is a function $f_{\mathcal{L}n}(x_1,\cdots,x_m)$ in α

which is not linear. Hence there exists an i $(1 \leq i \leq n)$, such that x_i is not a dummy variable, but such that a change in its value will not always cause a change in the function value. In other words, there are two m-tuple assignments $(\upsilon_1,\cdots,\upsilon_m)$ and $(\omega_1,\cdots,\omega_m)$ with $f_{\mathcal{L}n}(\upsilon_1,\cdots,\upsilon_m) = f_{\mathcal{L}n}(\upsilon_1,\cdots,\upsilon_{i-1},f_3(\upsilon_i),\upsilon_{i+1},\cdots,\upsilon_m)$ and $f_{\mathcal{L}n}(\omega_1,\cdots,\omega_m) \neq f_{\mathcal{L}n}(\omega_1,\cdots,\omega_{i-1},f_3(\omega_i),\omega_{i+1},\cdots,\omega_m)$.

Let us define x^*_j to be:

the constant 0	if $i \neq j$ and $\upsilon_j = \omega_j = 0$
the constant 1	if $i \neq j$ and $\upsilon_j = \omega_j = 1$
x	if $i \neq j$ and $\upsilon_j = 0$ and $\omega_j = 1$
$f_3(x)$	if $i \neq j$ and $\upsilon_j = 1$ and $\omega_j = 0$
y	if $i = j$

Then define $g(x,y)$ as $f_{\mathcal{L}n}(x^*_1,\cdots,x^*_n)$. Then $g(0,0) = f_{\mathcal{L}n}(\upsilon_1,\cdots,\upsilon_{i-1},0,\upsilon_{i+1},\cdots,\upsilon_m)) = f_{\mathcal{L}n}(\upsilon_1,\cdots,\upsilon_{-1},1,\upsilon_{i+1},\cdots,\upsilon_m)) = g(0,1)$. On the other hand, $g(1,0) = f_{\mathcal{L}n}(\omega_1,\cdots,\omega_{i-1},0,\omega_{i+1},\cdots,\omega_m) \neq f_{\mathcal{L}n}(\omega_1,\cdots,\omega_{i-1},1,\omega_{i+1},\cdots,\omega_m) = g(1,1)$.

Consequently, $g(x,y)$ takes 1 for an odd number of cases, and by theorem 3-18, α is functionally complete.

A systematic line-up of possible and relevant cases for purposes of expressing a function is usually called a **truth-table**. Perhaps the easiest arrangement will be in ascending (or descending) order as binary numbers. To illustrate how this works, suppose we have 3 variables x_1, x_2 and x_3. Then the input rows are: 000, 001, 010, 011, 100, 101, 110 and 111, in that order. It is obvious that this procedure will generate all possible cases once and only once and that the number of rows will be 2^n, where n is the number of variables and that consequently the number of functions will be 2^{2^n}. Our table is then:

x_1	x_2	x_3
0	0	0
0	0	1
0	1	0
0	1	1

1	0	0
1	0	1
1	1	0
1	1	1

With the truth table arranged in this fashion it is relatively easy to detect the five properties of the Post theorem, specifically:

1. A function $\mathbf{f}(x_1,\cdots,x_n)$ is 0-preserving if its top line, $\mathbf{f}(0,\cdots,0)$ is 0.
2. A function $\mathbf{f}(x_1,\cdots,x_n)$ is 1-preserving if its bottom line, $\mathbf{f}(1,\cdots,1)$ is 1.
3. A function is self-dual provided its result column, read top-to-bottom, is item-for-item opposite to its result column, read bottom-to-top.
4. Determining monotonicity is a little more complicated. Looking at the result column of the truth table, we find all pairs of lines that take respectively 0 and 1. For each such pair of lines, we see if thereis an input column with 0 and 1 at corresponding places (0 where the output is 0, 1 where it is 1); if there is not, the function is **not** monotonic, but if the corresponding column criterion is met for all pairs, the function is monotonic. (Of course different pairs can be satisfied by different columns.) Note that if the function is constant, there are no 0-1 pairs and the function is trivially monotonic.
5. Perhaps the most difficult test is for linearity. The easiest test we know is the following:

Choose a reference line, perhaps $\mathbf{f}(0,\cdots,0)$. Note its value. Now look at each line whose input differs from the reference line in exactly one argument position, i.e. $\mathbf{f}(1,0,\cdots,0)$, $\mathbf{f}(0,1,0,\cdots,0),\cdots,\mathbf{f}(0,\cdots,0,1)$. If the function were linear and the value does not change, that argument position is a dummy variable position; if the value does change, it is of course not a dummy variable. Since a change in any one non-dummy variable position will always occasion a change in the function value if the function is linear, we will have exactly one linear function which (1) agrees with the given function at the reference row, and (2) has dummy and non-dummy positions as indicated. If that is the function f we started with, f is indeed linear; if not, by reductio ad absurdum, it is not.

To illustrate, let us consider the singleton $\mathbf{f}(x,y)$ such that $\mathbf{f}(x,y) = 1$ if and only if $x = y = 0$ (in the usual reading, "neither-nor"). Its table is:

x	y	**f**(x,y)
0	0	1
0	1	0
1	0	0
1	1	0

1. Since **f**(0,0) = 1, **f** is not 0-preserving.
2. Similarly, since **f**(1,1) = 0, f is not 1-preserving.
3. Reading down the the table we get 1000, upwards, we get 0001; since the second elements are both 0, **f** is not self-dual.
4. Looking at the first two lines (in reverse order), we have an output pair 0-1, with no corresponding input. Hence **f** is not monotonic.
5. Since the first and second lines differ as do the first and third lines, neither variable is "dummy." Now the only linear two-place function with no dummy variables and **g**(0,0) = 1 is:

x	y	**g**(x,y)
0	0	1
0	1	0
1	1	0
1	1	1

Since this function is clearly not **f**, **f** is also not linear.

Hence {**f**(x,y)} is functionally complete.

From Post's theorem it follows that a function's singleton is functionally complete if and only if the function is not 0-preserving, 1-preserving, not self-dual, not monotonic and not linear. We call a function whose singleton is functionally complete a **Sheffer function** (earlier usage limited the term to two-place functions; in the last decade or so, this restriction has generally not been used).

It is easy to see that there are exactly two two-place Sheffer functions in two-valued logic. To be a Sheffer, **f**(x,y) must be such that **f**(0,0) = 1 and **f**(1,1) = 0. Then to avoid being self dual (and linear) **f**(0,1) must equal **f**(1,0) and hence there are exactly 2 such functions.

The corresponding problem as to which conditions functions must satisfy to be functionally complete for other values of m (and for every value of m) has been posed and in recent years, solved. Readers who are interested in the details are referred to the appendix .

Turning now to non-algebraic issues, we note that m-valued zero-order logics are not DZOS's in the sense defined in chapter 2. This situation (namely, the availability of two basically different types of zero-order logic) raises a number of questions concerning the relation between them.

The first of these is whether every DZOS is equivalent to some m-valued logic.

Theorem 3-20. There is a DZOS not equivalent to any m-valued logic.

Proof: Let $\mathcal{L}$ be a DZOS with "$\supset$" as its only connective and $\aleph_0$ variables. Let the rules of $\mathcal{L}$ be:

1. $\vdash A \supset A$

2. $A, A \supset B \vdash B$

Clearly, all theorems that can be generated are instances of 1. Suppose $\mathcal{L}$ were equivalent to an m-valued logic. Let $\mathbf{g_r}(\supset) = \mathbf{f}(x,y)$. Because of rule 1, $\mathbf{f}(x,x) \in \mathbf{D}$ for all values of x. Let $A_1, \cdots, A_{m^m}, A_{m^m+1}$ be distinct wffs of one and the same variable, with no A_i an instance of $A \supset A$. Since there are only m^m one-place functions, there must be A_i and A_j such that $i \neq j$ and $\mathbf{g'_r}(A_i) = \mathbf{g'_r}(A_j)$ for all $\mathbf{r} \in \mathbf{R}$. Thus $\mathbf{g'_r}(A_i \supset A_j) = \mathbf{g'_r}(A \supset A)$ for $\mathbf{r} \in \mathbf{R}$. and $\mathbf{g'_r}(A_i \supset A_j) \in \mathbf{D}$, for all $\mathbf{r} \in \mathbf{R}$. As we have seen not- $(\vdash_{\mathcal{L}} A_i \supset A_j)$.

The converse question as to whether every m-valued logic is equivalent to a DZOS is not completely solved. Slupecki has shown that if the set of functions correlated with connectives is functionally complete the answer is positive, and Rosser and Turquette have proven that this is true for somewhat weaker conditions.

One of the most significant uses of m-valued logic is as a tool in independence proofs concerning DZOS's. Given two DZOS's $\mathcal{L}_1$ and $\mathcal{L}_2$ such that $\mathcal{L}_1$ R-includes $\mathcal{L}_2$, their non-equivalence can sometimes be shown by defining an m-valued logic $\mathcal{L}_3$ such that $\mathcal{L}_3$ includes $\mathcal{L}_2$ (i.e. $\alpha \vdash_{\mathcal{L}_2} A$ implies $\alpha \vdash_{\mathcal{L}_3} A$), but nevertheless there is a β and a B such that $\beta \vdash_{\mathcal{L}_1} B$ and not $(\beta \vdash_{\mathcal{L}_3} B)$. Although this does not differ in principle from similarly interposing any logic, m-valued or not, m-valued logic has the special advantage that the non-derivability statement can be proved by calculation.

This raises the question as to whether whenever we have DZOS's $\mathcal{L}_1$ and $\mathcal{L}_2$ and $\mathcal{L}_1$ R-includes $\mathcal{L}_2$, but not conversely, an m-valued logic

$\mathcal{L}_3$ can always be interposed. To the best of our knowledge, this question has not been solved. There are some distinct DZOS, (for example, versions of Lewis's $\mathbf{S1}$ which differ only in the primitive equivalence theorem) which are non-equivalent but so closely related that it seems difficult to see how one could interpose an m-valued logic; hence, our conjecture is that the question has a negative answer. This however does not constitute a proof. Of course, even if we are right, interposition of m-valued logics has a wide applicability.

One final word before leaving this topic. Since two-valued logic took its origin from certain semantic assumptions (about truth and falsity), the impression has sometimes been given that a necessary condition for the applicability of an m-valued logic should be a semantic (or linguistic) interpretation for the m values. This view is, I believe, mistaken. Even if the individual values have no interesting meaning, if the deductive relations they specify are correct, we are justified in using an m-valued logic.

4
Positive Implication

The first of the deductive systems we shall consider has its motivation in the **conditional** connective, which is generally represented in English by the phrase "if___then___." As we have already indicated, any resemblance to the English phrase is only incidental, and the only meaning assigned to the connectives is what stems from the rules of the system. The system in question will be called **PI1** (the letters refer to "positive implication" and the wff function associated with the connective is indeed a positive implication, as we shall see). It is characterized by a single connective " ⊃ ," a denumerable infinity of variables and two rules, the first of which allows for any wffs A and B, the inference to B from A ⊃ B and A. This will be recognized as the familiar inference form "modus ponens," as in:

If the cavalry arrives in time, the wagon train will be saved.
The cavalry will arrive in time.
Therefore, the wagon train will be saved.

The second rule of inference is frequently termed "conditionalization". It allows the inference to A ⊃ B provided B can be deduced when A is added as an hypothesis (whether or not there are other hypotheses).

In more formal terms, **PI1** can be characterized as a DZOS with S_0 being a denumerably infinite set of variables, one two-place connective " ⊃ " and the following rules:

1. $A, A \supset B \vdash B$ (referred to as **MP**)
2. $\alpha, A \vdash B \Rightarrow \alpha \vdash A \supset B$ (referred to as **C**)

A large number of the better known "if___then___" inferences are provable in **PI1**. Before we proceed with the proofs, let us explain the numbering of theorems. In general, we shall prove three types of theorems, all of which are strictly speaking metatheorems, i.e. theorems concerning the systems involved, rather than provable in the system involved:

1. Theorems asserting that all well-formed formulae (wffs) of a given form are provable. These will be numbered with the suffix T (e.g. **PI1**-1T).

2. Theorems asserting that wffs of a given form are derivable from

other wffs of a given form. These will be numbered with the suffix D (e.g., P𝔗1-1D). Where modus ponens is a derived or primitive rule, some D-theorems can be proved from T-theorems by one or more applications of modus ponens; in this case, the proof of the D-theorem will normally be omitted. Similarly, we will omit the proofs of T-theorems when the corresponding D-theorems have been proved, providing of course conditionalization is a rule. When, as in P𝔗1 both modus ponens and conditionalization hold, we will choose one or the other, depending on which form is more convenient.

3. More complicated metatheorems. These will have the suffix M (e.g. P𝔗1-1M)

In accordance with the definitions of a DZOS, it is possible to give a complete characterization of P𝔗1.

1. **Arabic Numerals**

a. "0," "1," "2," "3," "4,""5," "6," "7," "8," and "9" are arabic numerals.

b. If α is an arabic numeral and β is an arabic numeral $\alpha^\frown\beta$ (i.e., α followed by β) is also.

c. There are no arabic numerals except by a and b above.

d. If α and β are arabic numerals they are the same arabic numeral if and only if $\alpha = \beta$.

e. If α, β, and γ are arabic numerals, the following are equivalent:

(i) α and β are the same numeral, (ii) $\alpha^\frown\gamma$ and $\beta^\frown\gamma$ are the same numeral, (iii) $\gamma^\frown\alpha$ and $\gamma^\frown\beta$ are the same numeral.

2. **Variables**

a. "p","q" and "r" are variables.

b. If n is an arabic numeral, p_n, q_n and r_n are variables.

c. There are no variables except by a and b above.

3. **Well-Formed Formulae (Wffs)**

a. If v is a variable, v is a well-formed formula of P𝔗1.

b. If A and B are well-formed formulae of P𝔗1, so is $\supset$AB.

4. **Derivation**

D is a **derivation of the wff** A **from the set of wffs** α **in** P𝔗1 provided, D is a finite sequence $F_1,\cdots,F_n$ of finite sequences of wffs (of P𝔗1), $A_{i1},\cdots,A_{im(i)}$ $(1 \le i \le n)$ and for each F_i, there is a sequence α_i of elements of F_i, such that for every j $(1 \le j \le m(i))$,

(1) $\alpha_n \subset \alpha$

(2) A is the last wff of F_n;

and either:

(3) A_i is an element of α_i,

(4) There exist k_1 and k_2 such that $k_1 < j$, $k_2 < j$ and A_{ik_2} is $\supset A_{ik_1} A_{ij}$,

(5) There exists a $k < i$ such that B is the last wff of a sequence of wffs F_k, α_k is $\{C\} \cup \alpha_i$ and A_{ij} is $\supset CB$, where C is a wff, or

(6) Every element of α_i is an element of F_i

The set α is called the **premise set** of D (and elements of α are called **premises**). A is called the **conclusion**.

5. **Derivability**

A is derivable from α in $\mathcal{P}\mathcal{l}1$ (in symbols $\alpha \vdash_{\mathcal{P}\mathcal{l}1} A$) provided there is a derivation of A from α in $\mathcal{P}\mathcal{l}1$.

6. Y-statement

Z is a Y-statement of $\mathcal{P}\mathcal{l}1$ provided Z is an expression for a set of wffs followed by " $\vdash$ " followed by a wff of $\mathcal{P}\mathcal{l}1$.

7. Y-derivation

D is a Y-derivation of A from α provided D is a finite sequence of Y-statements $\alpha_1 \vdash A_1, \cdots, \alpha_n \vdash A_n$ satisfying for $1 \leq i \leq n$:

(1) A is the last wff of F_n, and either:

(2) A_i is an element of α_i

(3) There is a $j < i$ such that $A_j = A_i$ and $\alpha_j \subset \alpha$

(4) There is a $j < i$ and a $k < i$ such that $\alpha_j = \alpha_k = \alpha_i$ and A_k is $\supset A_j A_i$

(5) There is a $j < i$ such that there is a wff B and $\alpha_j = \alpha_i \cup \{B\}$ and $A_i = \supset BA_j$.

One kind of result that might be provable about a system like $\mathcal{P}\mathcal{l}1$ establishes that a certain class of derivations can always be carried out in that system. While there are many conceivable ways this might be shown, one particularly effective way to demonstrate this is by providing a series of instructions (sufficiently unambiguous) for constructing a Y-derivation (and hence, by theorem 2-3, is also a derivation). In this process, it is convenient to provide notes as to what is being done: reference is thus made to 7(1) by the word "premise"; to 7(2) by the word "closure"; to 7(3) by "**MP**;" and to 7(4) by "**C**." These proofs take the form of a "telescoped" Y-derivation.

The "telescoping" consists of (1) allowing several steps to be performed on one line when the result is clear, and (2) allowing any transformation whose validity has already been shown as a step in the derivation. This represents no departure from the definition of derivation and Y-derivation; what is being presented is not the literal presentation of the Y-derivation (let alone the derivation) itself, but rather a proof (in the "metalanguage") that a Y-derivation can be produced.

Let us illustrate this in detail by presenting a first theorem:

PI1-1T. If A, B and C are wffs of **PI1**,

$\vdash_{\mathbf{PI1}}$ (B ⊃ C) ⊃ [(A ⊃ B) ⊃ (A ⊃ C)].

Normally, if there is no likelihood of misunderstanding, we would state this as:

PI1-1T. ⊢ (B ⊃ C) ⊃ [(A ⊃ B) ⊃ (A ⊃ C)]

Proof:	1. B ⊃ C, A ⊃ B, A ⊢ B	MP
	2. B ⊃ C, A ⊃ B, A ⊢ B ⊃ C	Premise
	3. B ⊃ C, A ⊃ B, A ⊢ C	1,2, MP
	4. ⊢ (B ⊃ C) ⊃ [(A ⊃ B) ⊃ (A ⊃ C)]	3,C(3)

What the proof establishes is that line 4 can be obtained by a single application of MP after "calling up" the obvious premises (in this case A and A⊃B), then "calling up" B ⊃ C, applying MP again and then applying C three times. Let us produce the Y-derivation which is spelled out by this procedure – the Y-derivation is not actually unique, since, for example, some interchange of lines is possible and, because there are an infinite number of choices for A, B and C. We will choose a Y-derivation where A is p, B is q and C is ⊃pq.

1. p, ⊃pq, ⊃q⊃pq ⊢ p
2. p, ⊃pq, ⊃q⊃pq ⊢ ⊃pq
3. p, ⊃pq, ⊃q⊃pq ⊢ q
4. p, ⊃pq, ⊃q⊃pq ⊢ ⊃q⊃pq
5. p, ⊃pq, ⊃q⊃pq ⊢ ⊃pq
6. ⊃pq, ⊃q⊃pq ⊢ ⊃p⊃pq
7. ⊃q⊃pq ⊢ ⊃⊃pq⊃p⊃pq
8. ⊢ ⊃⊃q⊃pq⊃⊃pq⊃p⊃pq

For this case, a shorter Y-derivation could be obtained by starting with line 5, but this could not be done if B were ⊃pq and C were q. The original proof would still hold, as can be seen in the following:

1. p, ⊃p⊃pq, ⊃⊃pqq ⊢ p
2. p, ⊃p⊃pq, ⊃⊃pqq ⊢ ⊃p⊃pq
3. p, ⊃p⊃pq, ⊃⊃pqq ⊢ ⊃pq
4. p, ⊃p⊃pq, ⊃⊃pqq ⊢ ⊃⊃pqq
5. p, ⊃p⊃pq, ⊃⊃pqq ⊢ q
6. ⊃p⊃pq, ⊃⊃pqq ⊢ ⊃pq
7. ⊃⊃pqq ⊢ ⊃⊃p⊃pq⊃pq
8. ⊢ ⊃⊃⊃pqq⊃⊃p⊃pq⊃pq

A derivation corresponding to the last Y-derivation mentioned is:
F1: (1) p, (2) ⊃p⊃pq, (3) ⊃⊃pqq, (4) ⊃pq, (5) q
F2: (1) ⊃p⊃pq, (2) ⊃⊃pqq, (3) ⊃pq
F3: (1) ⊃⊃pqq, (2) ⊃⊃p⊃pq⊃pq
F4: (1) ⊃⊃⊃pqq⊃⊃p⊃pq⊃pq

We can now claim that the sequences F1-F4 are a derivation of the formula "⊃⊃⊃pqq⊃⊃p⊃pq⊃pq" from the null set. We have already verified this in our original argument, but for the inordinately skeptical, we note (in accordance with that argument):

1. In F1, wff(4) can be obtained from wff(1) and wff(2) by **MP** and wff(5) from wff(3) and wff(4) by **MP**. Hence F1 is a sequence with (1)-(3) as premise set.

2. Hence, in F2, wff(3) follows from wff(1) and wff(2) and sequence F1 by **C**. Hence F2 is a sequence with wffs (1) and (2) as its premise set.

3. Then, in F3, wff(2) follows from wff(1) and sequence F2 by **C** and F3 is a sequence with the singleton of wff(1) as its premise set.

4. Hence, in F4, wff(1) follows from sequence F3 and F4 is a sequence with the null set as its premise set.

5. Therefore the sequence of sequences F1, F2, F3, F4 is a derivation of the last (and only) line of F4 from the null set.

𝔓𝔏1-1D. B ⊃ C ⊢ (A ⊃ B) ⊃ (A ⊃ C)
𝔓𝔏1-1Da. A ⊃ B, B ⊃ C ⊢ A ⊃ C

Note again that 𝔓𝔏1-1T and its variants establish an infinite class of Y-statements, namely all those that are uniform substitutions for the metalinguistic variables (in 𝔓𝔏1-1T, A, B and C). Their proof consists of making the same replacement in the steps of the indicated proofs. 𝔓𝔏1-1D is a familiar form of inference often called **chain inference**.

$\mathcal{PL}1$-2D. $(A \supset B) \vdash [(B \supset C) \supset (A \supset C)]$

Proof:	1. $A \supset B, B \supset C \vdash A \supset C$	$\mathcal{PL}1$-1Da
	2. $(A \supset B) \vdash [(B \supset C) \supset (A \supset C)]$	$\mathcal{P}\ell 1$-2D

$\mathcal{PL}1$-2T. $\vdash (A \supset B) \supset [(B \supset C) \supset (A \supset C)]$

$\mathcal{PL}1$-3M. $\mathcal{PL}1$ is an E- logic.

Proof: Suppose **Equiv**$_{\mathcal{PL}1}(A, B)$. By definition $A \vdash_{\mathcal{PL}1} B$ and $B \vdash_{\mathcal{PL}1} A$. Hence by C, $\vdash_{\mathcal{PL}1} A \supset B$ and $\vdash_{\mathcal{PL}1} B \supset A$. Then by $\mathcal{PL}1$-1D and $\mathcal{PL}1$-2D, $\vdash_{\mathcal{PL}1}(A \supset C) \supset (B \supset C)$, $\vdash_{\mathcal{PL}1} (B \supset C) \supset (A \supset C)$, $\vdash_{\mathcal{PL}1}(C \supset A) \supset (C \supset B)$ and $\vdash_{\mathcal{PL}1} (C \supset B) \supset (C \supset A)$. Therefore, by **MP**, we obtain $A \supset C \vdash_{\mathcal{PL}1} B \supset C, B \supset C \vdash_{\mathcal{PL}1} A \supset C, C \supset A \vdash_{\mathcal{PL}1} C \supset B$, and $C \supset B \vdash_{\mathcal{PL}1} C \supset A$. Thus, **Equiv**$(A \supset C, B \supset C)$ and **Equiv**$(C \supset A, C \supset B)$. Hence, since $\supset$ is the only connective, by theorem 2-17, $\mathcal{PL}1$ is an E-logic.

Note that if the wff function $\mathbf{f}(A,B) = A \supset B$, $\mathcal{PL}1$-1, $\mathcal{PL}1$-2 and $\mathcal{PL}1$-3M imply that f is a logical operation and hence by theorem 2-12, every positive implication expressible in $\mathcal{PL}1$ is equivalent to $\mathbf{f}$.

$\mathcal{PL}1$-4T. $\vdash A \supset A$

Proof:	1. $A \vdash A$	Premise
	2. $\vdash A \supset A$	1, C

$\mathcal{PL}1$-5D. $A \vdash B \supset A$

Proof:	1. $A, B \vdash A$	Premise
	2. $A \vdash B \supset A$	1, C

$\mathcal{PL}1$-5T. $\vdash A \supset (B \supset A)$

Proof: 1. $A \supset (B \supset C), (A \supset B), A \vdash B \supset C$ MP
2. $A \supset (B \supset C), (A \supset B), A \vdash B$ MP
3. $A \supset (B \supset C), (A \supset B), A \vdash C$ 1,2, MP
4. $A \supset (B \supset C) \vdash (A \supset B) \supset (A \supset C)$ 3, C(2)

PL1-6T. $\vdash [A \supset (B \supset C)] \supset [(A \supset B) \supset (A \supset C)]$

PL1-7D. $A \supset (B \supset C) \vdash B \supset (A \supset C)$ (The export-import law)

Proof: 1. $A \supset (B \supset C), A, B \vdash B \supset C$ MP
2. $A \supset (B \supset C), A, B \vdash B$ Premise
3. $A \supset (B \supset C), A, B \vdash C$ 1,2, MP

PL1-7M. $\vdash [A \supset (B \supset C)] \supset [B \supset (A \supset C)]$

PL1-8D. $(A \supset B) \supset (A \supset C) \vdash A \supset (B \supset C)$

Proof: 1. $(A \supset B) \supset (A \supset C), A, B \vdash A \supset B$ PL1-5D
2. $(A \supset B) \supset (A \supset C), A, B \vdash (A \supset B) \supset (A \supset C)$ Premise
3. $(A \supset B) \supset (A \supset C), A, B \vdash A \supset C$ 1, 2, MP
4. $(A \supset B) \supset (A \supset C), A, B \vdash A$ Premise
5. $(A \supset B) \supset (A \supset C), A, B \vdash C$ 3, 4, MP
6. $(A \supset B) \supset (A \supset C) \vdash A \supset (B \supset C)$ 5, C(2)

PL1-8T. $\vdash [(A \supset B) \supset (A \supset C)] \supset [A \supset (B \supset C)]$

PL1-9D. $A \supset B, C \supset (D \supset A) \vdash C \supset (D \supset B)$

Proof: 1. $A \supset B, C \supset (D \supset A), C, D \vdash D \supset A$ MP
2. $A \supset B, C \supset (D \supset A), C, D \vdash D$ Premise
3. $A \supset B, C \supset (D \supset A), C, D \vdash A$ 1,2, MP
4. $A \supset B, C \supset (D \supset A), C, D \vdash A \supset B$ Premise
5. $A \supset B, C \supset (D \supset A), C, D \vdash B$ 3,4, MP
6. $A \supset B, C \supset (D \supset A) \vdash C \supset (D \supset B)$ 5, C(2)

PL1-9Da. $A \supset B \vdash [C \supset (D \supset A)] \supset [C \supset (D \supset B)]$

PL1-9Db. $C \supset (D \supset A) \vdash (A \supset B) \supset [C \supset (D \supset B)]$

PL1-9T. $\vdash (A \supset B) \supset ([C \supset (D \supset A)] \supset [C \supset (D \supset B)])$

PL1-9Ta. $\vdash [C \supset (D \supset A)] \supset [(A \supset B) \supset [C \supset (D \supset B)]]$

PL1-10D. $A \supset (B \supset C), D \supset A, D \supset B \vdash D \supset C$

Proof:	1. $A \supset (B \supset C), D \supset A, D \supset B, D \vdash A$	MP
	2. $A \supset (B \supset C), D \supset A, D \supset B, D \vdash B$	MP
	3. $A \supset (B \supset C), D \supset A, D \supset B, D \vdash A \supset (B \supset C)$	Premise
	4. $A \supset (B \supset C), D \supset A, D \supset B, D \vdash B \supset C$	1, 3, MP
	5. $A \supset (B \supset C), D \supset A, D \supset B, D \vdash C$	2, 4, MP
	6. $A \supset (B \supset C), D \supset A, D \supset B \vdash D \supset C$	5, C

PL1-10Da. $A \supset (B \supset C), D \supset A \vdash (D \supset B) \supset (D \supset C)$

PL1-10Db. $A \supset (B \supset C) \vdash (D \supset A) \supset [(D \supset B) \supset (D \supset C)]$

PL1-10T $\vdash [A \supset (B \supset C)] \supset [(D \supset A) \supset [(D \supset B) \supset (D \supset C)]]$

PL1-11D. $(A \supset A) \supset B \vdash B$

Proof:	1. $(A \supset A) \supset B \vdash A \supset B$	PL1-4T
	2. $(A \supset A) \supset B \vdash (A \supset A) \supset B$	Premise
	3. $(A \supset A) \supset B \vdash B$	1,2, MP

PL1-11T. $\vdash [(A \supset A) \supset B] \supset B$

PL1-11D can of course be generalized.

PL1-12M. Suppose $\vdash_{\mathcal{L}} A$ and $\mathcal{L}$ R-includes **PL1**. Then

Equiv$_{\mathcal{L}}(A \rightarrow B, B)$ (where $\rightarrow$ is the translation of $\supset$ in $\mathcal{L}$)

Proof:	1. $A \rightarrow B \vdash_{\mathcal{L}} A \rightarrow B$	Premise
	2. $A \rightarrow B \vdash_{\mathcal{L}} A$	Hypothesis
	3. $A \rightarrow B \vdash_{\mathcal{L}} B$	1,2, MP
	4. $B \vdash_{\mathcal{L}} A \rightarrow B$	PL1-5d, Hypothesis

The parenthetic expression is necessary since the actual sign ⊃ may not be in the alphabet of 𝓛 or even worse may be in that alphabet, but not equivalent to ⊃ in a translation that preserves the rules of 𝒫𝓘1. Later on we shall indeed come across systems in which ⊃ is a "defined" term – i.e. it is not in the system proper, but rather represents a particular sentential form. Similarly, in many books of logic, signs (e.g. →) are used for the general purpose for which we use ⊃. When such a sign is a translation of ⊃ and the system ℝ-includes 𝒫𝓘1, the theorem applies.

𝒫𝓘1-13D. A ⊃ (A ⊃ B) ⊢ A ⊃ B

Proof:	1. A ⊃ (A ⊃ B), A ⊢ A ⊃ B	MP
	2. A ⊃ (A ⊃ B), A ⊢ A	Premise
	3. A ⊃ (A ⊃ B), A ⊢ B	1,2, MP
	4. A ⊃ (A ⊃ B) ⊢ A ⊃ B	3, C

𝒫𝓘1-13T. ⊢ [A ⊃ (A ⊃ B)] ⊃ (A ⊃ B)

𝒫𝓘1-11D and 𝒫𝓘1-3 together show the equivalence of A ⊃ (A ⊃ B) and A ⊃ B in 𝒫𝓘1 and systems which ℝ-include 𝒫𝓘1.

Some of the above theorems are regarded by some philosophers and even by a few logicians (e.g, C.I. Lewis and Alan Anderson) as "paradoxical." Apparently, this is to some degree a result of reading ⊃ as "logically implies." At this point, we shall not go into this dispute. But we do want to point out that our proofs show that the "implication" they have in mind could not be the implication of 𝒫𝓘1 or any system that ℝ-includes it. It could as a matter of fact not even be defined in such a system unless it were not a positive implication. We shall later consider some systems for which the "implication" does not satisfy C (and is indeed not positive).

It is sometimes useful to formulate a logical system in an alternative form. One form which is of interest is one in which MP is preserved as a rule and all other (primitive) deductive rules are axiom schemata. We will call one such system 𝒫𝓘2, and describe it as follows:

𝒫𝓘2: A DZOS with:

Alphabet: one connective: ⊃;

Variables: denumerably infinite

Rules: proper: A, A ⊃ B ⊢ B (MP)

axiom schemata: Ax1: $\vdash A \supset (B \supset A)$

Ax2: $\vdash [A \supset (B \supset C)] \supset [(A \supset B) \supset (A \supset C)]$

P12-1T. $\vdash A \supset A$

Proof: 1. $\vdash A \supset [(B \supset A) \supset A]$ Ax1

2. $\vdash A \supset [(B \supset A) \supset A] \supset ([A \supset (B \supset A)] \supset (A \supset A))$ Ax2

3. $\vdash ([A \supset (B \supset A)] \supset (A \supset A))$ 1,2, MP

4. $\vdash A \supset (B \supset A)$ Ax1

5. $\vdash A \supset A$ 3,4, MP

With the help of P12-1T, we can prove the deduction theorem (or in other words, that the rule C holds in P12).

P12-2M. Let $\mathcal{L}$ be a DZOS which R-includes P12 and which has only MP as a proper rule (i.e., a rule which is not an axiom schema specification). Then $\alpha, A \vdash_{\mathcal{L}} B \Rightarrow \alpha \vdash_{\mathcal{L}} A \supset B$.

Proof: Let F be a derivation. Since no rule refers to previous sequences, we can without loss of generality assume there is only one sequence. Then F is a sequence $w_1,\cdots,w_n$ such that for each i $(1 \le i \le n)$, either (1) $w_i \in \alpha$, or (2) $w_i = A$, or (3) w_i is an instance of an axiom schema, or (4) there exists a j and a k such that $j < i$ and $k < i$ and w_k is $w_j \supset w_i$. Let F^*_i be a sequence of wffs as follows:

(1) If w_i is an instance of an axiom or an element of α, F^*_i is:

w_i

$w_i \supset (A \supset w_i)$

$A \supset w_i$

(2) If w_i is A, F^*_i is the proof of $A \supset A$ (P12-1T)

(3) Otherwise, F^*_i is:

$[A \supset (w_j \supset w_i)] \supset [(A \supset w_j) \supset (A \supset w_i)]$

$(A \supset w_j) \supset (A \supset w_i)$

$A \supset w_i$

We now show by induction on the i (the length of the proof) that $\alpha \vdash w_i$.

(α) i = 1. Then only case (1) applies. But:

1. $\alpha \vdash w_i$ Premise(axiom)

2. $\alpha \vdash w_i \supset (A \supset w_i)$ Ax1

3. $\alpha \vdash A \supset w_i$ 1,2, MP

(β) Let $\alpha \vdash A \supset w_m$ hold for all $m < i$. We will show that $\alpha \vdash w_i$ holds also.

Case I. w_i is an axiom or an element of α. The proof is the same as (α) above.

Case II. w_i is A.

1. $\alpha \vdash A \supset A$ PI2-1T

Case III. There exist a j and a k, $j < i$, $k < i$ such that w_k is $w_j \supset w_i$ and $\alpha \vdash A \supset w_j$ and $\alpha \vdash w_k$

1. $\alpha \vdash A \supset w_j$ Ind.hyp.
2. $\alpha \vdash A \supset (w_j \supset w_i)$ Ind.hyp.
3. $\alpha \vdash [A \supset (w_j \supset w_i)] \supset [(A \supset w_j) \supset (A \supset w_i)]$ Ax2
4. $\alpha \vdash (A \supset w_j) \supset (A \supset w_i)$ 1,3, MP
5. $\alpha \vdash A \supset w_i$ 2,4, MP

Hence the last line of F^*_i is derivable from α ($\alpha \vdash A \supset w_i$) and $F^*_1 \cdots F^*_n$ is a derivation of $A \supset B$ from α.

PI2-3M. PI1 and PI 2 are equivalent

Proof: By PI1-5T and PI1-6T, the axioms of PI 2 are provable in PI1. MP, the only non-axiom rule of PI2 is also a rule of PI1. On the other hand, MP is a rule of PI2 and, by PI2-2M, C holds in PI2. Hence each R-includes the other.

By virtue of PI2-3M, PI1 and PI2 may be regarded as variant formulations of the same system which we shall term PI. In recognition of this, we shall omit the distinguishing numbers while proceeding with the theorem order of PI1.

One further interesting property which holds for PI and many of its extensions is replaceability on the basis of equivalence. We have already seen from PI1-3M, that this holds when the equivalence relation is Equiv_{PI}. We will now prove a related theorem in which the equivalence relation involved is defined by ⊃ holding in both directions. When we refer to systems which R-include PI, caution is required, since it is possible that replaceability may hold for some, but not all of the connectives. We shall proceed to prove the basic theorem (frequently termed "the equivalence theorem") in a rather general form.

PL-14M. Let $\mathcal{L}$ be a DZOS which R-contains **PL**. Let $f_{1m(1)},\cdots,f_{nm(n)}$ be connectives of $\mathcal{L}$ such that for every $i(1 \le i \le n)$, $f_{im(i)}$ is an $m(i)$-place connective.Then if: for every i $(1 \le i \le n)$ and every j $(1 \le j \le m(i))$, $A \supset B,\ B \supset A \vdash_{\mathcal{L}} f_{im(i)} v_1 \cdots v_{j-1} A v_{j+1} \cdots v_{m(i)} \supset f_{im(i)} v_1 \cdots v_{j-1} B v_{j+1} \cdots v_{m(i)}$, then if C is a wff containing no connectives other than $f_{1m(1)},\cdots,f_{nm(n)}$, then $A \supset B,\ B \supset A \vdash_{\mathcal{L}} \mathsf{S}^{v}_{A}C \supset \mathsf{S}^{v}_{B}C$.

Proof: The proof is analogous to that of theorem 2-11 and 2-17. By induction on $\ell(C)$:

(α) $\ell(C) = 1$. Then $C \in S_0$.

Case 1. $C = v$. Then $\mathsf{S}^{v}_{A}C = \mathsf{S}^{v}_{A}v = A$ and $\mathsf{S}^{v}_{B}C = \mathsf{S}^{v}_{B}v = B$.

Case 2. $C \ne v$. Then $\mathsf{S}^{v}_{A}C = C = \mathsf{S}^{v}_{B}C$.

(β) Assume that the result holds if $\ell(C) < k$. We prove it for $\ell(C) = k > 1$. Then $C = f w_1 \cdots w_m$, where f is one of the $f_{im(i)}$ and the w_j are wffs containing no connectives other than the $f_{im(i)}$. Since $\ell(w_j) < k$, we get by the hypothesis of induction:

$A \supset B,\ B \supset A \vdash \mathsf{S}^{v}_{A}w_j \supset \mathsf{S}^{v}_{B}w_j$ and by reversing the order of B and A, $A \supset B,\ B \supset A \vdash \mathsf{S}^{v}_{B}w_j \supset \mathsf{S}^{v}_{A}w_j$. Now let $G_j = f\mathsf{S}^{v}_{B}w_1 \cdots \mathsf{S}^{v}_{B}w_j \mathsf{S}^{v}_{A}w_{j+1} \cdots \mathsf{S}^{v}_{A}w_m$. Then let $D(i) = \mathsf{S}^{v}_{A}w_i$ and $E(i) = \mathsf{S}^{v}_{B}w_i$. Then

$$G_j = f\mathsf{S}^{v(1)}_{E(1)}v_1 \cdots \mathsf{S}^{v(j)}_{E(j)}v_j \mathsf{S}^{v(j+1)}_{D(j+1)}v_{j+1} \cdots \mathsf{S}^{v(m)}_{D(m)}v_m$$
$$= \mathsf{S}^{v(1)}_{E(1)} \cdots {}^{v(j)}_{E(j)} {}^{v(j+1)}_{D(j+1)} \cdots {}^{v(m)}_{D(m)} f v(1) \cdots v(m)$$

and $A \supset B,\ B \supset A \vdash_{\mathcal{L}} G_j \supset G_{j+1}$ and hence $A \supset B,\ B \supset A \vdash_{\mathcal{L}} G_0 \supset G_m$.

Therefore, $A \supset B,\ B \supset A \vdash_{\mathcal{L}} \mathsf{S}^{v}_{A}C \supset \mathsf{S}^{v}_{B}C$.

It is desirable to point out the force of the conditions on **PL**-14M. Given a DZOS $\mathcal{L}$ which R-contains **PL**, $\mathcal{L}$ will have a number of connectives. A subset κ of these (conceivably empty, but then the result is of no interest), will satisfy the condition that for every n-place connective in κ, the fact that the conditional holds between wffs A and B in both directions, justifies the replacement of A by B in any of the n positions in an "atomic" wff (i.e. one with at most one occurrence of a connective). When this holds, the same replacement is justified in any context which contains no connectives that are not in κ. There are logics in which some, but not all of the connectives satisfy our conditions (e.g. some modal logics). In these cases, our theorems allow replacements, but they are limited to the kind of context referred to. Of course, there are logics in which all of the connectives satisfy the stated conditions. When this is so, we say that **the equivalence theorem holds unrestrictedly** in that logic.

P1-15M. The equivalence theorem holds unrestrictedly in **P1**.

Proof: ⊃ is the only connective in **P1** and is a two-place connective. Hence, since by **P1**1-1D and **P1**1-2D, the hypothesis of **P1**-14M is satisfied for ⊃, our result follows.

The function $f(p,q)$ of two-valued arithmetic which takes the value 0 if and only if p takes 1 and q takes 0 is frequently called **material implication**. We will prove a number of results concerning the relations of material implication and ⊃.

P1-16M. If **R** is the realization family such that $g_r(\supset)$ is material implication for every $r \in R$, $\alpha \vdash_{P1} A$ implies $\alpha \models_R A$.

Proof: If $g_r(A) = 1$ and $g_r(B) = 0$, $g_r(A \supset A) = 0$ and hence **MP** is 1-preserving. Likewise, suppose α, A ⊨ B. Suppose **r** is a model of α, but not of A ⊃ B. Then $g'_r(A \supset B) = 0$. Hence, $g'_r(A) = 1$ and $g'_r(B) = 0$. But then **r** is a model of α and of A and hence $g'_r(B) = 1$.

P1-17M. Let **R** be a realization family of **P1** with 2 values, such that $\alpha \vdash_{P1} A$ implies $\alpha \models_R A$. Then $r \in R$ implies $g_r(\supset)$ is material implication.

Proof: For MP to be valid, it is necessary (and sufficient) that $g'_r(A \supset B) = 0$ when $g'_r(A) = 1$ and $g'_r(B) = 0$. Since by **PI**1-4T, $\vdash A \supset A$, $g'_r(A \supset B) = 1$, whenever $g'_r(A) = g'_r(B)$. Finally since by **PI**1-5T, we have $\vdash A \supset (B \supset A)$, $g'_r(A \supset (B \supset A)) = 1$, regardless of the values of A and B. Hence when $g'_r(A) = 1$ and $g'_r(B) = 0$, $g'_r(B \supset A)$ must equal 1 and hence $g_r(\supset)$ is material implication.

The close relation between ⊃ and material implication might lead us to wonder whether positive implication fully specifies material implication. That this is not so is seen in our next result.

PI-18M. With $g_r(\supset)$ material implication, **PI** is not model-theoretically complete (i.e., $\alpha \models_R A$ does not imply $\alpha \vdash_{PI} A$).

Proof: Consider the following 3-valued truth table for ⊃:

p\q	0	1	2
0	2	2	2
1	0	2	2
2	0	1	2

and let 2 be the only designated value. Then if $g'_r(A) = 2$ and $g'_r(A \supset B) = 2$, it follows that $g'_r(B) = 2$ and hence MP holds. Suppose $g'_r(A \supset (B \supset A)) = 1$ then $g'_r(A) = 2$ and $g'_r(B \supset A) = 1$. But then $g'_r(A) = 1$, which is impossible. Suppose $g'_r(A \supset (B \supset A)) = 0$. Then $g'_r(A) \neq 0$ and $g'_r(B \supset A) = 0$. But if $g'_r(B \supset A) = 0$, $g'_r(A) = 0$. Hence $g'_r(A \supset (B \supset A)) = 2$, for all argument values. Now suppose $g'_r([A \supset (B \supset C)] \supset [(A \supset B) \supset (A \supset C)]) = 0$.Then $g'_r(A \supset (B \supset C)) \neq 0$ and $g'_r((A \supset B) \supset (A \supset C)) = 0$. But then $g'_r(A \supset B) \neq 0$ and $g'_r(A \supset C) = 0$ and hence $g'_r(A) \neq 0$ and $g'_r(C) = 0$. Then $g'_r(B \supset C) \neq 0$ and $g'_r(B) = 0$. But then $g'_r(A \supset B) = 0$. If however, $g'_r([A \supset (B \supset C)] \supset [(A \supset B) \supset (A \supset C)]) = 1$, we have $g'_r((A \supset B) \supset (A \supset C)) = g'_r(A \supset C) = g'_r(C) = 1$ and $g'_r(A \supset (B \supset C)) = g'_r(A \supset B) = g'_r(A) = 2$. But then $g'_r(B \supset C) = g'_r(B) = g'_r(C) = 2$, which is impossible. Hence $g'_r([A \supset (B \supset C)] \supset [(A \supset B) \supset (A \supset C)]) = 2$. Hence **PI** is sound relative to the indicated realization family. Consider now $[(p \supset q) \supset p] \supset p$, a formula frequently called **Peirce's**

law. This always takes 1 in two-valued arithmetic (proof will be left to the student as an exercise), but takes the value 1 when $g'_r(p) = 1$ and $g'_r(q) = 0$. Hence Peirce's law is not provable in $\mathcal{P}\mathcal{I}$ and $\mathcal{P}\mathcal{I}$ is not complete.

$\mathcal{P}\mathcal{I}$-19M. $\mathcal{P}\mathcal{I}$ is not deductively complete.

Proof: As we have seen Peirce's law is not provable. But since it always takes 1 in 2-valued arithmetic and the rules of $\mathcal{P}\mathcal{I}$ preserve 1, adding it will not make the logic inconsistent.

$\mathcal{P}\mathcal{I}$-20M. $\mathcal{P}\mathcal{I}$ is deductively (and model theoretically) consistent.

Proof: This follows trivially from $\mathcal{P}\mathcal{I}$-16, since wffs that sometimes take 0 in two-valued arithmetic are expressible in $\mathcal{P}\mathcal{I}$.

Exercises
Chapter 4

1. Prove $A \vdash_{\mathcal{P}\mathcal{I}1} (A \supset B) \supset B$.

2. Let $\bigsupset^{1}_{i=1} A_i = A_1$ and $\bigsupset^{k}_{i=1} A_i = \left[A_1 \supset \bigsupset^{k-1}_{i=1} A_{i+1}\right]$ if $k > 1$. Prove

$$A_1 \supset A_k \vdash_{\mathcal{P}\mathcal{I}} \bigsupset^{k}_{i=1} A_i, \text{ for any wffs } A_2, \cdots, A_{k-1}.$$

5
Negation

We shall now consider systems which extend $\mathbf{P1}$ by including a second connective, this time one that takes one argument. This connective is suggested by the ordinary word "not." As in the case of $\supset$, its properties in each system are precisely those given by the rules of the system; the degree to which it otherwise corresponds to the usage of "not" will not interest us in our systematic considerations. It is our intention, however, to introduce a series of systems with progressively greater specification of the connective (which we symbolize by $\sim$). As a first step, then, we wish to introduce the weakest plausible negation consistent with $\mathbf{P1}$. Here we are helped by the relation between negation and what is sometimes referred to as "absurdity" (sometimes also as "inconsistency"). One of our strongest presystematic agreements concerning negation is that the result of simultaneously asserting a sentence A and its negation $\sim$A is absurdity. In this connection, it is irrelevant as to which sentence we started from. There does appear to be a minority intuition, namely, that A and not-A is very different from B and not-B; this however appears to be correlated with a strong rejection of positive implication and we will not consider it at the present time. If we accept the first view, we might consider "absurdity" as a constant (i.e. a zero-place connective), $\mathcal{F}$, such that A, $\sim$A $\vdash$ $\mathcal{F}$. If we deal with systems that $\mathbf{R}$-include $\mathbf{P1}$, this can hold only if $\sim$A $\vdash$ A $\supset$ $\mathcal{F}$. On the other hand, if A $\supset$ $\mathcal{F}$ is accepted, we normally would wish to say that A is thereby refuted and presumably $\sim$ A accepted. These considerations appear to lead to the weakest system for positive implication and negation in which $\sim$A is still to be regarded as the negation of A, namely, one in which $\supset$ and $\mathcal{F}$ are the primitive connectives and $\sim$A is introduced as an abbreviation for A $\supset$ $\mathcal{F}$. This still leaves unspecified the conditions to be placed on $\mathcal{F}$.

Of course, the weakest possible of such conditions would be to make no attempt to specify $\mathcal{F}$ at all beyond its status as a "constant," that is to simply append $\mathcal{F}$ to $\mathbf{P1}$ as a second connective (and hence a wff), with no further specification. This leads to a system which we shall term **P1A**:

P1A: a DZOS, with:

Connectives: ⊃ (2-place), $\mathcal{F}$ (0-place)

Rules: 1. A, A ⊃ B ⊢ B MP

2. α, A ⊢ B ⇒ ⊢ A ⊃ B C

We shall allow ourselves to write ~A as a shorthand expression for A ⊃ $\mathcal{F}$ when A is a wff of **P1A**.

P1A-1M. Every D or T theorem of **P1** holds in **P1A**.

Proof: This is trivial since **P1A** R-includes **P1**.

P1A-2M. The equivalence theorem holds unrestrictedly in **P1A**.

Proof: Since the equivalence theorem holds unrestrictedly in **P1** and $\mathcal{F}$ is a zero-place connective, the conditions on the connectives in **P1**-14M are satisfied and the result follows by **P1**-14M.

P1A-3M. **P1A** is an E-logic.

Proof: Suppose $\mathbf{Equiv}_{\mathbf{P1A}}$(A,B). Then A $\vdash_{\mathbf{P1A}}$ B and B $\vdash_{\mathbf{P1A}}$ A. By C, $\vdash_{\mathbf{P1A}}$ A ⊃ B and $\vdash_{\mathbf{P1A}}$ B ⊃ A. Hence by **P1A**-2M, $\mathbf{Equiv}_{\mathbf{P1A}}$(A⊃C,B⊃C) and $\mathbf{Equiv}_{\mathbf{P1A}}$(C ⊃ A,C ⊃ B) and by theorem 2-17, the result follows.

P1A-4M. If α and A are expressible in **P1** and α $\vdash_{\mathbf{P1A}}$ A, then α $\vdash_{\mathbf{P1}}$ A.

Proof: Let α $\vdash_{\mathbf{P1A}}$ A. Then there exists a Y-derivation of α ⊢ A in **P1A**, $\alpha_1 \vdash A_1, \cdots, \alpha_n \vdash A_n$, such that $\alpha_n = \alpha$, $A_n = A$. Without loss of generality, we can assume $\alpha_1, \cdots, \alpha_n$ to be finite and hence only a finite number of variables are used in $\alpha_1, \cdots, \alpha_n, A_1, \cdots, A_n$. For every wff B, let B* be the result of replacing $\mathcal{F}$ by a variable v not occurring in the derivation (the same variable throughout). Let β* be $\{B^*: B \in \beta\}$. Then $\alpha_1^* \vdash A_1^*, \cdots, \alpha_n^* \vdash A_n^*$ is also a Y-derivation. But since α and A have no $\mathcal{F}$, $\alpha_n^* = \alpha$ and $A_n^* = A$; hence, $\alpha \vdash_{\mathbf{PL}} A$.

PLA-5M. **PLA** is model-theoretically incomplete relative to two-valued logic if $\supset$ is interpreted as material implication.

Proof: By the proof of **PL**-18M, Peirce's law is not provable in **PL**. Hence by **PLA**-4M, it is also unprovable in **PLA** and the incompleteness of **PLA** follows immediately.

From properties like that proved in **PLA**-4M, one might get the impression that no properties of negation are deducible in **PLA**. Consider however the following theorems. Because of the ease in proving them, we will prove a few, but leave most of them for the student as practice.

PLA-6T. $\vdash_{\mathbf{PLA}} \sim\mathcal{F}$

Proof: $\vdash \mathcal{F} \supset \mathcal{F}$ — **PL1**-4T, **PLA**-1M

PLA-7D. $A \sim B, \sim B \vdash \sim A$

This is a variety of modus tollens.

Proof: 1. $A \supset B, B \supset \mathcal{F} \vdash A \supset \mathcal{F}$ — **PL1**-1Da, **PLA**-1M

PLA-7T. $\vdash (A \supset B) \supset (\sim B \supset \sim A)$

PLA-7Da. $A \supset B \vdash \sim B \supset \sim A$

This is sometimes called "the first form of contraposition."

PLA-8D. $A \supset \sim B \vdash B \supset \sim A$ — Exercise

PLA-8Da. $A \supset \sim B, B \vdash \sim A$

PLA-8T. $\vdash (A \supset \sim B) \supset (B \supset \sim A)$

PLA-9D. $A \vdash \sim\sim A$ — Exercise

PLA-9T. $\vdash A \supset \sim\sim A$

PLA-10D. $\sim\sim\sim A \vdash \sim A$ — Exercise

PLA-10T. $\vdash \sim\sim\sim A \supset \sim A$

PlA-11D. $\mathcal{F} \vdash \sim A$ Exercise

PlA-11T. $\vdash \mathcal{F} \supset \sim A$

PlA-12D. $A \supset \sim A \vdash \sim A$ Exercise

From the considerations that went into our construction of **PlA**, it is clear that we can easily construct a system in which negation is primitive rather than defined. Let us call this system **PlAN**:

PlAN: A DZOS, with:

Connectives: $\supset$ (2-place), $\mathcal{F}$ (0-place), $\sim$ (1-place)

Rules:
1. $A, A \supset B \vdash B$ — MP
2. $\alpha, A \vdash B \Rightarrow \alpha \vdash A \supset B$ — C
3. $A, \sim A \vdash \mathcal{F}$ — R(for Reduction)
4. $A \supset \mathcal{F} \vdash \sim A$ — N(for Negation)

As in the last system, simple theorems are easy to prove and are left to the reader.

PlAN-1T. $\vdash (A \sim \mathcal{F}) \supset \sim A$ Exercise

PlAN-2D. $\sim A \vdash A \supset \mathcal{F}$ Exercise

PlAN-2T. $\vdash \sim A \supset (A \supset \mathcal{F})$

PlAN-3D. $A \supset B \vdash \sim B \supset \sim A$ Exercise

PlAN-3Da. $A \supset B, \sim B \vdash \sim A$

PlAN-3T. $\vdash (A \supset B) \supset (\sim B \supset \sim A)$

PlAN-4D. $\mathcal{F} \vdash \sim B$ Exercise

PlAN-4T. $\vdash \mathcal{F} \supset \sim B$

PlAN-5M. Every T and D theorem of **Pl** holds in **PlAN**.

Proof: This is trivial, since **PlAN** R-includes **Pl**.

PlAN-6M. The equivalence theorem holds unrestrictedly in **PlAN**.

Proof: This follows directly from **PLAN**-3D, **PLAN**-5M, the fact that $\mathcal{F}$ is zero-place and **PL**-14M.

PLAN-7M. **PLAN** is an E-logic.

Proof: Suppose $\text{Equiv}_{PLAN}(A,B)$. Then $A \vdash_{PLAN} B$ and $B \vdash_{PLAN} A$. By C, $\vdash_{PLAN} A \supset B$ and $\vdash_{PLAN} B \supset A$. Hence by **PL1**-1D and **PL1**-2D and **PLAN**-5M, $\text{Equiv}_{PLAN}(A \supset C, B \supset C)$ and $\text{Equiv}_{PLAN}(C \supset A, C \supset B)$. Similarly, by **PLAN**-3D, we get $\text{Equiv}_{PLAN}(\sim A, \sim B)$. Hence, by theorem 2-17, the result follows.

PLAN-8M. Let B be a wff of **PLAN** and $g(A)$ be a transformation from wffs to wffs as follows: If v is a variable of **PLAN**, $g(v) = v$, $g(A \supset B) = g(A) \supset g(B)$, $g(\mathcal{F}) = \mathcal{F}$ and $g(\sim A) = A \supset \mathcal{F}$. Then $\text{Equiv}_{PLAN}(g(B),B)$.

Proof: By induction on $\ell(B)$:

(α) $\ell(B) = 1$. Then $B \in S_0$. Then B is $\mathcal{F}$ or a variable and hence $g(B) = B$ and the result is trivial.

(β) Assume the theorem is true for all wffs A with $\ell(A) \leq K$. Prove that the theorem holds for a wff C with $\ell(C) = K+1$. Then either $C = D \supset E$, in which case, $g(C) = g(D) \supset g(E)$ and the result follows by **PLAN**-6M and the hypothesis of induction, or else $C = \sim D$ and $g(C) = g(D) \supset \mathcal{F}$, and by N and **PLAN**-2D, $\text{Equiv}_{PLAN}(\sim D, g(D) \supset \mathcal{F})$. Then, by the hypothesis of induction and **PLAN**-6M, the result follows.

PLAN-9M. $\alpha \vdash_{PLAN} A$ if and only if $g(\alpha) \vdash_{PLA} g(A)$.

Proof: Let $g(\alpha) \vdash_{PLA} g(A)$. Then since **PLAN** R-includes **PLA**, $g(\alpha) \vdash_{PLAN} g(A)$. Then by **PLAN**–8M, $\alpha \vdash_{PLAN} A$. Now assume $\alpha \vdash_{PLAN} A$. Then there exists a Y-derivation $\alpha_1 \vdash A_1, \cdots, \alpha_n \vdash A_n$. We show by induction on the length of the derivation n that every Y-statement $\alpha_i \vdash A_i$ $(1 \leq i \leq n)$ holds in **PLA**.

(α) $n = 1$. Then $A_1 \in \alpha_1$. Hence $g(A_1) \in g(\alpha_1)$. Therefore,

$g(\alpha_1) \vdash_{PLA} g(A_1)$.

(β) Assume the theorem holds for $n \leq k$. We will prove it for $n = k+1$. Then the k+1st Y-statement follows from a subset of $g(\alpha_1) \vdash g(A_1), \cdots, g(\alpha_k) \vdash g(A_k)$, by one of the rules of PLAN. There are five cases:

Case 1. $A_{k+1} \in \alpha_{k+1}$. Then obviously $g(A_{k+1}) \in g(\alpha_{k+1})$ and $g(\alpha_{k+1}) \vdash_{PLA} g(A_{k+1})$.

Case 2. The k+1st step follows by MP. Then there exist i and j $(1 \leq i,j \leq k)$ such that $\alpha_i = \alpha_j = \alpha_{k+1}$ and $A_i = A_j \supset A_{k+1}$. But then $g(\alpha_i) = g(\alpha_j) = g(\alpha_{k+1})$ and $g(A_i) = g(A_j \supset A_{k+1}) = g(A_j) \supset g(A_{k+1})$. Hence $g(\alpha_{k+1}) \vdash_{PLA} g(A_{k+1})$, by MP.

Case 3. The k+1st step follows by C. Then there exist an $i \leq k$ and a wff A such that $\alpha_i = \alpha_j \cup \{A\}$ and $A_{k+1} = A \supset A_j$. Then $g(\alpha_i) = g(\alpha_j) \cup \{g(A)\}$ and $g(A_{k+1}) = g(A \supset A_j) = g(A) \supset g(A_j)$ and hence $g(\alpha_{k+1}) \vdash_{PLA} g(A_{k+1})$, by C.

Case 4. The k+1st step follows by R. Then there exist i and j $(1 \leq i,j \leq k)$ such that $\alpha_i = \alpha_j = \alpha_{k+1}$ and $A_j = {\sim}A_i$ and $A_{k+1} = \mathcal{F}$. Then $g(A_j) = g({\sim}A_i) = g(A_i) \supset \mathcal{F}$ and $g(A_{k+i}) = g(\mathcal{F}) = \mathcal{F}$ and hence $g(A_j) = g(A_i) \supset g(\mathcal{F})$ and therefore $g(\alpha_{k+1}) \vdash_{PLA} g(A_{k+1})$, by MP.

Case 5. The k+1st step follows by N. Then there exist an $i \leq k$ and a wff A such that $\alpha_i = \alpha_{k+1}$, $A_i = A \supset \mathcal{F}$ and $A_{k+1} = {\sim}A$. But then $g(A_i) = g(A \supset \mathcal{F}) = g(A) \supset g(\mathcal{F}) = g(A) \supset \mathcal{F} = g({\sim}A) = g(A_{k+1})$ and the result follows trivially.

PLAN-10M. If α and A are expressible in PL, $\alpha \vdash_{PLAN} A$ if and only if $\alpha \vdash_{PL} A$.

Proof: If $\alpha \vdash_{PL} A$, then $\alpha \vdash_{PLAN} A$, by PLAN-5M. If B is expressible in PL, $g(A) = A$, hence if $\alpha \vdash_{PLAN} A$, then $\alpha \vdash_{PLA} A$, by PLAN-9M. Therefore, $\alpha \vdash_{PL} A$, by PLA-4M.

PLAN-9M and -10M show that PLA can be considered to be the part of PLAN that has no negations.

PLAN-11M. **PLAN** is deductively incomplete and if **R** is a 2-valued realization family such that **PLAN** is sound relative to **R**, it is also model theoretically incomplete relative to **R**.

Proof: By **PLAN**-10M and **PL**-18M, Peirce's law is not provable in **PLAN**. Hence **PLAN** is deductively incomplete. Since by **PL**-17M, material implication is the only interpretation available for ⊃, it is also model-theoretically incomplete relative to any 2-valued interpretation.

PLAN-12D. $\sim(A \supset A) \vdash \mathcal{F}$ Exercise

PLAN-12T. $\vdash \sim(A \supset A) \supset \mathcal{F}$

One can also construct a system which is of the same strength as **PLAN** (and hence also of **PLA**), but without the constant $\mathcal{F}$. This system will be called **PLN**.

PLN: A DZOS, with:

Connectives: ⊃ (2-place), ~ (1-place)

Rules: 1. $A, A \supset B \vdash B$ MP

2. $\alpha, A \vdash B \Rightarrow \alpha \vdash A \supset B$ C

3. $\alpha, A \vdash \sim B \Rightarrow \alpha, B \vdash \sim A$ Con (Contraposition)

PLN-1M. Every T and D theorem of **PL** is a theorem of **PLN**.

Proof: This is trivial, since **PLN** **R**-includes **PL**.

PLN-2D. $B, A \supset \sim B \vdash \sim A$

Proof: 1. $A, A \supset \sim B \vdash \sim B$ MP

2. $B, A \supset \sim B \vdash \sim A$ 1, Con

PLN-2Da. $A \supset \sim B \vdash B \supset \sim A$

PLN-2Db. $B \vdash (A \supset \sim B) \supset \sim A$

PLN-2T. $\vdash (A \supset \sim B) \supset (B \supset \sim A)$

PLN-2Ta. $\vdash B \supset [(A \supset \sim B) \supset \sim A]$

PlN-3D. A ⊢ ~~A

Proof: 1. ~A⊢~A — Premise
2. A⊢~~A — 1, Con

PlN-3T. ⊢ A ⊃ ~~A

PlN-4D. A ⊃ B ⊢ ~B ⊃ ~A

Proof: 1. A ⊃ B, A, ~B ⊢ B — MP
2. A ⊃ B, A, ~B ⊢ ~~B — 1, PlN-3D
3. A ⊃ B, ~B ⊢ A ⊃ ~~B — 2, C
4. A ⊃ B, ~B ⊢ ~B — Premise
5. A ⊃ B, ~B ⊢~A — 3, 4, PlN-2D
6. A ⊃ B ⊢~B ⊃ ~A — 5, C

PlN-4T. ⊢ (A ⊃ B) ⊃ (~B ⊃ ~A)

PlN-4Da. A ⊃ B, ~B ⊢ ~A

PlN-5M. The equivalence theorem holds unrestrictedly in **PlN**.

Proof: This follows by **Pl**-14M, **PlN**-1M and **PlN**-4D.

PlN-6M. **PlN** is an E-logic.

Proof: Let Equiv_{PlN}(A,B). Hence by **Pl**1-3M, **PlN**-1M and **PlN**-2D and the fact that the set of connectives of **PlN** is {⊃, ~}, the result follows by theorem 2-17.

PlN-7D. ~A, A ⊢ ~(B ⊃ B)

Proof: 1. ~A, A ⊢ ~A — Premise
2. ⊢ B ⊃ B — **Pl**1-4T, **PlN**-1M
3. ~A, A ⊢ (B ⊃ B) ⊃ ~A — 1, 2, **Pl**1-12M
4. ~A, A ⊢ A — Premise
5. ~A, A ⊢ ~(B ⊃ B) — 3,4, **PlN**-2D

PLN-7Da. $\sim A \vdash A \supset \sim(B \supset B)$
PLN-7Db. $A \vdash \sim A \supset \sim(B \supset B)$
PLN-7T. $\vdash \sim A \supset [A \supset \sim(B \supset B)]$
PLN-7Ta. $\vdash A \supset [\sim A \supset \sim(B \supset B)]$

PLN-8D. $A \supset \sim(B \supset B) \vdash \sim A$

Proof:	1. $A \supset \sim(B \supset B) \vdash A \supset \sim(B \supset B)$	**Premise**
	2. $A \supset \sim(B \supset B) \vdash B \supset B$	**PL**1-4T, **PLN**-1M
	3. $A \supset \sim(B \supset B) \vdash \sim A$	1,2, **PLN**-2D

PLN-8T. $\vdash A \supset \sim(B \supset B) \supset \sim A$

PLN-9M. If $\alpha \vdash_{PLN} A$, then $\alpha \vdash_{PLAN} A$

Proof: MP and C are rules of **PLAN**. With the function g of **PLAN**-8M, $g(A \supset \sim B) = g(A) \supset (g(B) \supset \mathcal{F})$ and $g(\sim A) = A \supset \mathcal{F}$ Hence α, $A \vdash_{PLAN} \sim B$ implies $\alpha \vdash_{PLAN} A \supset (B \supset \mathcal{F})$, by **PLAN**-8M and C. Then, by **PL**-7D, **PLAN**-5M and MP, α, $B \vdash_{PLAN} \sim A$. Therefore, **PLAN** R-includes **PLN** and the theorem follows.

PLN-10M. Let A be a wff of **PLAN** and g be the following transformation: If v is a variable, $g(v) = v$, $g(\sim A) = \sim g(A)$, $g(A \supset B) = g(A) \supset g(B)$ and $g(\mathcal{F}) = \sim(p \supset p)$. Then $\alpha \vdash_{PLAN} A$ if and only if $g(\alpha) \vdash_{PLN} g(A)$, if α is a set of wffs of **PLAN** and $g(\alpha)$ is the set of wffs $g(B)$ such that $B \in \alpha$.

Proof: Let $g(\alpha) \vdash_{PLN} g(A)$. Then by **PLN**-9M, $g(\alpha) \vdash_{PLAN} g(A)$. But for any wff B of **PLN**, $g(B)$ differs from B at most by having $\sim(p \supset p)$ at a finite number of places where B has $\mathcal{F}$. Hence by **PLAN**-4T, **PLAN**-12T, and the equivalence theorem, $\alpha \vdash_{PLAN} A$. Now let $\alpha \vdash_{PLAN} A$. Then there is a Y-derivation $\alpha_1 \vdash A_1, \cdots, \alpha_n \vdash A_n$ of **PLAN** whose last line is $\alpha \vdash A$. We will show by induction on i that for every i $(1 \le i \le n)$,

$g(\alpha_i) \vdash_{\mathcal{PLN}} g(A_i)$:

(α) i = 1. $A_1 \in \alpha_1$, $g(A_1) \in g(\alpha_1)$ and $g(\alpha_1) \vdash_{\mathcal{PLN}} g(A_1)$.

(β) Assume $g(\alpha_1) \vdash_{\mathcal{PLN}} g(A_1), \cdots, g(\alpha_n) \vdash_{\mathcal{PLN}} g(A_n)$ and $\alpha_{n+1} \vdash_{\mathcal{PLAN}} A_{n+1}$. One of the following six cases holds:

Case 1. $A_{n+1} \in \alpha_{n+1}$. Then $g(A_{n+1}) \in g(\alpha_{n+1})$ and $g(\alpha_{n+1}) \vdash_{\mathcal{PLN}} g(A_{n+1})$.

Case 2. There is a $j \leq n$ such that $A_j = A_{n+1}$ and $\alpha_j \subset \alpha_{n+1}$. Hence $g(A_j) = g(A_{n+1})$ and $g(\alpha_j) \subset g(\alpha_{n+1})$ and $g(\alpha_{n+1}) \vdash_{\mathcal{PLN}} g(A_{n+1})$.

Case 3. There is a $j \leq n$ and a $k \leq n$ such that $\alpha_j = \alpha_k = \alpha_{n+1}$ and $A_k = A_j \supset A_{n+1}$. Then $g(\alpha_j) = g(\alpha_k) = g(\alpha_{n+1})$ and $g(A_k) = g(A_j) \supset g(A_{n+1})$. Since MP is a rule of $\mathcal{PLN}$, this gives us $g(\alpha_{n+1}) \vdash_{\mathcal{PLN}} g(A_j)$ and $g(\alpha_{n+1}) \vdash_{\mathcal{PLN}} g(A_j) \supset g(A_{n+1})$ and hence $g(\alpha_{n+1}) \vdash_{\mathcal{PLN}} g(A_{n+1})$.

Case 4. There is a $j \leq n$ and a wff B such that $\alpha_j = \alpha_{n+1} \cup \{B\}$ and $A_{n+1} = B \supset A_j$. Then $g(\alpha_j) = g(\alpha_{n+1}) \cup \{g(B)\}$ and $g(A_{n+1}) = g(B) \supset g(A_j)$. Hence we have $g(\alpha_{n+1}), g(B) \vdash_{\mathcal{PLN}} g(A_j)$ and hence by C, $g(\alpha_{n+1}) \vdash_{\mathcal{PLN}} g(B) \supset g(A_j)$, i.e. $g(\alpha_{n+1}) \vdash_{\mathcal{PLN}} g(A_{n+1})$.

Case 5. There is a $j \leq n$ and a $k \leq n$ such that $\alpha_j = \alpha_k = \alpha_{n+1}$ and $A_k = {\sim}A_j$ and $A_{n+1} = \mathcal{F}$. Then $g(\alpha_j) = g(\alpha_k) = g(\alpha_{n+1})$ and $g(A_k) = {\sim}g(A_j)$ and $g(A_{n+1}) = {\sim}(p \supset p)$. Then we have $g(\alpha_{n+1}) \vdash_{\mathcal{PLN}} g(A_j)$ and $g(\alpha_{n+1}) \vdash_{\mathcal{PLN}} {\sim}g(A_j)$. Hence by $\mathcal{PLN}$-7Da, $g(\alpha_{n+1}) \vdash_{\mathcal{PLN}} g(A_j) \supset {\sim}(p \supset p)$. Therefore, by MP, $g(\alpha_{n+1}) \vdash_{\mathcal{PLN}} {\sim}(p \supset p)$, i.e. $g(\alpha_{n+1}) \vdash_{\mathcal{PLN}} g(A_{n+1})$.

Case 6. There is a $j \leq n$ and a wff B such that $\alpha = \alpha_{n+1}$ and $A_j = B \supset \mathcal{F}$ and $A_{n+1} = {\sim}B$. Hence $g(\alpha_j) = g(\alpha_{n+1})$ and $g(A_j) = g(B) \supset {\sim}(p \supset p)$ and $g(A_{n+1}) = {\sim}g(B)$. Hence we have $g(\alpha_{n+1}) \vdash_{\mathcal{PLN}} g(B) \supset {\sim}(p \supset p)$. By MP, $g(\alpha_{n+1}), g(B) \vdash_{\mathcal{PLN}} {\sim}(p \supset p)$. By $\mathcal{PLN}$-1M and $\mathcal{PL}$1-4T, we have $g(\alpha_{n+1}) \vdash_{\mathcal{PLN}} (p \supset p)$. Hence, by Con, $g(\alpha_{n+1}) \vdash_{\mathcal{PLN}} {\sim}g(B)$, i.e. $g(\alpha_{n+1}) \vdash_{\mathcal{PLN}} g(A_{n+1})$.

Since g(A) is always equivalent to A in **P1AN**, **P1N** might be regarded as an implication-negation system which is of the same strength as **P1AN**.

P1N-11M. **P1N** is deductively (and, if ⊃ is interpreted as material implication, model theoretically) incomplete.

Proof: This follows immediately from **P1N**-10M and **P1AN**-11M.

Not too surprisingly, **P1N** can be represented axiomatically.

P1N2: A DZOS, with

Connectives: ⊃ (2-place), ~ (1-place)

Rules: 1. A, A ⊃ B ⊢ B   MP

Axiom Schemata:

1. ⊢ A ⊃ (B ⊃ A)
2. ⊢ [A ⊃ (B ⊃ C)] ⊃ [(A ⊃ B) ⊃ (A ⊃ C)]
3. ⊢ (A ⊃ ~B) ⊃ (B ⊃ ~A)

P1N2-1M: α, A $\vdash_{P1N2}$ B ⇒ $\alpha \vdash_{P1N2}$ A ⊃ B.

Proof: This follows from **P1**-2M, since **P1N2** **R**-includes **P12**.

P1N2-2D: A ⊃ ~B, B ⊢ ~A

Proof:	1. A ⊃ ~B, B ⊢ (A ⊃ ~B) ⊃ (B ⊃ ~A)	Ax2
	2. A ⊃ ~B, B ⊢ A ⊃ ~B	Premise
	3. A ⊃ ~B, B ⊢ B ⊃ ~A	1,2, MP
	4. A ⊃ ~B, B ⊢ B	Premise
	5. A ⊃ ~B, B ⊢ ~A	3,4, MP

P1N2-3D: α, A ⊢ ~B ⇒ α, B ⊢ ~A

Proof:	1. α, A, B ⊢ ~B	Assumption
	2. α, B ⊢ A ⊃ ~B	1, **P1N2**-1M
	3. α, B ⊢ (A ⊃ ~B) ⊃ (B ⊃ ~A)	Ax2
	4. α, B ⊢ B ⊃ ~A	2,3, MP
	5. α, B ⊢ B	Premise

6. α, B ⊢ ~A 4,5, MP

PLN2-4M: PLN and PLN2 are equivalent.

Proof: By PLN-1M, PL1-5T, PL1-6T, Ax1 and Ax2 are provable in PLN. By PLN–9M, PLAN-7M and PLA-8T, Ax3 is also. Hence PLN R-includes PLN2. By PLN2-1M PLN2-3D, the converse holds.

PLN-12D. A, ~B ⊢ ~(A ⊃ B) Exercise
PLN-12Da. A ⊢ ~B ⊃ ~(A ⊃ B)
PLN-12Db. ~B ⊢ A ⊃ ~(A ⊃ B)
PLN-12T. ⊢ A ⊃ [~B ⊃ ~(A ⊃ B)]
PLN-12Ta. ⊢ ~B ⊃ [A ⊃ ~(A ⊃ B)]

PLN-13D. ~~A, ~B ⊢ ~(A ⊃ B)

Proof: 1. A ⊃ B, ~B ⊢ ~B PLN-4Da
2. A ⊃ B, ~B ⊢ ~~~A 1, PLN-3D
3. ~B, ~~A ⊢ ~(A ⊃ B) 2, Con

PLN-13Da. ~~A ⊢ ~B ⊃ ~(A ⊃ B)
PLN-13Db. ~B ⊢ ~~A ⊃ ~(A ⊃ B)
PLN-13T. ⊢ ~~A ⊃ [~B ⊃ ~(A ⊃ B)]
PLN-13Ta. ⊢ ~B ⊃ [~~A ⊃ ~(A ⊃ B)]

PLN-14D. ~(A ⊃ B) ⊢ ~B

Proof: 1. B ⊢ A ⊃ B PL1-5D, PLN-1M
2. B ⊢ ~~(A ⊃ B) 1, PLN-3D
3. ~(A ⊃ B) ⊢ ~B 2, Con

PLN-14D. ⊢ ~(A ⊃ B) ⊃ ~B

PLN-15D. A, ~A ⊢ ~B Exercise
PLN-15Da. A ⊢ ~A ⊃ ~B
PLN-15Db. ~A ⊢ A ⊃ ~B

PIN-15T. ⊢ A ⊃ (~A ⊃ ~B)
PIN-15Ta. ⊢ ~A ⊃ (A ⊃ ~B)

PIN-16D. A ⊃ ~A ⊢ ~A Exercise
PIN-16T. ⊢ (A ⊃ ~A) ⊃ ~A

PIN-17D. ~A ⊃ A ⊢ ~~A Exercise
PIN-17T. ⊢ (~A ⊃ A) ⊃ ~~A

PIN-18D. ~(A ⊃ ~B) ⊢ ~~(A ⊃ B) Exercise
PIN-18T. ⊢ ~(A ⊃ ~B) ⊃ ~~(A ⊃ B)

PIN-19D. ~(A ⊃ B) ⊢ ~~(A ⊃ ~B) Exercise
PIN-19T. ⊢ ~(A ⊃ B) ⊃ ~~(A ⊃ ~B)

Despite the fact that many common rules of inference are derivable in **PIN**, one cannot conclude that the degree to which the rules of **PIN** determine the meaning of ⊃ and ~ is very great. To be specific, given any interpretation $\mathfrak{g}$ which satisfies **PI** and any individual a, which is a possible interpretation of a variable, that extension of $\mathfrak{g}$ which interprets $\mathcal{F}$ as a will satisfy **PIA**, since no condition is placed on $\mathcal{F}$ other than its being a constant. By virtue of **PIAN**-9M and **PIN**-10M, this also generates an interpretation for ~. Even if we are limited to two-valued truth functional interpretations, $\mathcal{F}$ can be interpreted as the constant 1 (in which case ~A is also equal to the constant 1).

Having determined the strength that negation must have to be equivalent to the "defined" negation of **PIA**, it is perhaps worth noting that a rather trivial DZOS with that strength (which we earlier termed "minimal negation") can be specified with negation as its only connective. The rule CM expresses a form that medieval logicians called the "consequentia mirabilis."

MN: A DZOS, with

Connectives: ~ (1-place)

Rules: 1. α, A ⊢ ~B ⇒ α, B ⊢ ~A Con

2. α, A ⊢ ~A ⇒ α ⊢ ~A CM

The only wffs in $\mathcal{MN}$ consist of variables and finite strings of ~ followed by a variable. Nevertheless, some non-trivial results hold.

$\mathcal{MN}$-1D. $A \vdash \sim\sim A$

Proof:

1. $\sim A \vdash \sim A$	Premise
2. $A \vdash \sim\sim A$	1, Con

$\mathcal{MN}$-2D. $\sim\sim\sim A \vdash \sim A$

Proof:

1. $A \vdash \sim\sim A$	$\mathcal{MN}$-1D
2. $\sim\sim A \vdash \sim\sim\sim\sim A$	$\mathcal{MN}$-1D
3. $A \vdash \sim\sim\sim\sim A$	1,2, closure
4. $\sim\sim\sim A \vdash \sim A$	3, Con

$\mathcal{MN}$-3M. $\mathrm{Equiv}_{\mathcal{MN}}(\sim A, \sim\sim\sim A)$

Proof: The conclusion follows from $\mathcal{MN}$-1D and $\mathcal{MN}$-2D.

$\mathcal{MN}$-4D. $A, \sim A \vdash \sim B$

Proof:

1. $\sim A, B \vdash \sim A$	Premise
2. $A, \sim A \vdash \sim B$	1, Con

$\mathcal{MN}$-5M. If v is a variable, not ($\sim\sim v \vdash_{\mathcal{MN}} v$).

Proof: Let $\mathbf{R}$ be a realization family such that $\mathbf{r} \in \mathbf{R}$ implies $g_{\mathbf{r}}(\sim)$ is the constant function 1. Then both Con and CM are 1-preserving . Let $g_{\mathbf{r}}(v) = 0$. Then $g'_{\mathbf{r}}(\sim\sim v) = 1$, but $g'_{\mathbf{r}}(v) = g_{\mathbf{r}}(v) = 0$.

We will find $\mathcal{MN}$ of additional interest when negation is combined with other connectives. The reader may have noticed that the rule CM was not used in any of the $\mathcal{MN}$ theorems; however, CM will be used in later systems with connectives other than negation.

Let us assume we want to specify ~ formally so that the rules are acceptability-preserving (or, in a rough sense, truth-preserving), and also for every A, ~A is unacceptable for every interpretation for which A is acceptable. To do this, it is necessary that our formal system be such that for every interpretation there exist a wff B which is unacceptable as interpreted and such that A, ~A ⊢ B.

Certainly the easiest way of accomplishing this is to provide that A, ~A ⊢ B, for every B. Some have expressed some suspicion of this because of the fact that the wff B might be quite independent of A. Since, however, as we have seen, A, ~A ⊢ ~B is already derivable in **PIN** (by **PIN**-15D), this type of objection loses some of its force.

The next system we shall consider (and the first with a rejective negation) will be called **WIN** (for "weak implication negation").

WIN: A DZOS, with:

Connectives: ⊃ (2-place), ~ (1-place)

Rules:	1. A, A ⊃ B ⊢ B	MP
	2. α, A ⊢ B ⇒ α ⊢ A ⊃ B	C
	3. α, A ⊢ ~B ⇒ α, B ⊢ ~A	Con
	4. A, ~A ⊢ B	RA (for reductio ad absurdum)

WIN-1M. Every T and D theorem of **PIN** (and hence also of **PI**) is also one of **WIN**.

Proof: This is trivial, since **WIN** R-includes **PIN**.

WIN-2M. The equivalence theorem holds unrestrictedly in **WIN**

Proof: This follows by **WIN**-1M, **PIN**- 4D and **PI**-14M.

WIN-3M. **WIN** is an E-logic.

Proof: Let Equiv_{WIN}(A,B). By C, $\vdash_{WIN}$ A⊃B and $\vdash_{WIN}$ B⊃A. Hence, by **WIN**-2M, $\vdash_{WIN} \check{S}_A C \supset \check{S}_B C$ and $\vdash_{WIN} \check{S}_B C \supset \check{S}_A C$ and hence, by MP, $\mathrm{Equiv}_{WIN}(\check{S}_A C, \check{S}_B C)$.

WIN-4D. $A \vdash \sim A \supset B$

Proof:	1. $A, \sim A \vdash B$	RA
	2. $A \vdash \sim A \supset B$	1, C

WIN-4Da. $\sim A \vdash A \supset B$
WIN-4T. $\vdash A \supset (\sim A \supset B)$
WIN-4Ta. $\vdash \sim A \supset (A \supset B)$

WIN-5D. $\sim(A \supset B) \vdash \sim\sim A$

Proof:	1. $\sim A \vdash A \supset B$	WIN-4Da
	2. $\sim A \vdash \sim\sim(A \supset B)$	1, PIN-3D, WIN-1M
	3. $\sim(A \supset B) \vdash \sim\sim A$	2, Con

WIN-5T. $\vdash \sim(A \supset B) \supset \sim\sim A$

WIN-6T. $\vdash \sim\sim(\sim\sim A \supset A)$

Proof:	1. $\sim(\sim\sim A \supset A) \vdash \sim\sim\sim\sim A$	WIN-5D
	2. $\sim(\sim\sim A \supset A) \vdash \sim A$	PIN-14D, WIN-1M
	3. $\sim(\sim\sim A \supset A) \vdash \sim\sim\sim A$	2, PIN-2D, WIN-1M
	4. $\sim(\sim\sim A \supset A) \vdash \sim(A \supset A)$	1,3, RA
	5. $\vdash \sim\sim(\sim\sim A \supset A)$	4, Con, PI1-4T, WIN 1M

WIN-7D. $\sim(A \supset A) \vdash B$

Proof:	1. $\sim(A \supset A) \vdash \sim(A \supset A)$	Premise
	2. $\sim(A \supset A) \vdash (A \supset A)$	PI-4T, WIN-1M
	3. $\sim(A \supset A) \vdash B$	1, 2, RA

WIN-7T. $\vdash \sim(A \supset A) \supset B$

WIN-8D. $\sim A \supset \sim B \vdash \sim\sim(B \supset A)$ Exercise
WIN-8T. $\vdash (\sim A \supset \sim B) \supset \sim\sim(B \supset A)$

WIN-9D. $A \supset \sim\sim B \vdash \sim\sim(A \supset B)$ Exercise

WIN-9T. ⊢ (A ⊃ ~~B) ⊃ ~~(A ⊃ B)

WIN-10D. ~~A ⊃ ~~B ⊢ ~~(A ⊃ B) Exercise
WIN-10T. ⊢ (~~A ⊃ ~~B) ⊃ ~~(A ⊃ B)

WIN-11D. (A ⊃ B) ⊃ A ⊢ ~~A Exercise
WIN-11T. ⊢ [(A ⊃ B) ⊃ A] ⊃ ~~A

WIN-12D. A ⊃ B, A ⊃ ~B ⊢ A ⊃ C Exercise
WIN-12T. ⊢ (A ⊃ B) ⊃ [(A⊃ ~B) ⊃ (A ⊃ C)]

Many alternative forms of **WIN** can be formulated. For example:

WIN1: A DZOS with:

Connectives: ⊃ (2-place), ~ (1-place)

Rules: 1. A ⊃ B, A ⊢ B — **MP**

2. α, A ⊢ B ⇒ α ⊢ A ⊃ B — **C**

3. A ⊃ B, A ⊃ ~B ⊢ A ⊃ C — **RA1**

4. A ⊃ ~(B ⊃ B) ⊢ ~A — **DA** (Denial of above)

WIN 1-1M. All T and D theorems of **PL** are theorems of **WIN**1.

Proof: **WIN**1 R-includes **PL**.

WIN 1-2M. α, A ⊢ ~B ⇒ α, B ⊢ ~A

Proof:

1. α, A, B ⊢ ~B	Hypothesis
2. α, B ⊢ A ⊃ ~B	1, C
3. α, A, B ⊢ B	Premise
4. α, B ⊢ A ⊃ B	3, C
5. α, B ⊢ A ⊃ ~(B ⊃ B)	2,4, RA1
6. α, B ⊢ ~A	5, DA

WIN 1-3D. A, ~A ⊢ B

Proof:

1. A, ~A ⊢ A	Premise
2. A, ~A ⊢ ~A	Premise
3. A, ~A ⊢ (A ⊃ A) ⊃ A	1, PL1-5D, WIN-1M

4. A, ~A ⊢ (A ⊃ A) ⊃ ~A	1, PL1-5D, WLN-1M
5. A, ~A ⊢ (A ⊃ A) ⊃ B	3,4, RA1
6. A, ~A ⊢ A ⊃ A	PL1-4T, WLN-1M
7. A, ~A ⊢ B	5,6, MP

WLN 1-4M. WLN and WLN1 are equivalent.

Proof: Since MP and C hold in both, WLN1 R-includes WLN by WLN1-2M and WLN1-3D. On the other hand, WLN R-includes WLN1 by WLN-12D, PLN-8D and WLN-1M.

Of course, WLN can also be expressed in various axiomatic forms. One such example is:

WLN2: A DZOS, with

Connectives: ⊃ (2-place), ~(1-place)

Rule: 1. A, A ⊃ B ⊢ B — MP

Axiom Schemata:

1. ⊢ A ⊃ (B ⊃ A)
2. ⊢ [A ⊃ (B ⊃ C)] ⊃ [(A ⊃ B) ⊃ (A ⊃ C)]
3. ⊢ (A ⊃ ~B) ⊃ (B ⊃ ~A)
4. ⊢ ~A ⊃ (~~A ⊃ B)

WLN 2-1M. All T and D theorems of PLN are theorems of WLN2.

Proof: WLN2 R-includes PLN2.

WLN 2-2T. ⊢ A ⊃ (~A ⊃ B)

Proof:

1. ⊢ A ⊃ ~~A	PLN-3T, WLN2-1M
2. ⊢ ~A ⊃ (~~A ⊃ B)	Ax 4
3. ⊢ ~~A ⊃ (~A ⊃ B)	2, PL1-7D, WLN2-1M
4. ⊢ A ⊃ (~A ⊃ B)	1,3, PL-1Da, WLN2-1M

WLN 2-3M. WLN and WLN2 are equivalent.

Proof: By WLN-1M and WLN-4T, WLN R-includes WLN2. By WLN2-1M and WLN2-2T, WLN2 R-includes WLN.

$\mathcal{WIN}$-13M. $\mathcal{WIN}$ is deductively (and with $\supset$ interpreted as material implication, model theoretically) incomplete.

Proof: This is left to the reader as an exercise .

Some additional metatheorems concerning $\mathcal{WIN}$ are dependent on theorems concerning complete implication-negation logic and hence will be treated in Chapter 6.

Exercises Chapter 5

1. Prove the theorems that were left as exercises.

2. Prove: (a) $A \supset B, A \supset \sim B \vdash_{\mathcal{PIN}} \sim A$

   (b) $A \supset B, \sim A \supset B \vdash_{\mathcal{PIN}} \sim\sim A$

   (c) $A \supset \sim B, \sim A \supset \sim B \vdash_{\mathcal{PIN}} \sim B$

   (d) $A \vdash_{\mathcal{MIN}} B \Rightarrow \sim B \vdash_{\mathcal{MIN}} \sim A$

6
Complete Implication-Negation Logic

As we have seen, none of the logics considered in the last two chapters have been complete relative to the two-valued truth functional interpretation of their connectives (i.e., implication and negation). It may also have occurred to the careful reader that one common form of argument, sometimes called dilemma, was never used or derived. The particular form of dilemma we have in mind, at least for the present, is the one that consists of establishing B by showing that it follows from A, and also that it follows from ~A. Perhaps the most general form of this principle is: (α, A $\vdash$ B and α, ~A $\vdash$ B) $\Rightarrow$ $\alpha \vdash$ B. To examine the effect of adding this principle we will introduce a system we will call **INC**, which is the result of adding that rule, which we will call **NgC** (for Negation Cases), to **WIN**.

INC: A DZOS with:

Connectives: $\supset$ (2-place), ~ (1-place)

Rules:

1.	$A \supset B, A \vdash B$	MP
2.	$\alpha, A \vdash B \Rightarrow \alpha \vdash A \supset B$	C
3.	$A, {\sim}A \vdash B$	RA
4.	$(\alpha, A \vdash B$ and $\alpha, {\sim}A \vdash B) \Rightarrow \alpha \vdash B$	NgC

INC-1M. $\alpha, A \vdash {\sim}B \Rightarrow \alpha, B \vdash {\sim}A$

Proof:

1.	$\alpha, B, A \vdash {\sim}B$	Assumption
2.	$\alpha, B, A \vdash B$	Premise
3.	$\alpha, B, A \vdash {\sim}A$	1,2,RA
4.	$\alpha, B, {\sim}A \vdash {\sim}A$	Premise
5.	$\alpha, B \vdash {\sim}A$	3,4, NgC

INC-2M. Every T and D theorem of **WIN** (and hence also of **PIN**, **MN** and **PI**) is a theorem of **INC**.

Proof: This follows by **INC**-1M and the definitions of the systems.

INC-3D. $\sim A \supset B, \sim A \supset \sim B \vdash A$

Proof:	1. $\sim A \supset B, \sim A \supset \sim B, \sim A \vdash B$	MP
	2. $\sim A \supset B, \sim A \supset \sim B, \sim A \vdash \sim B$	MP
	3. $\sim A \supset B, \sim A \supset \sim B, \sim A \vdash A$	1,2, RA
	4. $\sim A \supset B, \sim A \supset \sim B, A \vdash A$	Premise
	5. $\sim A \supset B, \sim A \supset \sim B \vdash A$	3,4, NgC

INC-3Da. $\sim A \supset B \vdash (\sim A \supset \sim B) \supset A$
INC-3Db. $\sim A \supset \sim B \vdash (\sim A \supset B) \supset A$
INC-3T. $\vdash \sim A \supset B \supset [(\sim A \supset \sim B) \supset A]$

INC-4D. $\sim A \supset A \vdash A$

Proof:	1. $\sim A \supset A, \sim A \vdash A$	MP
	2. $\sim A \supset A, A \vdash A$	Premise
	3. $\sim A \supset A \vdash A$	1,2, NgC

INC-4T. $\vdash (\sim A \supset A) \supset A$

INC-5D. $\sim A \supset \sim\sim A \vdash A$

Proof:	1. $\sim A \supset \sim\sim A \vdash \sim A \supset \sim\sim A$	Premise
	2. $\sim A \supset \sim\sim A \vdash \sim A \supset \sim A$	INC-2M, PI1-4T
	3. $\sim A \supset \sim\sim A \vdash A$	1,2, INC-3D

INC-5T. $\vdash (\sim A \supset \sim\sim A) \supset A$

INC-6D. $\sim\sim A \vdash A$ — Exercise
INC-6T. $\vdash \sim\sim A \supset A$

INC-7D. $\sim A \supset \sim B, B \vdash A$ — Exercise
INC-7Da. $\sim A \supset \sim B \vdash B \supset A$
INC-7Db. $B \vdash (\sim A \supset \sim B) \supset A$
INC-7T. $\vdash (\sim A \supset \sim B) \supset (B \supset A)$
INC-7Ta. $\vdash B \supset (\sim A \supset \sim B) \supset A$

INC-8D. $A \supset B, \sim A \supset B \vdash B$

Proof:

1.	$A \supset B, \sim A \supset B, A \vdash B$	MP
2.	$A \supset B, \sim A \supset B, \sim A \vdash B$	MP
3.	$A \supset B, \sim A \supset B \vdash B$	1,2, NgC

INC-8Da. $A \supset B \vdash (\sim A \supset B) \supset B$

INC-8Db. $\sim A \supset B \vdash (\sim A \supset B) \supset B$

INC-8T. $\vdash (A \supset B) \supset [(\sim A \supset B) \supset B]$

INC-8Ta. $\vdash (\sim A \supset B) \supset [(A \supset B) \supset B]$

INC-9M. The equivalence theorem holds unrestrictedly for INC.

Proof: This follows immediately from PI-14M, INC-2M and WIN-2M.

INC-10M. INC is an E-logic.

Proof: This follows immediately from INC-9M, MP and C (see WIN-3M).

INC-11M. $\mathrm{Equiv}_{INC}(A, \sim\sim A)$

Proof: This follows from PIN-3D, INC-2M and INC-6D.

INC-12D. $(A \supset B) \supset A \vdash A$

Proof:

1.	$(A \supset B) \supset A, A \vdash A$	Premise
2.	$(A \supset B) \supset A, \sim A \vdash \sim(A \supset B)$	PIN-4Da, ANC-2M
3.	$(A \supset B) \supset A, \sim A \vdash \sim\sim A$	2, WIN-5D, ANC-2M
4.	$(A \supset B) \supset A, \sim A \vdash A$	3, INC-11M.
5.	$(A \supset B) \supset A \vdash A$	1,4, NgC

INC-12T. $\vdash [(A \supset B) \supset A] \supset A$

Note that INC-12T (Peirce's law) is not provable in WIN and weaker systems.

INC-13M. If $r \in \mathbf{R}$ implies $g_r(\supset)$ is material implication and $g_r(\sim)$ is two-valued negation, then $\alpha \vdash_{\mathbf{INC}} A \Rightarrow \alpha \models_{\mathbf{R}} A$.

Proof: By the argument of **PI**-16M, **MP** and **C** are 1-preserving. Since $g'_r(\sim A) \neq g'_r(A)$, no realization satisfies both A and $\sim A$ and **RA** is (trivially) 1- preserving. Finally, assume $\alpha, A \models_{\mathbf{R}} B$ and $\alpha, \sim A \models_{\mathbf{R}} B$. Now assume $r \Vdash \alpha$ (i.e. r is a model of α). Then since $r \Vdash A$ or $r \Vdash \sim A$, $r \Vdash B$. Hence, **NgC** is 1-preserving.

INC-14M. Let α be a (proof-theoretically) consistent set of wffs. Let the set $\{w_1, w_2, \cdots\}$ be an enumeration of the wffs of **INC**. Let $\alpha_0 = \alpha$ and α_{n+1} be $\alpha_n \cup \{w_{n+1}\}$ provided $\alpha_n \vdash_{\mathbf{INC}} \sim w_{n+1}$ does not hold, and let α_{n+1} be α_n, otherwise. Then for every i, α_i is consistent.

Proof: By induction on i:

(α) $i = 0$. Then $\alpha_i = \alpha$, which is consistent by assumption.

(β) Suppose the theorem is true for $i < k$. Let us prove it for $i = k > 0$. α_{k-1} is consistent by the hypothesis of induction. Suppose α_k were inconsistent. Then obviously $\alpha_k \neq \alpha_{k-1}$. Hence $\alpha_{k-1} \vdash_{\mathbf{INC}} \sim w_k$ does not hold and $\alpha_k = \alpha_{k-1} \cup \{w_k\}$. Since α_k is inconsistent, $\alpha_k \vdash_{\mathbf{INC}} \sim w_k$. Hence $\alpha_{k-1}, w_k \vdash_{\mathbf{INC}} \sim w_k$. By **C**, we get $\alpha_{k-1} \vdash_{\mathbf{INC}} w_k \supset \sim w_k$. By **PIN**-16D and **INC**-2M, $\alpha_{k-1} \vdash \sim w_k$.

INC-15M. With the set of sets $\{\alpha_n\}$ defined as in INC-14M, $\beta = \cup\{\alpha_n\}$ is (proof-theoretically) consistent.

Proof: Suppose β were inconsistent. Then for some (actually for any) wff A, $\beta \vdash_{\mathbf{INC}} A$ and $\beta \vdash_{\mathbf{INC}} \sim A$. Let D be a derivation in **INC** of A from β and D' a derivation in **INC** of $\sim A$ from β. Let γ be the set of all wffs that occur in either D or D'. Clearly γ is finite and hence $\beta' = \gamma \cap \beta$ is also. Then $\beta' \vdash_{\mathbf{INC}} A$ and $\beta' \vdash_{\mathbf{INC}} \sim A$. Then there exists a natural number i such that $w_j \in \beta'$ implies $j \leq i$. Hence $\beta' \subset \alpha_i$ and β' is consistent, which is a contradiction.

INC-16M. The set β as defined in INC-15M is maximally consistent.

Proof: Suppose A is a wff not in β. By the construction in 𝓘𝓝𝓒-14M, there exists an i such that w_{i+1} = A. Then $A \notin \alpha_{i+1}$ and hence $\alpha_i \vdash \sim A$. Hence $\beta \vdash \sim A$. But if $\beta \vdash A$, then β would be inconsistent, contrary to 𝓘𝓝𝓒-15M.

𝓘𝓝𝓒-17M. Every consistent set of wffs of 𝓘𝓝𝓒 is contained in a maximally consistent superset. (**Lindenbaum's Theorem**)

Proof: By 𝓘𝓝𝓒-14M, 𝓘𝓝𝓒-15M and 𝓘𝓝𝓒-16M.

𝓘𝓝𝓒-18M. If β is a maximally consistent set of wffs, it is deductively closed (i.e. $\beta \vdash A \Rightarrow A \in \beta$).

Proof: Suppose $\beta \vdash A$ and β is maximally consistent. Hence not-($\beta \vdash \sim A$); then $\beta \cup \{A\}$ is consistent and, since β is maximal, $A \in \beta$.

𝓘𝓝𝓒-19M. Let β be maximally consistent. Then

(a) $\sim A \in \beta$ if and only if $A \notin \beta$.

(b) $A \supset B \in \beta$ if and only if $A \notin \beta$ or $B \in \beta$.

Proof: (a) Suppose $\sim A \in \beta$. Then $A \notin \beta$ since otherwise β would be inconsistent. Now suppose $A \notin \beta$. By 𝓘𝓝𝓒-18M, not-($\beta \vdash_{\mathcal{INC}} A$). Hence $\beta \cup \{A\}$ is consistent and, since β is maximal, $A \in \beta$.

(b) Suppose $A \supset B \in \beta$ and $A \in \beta$. Hence, $\beta \vdash_{\mathcal{INC}} A \supset B$ and $\beta \vdash_{\mathcal{INC}} A$. Thus, by **MP**, $\beta \vdash_{\mathcal{INC}} B$. Suppose $A \notin \beta$. By part (a), $\sim A \in \beta$. Hence $\beta \vdash_{\mathcal{INC}} \sim A$. By 𝓦𝓘𝓝-4Da and 𝓘𝓝𝓒-2M, $\beta \vdash_{\mathcal{INC}} A \supset B$. By 𝓘𝓝𝓒-18M, $A \supset B \in \beta$. Now suppose $B \in \beta$. Then $\beta \vdash_{\mathcal{INC}} B$. Hence, by 𝓟𝓘1-5D and 𝓘𝓝𝓒-2M, $\beta \vdash_{\mathcal{INC}} A \supset B$. Therefore, by 𝓘𝓝𝓒-18M, $A \supset B \in \beta$.

We will call a wff which is either a variable or is $\sim A$ (where A is a variable) a **literal**. If β is a maximally consistent set and λ is the set of literals in β, λ is called the **literal set** of β.

ℒNC-20M. Let λ be the literal set of a maximally consistent set β. Let **R** be the realization family of ℒNC-13M (i.e., **R** is the normal two-valued logic). Then, $(\mathbf{r} \in \mathbf{R}) \Rightarrow (\mathbf{r} \Vdash \lambda \Leftrightarrow \mathbf{r} \Vdash \beta)$.

Proof: Since $\lambda \subset \beta$, the implication from right to left is trivial. Now suppose $\mathbf{r} \vdash \lambda$. We will prove that for every wff A, $A \in \beta$ if and only if $g'_{\mathbf{r}}(A) = 1$. By induction on $\ell(A)$:

(α) $\ell(A) = 1$. Then A is a variable and $g'_{\mathbf{r}}(A) = 1$ if and only if $A \in \lambda$ and hence $A \in \beta$.

(β) Suppose the assertion is true for all wffs B such that $\ell(B) < k$. We will prove it for $\ell(A) = k > 1$. Then there exist wffs C and D such that either $A = {\sim}C$ or $A = C \supset D$. In either case, $\ell(C) < k$ and $\ell(D) < k$. Hence, by the hypothesis of induction, $C \in \beta$ if and only if $g'_{\mathbf{r}}(C) = 1$, and $D \in \beta$ if and only if $g'_{\mathbf{r}}(D) = 1$. Now suppose $A = C \supset D$ and $A \in \beta$. Then $C \notin \beta$ or $D \in \beta$, by ℒNC-19M. Hence, $g'_{\mathbf{r}}(C) = 0$ or $g'_{\mathbf{r}}(D) = 1$. Therefore, by the definition of **R**, $g'_{\mathbf{r}}(C \supset D) = 1$. Now suppose $C \supset D \notin \beta$. By ℒNC-19M, $C \in \beta$ and $D \notin \beta$. Hence, $g'_{\mathbf{r}}(C) = 1$ and $g'_{\mathbf{r}}(D) = 0$ and therefore $g'_{\mathbf{r}}(C \supset D) = 0$. Assume $A = {\sim}C$ and $A \in \beta$. By ℒNC-19M, $C \notin \beta$ and hence $g'_{\mathbf{r}}(C) = 0$ and $g'_{\mathbf{r}}({\sim}C) = 1$. Now assume $A \notin \beta$. By ℒNC-19M, $C \in \beta$ and hence $g'_{\mathbf{r}}(C) = 1$ and $g'_{\mathbf{r}}({\sim}C) = 0$.

ℒNC-21M. Let β be a maximally consistent set of wffs of ℒNC. Then β has a (unique) model (in two-valued logic).

Proof: Let **r** be the realization satisfying $g_{\mathbf{r}}(v) = 1$ if and only if $v \in \lambda$, for every variable v. Then $A \in \beta$ if and only if $g'_{\mathbf{r}}(A) = 1$. Let $\mathbf{r}' \in \mathbf{R}$ and $\mathbf{r} \neq \mathbf{r}'$. Then for some literal β in λ, **r** fails to satisfy B and hence is not a model of λ. Hence **r** (and only **r**) is a model of β.

ℒNC-22M. Every consistent set of wffs has a model.

Proof: By ℒNC-17M, if α is a consistent set of wffs of ℒNC, it is contained in a maximally consistent set β which has a model. Hence α has a model.

INC-23M. Let **R** be standard two-valued logic. Then $\alpha \vDash_{R} A$ implies $\alpha \vdash_{INC} A$. **(The Completeness Theorem)**

Proof: Suppose $\alpha \vDash_{R} A$. Then $\alpha \cup \{\sim A\}$ can have no models. Hence, by INC- 22M, it is (proof-theoretically) inconsistent. Hence, $\alpha, \sim A \vdash_{INC} A$. Obviously, $\alpha, A \vdash_{INC} A$. Hence, by **NgC**, it follows that $\alpha \vdash_{INC} A$.

We will be looking at techniques for applying our completeness results to extensions of INC. Before we do, however, let us consider a number of alternative ways of characterizing INC. We noted that INC-6D and INC-12D are not provable in WIN. Let us demonstrate that the addition of either rule to WIN will generate INC. We will do this by constructing two systems.

INC1: a DZOS, with

Connectives: $\supset$ (2-place), $\sim$ (1-place)

Rules: 1. $A, A \supset B \vdash B$	MP
2. $\alpha, A \vdash B \Rightarrow \alpha \vdash A \supset B$	C
3. $\alpha, A \vdash \sim B \Rightarrow \alpha, B \vdash \sim A$	Con
4. $\sim\sim A \vdash A$	DN (Double negation)

INC1-1M. Every D and T theorem of PIN is a theorem of INC1.

Proof: This is obvious, since INC1 R-includes WIN.

INC1-2D. $A, \sim A \vdash B$

Proof: 1. $A, \sim A \vdash \sim\sim B$	PIN-15D
2. $A, \sim A \vdash B$	1, DN

INC1-3M. Every D and T theorem of WIN is a theorem of INC1.

Proof: This follows from INC1-1M and INC1-2D.

INC1-4M. $(\alpha, A \vdash B \text{ and } \alpha, \sim A \vdash B) \Rightarrow a \vdash B$

Proof:

1. $\alpha, A \vdash B$	Hypothesis
2. $\alpha, \sim A \vdash B$	Hypothesis
3. $\alpha \vdash A \supset B$	1, C
4. $\alpha \vdash \sim A \supset B$	2,C
5. $\alpha \vdash \sim B \supset \sim A$	3, PIN-4D
6. $\alpha \vdash \sim B \supset \sim\sim A$	4, PIN-4D
7. $\alpha \vdash \sim B \supset \sim\sim B$	5,6, WIN-12D
8. $\alpha \vdash \sim\sim B$	7, PIN-16D
9. $\alpha \vdash B$	DN

INC1-5M. INC and INC1 are equivalent.

Proof: By INC-2M and INC-6D, INC R-includes INC1. By INC1-3M and INC1-4M, the theorem follows.

INC2: a DZOS, with
Connectives: $\supset$ (2-place), $\sim$ (1-place)

Rules:	
1. $A, A \supset B \vdash B$	MP
2. $\alpha, A \vdash B \Rightarrow \alpha \vdash A \supset B$	C
3. $\alpha, A \vdash \sim B \Rightarrow \alpha, B \vdash \sim A$	Con
4. $A, \sim A \vdash B$	RA
5. $(A \supset B) \supset A \vdash A$	PL (Peirce's Law)

INC2-1M. Any D or T theorem of WIN is a theorem of INC2.

Proof: INC2 obviously R-includes WIN.

INC2-2M. $(\alpha, A \vdash B \text{ and } \alpha, \sim A \vdash B) \Rightarrow \alpha \vdash B$

Proof:

1. $\alpha, A \vdash B$	Hypothesis
2. $\alpha, \sim A \vdash B$	Hypothesis
3. $\alpha \vdash A \supset B$	1, C
4. $\alpha \vdash \sim A \supset B$	2, C
5. $\alpha \vdash \sim B \supset \sim A$	3, PIN1-4D
6. $\alpha \vdash \sim B \supset B$	4, 5, PI1-1Da
7. $\alpha \vdash [B \supset \sim(A \supset A)] \supset B$	6, PIN-7Da, PIN-8D

8. $\alpha \vdash B$ 7, PL

ℑNC2-3M. ℑNC and ℑNC2 are equivalent.

Proof: By ℑNC-2M and ℑNC-12D, ℑNC R-includes ℑNC2. By ℑNC2-2D and ℑNC2-1M, ℑNC2 R-includes ℑNC.

The equivalence of the two latter systems is particularly interesting because, although in both cases all the rules govern only one connective, the strengthening from WℑN to ℑNC or ℑNC1 involves a rule with negation only, while for ℑNC2, the added rule involves implication only.

It is perhaps no surprise that there are axiomatic systems equivalent to ℑNC. One well known system is:

ℑNC3: a DZOS, with

Connectives: $\supset$ (2-place), $\sim$ (1-place)

Rules: 1. $A, A \supset B \vdash B$ MP

Axiom 1. $\vdash A \supset (B \supset A)$

2. $\vdash [A \supset (B \supset C)] \supset [(A \supset B) \supset (A \supset C)]$

3. $\vdash (\sim A \supset \sim B) \supset (B \supset A)$

ℑNC3-1M. All T and D theorems of Pℑ are theorems of ℑNC3.

Proof: ℑNC3 clearly R-includes Pℑ2.

ℑNC3-2M. C holds in ℑNC3.

Proof: The theorem follows by ℑNC3-1M and Pℑ2-2M.

ℑNC3-3D. $A, \sim A \vdash B$

Proof:	1. $A, \sim A \vdash \sim A$	Premise
	2. $A, \sim A \vdash \sim B \supset \sim A$	1, ℑNC3-1M, Pℑ1-5D
	3. $A, \sim A \vdash (\sim B \supset \sim A) \supset (A \supset B)$	Ax3
	4. $A, \sim A \vdash A \supset B$	2,3, MP
	5. $A, \sim A \vdash A$	Premise
	6. $A, \sim A \vdash B$	4,5, MP

INC3-4M. (α, A ⊢ B and α, A ⊢ ~B) ⇒ α ⊢ B

Proof:

1.	α, A ⊢ B	Hypothesis
2.	α, ~A ⊢ B	Hypothesis
3.	α, ~A, ~B ⊢ B	1, closure
4.	α, ~A, ~B ⊢ ~B	Premise
5.	α, ~A, ~B ⊢ ~(A ⊃ A)	3,4, INC3-3D
6.	α, ~B ⊢ ~A ⊃ ~(A ⊃ A)	5, C
7.	α, ~B ⊢ ~[~A ⊃ ~(A ⊃ A)] ⊃ [(A ⊃ A) ⊃ A]	Ax3
8.	α, ~B ⊢ (A ⊃ A) ⊃ A	6,7, MP
9.	α, ~B ⊢ (A ⊃ A)	PI1-4T, INC3-1M
10.	α, ~B ⊢ A	8,9, MP
11.	α, ~B ⊢ B	1,10, closure
12.	α, ~B ⊢ ~B	Premise
13.	α, ~B ⊢ ~(A ⊃ A)	11,12, INC3-3D
14.	α ⊢ ~B ⊃ ~(A ⊃ A)	13, C
15.	α ⊢ [~B ⊃ ~(A ⊃ A)] ⊃ [(A ⊃ A) ⊃ B]	Ax3
16.	α ⊢ (A ⊃ A) ⊃ B	14,15, MP
17.	α ⊢ (A ⊃ A)	PI1-4T, INC3-1M
18.	α ⊢ B	16,17, MP

INC3-5M. INC and INC3 are equivalent.

Proof: By INC-2M and INC-7T, INC R-includes INC3. By INC3-1M through INC3-4M, INC3 R-includes INC.

We have seen that INC (and its equivalents) are model-theoretically complete relative to two-valued logic of the standard kind – and, in addition, that the only possible two valued interpretation is the standard one. We will now show that we cannot strengthen INC as a DZOS without either adding connectives, or making it inconsistent.

INC-24M. Let L be a DZOS with ⊃ and ~ as the only connectives such that L R-includes INC, but is not equivalent to it. Then L is inconsistent. (In other words, INC is deductively complete.)

Proof: Given L as described, there exists a finite α and an A such that α $\vdash_{L}$A, but not- (α $\vdash_{INC}$A). By the completeness theorem, not-

($\alpha \models_{\mathbf{R}} A$). Hence there is a realization $\mathbf{r}$ which satisfies α, but not A. Let $v_1,\cdots,v_m$ be all the variables in α or A. For each i, let A'_i be $p \supset p$ if $\mathbf{g_r}(v_i) = 1$, and $\sim(p \supset p)$ if $\mathbf{g_r}(v_i) = 0$. For every wff B, let B^* be the result of uniformly substituting A'_i for v_i in B. Let α^* be the set $\{x$: There is a $y(y \subset \alpha$ and $x = y^*)\}$. Then for every $\mathbf{r}' \subset \mathbf{R}$ and every wff B, $\mathbf{g'_{r'}}(B^*) = \mathbf{g'_r}(B)$. Hence $\alpha^* \models_{\mathbf{R}} \sim A^*$. By the completeness theorem, $\alpha^* \vdash_{\mathcal{INC}} \sim A^*$. Since $\mathcal{L}$ $\mathbf{R}$-includes $\mathcal{INC}$, $\alpha^* \vdash_{\mathcal{L}} \sim A^*$. But since $\mathcal{L}$ is a DZOS and $\alpha^* \vdash A^*$ is a substitution instance of $\alpha \vdash A$, $\alpha^* \vdash_{\mathcal{L}} A^*$. Hence for every wff C, $\alpha^* \vdash_{\mathcal{L}} C$. But since $B \in \alpha$ implies $\mathbf{g'_r}(B) = 1$, $\mathbf{g'_{r'}}(B^*) = 1$ for every $\mathbf{r}' \subset \mathbf{R}$. Hence $\models_{\mathbf{R}} B^*$ and by the completeness theorem, $\vdash_{\mathcal{INC}} B^*$. Since $\mathcal{L}$ $\mathbf{R}$-includes $\mathcal{INC}$, $\vdash_{\mathcal{L}} C$, also. Hence every wff is a theorem of $\mathcal{L}$ and $\gamma \vdash C$ for every wff C and every set of wffs γ.

$\mathcal{INC}$-25M. $\mathcal{INC}$ is consistent.

Proof: This is a trivial consequence of $\mathcal{INC}$-13M, since $\vdash \sim(p \supset p)$ does not hold.

The soundness and completeness results $\mathcal{INC}$-13M, $\mathcal{INC}$-23M and $\mathcal{INC}$-24M, establish that the two-valued truth-tables constitute a decision procedure for derivability in $\mathcal{INC}$. By virtue of the functional completeness of negation and material implication, this result can be extended to any other two-valued connectives, by introducing them by means of definitions using negation and implication. The same effect can be obtained when the other connectives are introduced by rules instead .

$\mathcal{INC}$-26M. Let $\mathcal{L}$ be a DZOS which $\mathbf{R}$-includes $\mathcal{INC}$ and for which the equivalence theorem holds unrestrictedly (cf. $\mathcal{PL}$-14M). For each connective F in $\mathcal{L}$, if F is n-place, let there exist a wff A_F of $\mathcal{L}$ which contains no connective other than $\supset$ and $\sim$, such that if $v_1,\cdots,v_n$ are variables,

(1) $\vdash_{\mathcal{L}} Fv_1\cdots v_n \supset A_F$

(2) $\vdash_{\mathcal{L}} A_F \supset Fv_1\cdots v_n$.

Then $\mathcal{L}$ is deductively complete. Furthermore, suppose $\mathbf{R}$ is a realization family, $\mathbf{r} \in \mathbf{R}$ imply $\mathbf{g_r}(\supset)$ is material implication and

$\mathbf{g}_{\mathbf{r}}(\sim)$ is negation. Then if $\mathbf{r}' \subset \mathbf{R}$ implies $\mathbf{g}'_{\mathbf{r}'}(Fv_1 \cdots v_n \supset A_F) = 1$ and $\mathbf{g}'_{\mathbf{r}'}(A_F \supset Fv_1 \cdots v_n) = 1$, it follows that $\mathcal{L}$ is model-theoretically complete (relative to standard two-valued logic).

Proof: Let $\mathcal{L}'$ be a DZOS which R-includes $\mathcal{L}$ and A be a wff and α be a finite set of wffs such that $\alpha \vdash_{\mathcal{L}'} A$ and not-($\alpha \vdash_{\mathcal{L}} A$). Since $\mathcal{L}'$ is a DZOS, α can be restricted to a finite set due to the definition of derivation. (Since $\mathcal{L}$ R-includes **WIN**, if it is deductively inconsistent, it must be deductively and model-theoretically complete.) We will prove, for any wff C, by induction on the number m of distinct sub-wffs in C whose main connectives are neither $\supset$ nor $\sim$, that there exists a wff B_C such that B_C has no connectives other than $\supset$ and $\sim$, and furthermore $\vdash_{\mathcal{L}} C \supset B_C$ and $\vdash_{\mathcal{L}} B_C \supset C$.

(α) m = 0. Then C has no connectives other than $\supset$ and $\sim$. If B_C is C and the result follows by **PI**1-4T and the R-inclusion of **INC** and, hence, that of **PI**.

(β) Assume the result is true for m < k. Let us prove that it holds for m = k > 0. Then there exists at least one sub-wff D (possibly identical with C) such that there is a connective F which is neither $\supset$ nor $\sim$ such that D = Fw(1)$\cdots$w(n) where w(1),$\cdots$,w(n) are wffs. Let C^* be $\mathbf{S}^{v_1}_{w(1)} \cdots ^{v_n}_{w(n)} A_F$. Then $C \supset C^* =$ $\mathbf{S}^{v_1}_{w(1)} \cdots ^{v_n}_{w(n)}(Fv_1 \cdots v_n \supset A_F) =$ $\mathbf{S}^{v_1}_{w(1)} \cdots ^{v_n}_{w(n)} Fv_1 \cdots v_n \supset \mathbf{S}^{v_1}_{w(1)} \cdots ^{v_n}_{w(n)} A_F$ and $C^* \supset C =$ $\mathbf{S}^{v_1}_{w(1)} \cdots ^{v_n}_{w(n)}(A_F \supset Fv_1 \cdots v_n)$. Hence $\vdash_{\mathcal{L}} C \supset C^*$ and $\vdash_{\mathcal{L}} C^* \supset C$. Since C^* has no sub-wffs not in C, it has at most k-1 distinct sub-wffs whose main connective is neither $\supset$ nor $\sim$. Then B_C is B_{C^*} and has no connectives other than $\supset$ and $\sim$.

Suppose not-($\alpha \vdash_{\mathcal{L}} A$) and $\alpha \vdash_{\mathcal{L}'} A$. Since $\mathcal{L}'$ R-includes $\mathcal{L}$, we get $\alpha^* \vdash_{\mathcal{L}'} A^*$, and hence by the argument of **INC**-24M, $\mathcal{L}'$ is inconsistent and $\mathcal{L}$ is deductively complete.

Finally, if the model-theoretic assumption is true, $\mathbf{g}'_{\mathbf{r}}(C) = \mathbf{g}'_{\mathbf{r}}(B_C)$, for all wffs C and hence $\alpha \vdash_{\mathcal{L}} A$ if and only if $\alpha^* \vdash_{\mathcal{L}} A^*$. Since the "starred" wffs contain no connectives other than $\supset$ and

$\sim$, $\alpha^* \vdash_{\mathcal{L}} A^*$ if and only if $\alpha^* \vdash_{\mathcal{INC}} A^*$, and by $\mathcal{INC}$-13M and $\mathcal{INC}$-23M, $\alpha^* \vdash_{\mathcal{INC}} A^*$ if and only if $\alpha^* \vDash_{\mathbf{R}} A^*$. But then $\alpha \vdash_{\mathcal{L}} A$ if and only if $\alpha \vDash_{\mathbf{R}} A$.

Under appropriate conditions, $\mathcal{INC}$-26M allows us to extend our completeness results with regard to $\mathcal{INC}$ to systems containing connectives in addition to $\supset$ and $\sim$ in a rather straightforward way – i.e., by proving $\mathcal{R}$-inclusion of $\mathcal{INC}$, the equivalence theorem and suitable equivalences for each connective. It can be extended even further, though at the cost of some additional complexity of statement.

$\mathcal{INC}$-27M. Let $\mathcal{L}$ be a DZOS. Let A be a wff of $\mathcal{L}$ containing the variables v_1 and v_2 and B a wff containing the variable v_1. Let **T** be the least subset of wffs of $\mathcal{L}$ containing the variables, also A and B, and for every A(1) and A(2) in **T**, containing also $\mathbf{S}^{v_1}_{A(1)}{}^{v_2}_{A(2)}A$ and $\mathbf{S}^{v_1}_{A(1)}B$. Now let the following hold for each B(1) and B(2) of $\mathcal{L}$:

(1) $B(1), \mathbf{S}^{v_1}_{B(1)}{}^{v_2}_{B(2)}A \vdash_{\mathcal{L}} B(2)$

(2) $\alpha, B(1) \vdash_{\mathcal{L}} B(2) \Rightarrow \alpha \vdash_{\mathcal{L}} \mathbf{S}^{v_1}_{B(1)}{}^{v_2}_{B(2)}A$

(3) $B(1), \mathbf{S}^{v_1}_{B(1)}B \vdash_{\mathcal{L}} B(2)$

(4) $[\alpha, B(1) \vdash_{\mathcal{L}} B(2)$ and $\alpha, \mathbf{S}^{v_1}_{B(1)}B \vdash_{\mathcal{L}} B(2)] \Rightarrow \alpha \vdash_{\mathcal{L}} B(2)$

(5) For every n-place connective F of $\mathcal{L}$, if $w_1,\cdots,w_n$ are variables, there exists a wff A(F) in **T** such that:

(a) $\vdash_{\mathcal{L}} \mathbf{S}^{v_1}_{Fw_1\cdots w_n}{}^{v_2}_{A(F)}A$, and

(b) $\vdash_{\mathcal{L}} \mathbf{S}^{v_1}_{A(F)}{}^{v_2}_{Fw_1\cdots w_n}A$

(6) For each n-place connective F of $\mathcal{L}$ and all wffs A_1 and A_2 the following n theorems hold (for $k = 1,\cdots,n$)

$$\mathbf{S}^{v_1}_{A_1}{}^{v_2}_{A_2}A, \mathbf{S}^{v_1}_{A_2}{}^{v_2}_{A_1}A \vdash_{\mathcal{L}} \mathbf{S}^{v_1}_{A_{1k}}{}^{v_2}_{A_{2k}}A$$

where $A_{jk} = Fw_1\cdots w_{k-1}A_j w_{k+1}\cdots w_n$. Then $\mathcal{L}$ is deductively complete.

Proof: Let **H**(x) be defined as follows: If v is a variable, then **H**(v) = v. $\mathbf{H}(\mathbf{S}^{v_1}_{A_1}{}^{v_2}_{A_2}A) = \mathbf{H}(A_1) \supset \mathbf{H}(A_2)$. $\mathbf{H}(\mathbf{S}^{v_1}_{A_1}B) = \sim\mathbf{H}(A_1)$. Let $\mathcal{L}^*$ be the result of adding ⊃ and ~ to the list of connectives of $\mathcal{L}$ together with the following rules: (1*) **MP**, (2*)**C**, (3*)**RA**, (4*) **NgC**, (5*) For every n - place connective F: $\vdash Fw_1 \cdots w_n \supset H(A_F)$ and $\vdash H(A_F) \supset Fw_1 \cdots w_n$, and (6*) For each n-place connective F and each i ($1 \leq i \leq n$), we have:

$C \supset D,\ D \supset C \vdash Fv_1 \cdots v_{i-1} C v_{i+1} \cdots v_n \supset Fv_1 \cdots v_{i-1} D v_{i+1} \cdots v_n$.

Then $x \in \mathbf{T}$ implies **H**(x) contains only variables, ⊃ and ~. Then $\mathcal{L}^*$ $\mathcal{R}$-includes **INC** and by **PI**-14M, the equivalence theorem holds unrestrictedly. Hence by **INC**-26M, $\mathcal{L}^*$ is deductively complete. Since $f(x,y) = \mathbf{S}^{v_1}{}_x{}^{v_2}{}_y A$ is a positive implication and $g(x) = \mathbf{S}^{v_1}{}_x B$ is a rejective (indeed a classical) negation, f is equivalent to ⊃ and g to ~, by theorems 2-12 and 2-16. Let C be a wff of $\mathcal{L}^*$and α a set of wffs of $\mathcal{L}^*$ and $\alpha \vdash_{\mathcal{L}^*} C$. Then there is a Y-derivation of $\alpha \vdash C$ using only rules (1) - (6). Now we define **G**(A) as follows: let $G(v) = v$ for all variables v, $G(C \supset D) = \mathbf{S}^{v_1}{}_C{}^{v_2}{}_D A$, $G(\sim C) = \mathbf{S}^{v_1}{}_C{}^{v}B$ and $G(Fw_1 \cdots w_n) = FG(w_1) \cdots G(w_n)$. Then the result of substituting **G**(C) for C throughout constitutes a Y-derivation of $G(\alpha) \vdash G(C)$ in $\mathcal{L}$. Since for any wff C in $\mathcal{L}$, $G(C) = C$, we have $\alpha \vdash_{\mathcal{L}^*} C \Leftrightarrow \alpha \vdash_{\mathcal{L}} C$ for wffs α and C and the result follows.

The significance of **INC**-27M is that the status of ⊃ and ~ as primitive connectives is not required for the deductive completeness demonstrated in **INC**-27M. It is sufficient that one be able to define within the systems connectives (not necessarily primitive) which satisfy the properties (1) - (6) of ⊃ and ~. When in later chapters we deal with complete systems (that are also functionally complete) which lack one or both of these primitives, we will consequently be freed of the necessity of producing complex constructions. That is not to say that if we had started with such a system that we would necessarily have first proved **INC**--23M and **INC**--27M. In most cases it would be more expedient to use a more direct method. Having, however, already proved **INC**--23M and **INC**--26M, the extra convenience of a theorem of the strength of **INC**--27M is attractive.

Before turning to other connectives, let us look at the connection between completeness and the systems without ~ that we have considered. As we saw in Chapters 4 and 5, **PI** and the related system **PIA** are not complete relative to two-valued logic, i.e. there are valid inference schemes not provable. We will now examine how rules sufficient to complete them can be added. It might be wise here to emphasize that there is nothing wrong per se with a system being incomplete. If it is our intention that our connectives have truth functional meanings, completeness relative to a truth-functional interpretation is a goal to be wished for. But we need not have that motivation. If, for some reason such as loyalty to certain ordinary language locutions we wish to avoid requiring a truth functional interpretation, we might deliberately wish to avoid completeness. In either event, it seems desirable to know what rules, if added to the systems in question, will result in completeness.

We will first consider an extension of **PIA**. If our connectives are to be interpreted as (two-valued) truth functions, the interpretation of $\supset$ as material implication has already been established (**PI**-17M). $\mathfrak{F}$ is open to two possible interpretations, namely the two constants, and hence our purpose is to add rules sufficient to exclude the constant 1 while still allowing the constant 0. The rule we shall choose is related to double negation (were it not for the fact that we are able to prove completeness, we would be inclined to think it a bit weaker than double negation). The rule in question is: $\alpha, A \supset \mathfrak{F} \vdash \mathfrak{F} \Rightarrow \alpha \vdash A$ (in words: if assuming that A leads to absurdity itself leads to absurdity, A holds).

Our formal system then is:

IAC: A DZOS with:

Connectives: $\supset$ (2-place), $\mathfrak{F}$ (0-place)

Rules: 1. $A \supset B, A \vdash B$ MP

IAC-1M. Every T and D theorem of **PIA** (and hence also of **PI**) is a theorem of **IAC**.

Proof: This is trivial, since every rule of **PIA** is a rule of **IAC**.

IAC-2M. The equivalence theorem holds unrestrictedly in **IAC**.

Proof: This is trivial, since **IAC** R-includes **PI** and the only other connective is $\mathfrak{F}$ which, since it is 0-place, satisfies the requirements of **PI**-14M.

𝔍𝔄ℭ-3D. $A, A \supset \mathfrak{F} \vdash B$

Proof:

1. $A, A \supset \mathfrak{F}, B \supset \mathfrak{F} \vdash \mathfrak{F}$	MP
2. $A, A \supset \mathfrak{F}, \vdash B$	1, EA

𝔍𝔄ℭ-4M. $(\alpha, A \vdash B$ and $\alpha, A \supset \mathfrak{F} \vdash B) \Rightarrow \alpha \vdash B$

Proof:

1. $\alpha, A, B \supset \mathfrak{F} \vdash B$	Hypothesis
2. $\alpha, A \supset \mathfrak{F}, B \supset \mathfrak{F} \vdash B$	Hypothesis
3. $\alpha, A \supset \mathfrak{F}, B \supset \mathfrak{F} \vdash B \supset \mathfrak{F}$	Premise
4. $\alpha, A \supset \mathfrak{F}, B \supset \mathfrak{F} \vdash \mathfrak{F}$	2, 3, MP
5. $\alpha, B \supset \mathfrak{F} \vdash A$	4, EA
6. $\alpha, B \supset \mathfrak{F} \vdash B$	1,5, Closure
7. $\alpha, B \supset \mathfrak{F} \vdash B \supset \mathfrak{F}$	Premise
8. $\alpha, B \supset \mathfrak{F} \vdash \mathfrak{F}$	6, 7, MP
9. $\alpha \vdash B$	8, EA

𝔍𝔄ℭ-5T. $\vdash \mathfrak{F} \supset [(p \supset p) \supset \mathfrak{F}]$

Proof:

1. $\vdash \mathfrak{F} \supset [(p \supset p) \supset \mathfrak{F}]$	𝔍𝔄ℭ-1M, 𝔓𝔍-5T

𝔍𝔄ℭ-6T. $\vdash [(p \supset p) \supset \mathfrak{F}] \supset \mathfrak{F}$

Proof:

1. $(p \supset p) \supset \mathfrak{F} \vdash (p \supset p) \supset \mathfrak{F}$	Premise
2. $(p \supset p) \supset \mathfrak{F} \vdash p \supset p$	𝔍𝔄ℭ-1M, 𝔓𝔍-4T
3. $(p \supset p) \supset \mathfrak{F} \vdash \mathfrak{F}$	1, 2, MP
4. $\vdash [(p \supset p) \supset \mathfrak{F}] \supset \mathfrak{F}$	3, C

𝔍𝔄ℭ-7M. 𝔍𝔄ℭ is deductively complete.

Proof: Let us consider the conditions of 𝔍𝔑ℭ-27M. Let A be $p \supset q$ and B be $p \supset \mathfrak{F}$. Let the set T consist of all wffs of 𝔍𝔄ℭ which can be expressed in terms of variables, $\supset$ and the ~ of 𝔓𝔍𝔄; i.e., which when expressed in the abbreviated notation mentioned in our discussion of 𝔓𝔍𝔄 need contain **no** explicit mention of $\mathfrak{F}$. Then the result follows by 𝔍𝔑ℭ-27M.

𝔍𝔄ℭ-8M. If $\mathfrak{g}_r(\supset)$ is material implication and $\mathfrak{g}_r(\mathfrak{F}) = 0$, $r \in \mathbf{R}$ implies that $\alpha \vdash_{\mathcal{INC}} A$ implies $\alpha \models_{\mathbf{R}} A$.

Proof: This follows by $\mathcal{PI}$-16M and the fact that $\mathbf{g}'_{\mathbf{r}}((A \supset \mathcal{F}) \supset \mathcal{F}) = \mathbf{g}'_{\mathbf{r}}(A)$.

$\mathcal{IAC}$-9M. $\mathcal{IAC}$ is model-theoretically complete (with $\supset$ interpreted as material implication and $\mathcal{F}$ as the constant 0).

Proof: Under the stated interpretation **R**, all of the rules are 1-preserving. Suppose that $\alpha \models_{\mathbf{R}} A$, for some particular α and A. Then $\alpha \vdash A$ could be added without making the result inconsistent. But since $\mathcal{IAC}$ is deductively complete, that implies $\alpha \vdash_{\mathcal{IAC}} A$.

We now turn to pure implicational logic. Considering the fact that we have used Peirce's law as a counterexample to completeness several times, it may be less than surprising that it provides the principle sufficient to complete implicational logic.

$\mathcal{IC}$: a DZOS, with:

Connectives: $\supset$ (2-place)

Rules:	1. $A \supset B, A \vdash B$	**MP**
	2. $\alpha, A \vdash B \Rightarrow \alpha \vdash A \supset B$	**C**
	3. $(A \supset B) \supset A \vdash A$	**PL** (Peirce's Law)

$\mathcal{IC}$-1M. $\mathcal{IC}$ is model-theoretically complete (if $\supset$ is interpreted as material implication).

Proof: Let $\alpha \models_{\mathbf{R}} A$ (where **R** is the standard two-valued realization family). By $\mathcal{IAC}$-8M, $\alpha \vdash_{\mathcal{IAC}} A$. Then there exists a Y-derivation $\alpha_1 \vdash A_1, \cdots, \alpha_n \vdash A_n$ in $\mathcal{IAC}$. Then each step is either a premise step, or an application of **MP**, or of **C**, or of **EA** [i.e., in the latter case, it is a line $\alpha_i \vdash A_i$ such that there is a $j < i$ with $\alpha_j = \alpha_i \cup \{A_i \supset \mathcal{F})\}$ and $A_j = \mathcal{F}$]. For each i, such that the ith step is the jth application of **EA**, let $C_j = ((A_i \supset \mathcal{F}) \supset \mathcal{F}) \supset A_i$. Let β_i be the union of α_i and all C_j's such that the jth application of **EA** is the ith step or earlier. We will establish that $\beta_i \vdash A_i$, for every $i \leq n$. Assume that it holds for $j < i$. Then, if the ith step is a premise step or an application of **MP** or **C**, the result obviously follows. If the ith step is an application of **EA**, there is a $j<i$ such that $\alpha_j = A_i \supset \mathcal{F} \in \alpha_j$ and $\mathcal{F} = A_j$. Hence by the hypothesis of induction, we can obtain $\alpha_i, A_i \supset \mathcal{F}, C_1,\cdots,C_K \vdash_{\mathbf{PL}\mathcal{A}} \mathcal{F}$. Hence by **C**,

$\alpha_i, C_1,\cdots,C_K, [(A_i \supset \mathcal{F}) \supset \mathcal{F}] \supset A_i \vdash_{\mathbf{PL}\mathcal{A}} (A_i \supset \mathcal{F}) \supset \mathcal{F}$ and

$\alpha_i, C_1,\cdots,C_K, [(A_i \supset \mathcal{F}) \supset \mathcal{F}] \supset A_i \vdash_{\mathbf{PL}\mathcal{A}} [(A_i \supset \mathcal{F}) \supset \mathcal{F}] \supset A_i$.

Hence by **MP**, $\alpha_i, C_1,\cdots,C_K, [(A_i \supset \mathcal{F}) \supset \mathcal{F}] \supset A_i \vdash_{\mathbf{PL}\mathcal{A}} A_i$, i.e. $\beta_i \vdash A_i$. Hence $\alpha, C_1,\cdots,C_K \vdash_{\mathbf{PL}\mathcal{A}} A_i$ in which all of the C's are of the form $[(A_j \supset \mathcal{F}) \supset \mathcal{F}] \supset A_j$ where the jth step of the original Y-derivation is an application of **EA**. Now let v be a variable that does not occur in any of $\alpha_1,\cdots,\alpha_n, A_1,\cdots,A_n$. Then for each i, $\mathbf{S}^{\mathcal{F}}{}_{v}(\alpha_i)$ and $\mathbf{S}^{\mathcal{F}}{}_{v}(A_i)$ contains no $\mathcal{F}$, by 1-9. Since $\mathbf{PL}$ and $\mathbf{PL}\mathcal{A}$ have the same rules and $\mathbf{PL}\mathcal{A}$ has no primitive rule mentioning $\mathcal{F}$, we therefore get:

$\mathbf{S}^{\mathcal{F}}{}_{v}(\alpha_i), \mathbf{S}^{\mathcal{F}}{}_{v}(C_1),\cdots, \mathbf{S}^{\mathcal{F}}{}_{v}(C_{k+1}) \vdash_{\mathbf{PL}} \mathbf{S}^{\mathcal{F}}{}_{v}(A_i)$. Then each $\mathbf{S}^{\mathcal{F}}{}_{v}(C_i)$ is $[(\mathbf{S}^{\mathcal{F}}{}_{v}(A_{k(i)}) \supset v) \supset v] \supset \mathbf{S}^{\mathcal{F}}{}_{v}(A_{k(i)})$, for some $k(i)$ which was the ith application of **EA**. Let D_j be: $\mathbf{S}^{v}{}_{A}\mathbf{S}^{\mathcal{F}}{}_{v}(C_j)$, i.e., $[(\mathbf{S}^{\mathcal{F}}{}_{A}(A_{k(j)}) \supset A) \supset A] \supset \mathbf{S}^{\mathcal{F}}{}_{A}(A_{k(j)})$. Since $\mathbf{PL}$ is a DZOS and hence closed under uniform substitution for variables, it follows that $\alpha, D_1,\cdots,D_m \vdash_{\mathbf{PL}} A$ and hence $\alpha, D_1,\cdots,D_m \vdash_{\mathbf{LC}} A$. (Since any derivation uses only a finite number of wffs and hence only a finite number of variables, no loss of generality occurs from assuming, as we have done, that the α_i do not contain v.) For every j, by $\mathbf{PL}$1−1D and the **R**-inclusion of $\mathbf{PL}$:

$$(\mathbf{S}^{\mathcal{F}}{}_{A}(A_{k(j)}) \supset A) \supset A,\ A \supset \mathbf{S}^{\mathcal{F}}{}_{A}(A_{k(j)}) \vdash_{\mathbf{LC}} (\mathbf{S}^{\mathcal{F}}{}_{A}(A_{k(j)}) \supset A) \supset \mathbf{S}^{\mathcal{F}}{}_{A}(A_{k(j)})$$

and hence by **PL**:

$$(\mathbf{S}^{\mathcal{F}}{}_{A}(A_{k(j)}) \supset A) \supset A,\ A \supset \mathbf{S}^{\mathcal{F}}{}_{A}(A_{k(j)}) \vdash_{\mathbf{LC}} \mathbf{S}^{\mathcal{F}}{}_{A}(A_{k(j)}).$$

Thus by **C**:

$$A \supset \mathbf{S}^{\mathcal{F}}_{A}(A_{k(j)}) \vdash_{\mathcal{IC}} [(\mathbf{S}^{\mathcal{F}}_{A}(A_{k(j)}) \supset A) \supset A] \supset \mathbf{S}^{\mathcal{F}}_{A}(A_{k(j)})]$$

Therefore, we have, by closure:

$$\alpha, A \supset \mathbf{S}^{\mathcal{F}}_{A}(A_{k(1)}), \cdots, A \supset \mathbf{S}^{\mathcal{F}}_{A}(A_{k(m)}) \vdash_{\mathcal{IC}} A$$

Then, by **C**:

$$\alpha, A \supset \mathbf{S}^{\mathcal{F}}_{A}(A_{k(1)}), \cdots, A \supset \mathbf{S}^{\mathcal{F}}_{A}(A_{k(m-1)}) \vdash_{\mathcal{IC}} [A \supset \mathbf{S}^{\mathcal{F}}_{A}(A_{k(m)})] \supset A.$$

Hence by **PL**:

$$\alpha, A \supset \mathbf{S}^{\mathcal{F}}_{A}(A_{k(1)}), \cdots, A \supset \mathbf{S}^{\mathcal{F}}_{A}(A_{k(m-1)}) \vdash_{\mathcal{IC}} A$$

Consequently, by induction:

$$\alpha \vdash_{\mathcal{IC}} A$$

$\mathcal{IC}$-2M. $\mathcal{IC}$ is deductively complete.

Proof: Let not-($\beta \vdash_{\mathcal{IC}} B$). Then not-($\beta \vdash_{\mathcal{IAC}} B$). Suppose $\mathcal{L}$ is the DZOS that results by adding $\beta \vdash B$ to $\mathcal{IAC}$. Since $\mathcal{IAC}$ is deductively complete by $\mathcal{IAC}$-7M, $\mathcal{L}$ is deductively inconsistent. Hence $\vdash_{\mathcal{L}} w$ where w is a variable. Let $\mathcal{L}'$ be the result of adding $\beta \vdash B$ to $\mathcal{IC}$. By the construction in $\mathcal{IC}$-1M, we get $\mathbf{S}^{\mathcal{F}}_{v}(C_1), \cdots, \mathbf{S}^{\mathcal{F}}_{v}(C_m) \vdash_{\mathcal{L}'} w$, where $v \neq w$ and v is a variable not in the derivation and hence not in $C_1, \cdots, C_m$. By the argument of $\mathcal{IC}$-1M, we get:

$$w \supset \mathbf{S}^{\mathcal{F}}_{A}(A_{k(j)}), \cdots, w \supset \mathbf{S}^{\mathcal{F}}_{A}(A_{k(j)}) \vdash_{\mathcal{L}'} w$$

Hence by the argument of $\mathcal{IC}$-1M, $\vdash_{\mathcal{L}'} w$ and $\mathcal{L}'$ is inconsistent.

$\mathcal{IC}$-2M shows that deductive completeness can hold even for systems with a set of connectives which lack a functionally incomplete interpretation. One additional point is that the technique of $\mathcal{IC}$-1M and $\mathcal{IC}$-2M is applicable in a more general context.

$\mathcal{IC}$-3M. Let $\mathcal{L}$ be a DZOS not containing $\mathcal{F}$ as connective, but with rules **MP**, **C**, **PL** and additional rules $R_1, \cdots, R_n$. Let $\mathcal{L}'$ have as rules **MP**, **C**, **EA** and $R_1, \cdots, R_n$. Then if α and A are all expressible in $\mathcal{L}$ and $\alpha \vdash_{\mathcal{L}'} A$, then $\alpha \vdash_{\mathcal{L}} A$.

Proof: We omit the details of the proof except to indicate that the construction of IC-1M and IC-2M carries over without significant differences.

7
Disjunction

Let us turn to the examination of the logical characteristics of the particle represented by "or" and similar words. As usual, the actual results depend only on the rules chosen and hence they are more or less independent of the motivations involved.

While it is clear that the word "or" is used in various ways, including arguably in some cases the denying of the simultaneous acceptability of the sentences connected by it, there is at least one usage or family of usages (frequently called "inclusive or") for which admission of A commits one against denying or rejecting "A or B," or for that matter "B or A." We are actually inclined to believe this to be the basic meaning of "or," but whether we are right in this or not, it is this inclusive use of "or" which provides the colloquial basis for disjunction, as we shall use the term in this and succeeding chapters.

Our first, rather minimal, system for disjunction will have only one connective, with properties sufficient to make it a normal disjunction in the sense specified in chapter 2. We will call it $\mathcal{SA}$ for "simple alternation."

$\mathcal{SA}$: a DZOS with:

Connectives: $\vee$

Rules: 1. $A \vdash A \vee B$ **AR** (Addition,right)

2. $A \vdash B \vee A$ **AL** (Addition,left)

3. $(\alpha, A \vdash C \text{ and } \alpha, B \vdash C) \Rightarrow \alpha, A \vee B \vdash C$ **D** (Dilemma)

$\mathcal{SA}$-1M. Equiv$_{\mathcal{SA}}$(A,B) ⇒ Equiv$_{\mathcal{SA}}$(A ∨ C, B ∨ C)

Proof:
1. $A \vdash B$ Hypothesis
2. $A \vdash B \vee C$ 1,AR
3. $C \vdash C$ Premise
4. $C \vdash B \vee C$ 3,AL

5. A ∨ C ⊢ B ∨ C 2,4, D

Hence B ∨ C ⊢ A ∨ C, by the same argument and the theorem follows.

$\mathcal{SA}$-2M. $\mathrm{Equiv}_{\mathcal{SA}}$(A,B) ⇒ $\mathrm{Equiv}_{\mathcal{SA}}$(C ∨ A, C ∨ B)

Proof: The proof is analogous to that of $\mathcal{SA}$-1M.

$\mathcal{SA}$-3M. $\mathcal{SA}$ is an E-logic.

Proof: This follows by $\mathcal{SA}$-1M, $\mathcal{SA}$-2M and 2-17.

$\mathcal{SA}$-4D. A ∨ A ⊢ A

Proof: 1. A ⊢ A Premise

2. A ∨ A ⊢ A 1,1, D

$\mathcal{SA}$-5D. A ∨ B ⊢ B ∨ A

Proof: 1. A ⊢ B ∨ A AL

2. B ⊢ B ∨ A AR

3. A ∨ B ⊢ B ∨ A 1, 2, D

$\mathcal{SA}$-6D. A ∨ (B ∨ C) ⊢ (A ∨ B) ∨ C

Proof: 1. A ⊢ A ∨ B AR

2. A ⊢ (A ∨ B) ∨ C 1, AR

3. B ⊢ A ∨ B AL

4. B ⊢ (A ∨ B) ∨ C 3, AR

5. C ⊢ (A ∨ B) ∨ C AL

6. B ∨ C ⊢ (A ∨ B) ∨ C 4, 5, D

7. A ∨ (B ∨ C) ⊢ (A ∨ B) ∨ C 2, 6, D

Theorem **7-1**. Let $\mathcal{L}$ be a DZOS having a two-place connective ✡. Let ✡ be commutative and associative (i.e., $\mathrm{Equiv}_{\mathcal{L}}$(A ✡ B, B ✡ A) and $\mathrm{Equiv}_{\mathcal{L}}$(A ✡ (B ✡ C), (A ✡ B) ✡ C). Let the conditions of theorem 2-10 hold for $\mathcal{L}$. Let $v_1, \cdots, v_n$ be distinct variables of $\mathcal{L}$. Let A and B be wffs of $\mathcal{L}$ each containing no connectives other than m-1 occurrences of $\star$ and no more than one occurrence of each variable. Let $A_1, \cdots, A_n$ be wffs of $\mathcal{L}$. Then $\mathbf{Equiv}_{\mathcal{L}}(\mathbf{S}^{v_1 \cdots v_n}_{A_1, \cdots, A_n}A, \mathbf{S}^{v_1 \cdots v_n}_{A_1, \cdots, A_n}B))$.

Proof: Let B_1 be v_1 and B_{k+1} be $B_k \star v_{k+1}$. We will show that for every wff C satisfying the conditions on A and B, $\mathbf{Equiv}_{\mathcal{L}}(C, B_m)$. By induction on m:

(α) $m = 1$. Then $C = v_1 = B_1$ and the result follows trivially.

(β) Assume the assertion is true for all $m \leq k$. We prove it for $m = k+1$. By definition the main connective of B is $\star$. Hence there exist wffs D and E such that $C = D \star E$. By the hypothesis of induction, the number of variables n D is at most k and likewise for E. Let $v_{D(1)}, \cdots, v_{D(j)}$ be the variables of D in order of ascending index and $v_{E(1)}, \cdots, v_{E(j')}$ be those for E. Let D_i and E_i be defined analogously to B_i. Then by the hypothesis of induction, $\mathbf{Equiv}_{\mathcal{L}}(D, D_j)$ and $\mathbf{Equiv}_{\mathcal{L}}(E, E_{j'})$. Then $\mathbf{Equiv}_{\mathcal{L}}(D \star E, D_j \star E)$ and hence $\mathbf{Equiv}_{\mathcal{L}}(D_j \star E, D_j \star E_{j'})$. Thus $\mathbf{Equiv}_{\mathcal{L}}(C, D_j \star E_{j'})$. Either $D(j) = k+1$ or $E(j')$. Suppose the latter (case 1). Since then $E_{j'}$ is $E_{j'-1} \star v_{E(j')}$, we therefore obtain $\mathbf{Equiv}_{\mathcal{L}}(D_j \star E_{j'} (D_j \star E_{j'-1}) \star v_{k+1})$. Since the variables of $D_j \star E_{j'-1}$ are $v_1, \cdots, v_k$ by the hypothesis of induction, we have $\mathbf{Equiv}_{\mathcal{L}}(D_j \star E_{j'-1}, B_k)$ and hence $\mathbf{Equiv}_{\mathcal{L}}(D_j \star E_{j'} (D_j \star E_{j'-1}) \star v_{k+1})$, which is the same as $\mathbf{Equiv}_{\mathcal{L}}(D_j \star E_{j'}, B_{k+1})$ and therefore $\mathbf{Equiv}_{\mathcal{L}}(C, B_{k+1})$. If on the other hand $D(j) = k+1$ (case 2), then $D_j = D_{j-1} \star v_{k+1}$. But since $\mathbf{Equiv}_{\mathcal{L}}(D_j \star E_{j'}, E_{j'} \star D_j)$, the conditions of case 1 are satisfied and the proof concludes as in case 1.

Hence $\mathbf{Equiv}_{\mathcal{L}}(A, B_n)$ and $\mathbf{Equiv}_{\mathcal{L}}(B, B_n)$ and thus $\mathbf{Equiv}_{\mathcal{L}}(A, B)$. Therefore since $\mathcal{L}$ is a DZOS, $\mathbf{Equiv}_{\mathcal{L}}(\mathbf{S}^{v_1 \cdots v_n}_{A_1, \cdots, A_n}A, \mathbf{S}^{v_1 \cdots v_n}_{A_1, \cdots, A_n}B)$.

Theorem 7-1 can be reworded to state that the deductive properties of a connective (or for that matter a logical operation) which satisfies the conditions on $\star$ are such that a wff formed by repeated application of such a connective is independent of the order and grouping of the connected wffs. Under such circumstances, if a notation is being used which requires parentheses, it is customary to permit their omission on the basis of theorem 7-1. The theorem can be extended in the event $\star$ is also idempotent --i.e. $\mathrm{Equiv}_{\mathcal{L}}(A, A \star A)$, for all wffs A.

Theorem 7-2. Let $\mathcal{L}$ be a DZOS satisfying the conditions of theorem 7-1.Let $\star$ furthermore be idempotent. Let A be a wff containing no connectives other than $\star$. Let B be a wff containing every variable in A, but having no variables repeated. Then $\mathrm{Equiv}_{\mathcal{L}}(A,B)$.

Proof: By induction on $\ell(A)$, we get:

(α) $\ell(A) = 1$. Then A consists of a single variable and hence B consists of the same variable and A = B. Hence $\mathrm{Equiv}_{\mathcal{L}}(A,B)$.

(β) Suppose the theorem holds for all wffs C with $\ell(C) \leq k$. We prove that it holds for $\ell(A) = k+1 > 1$. Either A has no variable repeated and $\mathrm{Equiv}_{\mathcal{L}}(A,B)$ by theorem 7-1, or else A has at least one variable repeated. Then for some wff C and variable v, $A = C \star v$. Hence $\ell(C) = k-1$ and by the hypothesis of induction, there exists a wff B′ such that $\mathrm{Equiv}_{\mathcal{L}}(C,B')$ and B′ contains no variable repeated. Now either B′ contains no v and $B = B' \star v$, or else B′ contains v and hence, by theorem 7-1, there exists a wff B″ with $\mathrm{Equiv}_{\mathcal{L}}(B',B'')$ such that there exists a wff C′ such that $B'' = C' \star v$. Hence $\mathrm{Equiv}_{\mathcal{L}}(A,(C' \star v) \star v)$. Thus, by theorem 7-1, $\mathrm{Equiv}_{\mathcal{L}}(A,C' \star (v \star v))$ and by idempotency, $\mathrm{Equiv}_{\mathcal{L}}(A,C' \star v)$. Therefore $B = C' \star v$.

Theorem 7-2 can be expressed by stating that the deductive properties of wffs consisting of wffs connected with $\star$ are independent of order, grouping or repetition (when, of course, the conditions of theorem 7-2 are satisfied).

$\mathcal{SA}$-7M. The deductive properties of a wff A of $\mathcal{SA}$ are dependent only on the variables occurring in A and not on their order, grouping and repetition.

Proof: This follows immediately from theorem 7-2.

$\mathcal{SA}$-8M. If $\alpha \vdash_{\mathcal{SA}}$ A and $\mathbf{g_r}(\vee)$ is the truth function inclusive-or, $\mathbf{r} \in \mathbf{R}$ implies $\alpha \models_{\mathbf{R}}$ A.

Proof: This is left to the reader as an exercise.

$\mathcal{SA}$-9M. A $\vdash_{\mathcal{SA}}$ B if and only if every variable in A is also in B.

Proof: Suppose every variable of A is in B. Then either A = B, in which case the result is trivial, or not, in which case (by $\mathcal{SA}$-7M) there exist C and D such that $\mathbf{Equiv}_{\mathcal{L}}$(A,C) and $\mathbf{Equiv}_{\mathcal{L}}$(C $\vee$ D,B) and hence the result follows by **AR**.

$\mathcal{SA}$-10M. Let **R** be a realization family of $\mathcal{SA}$ with 2 values such that $\alpha \vdash_{\mathcal{SA}}$A implies $\alpha \models_{\mathbf{R}}$ A. Then $\mathbf{r} \in \mathbf{R}$ implies $\mathbf{g_r}(\vee)$ is inclusive-or.

Proof: Since **AR** must be 1-preserving, $\mathbf{g'_r}$(A) = 1 implies $\mathbf{g'_r}$(A $\vee$ B) = 1, independent of the value of $\mathbf{g'_r}$(B) and similarly, $\mathbf{g'_r}$(B $\vee$ A) = 1, mutatis mutandis, by **AL**. Hence $\mathbf{g'_r}$(A $\vee$ B) = 1 unless $\mathbf{g'_r}$(A) = $\mathbf{g'_r}$(B) = 0. Let A, B and C be wffs and r a realization such that $\mathbf{g'_r}$(A $\vee$ B) = 1 and $\mathbf{g'_r}$(C) = 0. Then since D must be validity-preserving either $\mathbf{g'_r}$(A) = 1 or $\mathbf{g'_r}$(B) = 1 and hence $\mathbf{g_r}(\vee)$ is inclusive-or.

$\mathcal{SA}$-11M. If $\mathbf{g_r}(\vee)$ is (two-valued) inclusive or and $\mathbf{r} \in \mathbf{R}$, $\alpha \models_{\mathbf{R}}$ A implies $\alpha \vdash_{\mathcal{SA}}$ A (in other words, $\mathcal{SA}$ is model-theoretically complete).

Proof: Suppose there exists a wff B $\in \alpha$ such that every variable in B is in A. Then by $\mathcal{SA}$-9M, $\alpha \vdash_{\mathcal{SA}}$A. Suppose on the other hand, for every $B \in \alpha$, there exists a variable v_B in B that is not in A. Now let r be the realization with $g_r(v_B) = 1$ for every B in α and $g_r(v) = 0$ for all other variables v. Hence $g'_r(B) = 1$ for every $B \in \alpha$ and $g'_r(A) = 0$. Consequently, $\alpha \vdash_R A$ implies that there exists a $B \in A$ such that every variable in B is in A and hence $\alpha \vdash_{SA} A$.

SA-12M. SA is virtually deductively complete.

Proof: Let $\mathcal{L}$ R-include SA and $\alpha \vdash_{\mathcal{L}} A$, and not($\alpha \vdash_{SA} A$). By SA-9M, for every $B \in \alpha$, there is a variable in B not in A. Let C* be the result of substituting x for every variable that is also in A and w for all other variables. Then $\mathbf{Equiv}_{\mathcal{L}}(A^*, x)$ and $B \in \alpha$ implies $\mathbf{Equiv}_{\mathcal{L}}(B^*, w)$ or $\mathbf{Equiv}_{\mathcal{L}}(B^*, x \vee w)$. Therefore, if $\alpha \neq \emptyset$, then $x \vee w$, $w \vdash_{\mathcal{L}} x$ and hence $w \vdash_{\mathcal{L}} x$ and $\mathcal{L}$ is virtually deductively inconsistent, while if $\alpha = \emptyset$, then $\vdash_{\mathcal{L}} x$ and $\mathcal{L}$ is deductively inconsistent.

The completeness of SA is particularly interesting, because (as will become clear) it is primarily caused by the expressive weakness of the system, so that addition of further connectives can result in the incompleteness expanded system.

We will start by adding a negation of minimal strength, similar to that of PIN, by combining SA and MN into a system we will term MAN:

MAN: A DZOS with:

Connectives: $\vee$ (2-place), $\sim$ (1-place)

Rules:	1. $A \vdash A \vee B$	AR
	2. $A \vdash B \vee A$	AL
	3. $(\alpha, A \vdash C$ and $\alpha, B \vdash C) \Rightarrow \alpha, B \vee C \vdash C$	D
	4. $\alpha, A \vdash \sim B \Rightarrow \alpha, B \vdash \sim A$	Con
	5. $\alpha, A \vdash \sim A \Rightarrow \alpha \vdash \sim A$	CM

MAN-1M. Every D theorem of SA or MN is a theorem of MAN.

Proof: This is trivial since MAN R-includes both SA and MN.

MAN-2D. $A \vee \sim B, \sim A \vdash \sim B$

Proof: 1. A, ~A ⊦ ~B	MN-4D, MAN-1M
2. ~B, ~A ⊦ ~B	Premise
3. A ∨ ~B, ~A ⊦ ~B	1, 2, D

MAN-3D. ~A ∨ ~B, A ⊦ ~B

Proof: 1. ~A ∨ ~B, A ⊦ A	Premise
2. ~A ∨ ~B, A ⊦ ~~A	1, MN-1D, MAN-1M
3. ~A ∨ ~B, A ⊦ ~A ∨ ~B	Premise
4. A ∨ ~B, A ⊦ ~B	2, 3, MAN-2D

MAN-4D. A ∨ B, ~A ⊦ ~~B

Proof: 1. A, ~A ⊦ ~~B	MN-4D, MAN-1M
2. B, ~A ⊦ B	Premise
3. B, ~A ⊦ ~~B	1, MN-1D, MAN-1M
4. A ∨ B, ~A ⊦ ~~B	1, 4, D

MAN-5D. ~A ∨ B, A ⊦ ~~B — Exercise

MAN-6D. ~(A ∨ B) ⊦ ~A

Proof: 1. ~(A ∨ B), A ⊦ A ∨ B	AR
2. ~(A ∨ B), A ⊦ ~(A ∨ B)	Premise
3. ~(A ∨ B), A ⊦ ~A	1, 2, MN-4D, MAN-1M
4. ~(A ∨ B) ⊦ ~A	3, CM

MAN-7D. ~(A ∨ B) ⊦ ~B

MAN-8D. ~A, ~B ⊦ ~(A ∨ B)

Proof: 1. ~A, ~B, A ⊦ ~(A ∨ B)	MN-4D, MAN-1M
2. ~A, ~B, B ⊦ ~(A ∨ B)	MN-4D, MAN-1M
3. ~A, ~B, A ∨ B ⊦ ~(A ∨ B)	1, 2, D
4. ~A, ~B ⊦ ~(A ∨ B)	3, CM

𝔐𝔄𝔑-9D. A, B ⊢ ~(~A ∨ ~B) Exercise

𝔐𝔄𝔑-10M. A ⊢ B ⇒ A ∨ C ⊢ B ∨ C

Proof: 1. A ⊢ B Hypothesis
2. A ⊢ B ∨ C 1, AR
3. C ⊢ B ∨ C AL
4. A ∨ C ⊢ B ∨ C 2, 3, D

𝔐𝔄𝔑-11M. A ⊢ B ⇒ C ∨ A ⊢ C ∨ B Exercise

𝔐𝔄𝔑-12M. 𝔐𝔄𝔑 is an E-logic.

Proof: This follows by 𝔐𝔄𝔑−10M, 𝔐𝔄𝔑−11M and theorem 2-11.

𝔐𝔄𝔑-13D. ~(A ∨ ~A) ⊢ ~B

Proof: 1. ~(A ∨ ~A) ⊢ ~~A 𝔐𝔄𝔑-7D
2. ~(A ∨ ~A) ⊢ ~A 𝔐𝔄𝔑-6D
3. ~(A ∨ ~A) ⊢ ~B 1, 2, 𝔐𝔑-4D, 𝔐𝔄𝔑-1M

𝔐𝔄𝔑-14D. ⊢ ~~(A ∨ ~A) Exercise

𝔐𝔄𝔑-15M. α, A ∨ ~A ⊢ B ⇒ α ⊢ ~~B

Proof: 1. α, A ∨ ~A ⊢ B Hypothesis
2. α, A ∨ ~A ⊢ ~~B 1, 𝔐𝔑-1D, 𝔐𝔄𝔑-1M
3. α, ~B ⊢ ~(A ∨ ~A) 2, Con
4. α, ~B ⊢ ~~B 3, 𝔐𝔄𝔑-13D
5. α ⊢ ~~B 4, CM

If we strengthen the negation to rejective strength, we get a system which we will call 𝔚𝔄𝔑.

𝔚𝔄𝔑: a DZOS, with:
connectives: ∨ (2-place), ~ (1-place)
Rules: 1. A ⊢ A ∨ B AR
2. A ⊢ B ∨ A AL

3. (α, A ⊢ C and α, B ⊢ C) ⇒ α,B ∨ C ⊢ C **D**
4. α, A ⊢ ~B ⇒ α, B ⊢ ~A **Con**
5. α, A ⊢ ~A ⇒ α ⊢ ~A **CM**
6. A, ~A ⊢ B **RA**

WAN-1M. Every D- and T-theorem of MAN is a theorem of WAN.

Proof: This is trivial since all of the rules of MAN are also rules of WAN.

WAN-2D. ~A, A ∨ B ⊢ B

Proof: 1. ~A, A ⊢ B	RA
2. ~A, B ⊢ B	Premise
3. ~A, A ∨ B ⊢ B	1,2, D

WAN-3D. A, ~A ∨ B ⊢ B Exercise

WAN-4D. A ∨ B, ~B ∨ C ⊢ A ∨ C

Proof: 1. ~B ∨C, A ⊢ A ∨ C	AR
2. ~B ∨ C, B ⊢ C	WAN-3D
3. ~B ∨C, B ⊢ A ∨ C	2, AL
4. ~B ∨ C, A ∨ B ⊢ A ∨ C	1,3, D

WAN-5D. A ∨ (~B ∨ C), A ∨ B ⊢ A ∨ C

Proof: 1. A ∨ (~B ∨ C), A ⊢ A ∨ C	AR
2. A ∨ (~B ∨ C), B ⊢ A ∨ (~B ∨ C)	Premise
3. A ∨ (~B ∨ C), B ⊢ ~B ∨ (A ∨ C)	1,SA7M,WAN-1M
4. A ∨ (~B ∨ C), B ⊢ B	Premise
5. A ∨ (~B ∨ C), B ⊢~~B	4,WAN-1M,MN-1D
6. A ∨ (~B ∨ C), B ⊢ A ∨ C	3,5, WAN-2D
7. A ∨ (~B ∨ C), A ∨ B ⊢ A ∨ C	1,6, D

WAN-3D gives a form of inference akin to modus ponens. Since in two-valued logic, A ⊃ B represents the same function as ~A ∨ B, it is of interest to note that many, but not all of the familiar inference schemes, are derivable if we adopt it as an abbreviation (using the notation "⊃df").

WAN-6D. A, A ⊃ B ⊢ B	WAN-3D, ⊃df
WAN-7D. A ⊃ B, B ⊃ C ⊢ A ⊃ C	WAN-4D, ⊃df
WAN-8D. A ⊃ (B ⊃ C), A ⊃ B ⊢ A ⊃ C	WAN-5D, ⊃df
WAN-9D. A ⊃(B ⊃ C) ⊢ B ⊃(A ⊃ C)	SA-7M, WAN 1 M, ⊃df
WAN-10D. A ⊢ B ⊃ A	AL, ⊃df
WAN-11D. A ⊢ ~A ⊃ B	AR, ⊃df

WAN-12D. A ⊃ (A ⊃ B) ⊢ A ⊃ B

Proof: 1. A ⊃ (A ⊃ B) ⊢ ~A ∨ (~A ∨ B)	⊃df
2. A ⊃ (A ⊃ B) ⊢ ~A ∨ B	1, SA-7M, WAN-1M
3. A ⊃ (A ⊃ B) ⊢ A ⊃ B	2, ⊃df

WAN-13D. A ⊃ B, ~B ⊢ ~A

Proof: 1. A ⊃ B, ~B ⊢ ~A ∨ B	⊃def
2. A ⊃ B, ~B ⊢ B ∨ ~A	1, SA-5D, WAN-1M
3. A ⊃ B, ~B ⊢ ~B	Premise
4. A ⊃ B, ~B ⊢ ~A	2,3, WAN-2D

WAN-14M. If $g_r(\vee)$ is inclusive-or and $g_r(\sim)$ is two-valued negation, $\alpha \vdash_{WAN} A$ and $r \in R$ imply $\alpha \vDash_R A$ (Soundness Theorem).

Proof: Every rule of WAN is either a rule of SA and hence is validity-preserving by SA-10M or is a rule of INC and hence is validity-preserving by INC-13M.

WAN-15M. WAN is deductively consistent.

Proof: By WAN-14M, not ($v_1 \vdash_{WAN} v_2$) where v_1 and v_2 are distinct variables.

WAN-16M. With ∨ and ~ interpreted in the usual way, WAN is not model-theoretically complete; it is also not deductively complete.

Proof: Given a 3-valued logic with the following valuation rules: $g'_r(\sim A) = 4 - g'_r(A)$ and $g'_r(A \vee B) = \min(g'_r(A), g'_r(B))$ and 1 as the only designated value. It follows that no derivation holds in WAN unless the value of the conclusion is less than or equal to that of some premise. Hence the rules of WAN are 1-preserving. But A ∨ ~A takes the value 2 if A does. Hence not-($\vdash_{WAN}$ A ∨ ~A). But since A ∨ ~A is valid in two-valued logic, WAN is not complete relative to the standard 2-valued interpretation. Since by WAN-14M, adding A ∨ ~A as an axiom will only add entailments valid in two-valued logic, WAN is deductively consistent.

In connection with A ∨ ~A, it is worth noting that the deduction theorem (i.e. rule C) fails in WAN, since ~A ∨ A translates as A ⊃ A and hence, as we have seen, is not provable in WAN. A related theorem which follows easily in WAN by D is:

WAN-17M. (α, A ⊢ B and α, ~A ⊢ B) ⇒ α, A ∨ ~A ⊢ B.

Perhaps the most obvious principle to add to WAN might be the special case of dilemma we have already encountered as **NgC**. We will call that system ANC (for alternation, negation complete):

ANC: A DZOS, with:

connectives: ∨ (2-place), ~ (1-place)

Rules:	1. A ⊢ A ∨ B	**AR**
	2. A ⊢ B ∨ A	**AL**
	3. (α, A ⊢ C and α, B ⊢ C) ⇒ α,B ∨ C ⊢ C	**D**
	4. A, ~A ⊢ B	**RA**
	5. (α, A ⊢ B and α, ~A ⊢ B) ⇒ α ⊢ B	**NgC**

𝒜NC-1M. $\alpha, A \vdash \sim A \Rightarrow \alpha \vdash \sim A$

Proof: 1. $\alpha, A \vdash \sim A$	Hypothesis
2. $\alpha, \sim A \vdash \sim A$	Premise
3. $\alpha \vdash \sim A$	1, 2, NgC

𝒜NC-2M. $\alpha, A \vdash \sim B \Rightarrow \alpha, B \vdash \sim A$

1. $\alpha, A, B \vdash \sim B$	Hypothesis
2. $\alpha, A, B \vdash B$	Premise
3. $\alpha, A, B \vdash \sim A$	1, 2, RA
4. $\alpha, \sim A, B \vdash \sim A$	Premise
5. $\alpha, B \vdash \sim A$	3, 4, NgC

𝒜NC-3M. Every D- and T-theorem of 𝒲𝒜N is a theorem of 𝒜NC.

Proof: By 𝒜NC-1M and 𝒜NC-2M and the rules of 𝒜NC, 𝒜NC R-includes 𝒲𝒜N.

𝒜NC-4T. $\vdash A \vee \sim A$

Proof: 1. $A \vdash A \vee \sim A$	AR
2. $\sim A \vdash A \vee \sim A$	AL
3. $\vdash A \vee \sim A$	1, 2, NgC

𝒜NC-5T. $\vdash \sim A \vee A$	Exercise
𝒜NC-6T. $\vdash A \supset A$	𝒜NC-5T, $\supset$df

𝒜NC-7M. $\alpha, A \vdash B \Rightarrow \alpha \vdash A \supset B$

Proof: 1. $\alpha, A \vdash B$	Hypothesis
2. $\alpha, A \vdash \sim A \vee B$	1, AL
3. $\alpha, \sim A \vdash \sim A$	Premise
4. $\alpha, \sim A \vdash \sim A \vee B$	3, AR
5. $\alpha \vdash \sim A \vee B$	2, 4, NgC
6. $\alpha \vdash A \supset B$	5, $\supset$df

ANC-8D. $A \vdash \sim\sim A$

Proof: This follows by ANC-3M, WAN-1M, MAN-1M and MN-1D.

ANC-8T. $\vdash A \supset \sim\sim A$

ANC-9D. $\sim\sim A \vdash A$ — Exercise

ANC-9T. $\vdash \sim\sim A \supset A$

ANC-10D. $\sim A \supset \sim B, B \vdash A$

Proof:

1. $\sim A \supset \sim B, B \vdash \sim\sim A \vee \sim B$	$\supset$df
2. $\sim A \supset \sim B, B \vdash B$	Premise
3. $\sim A \supset \sim B, B \vdash \sim B \vee \sim\sim A$	1, SA-5D, ANC-3M
4. $\sim A \supset \sim B, B \vdash \sim\sim A$	2, 3, WAN-2D, ANC-3M
5. $\sim A \supset \sim B, B \vdash A$	4, ANC-9D

ANC-10Da. $\sim A \supset \sim B \vdash B \supset A$

ANC-10T. $\vdash (\sim A \supset \sim B) \supset (B \supset A)$

ANC-11M. $\alpha, A \vdash B \Rightarrow \alpha, \sim B \vdash \sim A$

Proof:

1. $\alpha, A, \sim B \vdash B$	Hypothesis
2. $\alpha, A, \sim B \vdash \sim B$	Premise
3. $\alpha, A, \sim B \vdash \sim A$	1, 2, RA
4. $\alpha, \sim A, \sim B \vdash \sim B$	Premise
5. $\alpha, \sim B \vdash \sim A$	3, 4, NgC

ANC-12M. $\alpha, \sim A \vdash \sim B \Rightarrow \alpha, B \vdash A$ — Exercise

ANC-13M. The equivalence theorem holds without restriction in ANC.

Proof: By ANC-3M, ANC-11M, MAN-10M, MAN-11M, the conditions on PL-14M are satisfied.

ANC-14M. ANC is an E-logic.

Proof: By ANC- 7M, WAN- 6D and ANC- 3M, $\vdash_{ANC}$ A ⊃ B ⇔ A $\vdash_{ANC}$ B. Hence the result follows by ANC-13M and theorem 2-17.

ANC-15M. The portion of ANC expressible in terms of ⊃ and ~ R-includes INC.

Proof: This follows immediately from ANC-3M, WAN-6D and ANC-7M.

ANC-16D. ~A ⊃ B ⊢ A ∨ B

Proof:
1. ~A ⊃ B ⊢ ~~A ∨ B — ⊃df
2. ~A ⊃ B ⊢ A ∨ B — 1, ANC-8D, ANC-9D, ANC-13M

ANC-16T. ⊢ (~A ⊃ B) ⊃ (A ∨ B)

ANC-17D. A ∨ B ⊢ ~A ⊃ B — Exercise

ANC-17T. ⊢ (A ∨ B) ⊃ (~A ⊃ B)

ANC-18M. If $g_r(\vee)$ is inclusive-or and $g_r(\sim)$ is negation, $\alpha \vdash_{ANC}$ A and **r** ∈ **R** imply $\alpha \vDash_{R}$ A.

Proof: Exercise

ANC-19M. Under the same conditions as in ANC-18M, ANC is model-theoretically consistent.

Proof: Exercise

ANC-20M. Under the same conditions as in ANC-18M, $\alpha \vDash_{R}$ A implies $\alpha \vdash_{ANC}$ A. Also ANC is deductively complete.

Proof: By ANC-15M, ANC-13M, ANC-16M, and ANC-17M, the conditions of INC-27M are satisfied.

There are many alternative formulations of ANC. The most obvious one, and one of special interest to many who have intuitionistic sympathies in the philosophy of mathematics is one we will call 𝒜𝒩𝒞1 which substitutes "the law of the excluded middle" for **NgC**.

𝒜𝒩𝒞1: A DZOS, with

connectives: ∨ (2-place), ~ (1-place)

axiom schemata: 1. ⊢ A ∨ ~A

Rules:	1. A ⊢ A ∨ B	**AR**
	2. A ⊢ B ∨ A	**AL**
	3. (α, A ⊢ B and α, ~A ⊢ B) ⇒ α ⊢ B	**D**
	4. A, ~A ⊢ B	**RA**

𝒜𝒩𝒞 1-1M. (α, A ⊢ B and α, ~A ⊢ B) ⇒ α ⊢ B

Proof: 1. α, A ⊢ B	Hypothesis
2. α, ~A ⊢ B	Hypothesis
3. α, A ∨ ~A ⊢ B	1, 2, D
4. α ⊢ A ∨ ~A	Ax 1
5. α ⊢ B	3, 4, closure

𝒜𝒩𝒞 1-2M. 𝒜𝒩𝒞 and 𝒜𝒩𝒞1 are equivalent.

Proof: By the rules and 𝒜𝒩𝒞1-2M, 𝒜𝒩𝒞1 R-includes 𝒜𝒩𝒞. By the rules, and 𝒜𝒩𝒞-4T, 𝒜𝒩𝒞 R-includes 𝒜𝒩𝒞1. Since the wffs agree, they are equivalent.

An historically more significant system (which is a little harder to prove equivalent) is one which originates with Whitehead and Russell's Principia Mathematica. We will call this 𝒜𝒩𝒞2. We will find it convenient to use the abbreviation we introduced in 𝒲𝒜𝒩, namely A ⊃ B for ~A ∨ B.

𝒜𝒩𝒞2: A DZOS, with:

connectives: ∨ (2-place), ~ (1-place)

axiom schemata:

1. ⊢ (A ∨ A) ⊃ A
2. ⊢ A ⊃ (A ∨ B)

3. ⊢ (A ∨ B) ⊃ (B ∨ A)
4. ⊢ (A ⊃ B) ⊃ [(C ∨ A) ⊃ (C ∨ B)]
Rules: 1. A, A ⊃ B ⊢ B MP 1

We call this rule **MP 1**, since strictly speaking it is not MP but rather A, ~A ∨ B ⊢ B.

𝒜NC2-1D. A ⊢ A ∨ B

Proof:	1. A ⊢ A ⊃ (A ∨ B)	Ax2
	2. A ⊢ A	Premise
	3. A ⊢ A ∨ B	1, 2, MP 1

𝒜NC2-2D. B ⊢ A ∨ B Exercise

𝒜NC2-3D. A ⊃ B, C ⊃ A ⊢ C ⊃ B

Proof:	1. A ⊃ B, C ⊃ A ⊢ (A ⊃ B) ⊃ [(C ⊃ A) ⊃ (C ⊃ B)]	Ax4
	2. A ⊃ B, C ⊃ A ⊢ (A ⊃ B)	Premise
	3. A ⊃ B, C ⊃ A ⊢ (C ⊃ A) ⊃ (C ⊃ B)	1,2, MP 1
	4. A ⊃ B, C ⊃ A ⊢ C ⊃ A	Premise
	5. A ⊃ B, C ⊃ A ⊢ C ⊃ B	3,4, MP 1

𝒜NC2-4T. ⊢ A ⊃ A

Proof:	1. ⊢ (A ∨ A) ⊃ A	Ax1
	2. ⊢ A ⊃ (A ∨ A)	Ax2
	3. ⊢ A ⊃ A	1, 2, 𝒜NC2-3D

𝒜NC2-5T. ⊢ A ∨ ~A

Proof:	1. ⊢ A ⊃ A	𝒜NC2-4T
	2. ⊢ ~A ∨ A	⊃df
	3. ⊢ (~A ∨ A) ⊃ (A ∨ ~A)	Ax3
	4. ⊢ A ∨ ~A	2, 3, MP 1

𝒜NC2-6T. ⊢ A ⊃ (B ⊃ A)

Proof: 1. $\vdash [(A \vee \sim B) \supset (\sim B \vee A)] \supset$
$[(A \supset [A \vee \sim B]) \supset (A \supset [\sim B \vee A])]$ Ax4
2. $\vdash (A \vee \sim B) \supset (\sim B \vee A)$ Ax3
3. $\vdash (A \supset [A \vee \sim B]) \supset (A \supset [\sim B \vee A])$ 1, 2, MP1
4. $\vdash A \supset (A \vee \sim B)$ Ax2
5. $\vdash A \supset (\sim B \vee A)$ 3, 4, MP1
6. $\vdash A \supset (B \supset A)$ 5, $\supset$def

𝒜NC2-7D. $A \vee (B \vee C) \vdash B \vee (A \vee C)$

Proof: 1. $A \vee (B \vee C) \vdash C \supset (C \vee A)$ Ax2
2. $A \vee (B \vee C) \vdash (C \vee A) \supset (A \vee C)$ Ax3
3. $A \vee (B \vee C) \vdash C \supset (A \vee C)$ 1,2, 𝒜NC2-3D
4. $A \vee (B \vee C) \vdash [C \supset (A \vee C)] \supset [(B \vee C) \supset (B \vee [\![A \vee C]\!])]$ Ax4
5. $A \vee (B \vee C) \vdash [B \vee C] \supset [B \vee (A \vee C)]$ 3,4, MP1
6. $A \vee (B \vee C) \vdash [(B \vee C) \supset (B \vee [\![A \vee C]\!])] \supset$
$[(A \vee [\![B \vee C]\!]) \supset (A \vee [\![B \vee [A \vee C]\!]\!])]$ Ax4
7. $A \vee (B \vee C) \vdash (A \vee [\![B \vee C]\!]) \supset (A \vee [\![B \vee [A \vee C]]\!])$ 5,6, MP1
8. $A \vee (B \vee C) \vdash A \vee (B \vee C)$ Premise
9. $A \vee (B \vee C) \vdash A \vee [B \vee (A \vee C)]$ 7,8, MP1
10. $A \vee (B \vee C) \vdash [\![A \vee [B \vee (A \vee C)]]\!] \supset [\![[B \vee (A \vee C)] \vee A]\!]$ Ax3
11. $A \vee (B \vee C) \vdash [B \vee (A \vee C)] \vee A$ 9,10, MP1
12. $A \vee (B \vee C) \vdash A \supset (A \vee C)$ Ax2
13. $A \vee (B \vee C) \vdash (A \vee C) \supset [(A \vee C) \vee B]$ Ax2
14. $A \vee (B \vee C) \vdash [(A \vee C) \vee B] \supset [B \vee (A \vee C)]$ Ax3
15. $A \vee (B \vee C) \vdash A \supset [(A \vee C) \vee B]$ 12,13, 𝒜NC2-3D
16. $A \vee (B \vee C) \vdash A \supset [B \vee (A \vee C)]$ 14,15, 𝒜NC2-3D
17. $A \vee (B \vee C) \vdash [\![A \supset [B \vee (A \vee C)]]\!] \supset$
$([\![[B \vee (A \vee C)]\!] \vee A] \supset [\![[B \vee (A \vee C)]\!] \vee [\![B \vee (A \vee C)]\!]\!])$ Ax4
18. $A \vee (B \vee C) \vdash [\![[B \vee (A \vee C)]\!] \vee A] \supset$
$[\![[B \vee (A \vee C)]\!] \vee [\![B \vee (A \vee C)]\!]\!]$ 16,17, MP1
19. $A \vee (B \vee C) \vdash [\![B \vee (A \vee C)]\!] \vee [\![B \vee (A \vee C)]\!]$ 11,18, MP1

20. $A \vee (B \vee C) \vdash [\![[B \vee (A \vee C)]\!] \vee [\![B \vee (A \vee C)]\!]\!] \supset$
$[\![B \vee (A \vee C)]\!]$ Ax1
21. $A \vee (B \vee C) \vdash B \vee (A \vee C)$ 19,20, MP1

$\mathcal{A}$NC2-8D. $A \supset (B \supset C) \vdash B \supset (A \supset C)$ Exercise

$\mathcal{A}$NC2-9D. $A \supset (B \supset C), A \supset B \vdash A \supset C$

Proof:	
1. $A \supset (B \supset C), A \supset B \vdash B \supset (A \supset C)$	$\mathcal{A}$NC2-8D
2. $A \supset (B \supset C), A \supset B \vdash A \supset B$	Premise
3. $A \supset (B \supset C), A \supset B \vdash A \supset (A \supset C)$	$\mathcal{A}$NC2-3D
4. $A \supset (B \supset C), A \supset B \vdash \sim A \vee (\sim A \vee C)$	3,⊃df
5. $A \supset (B \supset C), A \supset B \vdash (\sim A \vee C) \supset (C \vee \sim A)$	Ax3
6. $A \supset (B \supset C), A \supset B \vdash [(\sim A \vee C) \supset (C \vee \sim A)] \supset [(\sim A \vee [\sim A \vee C]) \supset (\sim A \vee [C \vee \sim A])]$	Ax4
7. $A \supset (B \supset C), A \supset B \vdash (\sim A \vee [\sim A \vee C]) \supset (\sim A \vee [C \vee \sim A])$	5,6, MP1
8. $A \supset (B \supset C), A \supset B \vdash \sim A \vee (C \vee \sim A)$	4,7, MP1
9. $A \supset (B \supset C), A \supset B \vdash C \vee (\sim A \vee \sim A)$	8, $\mathcal{A}$NC2-7D
10. $A \supset (B \supset C), A \supset B \vdash [(\sim A \vee \sim A) \supset \sim A] \supset [(C \vee [\sim A \vee \sim A]) \supset (C \vee \sim A)]$	Ax4
11. $A \supset (B \supset C), A \supset B \vdash (\sim A \vee \sim A) \supset \sim A$	Ax1
12. $A \supset (B \supset C), A \supset B \vdash [C \vee (\sim A \vee \sim A)] \supset (C \vee \sim A)$	9,10, MP1
13. $A \supset (B \supset C), A \supset B \vdash C \vee \sim A$	9,12, MP1
14. $A \supset (B \supset C), A \supset B \vdash (C \vee \sim A) \vee (\sim A \vee C)$	Ax3
15. $A \supset (B \supset C), A \supset B \vdash \sim A \vee C$	13,14, MP1
16. $A \supset (B \supset C), A \supset B \vdash A \supset C$	15, ⊃df

$\mathcal{A}$NC2-10M. The ⊃ and ~ subsystem of $\mathcal{A}$NC2 R-includes PL2.

Proof: This follows from $\mathcal{A}$NC2-9D, $\mathcal{A}$NC2-6T, and PL2-3M

$\mathcal{A}$NC2-11M. ($\alpha, A \vdash C$ and $\alpha, B \vdash C$) ⇒ $\alpha, A \vee B \vdash C$

Proof:	
1. $\alpha, A \vee B, A \vdash C$	Hypothesis
2. $\alpha, A \vee B, B \vdash C$	Hypothesis
3. $\alpha, A \vee B \vdash A \supset C$	1, $\mathcal{A}$NC2-10M
4. $\alpha, A \vee B \vdash B \supset C$	2, $\mathcal{A}$NC2-10M
5. $\alpha, A \vee B \vdash (A \supset C) \supset [(B \vee A) \supset (B \vee C)]$	Ax4
6. $\alpha, A \vee B \vdash (B \vee A) \supset (B \vee C)$	3, 5, MP1
7. $\alpha, A \vee B \vdash (A \vee B) \supset (B \vee A)$	Ax3

8. α, A ∨ B ⊢ A ∨ B	Premise
9. α, A ∨ B ⊢ B ∨ A	7, 8, MP 1
10. α, A ∨ B ⊢ B ∨ C	6, 9, MP 1
11. α, A ∨ B ⊢ (B ∨ C) ⊃ (C ∨ B)	10, MP 1
12. α, A ∨ B ⊢ C ∨ B	10, 11, MP 1
13. α, A ∨ B ⊢ (B ⊃ C) ⊃ [(C ∨ B) ⊃ (C ∨ C)]	Ax4
14. α, A ∨ B ⊢ (C ∨ B) ⊃ (C ∨ C)	10, 13, MP 1
15. α, A ∨ B ⊢ C ∨ C	12, 14, MP 1
16. α, A ∨ B ⊢ (C ∨ C) ⊃ C	Ax 1
17. α, A ∨ B ⊢ C	15, 16, MP 1

𝒜NC2-12D. A, ~A ⊢ B

Proof: 1. A, ~A ⊢ ~A ∨ B	𝒜NC2-1D
2. A, ~A ⊢ A	Premise
3. A, ~A ⊢ B	1, 2, MP 1

𝒜NC2-13M. $\alpha \vdash_{\mathcal{A}NC2} A \Rightarrow \alpha \vDash_{\mathbf{R}} A$ (where **R** is the usual 2-valued interpretation).

Proof: Exercise

𝒜NC2-14M. 𝒜NC and 𝒜NC2 are equivalent.

Proof: By 𝒜NC2-1D, 𝒜NC2-2D, 𝒜NC2-10D, 𝒜NC2-11D and 𝒜NC2-5T, 𝒜NC2 R-includes 𝒜NC. Since 𝒜NC2 is deductively consistent by 𝒜NC2-13M, then the result follows by 𝒜NC2-10M and ℒNC-24M.

Exercises
Chapter 7

1. Prove the theorems that were left as exercises. (SA-8M, MAN-5D, MAN-7D, MAN-9D, MAN-11D, MAN-14D, WAN-3D, ANC-9D, ANC-9T, ANC-12M, ANC-17D, ANC-17T, ANC-18M, ANC-19M, ANC2-13M)

2. Show that $A \vee B, \sim A \vdash B$ does not hold in MAN.

3. Show that $\sim(\sim A \vee \sim B) \vdash A$ does not hold in MAN.

4. Show that MAN is deductively consistent.

5. Show that MAN is incomplete relative to two-valued logic, and also is deductively incomplete.

8
Conjunction

The fourth of the connectives in common use in colloquial languages is "and" and there appears to be little problem in identifying it with the logical operation we termed "normal conjunction" in chapter 2. The formal system most obviously related to that we will call **SK** for "simple conjunction":

SK: a DZOS, with:

Connective: $\wedge$ (2-place)

Rules:	1. $A \wedge B \vdash A$	**LS** (left simplification)
	2. $A \wedge B \vdash B$	**RS** (right simplification)
	3. $A, B \vdash A \wedge B$	**A** (Adjunction)

SK-1D: $A \wedge B \vdash B \wedge A$

Proof:	1. $A \wedge B \vdash B$	RS
	2. $A \wedge B \vdash A$	LS
	3. $A \wedge B \vdash B \wedge A$	1, 2, A

SK-2D: $A \wedge (B \wedge C) \vdash (A \wedge B) \wedge C$

Proof:	1. $A \wedge (B \wedge C) \vdash A$	LS
	2. $A \wedge (B \wedge C) \vdash B \wedge C$	RS
	3. $A \wedge (B \wedge C) \vdash B$	2, LS
	4. $A \wedge (B \wedge C) \vdash A \wedge B$	1, 3, A
	5. $A \wedge (B \wedge C) \vdash C$	2, RS
	6. $A \wedge (B \wedge C) \vdash (A \wedge B) \wedge C$	4, 5, A

SK-3D: $(A \wedge B) \wedge C \vdash A \wedge (B \wedge C)$ Exercise

SK-4D: $A \vdash A \wedge A$

Proof:	1. $A \vdash A$	Premise

2. $A \vdash A \wedge A$ — 1, 1, A

SK-5M: The deductive properties of wffs of **SK** depend only on the variables.

Proof: This follows by theorem 7-2, utilizing **SK**-1D, **SK**-2D, **SK**-3D, **SK**-4D and **LS**.

SK-6M: $A \vdash B \Rightarrow A \wedge C \vdash B \wedge C$

Proof:
1. $A \wedge C \vdash A$ — LS
2. $A \wedge C \vdash B$ — 1, Hypothesis
3. $A \wedge C \vdash C$ — RS
4. $A \wedge C \vdash B \wedge C$ — 2, 3, A

SK-7M: $A \vdash B \Rightarrow C \wedge A \vdash C \wedge B$ — Exercise

SK-8M: **SK** is an E-logic

Proof: This follows by theorem 2-17, utilizing **SK**-6M and **SK**-7M.

SK-9M: If $\mathbf{g_r}(\wedge)$ is the truth-function "and" and $\mathbf{r} \in \mathbf{R}$, then $\alpha \vdash_{\mathbf{SK}} A$ implies $\alpha \models_{\mathbf{R}} A$.

Proof: Exercise

SK-10M: $\alpha \vdash_{\mathbf{SK}} A$ if and only if every variable in A is in one of the elements of α.

Proof: Suppose every variable in A is in one of the elements of α. Let $v_1,\cdots,v_n$ be all the variables in A. For each i ($1 \leq i \leq n$), let A_i be the element of α that contains v_i. Then for each i there exists a wff B_i $\mathbf{Equiv}_{\mathbf{SK}}(A_i, B_i \wedge v_i)$ by **SK**-5M. By **RS**, $B_i \wedge v_i \vdash v_i$. Hence $A_i \vdash v_i$ and $\alpha \vdash v_i$. Hence, by A (n-1 times), $\alpha \vdash v_1 \wedge \cdots \wedge v_n$. Hence by **SK**-5M, $\alpha \vdash A$. Suppose there is a variable v in A and in none of the elements of α. Let $\mathbf{g_r}(v) = 0$ and otherwise $\mathbf{g_r}(x) = 1$ if x is a variable. Then $\mathbf{r} \Vdash \alpha$ but not-($\mathbf{r} \Vdash A$). But then not-($\alpha \models A$) and by

SK-9M, not-($\alpha \vdash A$).

SK-11M: With $\wedge$ interpreted as "and," **SK** is model-theoretically complete.

Proof: Suppose not-($\alpha \vdash A$). Then by **SK**-10M, there exists a variable v in A which is not in any element of α. Let $g_r(v) = 0$ and $g_r(x) = 1$ for all other variables. Then **r** satisfies α but not A and not-($\alpha \vDash A$).

SK-12M: **SK** is virtually deductively complete.

Proof: This is left as an exercise for the reader (Cf. **SA-12M**).

If, as we have done with implication and disjunction, we add a negation of "minimal strength" to **SK**, we get a "minimal conjunction-negation" system which we will call **MKN**.

MKN: A DZOS, with

connectives: $\wedge$ (2-place), ~ (1-place)

rules:

	1. $A \wedge B \vdash A$	LS
	2. $A \wedge B \vdash B$	RS
	3. $A, B \vdash A \wedge B$	A
	4. $\alpha, A \vdash \sim B \Rightarrow \alpha, B \vdash \sim A$	Con
	5. $\alpha, A \vdash \sim A \Rightarrow \alpha \vdash \sim A$	CM

MKN-1M. Every D-theorem of **SK** and **MN** is a theorem of **MKN**.

Proof: This is trivial, since **MKN** R-includes both.

MKN-2M. $\alpha, A \vdash B \Rightarrow \alpha, A \wedge C \vdash B \wedge C$

Proof:

1. $\alpha, A \wedge C \vdash A$	RS
2. $\alpha, A \wedge C \vdash C$	LS
3. $\alpha, A \wedge C \vdash B$	1, Hypothesis
4. $\alpha, A \wedge C \vdash B \wedge C$	2, 3, A

MKN-3M. $\alpha, A \vdash B \Rightarrow \alpha, C \wedge A \vdash C \wedge B$ — Exercise

MKN-4M. $\alpha, A \vdash B \Rightarrow \alpha, \sim B \vdash \sim A$ — Exercise

$\mathcal{MKN}$-5M. $\mathcal{MKN}$ is an E-logic.

Proof: This follows by theorem 2-17, utilizing $\mathcal{MKN}$-2M, $\mathcal{MKN}$-3M and $\mathcal{MKN}$-4M.

$\mathcal{MKN}$-6D. $A \wedge {\sim}A \vdash {\sim}B$

Proof: 1. $A \wedge {\sim}A \vdash A$	RS
2. $A \wedge {\sim}A \vdash {\sim}A$	LS
3. $A \wedge {\sim}A \vdash {\sim}B$	1,2, $\mathcal{MKN}$-1M, $\mathcal{MN}$-4D

$\mathcal{MKN}$-7T. $\vdash {\sim}(A \wedge {\sim}A)$

Proof: 1. $A \wedge {\sim}A \vdash {\sim}(A \wedge {\sim}A)$	$\mathcal{MKN}$-6D
2. $\vdash {\sim}(A \wedge {\sim}A)$	1, CM

$\mathcal{MKN}$-8D. ${\sim}A \wedge {\sim\sim}A \vdash {\sim}B \wedge {\sim\sim}B$ Exercise

$\mathcal{MKN}$-9D. ${\sim}({\sim\sim}A \wedge B) \vdash {\sim}(A \wedge B)$

Proof: 1. $A \wedge B \vdash A$	LS
2. $A \wedge B \vdash {\sim\sim}A$	1, $\mathcal{MN}$-1D, $\mathcal{MKN}$-1M
3. $A \wedge B \vdash B$	RS
4. $A \wedge B \vdash {\sim\sim}A \wedge B$	2, 3, A
5. $A \wedge B \vdash {\sim\sim}({\sim\sim}A \wedge B)$	4, $\mathcal{MN}$-1D, $\mathcal{MKN}$-1M
6. ${\sim}({\sim\sim}A \wedge B) \vdash {\sim}(A \wedge B)$	5, Con

$\mathcal{MKN}$-10D. ${\sim}(A \wedge B) \vdash {\sim}({\sim\sim}A \wedge B)$ Exercise

$\mathcal{MKN}$-11D. ${\sim}(A \wedge B), A \vdash {\sim}B$

Proof: 1. ${\sim}(A \wedge B), A, B \vdash A \wedge B$	A
2. ${\sim}(A \wedge B), A, B \vdash {\sim\sim}(A \wedge B)$	1, $\mathcal{MN}$-1D, $\mathcal{MKN}$-1M
3. $A, B \vdash {\sim\sim}(A \wedge B)$	2, CM
4. ${\sim}(A \wedge B), A \vdash {\sim}B)$	3, Con

$\mathcal{MKN}$-12D. ${\sim\sim}(A \wedge B) \vdash {\sim\sim}A \wedge {\sim\sim}B$

Proof: 1. $A \wedge B \vdash A$ LS

2. $A \wedge B \vdash \sim\sim A$ 1,$\mathcal{MN}$-1D,$\mathcal{MKN}$-1M

3. $\sim A \vdash \sim(A \wedge B)$ 2, Con

4. $\sim A \vdash \sim\sim\sim(A \wedge B)$ 3,$\mathcal{MN}$-1D,$\mathcal{MKN}$-1M

5. $\sim\sim(A \wedge B) \vdash \sim\sim A$ 4, Con

6. $A \wedge B \vdash B$ RS

7. $A \wedge B \vdash \sim\sim B$ 6,$\mathcal{MN}$-1D,$\mathcal{MKN}$-1M

8. $\sim B \vdash \sim(A \wedge B)$ 7, Con

9. $\sim B \vdash \sim\sim\sim(A \wedge B)$ 8,$\mathcal{MN}$-1D,$\mathcal{MKN}$-1M

10. $\sim\sim(A \wedge B) \vdash \sim\sim B$ 9, Con

11. $\sim\sim(A \wedge B) \vdash \sim\sim A \wedge \sim\sim B$ 5, 10, A

$\mathcal{MKN}$-13D. $\sim\sim A \wedge \sim\sim B \vdash \sim\sim(A \wedge B)$

Proof: 1. $\sim\sim A \wedge \sim\sim B, \sim(A \wedge B) \vdash \sim(\sim\sim A \wedge B)$ $\mathcal{MKN}$-8D

2. $\sim\sim A \wedge \sim\sim B, \sim(A \wedge B) \vdash \sim\sim A$ LS

3. $\sim\sim A \wedge \sim\sim B, \sim(A \wedge B) \vdash \sim B$ 1,2, $\mathcal{MKN}$-10D

4. $\sim\sim A \wedge \sim\sim B, \sim(A \wedge B) \vdash \sim\sim B$ RS

5. $\sim\sim A \wedge \sim\sim B, \sim(A \wedge B) \vdash \sim\sim(A \wedge B)$ 1,$\mathcal{MN}$4D,$\mathcal{MKN}$-1M

6. $\sim\sim A \wedge \sim\sim B \vdash \sim\sim(A \wedge B)$ 6, CM

$\mathcal{MKN}$-14M: If $g_r(\wedge)$ is the truth-function "and", $g_r(\sim)$ is the truth function "not" and $r \in \mathbf{R}$, then $\alpha \vdash_{\mathcal{SK}} A$ implies $\alpha \vDash_{\mathbf{R}} A$.

Proof: Exercise

$\mathcal{MKN}$-15M: If $g_r(\wedge)$ is the truth-function "and", $g_r(\sim)$ is the truth function "not", then $\mathcal{MKN}$ is not model-theoretically complete and is also not deductively complete.

Proof: Soundness still holds with $\sim$ interpreted as the constant 1 and hence $A, \sim A \vdash B$ is not derivable.

We now consider a system with negation strengthened so that it is rejective.

WKN: A DZOS, with

connectives: $\wedge$ (2-place), $\sim$ (1-place)

rules:

1.	$A \wedge B \vdash A$	LS
2.	$A \wedge B \vdash B$	RS
3.	$A, B \vdash A \wedge B$	A
4.	$\alpha, A \vdash \sim B \Rightarrow \alpha, B \vdash \sim A$	Con
5.	$\alpha, A \vdash \sim A \Rightarrow \alpha \vdash \sim A$	CM
6.	$A, \sim A \vdash B$	RA

WKN-1M. Every D- and T-theorem of **MKN** is a theorem of **WKN**.

Proof: **WKN** R-includes **MKN**, by rules 1 to 5.

WKN-2D. $\sim(A \wedge \sim\sim A) \vdash \sim A$ [**MKN**-15D]

Proof:

1.	$A \vdash A$	Premise
2.	$A \vdash \sim\sim A$	1, **MN**-1D, **MKN**-1M
3.	$A \vdash A \wedge \sim\sim A$	1, 2, A
4.	$A \vdash \sim\sim(A \wedge \sim\sim A)$	3, **MN**-1D, **MKN**-1M
5.	$\sim(A \wedge \sim\sim A) \vdash \sim A$	4, Con

WKN-3M. **WKN** is an E-logic.

Proof: This follows by theorem 2-17, utilizing **MKN**-2M, **MKN**-3M, **MKN**-4M and **WKN**-1M.

WKN-4D. $\sim(A \wedge B), A \vdash \sim B$

Proof:

1.	$\sim(A \wedge B), A, B \vdash \sim(A \wedge B)$	Premise
2.	$\sim(A \wedge B), A, B \vdash A \wedge B$	A
3.	$\sim(A \wedge B), A, B \vdash \sim B$	1, 2, RA
4.	$\sim(A \wedge B), A \vdash \sim B$	3, CM

WKN-5M. $\alpha, A \vdash B \Rightarrow \alpha \vdash \sim(A \wedge \sim B)$

Proof:

1.	$\alpha, A \wedge \sim B \vdash A$	LS
2.	$\alpha, A \wedge \sim B \vdash B$	1, Hypothesis

3. α, A ∧ ~B ⊢ ~B	RS
4. α, A ∧ ~B ⊢ ~(A ∧ ~B)	2, 3, RA
5. α ⊢ ~(A ∧ ~B)	4, CM

WKN-6D. ~(A ∧ ~B), ~~A ⊢ ~~B

Proof: 1. ~(A ∧ ~B), A ⊢ ~~B	WKN-4D
2. ~(A ∧ ~B), ~B ⊢ ~A	1, Con
3. ~(A ∧ ~B), ~B ⊢ ~~~A	2, MN-1D, MKN-1M
4. ~(A ∧ ~B), ~~A ⊢ ~~B	3, Con

Since ~(A ∧ ~B) behaves much like A ⊃ B, we will adopt it as an abbreviation (much as we have done earlier for ~A ∨ B, calling the rule ⊃df).

WKN-7M. α, A ⊢ B ⇒ α ⊢ A ⊃ B WKN-5M, ⊃df

WKN-8D. A ⊃ (B ⊃ C) ⊢ B ⊃ (A ⊃ C)

Proof: 1. A ⊃ (B ⊃ C), A, B, C ⊢ B ∧ ~C	A
2. A ⊃ (B ⊃ C), A, B, ~C ⊢ ~~(B ∧ ~C)	1, MN-1D, MKN-1M
3. A ⊃ (B ⊃ C), A, B, ~C ⊢ A	Premise
4. A ⊃ (B ⊃ C), A, B, ~C ⊢ A ∧ ~~(B ∧ ~C)	2, 3, A
5. A ⊃ (B ⊃ C), A, B, ~C ⊢ ~[A ∧ ~~(B ∧ ~C))]	Premise
6. A ⊃ (B ⊃ C), A, B, ~C ⊢ C	4,5, RA
7. A ⊃ (B ⊃ C), A, B ⊢ ~(~C ∧ ~C)	6, WKN-5M
8. A ⊃ (B ⊃ C), A, B ⊢ ~~C	7, WKN-3M, LS, A
9. A ⊃ (B ⊃ C), B ⊢ ~(A ∧ ~~~C)	8, WKN-5M
10. A ⊃ (B ⊃ C), B ⊢ ~(A ∧ ~C)	9, WKN-1M, MN-3M
11. A ⊃ (B ⊃ C), B ⊢ A ⊃ C	10, ⊃df
12. A ⊃ (B ⊃ C) ⊢ B ⊃(A ⊃ C)	11, WKN-7M

WKN-9D. A ⊃ B , B ⊃ C ⊢ A ⊃ C

Proof: 1. A ⊃ B , B ⊃ C, A, ~C ⊢ ~(A ∧ ~B)	⊃df
2. A ⊃ B , B ⊃ C, A, ~C ⊢ ~(B ∧ ~C)	⊃df
3. A ⊃ B , B ⊃ C, A, ~C ⊢ A	Premise
4. A ⊃ B , B ⊃ C, A, ~C ⊢ ~~B	1,3, WKN-4D

5. $A \supset B, B \supset C, A, \sim C \vdash \sim\sim C$	2,4, WKN-6D
6. $A \supset B, B \supset C, A \vdash \sim(\sim C \wedge \sim\sim\sim C)$	5, WKN-5M
7. $A \supset B, B \supset C, A \vdash \sim(\sim C \wedge \sim C)$	6,WKN-1M,MN-3M
8. $A \supset B, B \supset C, A \vdash \sim\sim C$	7,WKN-3M,LS,A
9. $A \supset B, B \supset C \vdash \sim(A \wedge \sim\sim\sim C)$	8, WKN-5M
10. $A \supset B, B \supset C \vdash \sim(A \wedge \sim C)$	9,WKN-1M,MN-3M
11. $A \supset B, B \supset C \vdash A \supset C$	10, $\supset$df

WKN-10D. $A \supset B,\ A \supset (B \supset C) \vdash A \supset C$

Proof:

1. $A \supset B,\ A \supset (B \supset C), A, \sim C \vdash B \supset (A \supset C)$	WKN-8D
2. $A \supset B,\ A \supset (B \supset C), A, \sim C \vdash A \supset B$	Premise
3. $A \supset B,\ A \supset (B \supset C), A, \sim C \vdash A \supset (A \supset C)$	1,2, WKN-9D
4. $A \supset B,\ A \supset (B \supset C), A, \sim C \vdash A$	Premise
5. $A \supset B,\ A \supset (B \supset C), A, \sim C \vdash \sim\sim A$	4,MN-1M, WKN-1M
6. $A \supset B,\ A \supset (B \supset C), A, \sim C \vdash \sim\sim(A \supset C)$	5, WKN-6D
7. $A \supset B, A \supset (B \supset C), A, \sim C \vdash \sim\sim\sim(A \wedge \sim C)$	6, $\supset$df
8. $A \supset B, A \supset (B \supset C), A, \sim C \vdash \sim(A \wedge \sim C)$	7,MN-3M, WKN-3M
9. $A \supset B, A \supset (B \supset C), A, \sim C \vdash A \quad \wedge \sim C$	A
10. $A \supset B,\ A \supset (B \supset C), A, \sim C \vdash C$	8,9, RA
11. $A \supset B,\ A \supset (B \supset C), A \vdash \sim(\sim C \wedge \sim C)$	10,WKN-5M
12. $A \supset B,\ A \supset (B \supset C), A \vdash \sim\sim C$	11,WKN-3M, LS, A
13. $A \supset B,\ A \supset (B \supset C) \vdash \sim(A \wedge \sim\sim\sim C)$	12,WKN-5M
14. $A \supset B,\ A \supset (B \supset C) \vdash \sim(A \wedge \sim C)$	13,WKN-3M,MN-3M
15. $A \supset B,\ A \supset (B \supset C) \vdash A \supset C$	14, $\supset$df

WKN-11M. $(\alpha, A \vdash \sim B$ and $\alpha, \sim A \vdash \sim B) \Rightarrow \alpha \vdash \sim B$

Proof:

1. $\alpha, A \vdash \sim B$	Hypothesis
2. $\alpha, B \vdash \sim A$	1, Con
3. $\alpha, \sim A \vdash \sim B$	Hypothesis
4. $\alpha, B \vdash \sim B$	2, 3, closure
5. $\alpha \vdash \sim(B \wedge \sim\sim B)$	4, WKN-5M
6. $\alpha \vdash \sim B$	5, WKN-2D

WKN-12M. With ∧ and ~ interpreted in the usual two-valued way, WKN is sound.

Proof: This follows immediately from the soundness of WIN and MKN.

Not too surprisingly, adding **NgC** gives us a system which is complete (and incidentally allows us to drop **Con** and **CM**).

NKC: A DZOS, with

connectives: ∧ (2-place), ~(1-place)

rules:	1. A ∧ B ⊢ A	LS
	2. A ∧ B ⊢ B	RS
	3. A, B ⊢ A ∧ B	A
	4. A, ~A ⊢ B	RA
	5. (α, A ⊢ B and α, ~A ⊢ B) ⇒ α ⊢ B	NgC

NKC-1M. Every D-theorem of SK is a theorem of NKC.

Proof: This is obvious.

NKC-2D. ~(A ∧ ~B), A ⊢ B

Proof:	1. ~(A ∧ ~B), A, B ⊢ B	Premise
	2. ~(A ∧ ~B), A, ~B ⊢ A ∧ ~B	A
	3. ~(A ∧ ~B), A, ~B ⊢ ~(A ∧ ~B)	Premise
	4. ~(A ∧ ~B), A, ~B ⊢ B	2, 3, RA
	5. ~(A ∧ ~B), A ⊢ B	1, 4, NgC

NKC-2D suggests that ~(A ∧ ~B), viewed as a wff function may be a positive implication. As we shall see, that suggestion will turn out to be true. This leads to the convenience of adopting, as we did in WKN, the abbreviation A ⊃ B for it. Doing so allows us to state NKC-2D in a more familiar form:

NKC-3D. A ⊃ B, A ⊢ B   NKC-2D, ⊃df

NKC-4M. α, A ⊢ B ⇒ α ⊢ A ⊃ B

Proof:

1.	α, A ∧ ~B ⊢ A	LS
2.	α, A ∧ ~B ⊢ ~B	RS
3.	α, A ∧ ~B ⊢ B	1, Hypothesis
4.	α, A ∧ ~B ⊢ ~(A ∧ ~B)	2, 3, RA
5.	α, ~(A ∧ ~B) ⊢ ~(A ∧ ~B)	Premise
6.	α ⊢ ~(A ∧ ~B)	4, 5, NgC
7.	α ⊢ A ⊃ B	6, ⊃df

NKC-5M. α, A ⊢ ~B ⇒ α, B ⊢ ~A

Proof:

1.	α, A, B ⊢ B	Premise
2.	α, A, B ⊢ ~B	Hypothesis
3.	α, A, B ⊢ ~A	1, 2, RA
4.	α, ~A, B ⊢ ~A	Premise
5.	α, B ⊢ A	3, 4, NgC

NKC-6M. α, A ⊢ ~A ⇒ α ⊢ ~A

Proof:

1.	α, A ⊢ ~A	Hypothesis
2.	α, ~A ⊢ ~A	Premise
3.	α ⊢ ~A	1, 2, NgC

NKC-7M. Every D- and T-theorem of **WKN** is also one of **NKC**.

Proof: This follows by **NKC**-5M and **NKC**-6M.

NKC-8D. ~A ⊃ A ⊢ A

Proof:

1.	~A ⊃ A, A ⊢ A	Premise
2.	~A ⊃ A, ~A ⊢ A	**NKC**-3D
3.	~A ⊃ A ⊢ A	1, 2, NgC

NKC-9D. A ⊃ ~A ⊢ ~A — Exercise

NKC-10D. ~A ⊃ B, ~A ⊃ ~B ⊢ A

Proof:

1.	~A ⊃ B, ~A ⊃ ~B, ~A ⊢ B	**NKC**-3D
2.	~A ⊃ B, ~A ⊃ ~B, ~A ⊢ ~B	**NKC**-3D

3. ~A ⊃ B, ~A ⊃ ~B, ~A ⊢ A	1,2, RA
4. ~A ⊃ B, ~A ⊃ ~B ⊢ ~A ⊃ A	3, NKC-4M
5. ~A ⊃ B, ~A ⊃ ~B ⊢ A	4, NKC-8D

NKC-11D. A ⊃ B, ~B ⊢ ~A

Proof: 1. A ⊃ B, ~B, A ⊢ B	NKC-3D
2. A ⊃ B, ~B, A ⊢ ~B	Premise
3. A ⊃ B, ~B, A ⊢ ~A	1, 2, RA
4. A ⊃ B, ~B ⊢ A ⊃ ~A	3, NKC-4M
5. A ⊃ B, ~B ⊢ ~A	4, NKC-9D

NKC-11Da. A ⊃ B ⊢ ~B ⊃ ~A

NKC-11T. ⊢ (A ⊃ B) ⊃ (~B ⊃ ~A)

NKC-12D. A ⊃ B, A ∧ C ⊢ B ∧ C

Proof: 1. A ⊃ B, A ∧ C ⊢ A	LS
2. A ⊃ B, A ∧ C ⊢ A ⊃ B	Premise
3. A ⊃ B, A ∧ C ⊢ B	1, 2, NKC-3D
4. A ⊃ B, A ∧ C ⊢ C	RS
5. A ⊃ B, A ∧ C ⊢ B ∧ C	3, 4, A

NKC-12Da. A ⊃ B ⊢ (A ∧ C) ⊃ (B ∧ C)
NKC-12T. ⊢ (A ⊃ B) ⊃ [(A ∧ C) ⊃ (B ∧ C)]
NKC-12M. A ⊢ B ⇒ A ∧ C ⊢ B ∧ C

NKC-13D. A ⊃ B, C ∧ A ⊢ C ∧ B	Exercise
NKC-13M. A ⊢ B ⇒ C ∧ A ⊢ C ∧ B	Exercise

NKC-14M. The equivalence theorem holds unrestrictedly in NKC.

Proof: This follows by PL-14M, utilizing NKC-12D, NKC-13D and NKC-11Da.

NKC-15M. NKC is an E-logic.

Proof: This follows by Theorem 2-17, utilizing 𝒩𝒦𝒞-12M, 𝒩𝒦𝒞-13M and 𝒩𝒦𝒞-11Da.

𝒩𝒦𝒞-16D. A ⊢ ~~A

Proof:	1. A, ~A ⊢ ~~A	RA
	2. A, ~~A ⊢ ~~A	Premise
	3. A ⊢ ~~A	1, 2, NgC

𝒩𝒦𝒞-17M. $\text{Equiv}_{\mathcal{NKC}}$(A, ~~A)

Proof: This follows by 𝒩𝒦𝒞-7M, ℳ𝒩-1D and 𝒲𝒦𝒩-16D.

𝒩𝒦𝒞-18D. ~(A ⊃ ~B) ⊢ A ∧ B

Proof:	1. ~(A ⊃ ~B) ⊢ ~~(A ∧ ~~B)	⊃df
	2. ~(A ⊃ ~B) ⊢ A ∧ B	1, 𝒩𝒦𝒞-17M

𝒩𝒦𝒞-19D. A ∧ B ⊢ ~(A ⊃ ~B) Exercise

𝒩𝒦𝒞-20M. 𝒩𝒦𝒞 is sound relative to the standard two-valued interpretation.

Proof: Exercise

𝒩𝒦𝒞-21M. 𝒩𝒦𝒞 is deductively complete and also complete relative to the standard two- valued interpretation.

Proof: By 𝒩𝒦𝒞-3D, 𝒩𝒦𝒞-4M (together with **RA** and **NgC**), 𝒩𝒦𝒞-14M and 𝒩𝒦𝒞-17D and 𝒩𝒦𝒞-18D, 𝒩𝒦𝒞 satisfies the conditions of 𝓛𝒩𝒞-27M and hence is deductively closed. Since furthermore all of its D-theorems are 1-preserving, adding to 𝒩𝒦𝒞 any rule valid in two-valued logic would leave it consistent and hence it must be complete relative to two-valued logic.

Clearly an axiomatic formulation equivalent to 𝒩𝒦𝒞 can be given. We will give an example which uses the abbreviation ⊃df.

𝒩𝒦𝒞1: A DZOS, with :

connectives: $\wedge$ (two-place), $\sim$ (one-place)

rules: 1. $A, A \supset B \vdash B$ MP2

axiom schemata:

1. $\vdash A \supset (B \supset A)$
2. $\vdash [A \supset (B \supset C)] \supset [(A \supset B) \supset (A \supset C)]$
3. $\vdash (A \wedge B) \supset A$
4. $\vdash (A \wedge B) \supset B$
5. $\vdash A \supset (B \supset [A \wedge B])$
6. $\vdash A \supset (\sim A \supset B)$
7. $\vdash (A \supset B) \supset [(\sim A \supset B) \supset B]$

The following theorems follow easily:

NKC1-1D. $A \wedge B \vdash A$

NKC1-2D. $A \wedge B \vdash B$

NKC1-3D. $A, B \vdash A \wedge B$

NKC1-4D. $A, \sim A \vdash B$

NKC1-5M. $\alpha, A \vdash B \Rightarrow \alpha \vdash A \supset B$

Proof: This follows by the argument of PL2-2M, using Ax1, Ax2 and MP1.

NKC1-6M. ($\alpha, A \vdash B$ and $\alpha, \sim A \vdash B$) $\Rightarrow \alpha \vdash B$

Proof:

1.	$\alpha, A \vdash B$	Hypothesis
2.	$\alpha, \sim A \vdash B$	Hypothesis
3.	$\alpha \vdash A \supset B$	1, NKC1-5M.
4.	$\alpha \vdash \sim A \supset B$	2, NKC1-5M.
5.	$\alpha \vdash (A \supset B) \supset [(\sim A \supset B) \supset B]$	Ax7
6.	$\alpha \vdash (\sim A \supset B) \supset B$	3, 5, MP1
7.	$\alpha \vdash B$	4, 6, MP1

NKC1-7M. NKC and NKC1 are equivalent.

Proof: Since all the axioms are tautologies, $\mathcal{NKC}$ R-includes $\mathcal{NKC}1$ by $\mathcal{NKC}$- 20M. But by $\mathcal{NKC}1$-1D, $\mathcal{NKC}1$-2D, $\mathcal{NKC}1$-3D, $\mathcal{NKC}1$-4D and $\mathcal{NKC}1$-6M, $\mathcal{NKC}1$ $\mathbf{R}$-includes $\mathcal{NKC}$.

Even though WKN is not equivalent to NKC, as we shall see in the next chapter, there is an interesting, even remarkable relation between them which will be shown in the next theorem.

$\mathcal{NKC}$-22M. For any wff A of $\mathcal{NKC}$, let A^* be $\sim\sim A$. For any set of wffs α, let α^* be the set of wffs B such that $B \subset \alpha$. Then $\alpha \vdash_{\mathcal{NKC}} A \iff \alpha^* \vdash_{\mathcal{WKN}} A^*$.

Proof: Let $\alpha^* \vdash_{\mathcal{WKN}} A^*$. Then by $\mathcal{WKN}$-12M and $\mathcal{NKC}$-21M, $\alpha^* \vdash_{\mathcal{NKC}} A^*$.By virtue of the equivalence theorem and the deductive equivalence of B and $\sim\sim B$ in $\mathcal{NKC}$, $\alpha \vdash_{\mathcal{NKC}} A$. Let $\alpha_1 \vdash A_1, \cdots, \alpha_n \vdash A_n$ be a Y-derivation in $\mathcal{NKC}$ whose last line is $\alpha \vdash A$. We prove by induction on i that, for each i, $\alpha_i^* \vdash_{\mathcal{WKN}} A_i^*$:

(α) $i = 1$

Then $\alpha_1 \vdash A_1$ being the first line of a Y-derivation must satisfy $A_1 \subset \alpha_1$. Hence $A_1^* \subset \alpha_1^*$ and $\alpha_1^* \vdash_{\mathcal{WKN}} A_1^*$.

(β) Assume that the assertion is true for each of the first k lines. We will prove that it holds for $\alpha_{k+1} \vdash A_{k+1}$. Then $\alpha_{k+1} \vdash A_{k+1}$ is either an instance of **LS**, **RS**, **A** or **RA** or else follows from two previous lines by **NgC** (unless of course $\alpha_{k+1} \subset A_{k+1}$ and it follows by the argument of (α)):

Case 1: $\alpha_{k+1} \vdash A_{k+1}$ follows by **LS**. Then there exists a $j \le k$ and $\alpha_j = \alpha_{k+1}$ and $A_j = A_{k+1} \wedge B$, for some wff B. By the hypothesis of induction, $\alpha_{k+1}^* \vdash_{\mathcal{WKN}} \sim\sim(A_{k+1} \wedge B)$. Then by $\mathcal{MKN}$-12D, $\alpha_{k+1}^* \vdash_{\mathcal{WKN}} \sim\sim A_{k+1} \wedge \sim\sim B$. Hence we get by **LS**, $\alpha_{k+1}^* \vdash_{\mathcal{WKN}} \sim\sim A_{k+1}$, i.e., $\alpha_{k+1}^* \vdash_{\mathcal{WKN}} A_{k+1}^*$.

Case 2: $\alpha_{k+1} \vdash A_{k+1}$ follows by **RS**. The argument is analogous to that of case 1.

Case 3: $\alpha_{k+1} \vdash A_{k+1}$ follows by **A**. Then there exists $i \le k$ and $j \le k$ with $\alpha_i = \alpha_j = \alpha_{k+1}$ and $A_{k+1} = A_i \wedge A_j$. By the hypothesis of induction we get $\alpha_{k+1}{}^* \vdash_{\mathcal{WKN}} {\sim}{\sim}A_i$ and $\alpha_{k+1}{}^* \vdash_{\mathcal{WKN}} {\sim}{\sim}A_j$ and thus by A, $\alpha_{k+1}{}^* \vdash_{\mathcal{WKN}} {\sim}{\sim}A_i \wedge {\sim}{\sim}A_j$. Then by $\mathcal{MKN}$-13D, $\alpha_{k+1}{}^* \vdash_{\mathcal{WKN}} {\sim}{\sim}(A_i \wedge A_j)$, i.e. $\alpha_{k+1}{}^* \vdash_{\mathcal{WKN}} A_{k+1}{}^*$.

Case 4. $\alpha_{k+1} \vdash A_{k+1}$ follows by **RA**. Then there exist $i \leq k$ and $j \leq k$ with $\alpha_i = \alpha_j = \alpha_{k+1}$ and $A_i = {\sim}A_j$. By the hypothesis of induction, $\alpha_{k+1}{}^* \vdash_{\mathcal{WKN}} {\sim}{\sim}A_j$ and $\alpha_{k+1}{}^* \vdash_{\mathcal{WKN}} {\sim}{\sim}{\sim}A_j$. Hence by RA, $\alpha_{k+1}{}^* \vdash_{\mathcal{WKN}} A_{k+1}{}^*$.

Case 5. $\alpha_{k+1} \vdash A_{k+1}$ follows by **NgC**. Then there exist $i \leq k$ and $j \leq k$ and $\alpha_i = \alpha_{k+1} \cup \{B\}, \alpha_j = \alpha_{k+1} \cup \{{\sim}B\}$ and $A_i = A_j = A_{k+1}$. By the hypothesis of induction, we get:

1. $\alpha_{k+1}{}^*, {\sim}{\sim}B \vdash_{\mathcal{WKN}} {\sim}{\sim}A_{k+1}$	
2. $\alpha_{k+1}{}^*, {\sim}{\sim}{\sim}B \vdash_{\mathcal{WKN}} {\sim}{\sim}A_{k+1}$	
3. $\alpha_{k+1}{}^*, {\sim}{\sim}{\sim}A_{k+1} \vdash_{\mathcal{WKN}} {\sim}{\sim}{\sim}B$	1, Con
4. $\alpha_{k+1}{}^*, {\sim}{\sim}{\sim}A_{k+1} \vdash_{\mathcal{WKN}} {\sim}{\sim}A_{k+1}$	2,3,closure
5. $\alpha_{k+1}{}^*, {\sim}A_{k+1} \vdash_{\mathcal{WKN}} {\sim}{\sim}A_{k+1}$	4, $\mathcal{MN}$-3M
6. $\alpha_{k+1}{}^* \vdash_{\mathcal{WKN}} {\sim}{\sim}A_{k+1}$	5, CM
7. $\alpha_{k+1}{}^* \vdash_{\mathcal{WKN}} A_{k+1}{}^*$	

9
Multi-Connective Systems

In the deductive systems we have been studying, we have been concerned primarily with individual connectives, either alone or with negation. With systems of sufficient strength, particularly with complete ones, it is customary to define other connectives, as we indeed have done in a number of cases. A different approach to the basic connectives is possible, namely, to specify the properties of all the connectives in the general way we have been doing, by rules and axiom schemata, and allow the relations to emerge from this specification. We do not always realize how many of the properties of the connectives can be specified by such elementary properties, although the uniqueness theorems of chapter 2 might have led us to anticipate these possibilities. In this chapter we will consider a number of examples.

The first of these will consist of a combination of $\mathcal{SA}$ and $\mathcal{SK}$.

$\mathcal{AK}$: A DZOS, with

connectives: $\vee$ (two-place), $\wedge$ (two-place)

rules:	1. $A \vdash A \vee B$	AR
	2. $B \vdash A \vee B$	AL
	3. $(\alpha, A \vdash C$ and $\alpha, B \vdash C) \Rightarrow \alpha, A \vee B \vdash C$	D
	4. $A \wedge B \vdash A$	LS
	5. $A \wedge B \vdash B$	RS
	6. $A, B \vdash A \wedge B$	A

$\mathcal{AK}$-1M. Every D-theorem of $\mathcal{SA}$ or $\mathcal{SK}$ is a theorem of $\mathcal{AK}$.

Proof: This is obvious.

$\mathcal{AK}$-2D. $A \vee (A \wedge B) \vdash A$

Proof:	1. $A \vdash A$	Premise
	2. $A \wedge B \vdash A$	LS
	3. $A \vee (A \wedge B) \vdash A$	1, 2, D

𝒜𝒦-3D. $A \vdash A \wedge (A \vee B)$

Proof:	1. $A \vdash A$	Premise
	2. $A \vdash A \vee B$	AR
	3. $A \vdash A \wedge (A \vee B)$	1, 2, A

𝒜𝒦-4M. 𝒜𝒦 is an E-logic.

Proof: Since the conditions for theorem 2-11 were already satisfied in 𝒮𝒜 and in 𝒮𝒦, they are automatically satisfied here.

𝒜𝒦-5D. $A \wedge (B \vee C) \vdash (A \wedge B) \vee (A \wedge C)$

Proof:	1. $A \wedge (B \vee C) \vdash A$	LS
	2. $A \wedge (B \vee C) \vdash B \vee C$	RS
	3. $A \wedge (B \vee C), B \vdash B$	Premise
	4. $A \wedge (B \vee C), B \vdash A \wedge B$	1, 3, A
	5. $A \wedge (B \vee C), B \vdash (A \wedge B) \vee (A \wedge C)$	4, AR
	6. $A \wedge (B \vee C), C \vdash C$	Premise
	7. $A \wedge (B \vee C), C \vdash A \wedge C$	1, 6, A
	8. $A \wedge (B \vee C), C \vdash (A \wedge B) \vee (A \wedge C)$	7, AL
	9. $A \wedge (B \vee C), B \vee C \vdash (A \wedge B) \vee (A \wedge C)$	5, 8, D
	10. $A \wedge (B \vee C) \vdash (A \wedge B) \vee (A \wedge C)$	2,9, closure

𝒜𝒦-6D. $(A \wedge B) \vee (A \wedge C) \vdash A \wedge (B \vee C)$

Proof:	1. $A \wedge B \vdash A$	LS
	2. $A \wedge B \vdash B$	RS
	3. $A \wedge B \vdash B \vee C$	2, AR
	4. $A \wedge B \vdash A \wedge (B \vee C)$	2, 3, A
	5. $A \wedge C \vdash A$	LS
	6. $A \wedge C \vdash C$	RS
	7. $A \wedge B \vdash B \vee C$	2, AL
	8. $A \wedge B \vdash A \wedge (B \vee C)$	2, 3, A
	9. $(A \wedge B) \vee (A \wedge C) \vdash A \wedge (B \vee C)$	4, 8, D

𝒜𝒦-7D. $A \vee (B \wedge C) \vdash (A \vee B) \wedge (A \vee C)$

Proof:	1. $A \vdash A \vee B$	AR
	2. $A \vdash A \vee C$	AL
	3. $B \wedge C \vdash B$	LS
	4. $B \wedge C \vdash A \vee B$	3, AL
	5. $A \vee (B \wedge C) \vdash A \vee B$	1, 4, D
	6. $B \wedge C \vdash C$	RS
	7. $B \wedge C \vdash A \vee C$	6, AR
	8. $A \vee (B \wedge C) \vdash A \vee C$	2, 7, D
	9. $A \vee (B \wedge C) \vdash (A \vee B) \wedge (A \vee C)$	5, 8, A

𝒜𝒦-8D. $(A \vee B) \wedge (A \vee C) \vdash A \vee (B \wedge C)$

Proof:	1. $B, A \vdash A \vee (B \wedge C)$	AR
	2. $B, C \vdash B \wedge C$	A
	3. $B, C \vdash A \vee (B \wedge C)$	2, AL
	4. $B, A \vee C \vdash A \vee (B \wedge C)$	1, 3, D
	5. $A, A \vee C \vdash A \vee (B \wedge C)$	AR
	6. $A \vee B, A \vee C \vdash A \vee (B \wedge C)$	4, 5, D

𝒜𝒦-3D through 𝒜𝒦-8D represent, in view of the equivalences, the well known distributivity theorems. Through the use of them, we are able to determine some additional basic properties of 𝒜𝒦 and logics which include it. Let us say a wff of 𝒜𝒦 is in **disjunctive normal form (dnf)** if it consists exclusively of disjunctions of conjunctions (for 𝒜𝒦, this can be stated exactly by specifying that A is in disjunctive normal form provided that whenever $B \wedge C$ is a wff which occurs in A, neither B nor C is of the form $D \vee E$). We will say a wff of 𝒜𝒦 is in **reduced disjunctive normal form (rdnf)** provided no maximally disjunction-free well-formed part [i.e., **a well-formed part (wfp)** which consists only of variables and $\wedge$'s and which is not a proper part of any disjunction-free wfp] contains all variables in another maximally disjunction-free wfp and no maximally disjunction-free wfp contains any variable twice.

𝒜𝒦-9M. If $g_r(\wedge)$ is the truth function "and" and $g_r(\vee)$ is "inclusive-or" and $r \in \mathbf{R}$, $\alpha \vdash_{\mathcal{AK}} A$ implies $\alpha \models_{\mathbf{R}} A$.

Proof: This follows immediately from the corresponding theorems of $\mathcal{SK}$ and $\mathcal{SA}$ (viz., $\mathcal{SA}$-10M and $\mathcal{SK}$-9M).

$\mathcal{AK}$-10M. If A and B are deductively equivalent in $\mathcal{AK}$, they are model-theoretically equivalent relative to two-valued logic (i.e. they take the same value for any consistent assignment of values to the variables for two-valued logic).

Proof: This is a corollary of $\mathcal{AK}$-9M.

$\mathcal{AK}$-11M. Every wff of $\mathcal{AK}$ is deductively equivalent to a wff in disjunctive normal form.

Proof: Define the operations L, m and n as follows: if v is a variable, $\mathsf{L}(v) = \mathsf{m}(v) = \mathsf{n}(v) = 0$. $\mathsf{L}(A \vee B) = 1$. $\mathsf{L}(A \wedge B) = \mathsf{max}(\mathsf{L}(A), \mathsf{L}(B))$. $\mathsf{m}(A \wedge B) = \mathsf{max}(\mathsf{L}(A), \mathsf{L}(B))$. $\mathsf{m}(A \vee B) = \mathsf{max}(\mathsf{m}(A), \mathsf{m}(B))$. $\mathsf{n}(A \wedge B) = \mathsf{n}(A) + \mathsf{n}(B) + \mathsf{m}(A \wedge B)$. $\mathsf{n}(A \vee B) = \mathsf{n}(A) + \mathsf{n}(B) + \mathsf{m}(A \vee B)$. Thus defined, it follows that $\mathsf{L}(A) = 1$ if and only if A has a wfp which is of disjunctive form, $\mathsf{m}(A) = 1$ if and only if it has a wfp which is a conjunction of disjunctions, or in other words, is not in disjunctive normal form. Hence, $\mathsf{n}(A)$ is the number of wfps of A not in disjunctive normal form (remember that if A is a wff, it is a wfp of itself). Note that $\mathsf{n}(A) = 0$ is true if and only if A is in disjunctive normal form and that consequently our theorem will follow if we are able to show that for every wff A if $\mathsf{n}(A) > 0$, there exists a wff B such that $\mathsf{Equiv}_{\mathcal{AK}}(A,B)$ and $\mathsf{n}(A) > \mathsf{n}(B)$. We start by defining "continuing disjunction":

$$\bigvee_{i=1}^{1} A_i = A_1 \text{ and } \bigvee_{i=1}^{k+1} A_i = A_{k+1} \vee \bigvee_{i=1}^{k} A_i .$$

We now prove, by induction on n and m that (with $\approx$ being $\mathsf{Equiv}_{\mathcal{AK}}$):

$$\bigvee_{i=1}^{n} A_i \wedge \bigvee_{j=1}^{m} B_j \approx \bigvee_{i=1}^{n} \bigvee_{j=1}^{m} (A_i \wedge B_j)$$

(α) $n = 1$

($\alpha\alpha$) m = 1

$$\bigvee_{i=1}^{1} A_i \wedge \bigvee_{j=1}^{1} B_j = A_1 \wedge B_1 \approx \bigvee_{i=1}^{1} \bigvee_{j=1}^{1} (A_i \wedge B_j).$$

($\alpha\beta$) Let us assume the assertion is true for all wffs with $m \leq k$; we will prove it for m = k+1:

$$\bigvee_{i=1}^{1} A_i \wedge \bigvee_{j=1}^{k+1} B_j = A_1 \wedge \bigvee_{j=1}^{k+1} B_j = A_1 \wedge (B_{k+1} \vee \bigvee_{j=1}^{k} B_j) \approx$$

$$(A_1 \wedge B_{k+1}) \vee (A_1 \wedge \bigvee_{j=1}^{k} B_j) \approx \bigvee_{j=1}^{k+1} (A_1 \wedge B_j) =$$

$$\bigvee_{i=1}^{1} \bigvee_{j=1}^{k+1} (A_i \wedge B_j)$$

(β) By the hypothesis of induction,

$$\bigvee_{i=1}^{k} A_i \wedge \bigvee_{j=1}^{m} B_j = \bigvee_{i=1}^{k} \bigvee_{j=1}^{m} (A_i \wedge B_j)\text{. Hence}$$

$$\bigvee_{i=1}^{k+1} A_i \wedge \bigvee_{j=1}^{m} B_j = \left(A_{k+1} \vee \bigvee_{i=1}^{k} A_i\right) \wedge \bigvee_{j=1}^{m} B_j \approx$$

$$\left(A_{k+1} \wedge \bigvee_{j=1}^{m} B_j\right) \vee \left(\bigvee_{i=1}^{k} A_i \wedge \bigvee_{j=1}^{m} B_j\right) \approx$$

$$\bigvee_{j=1}^{m} (A_{k+1} \wedge B_j) \vee \bigvee_{i=1}^{k} \bigvee_{j=1}^{m} (A_i \wedge B_j) \approx \bigvee_{i=1}^{k+1} \bigvee_{j=1}^{m} (A_i \wedge B_j)$$

Hence, since $n(\bigvee A_i \wedge \bigvee B_j) \geq$

$1 + n(\bigvee\bigvee(A_i \wedge B_j))$, every wff not in dnf is equivalent to one with a smaller n and hence is equivalent to a wff in dnf.

𝒜𝒦-12M. Every wff of 𝒜𝒦 is equivalent to one in reduced disjunctive normal form.

Proof: Let A be a wff of 𝒜𝒦. By 𝒜𝒦-11M there exists a wff B equivalent to A which is in disjunctive normal form. Hence we can without loss of generality assume A to be in dnf. Let us call any occurrence of a variable which has appeared earlier in the same maximally disjunction-free well-formed part (md-fwfp) a **redundant occurrence**. We will call a wff D a **redundant term** in B provided B is a wff in dnf, D is a md-fwfps of B and there exists a wfp of B, C, such that (1)C is a md-fwfp and either (2a) every variable in D is in C, but there is a variable in C not in D, or else (2b) D and B have the same variables but C occurs earlier in B. We first prove that if A has redundant occurrences, there exists an equivalent A′ with fewer redundant occurrences. Obviously the number of redundant occurrences in A is equal to the sum of all redundant occurrences in its maximally disjunction-free wfps and hence it suffices to show that the assertion is true for md-fwfps. Suppose B is a md-fwfp that has k+1 redundant occurrences, then any rearrangement or regrouping will also have k+1 redundant occurrences. Suppose v is the first redundant variable in B. Then for some variables $v_1, \ldots, v_i, w_1, \ldots, w_j, x_1, \ldots, x_n$, $B = v_1 \wedge \ldots \wedge v_i \wedge v \wedge w_1 \wedge \ldots \wedge w_j \wedge v \wedge x_1 \wedge \ldots \wedge x_k$ (note that any or even all of i, j, and m could conceivably be 0). But then $v_1 \wedge \ldots \wedge v_i \wedge w_1 \wedge \ldots \wedge w_j \wedge x_1 \wedge \ldots \wedge x_m \wedge v \wedge v$, is equivalent to B, by 𝒜𝒦-1M and 𝒮𝒦-5M, and has k+1 redundant occurrences. Then by 𝒜𝒦-1M, 𝒮𝒦-4D, L S and 𝒜𝒦-4M, this is in turn equivalent to $v_1 \wedge \ldots \wedge v_i \wedge w_1 \wedge \ldots \wedge w_j \wedge x_1 \wedge \ldots \wedge x_m \wedge v$, which then has k redundant variables. Hence there exists a wff A′ in dnf with no redundant occurrences equivalent to A. Suppose A′ has k+1 redundant terms; there exist md-fwfps $A_1, \ldots, A_i$, $B_1, \ldots, B_j$, $C_1, \ldots, C_m$, B and C such that either (1) $B \approx C \wedge D$ or (2) $B = C$ and $A' = A_1 \vee \ldots \vee A_i \vee B \vee B_1 \vee \ldots \vee B_j \vee C \vee C_1 \vee \ldots \vee C_m$. Then $A' \approx A_1 \vee \ldots \vee A_i \vee B_1 \vee \ldots \vee B_j \vee C_1 \vee \ldots \vee C_m \vee B \vee C$ by 𝒜𝒦-1M and 𝒮𝒜-7M.

But then in case (2), $B \vee C$ is equivalent to $(C \wedge D) \vee C$ which is in turn equivalent to C, and since $\mathcal{AK}$ is an E-logic, A′ is equivalent to $A_1 \vee \ldots \vee A_i \vee B_1 \vee \ldots \vee B_j \vee C_1 \vee \ldots \vee C_m \vee C$, which has k redundant terms; in case (1), $A' = A_1 \vee \ldots \vee A_i \vee B \vee B_1 \vee \ldots \vee B_j \vee B \vee C_1 \vee \ldots \vee C_m$, and is equivalent to $A_1 \vee \ldots \vee A_i \vee B_1 \vee \ldots \vee B_j \vee C_1 \vee \ldots \vee C_m \vee B \vee B$ which by $\mathcal{AK}$-1M, $\mathcal{AK}$-4M and $\mathcal{SA}$-7M, is in turn equivalent to $A_1 \vee \ldots \vee A_i \vee B_1 \vee \ldots \vee B_j \vee C_1 \vee \ldots \vee C_m \vee B$ which has k redundant terms. Therefore there exists a wff A" in dnf that has no redundant variable occurrences and no redundant terms (and hence is in reduced dnf) and is equivalent to A.

$\mathcal{AK}$-13M. If $A = \bigvee_{i=1}^{n} A_i$ and $B = \bigvee_{j=1}^{m} B_j$ and all of the A_is and B_js are variables or conjunctions of variables, $A \vdash_{\mathcal{AK}} B$ if and only if every A_i has every variable in at least one B_j.

Proof: Suppose every A_i has every variable in at least one B_j, then for some C_{ij}, A_i is equivalent to $B_j \wedge C_{ij}$. Hence by **LS** and $\mathcal{SK}$-5M, $A_i \vdash B_j$, and by $\mathcal{SA}$-7M and **AL**, $A_i \vdash B$, leading by repeated use of **D** to $A \vdash B$. Suppose that there is an A_i such that for every B_j there is a variable in B_j which is not in A_i. Let **r** be the two-valued realization such that $g_r(v) = 0$ if v is a variable in B but not in A_i, and otherwise $g_r(v) = 1$. Then since each B_j is a conjunction and at least one conjunct takes 0, $g'_r(B_j) = 0$. But then since B is a disjunction, all of whose disjuncts take 0, $g'_r(B) = 0$. But since every variable in A_i takes the value 1, $g'_r(A_i) = 1$, and since A is a disjunction and A_i one of its disjuncts, $g'_r(A) = 1$. Hence not-$(A \models B)$ and therefore, by $\mathcal{AK}$-7M, not-$(A \vdash B)$.

Let $\bigwedge_{i=1}^{1} A_i = A_1$ and $\bigwedge_{i=1}^{k+1} A_i = A_{k+1} \wedge \bigwedge_{i=1}^{k} A_i$

𝒜𝒦-14M. $A_1,\cdots,A_n \vdash A$ if and only if $\bigwedge_{i=1}^{n} A_i \vdash A$

Proof: Exercise.

Because $\vee$ and $\wedge$ are interchangeable in each of the basic equivalences (distributivity, commutativity, associativity and idempotency), each step performed in the proofs of 𝒜𝒦-11M and 𝒜𝒦-12 can be applied "in reverse." We will consequently define a **conjunctive normal form (cnf)** as a wff of 𝒜𝒦 consisting exclusively of disjunctions of conjunctions (for 𝒜𝒦, whenever $B \vee C$ is a wff which occurs in A, neither B nor C is of the form $D \vee E$). Analogously, we can define **reduced conjunctive normal form (rcnf)**. This leads to theorems co-relative to 𝒜𝒦-11M and 𝒜𝒦-12:

𝒜𝒦-15M. Every wff of 𝒜𝒦 is equivalent to one in cnf (and indeed in rcnf).

Proof: The proofs are step-by-step the same as those of 𝒜𝒦-11M and 𝒜𝒦-12M. We will accordingly omit them here.

Similar to 𝒜𝒦-13M is a result concerning cnfs:

𝒜𝒦-16M. If $A = \bigwedge_{i=1}^{n} A_i$ and $B = \bigwedge_{j=1}^{m} B_j$ and all of the A_is and B_js are variables or disjunctions of variables, $A \vdash_{\mathcal{AK}} B$ if and only if every B_j contains every variable which is in at least one A_i.

Proof: Suppose every B_j has every variable in at least one A_i. Then since all A_is and B_js are disjunctions, there exists a C_{ij} such that $B_j \approx A_i \vee C_{ij}$. Hence $A_i \vdash B_j$ and thus $A \vdash B_j$, for all B_j. Then we have $A \vdash B$, by repeated use of A. Suppose there is a B_j such that for every A_i there exists a variable in A_i not in B_j. Since each of the A_is and B_js are disjunctions, if we assign 1 to all of the "exceptional" variables and 0 to all of the others, $g'_r(A) = 1$ and $g'_r(B) = 0$ and hence A does not entail B, and by virtue of soundness, A does not yield B.

𝒜𝒦-17M. If α is a set of wffs all of whose members are variables or disjunctions of variables and B is a wff of 𝒜𝒦 and $\alpha \vDash B$, then there is at least one element of α which consistsexclusively of variables which occur in B.

Proof: Suppose every element of α has at least one variable not in B. Then let **r** be a (two-valued) realization such that $g_r(v) = 0$ if v occurs in B and $g_r(v) = 1$ otherwise. Then for every element $A \in \alpha$, $g'_r(A) = 1$, but since both the truth-functions "disjunction" and "conjunction" are 0-preserving, $g'_r(B) = 0$, and α does not entail B.

𝒜𝒦-18M. If α is a set of variables or disjunctions of variables, and B a wff of 𝒜𝒦, and α' the set of elements of α which contain exclusively variables in B, then if $\alpha \vDash B$, $\alpha' \vDash B$.

Proof. Suppose **r** is a realization and **r** $\Vdash \alpha'$. Then let **r'** be the realization such that $g_{r'}(v) = 1$ for all variables v not in B and $g_{r'}(v) = g_r(v)$ for all variables in B. Then obviously if A is an element of α' and hence consists exclusively of variables in B, $g'_{r'}(A) = g'_r(A) = 1$, while if A is in α but not in α', $g'_{r'}(A) = 1$ by the fact that the truth-function "inclusive-or" is 1-preserving. Hence **r'** $\Vdash \alpha$ and by the entailment, **r** $\Vdash$ B. But since **r'** agrees with **r** on all variables in B, **r** $\Vdash$ B.

𝒜𝒦-19M. 𝒜𝒦 is model-theoretically complete relative to two-valued logic (with $\vee$ interpreted as "inclusive-or" and $\wedge$ as "and").

Proof: Suppose $\alpha \vDash B$. Since every wff is equivalent to one in cnf by 𝒜𝒦-15M, one can assume without loss of generality that all elements of α and B are in cnf. Furthermore, one can assume that all elements of α are variables or disjunctions of variables, since every wff in cnf is deductively equivalent to the set of its conjuncts. Furthermore, by 𝒜𝒦-18M, there is a subset α' which contains only variables in B such that $\alpha' \models B$. But since B contains only a finite number of variables, there are a finite number of non-equivalent disjunctions that contain exclusively variables in B. Hence there is a finite set $\{A_1, \cdots, A_n\}$ such that every element of α' is an A_i and vice versa. Hence $\bigwedge A_i \models B$ and $\bigwedge A_i$ is in cnf. Suppose there is a B_j such that for every A_i there is a variable v_{ij} which occurs in A_i but not in B_j; let every such v_{ij} take 1 and all variables in B_j take 0. Then every A_i takes 1 while B takes 0 and the entailment does not hold. But if for every B_j there is an A_i such that every variable in A_i is also in B_j, by 𝒜𝒦-16M and 𝒜𝒦-14M, $A_1, \cdots, A_n \vdash B$. Since $\{A_1, \cdots, A_n\} \subset \alpha'$ and the elements of α are equivalent to elements of α' or their conjunctions, $\alpha \vdash B$.

We will now consider the systems which have four or five primitive connectives. It would indeed have been possible to consider first the various possibilities of three connective systems as well as implication-disjunction and implication-conjunction systems, but lack of space prevents us. Interested students are encouraged to try some of these systems as an exercise. We will turn to five connective systems, in particular, systems with the connectives $\vee$, $\wedge$, $\supset$, $\sim$ and $\equiv$. These represent what might be called the normal zero-order or sentential mechanism (leaving aside such refinements as modality). It may seem to some that we are not paying much attention to the connective $\equiv$. This is indeed true to a degree. However, so many of the characteristics of the resulting systems are independent of the presence or absence of $\equiv$ (as an undefined connective), that it seems superfluous to cconsider that connective in detail here. The first system we will introduce is, in a sense, the combination of the weakest systems we have considered in chapters 5 through 8. We will call it 𝒫𝒤𝒩ℰ𝒜𝒦 (the corresponding system without $\equiv$ might be called 𝒫𝒤𝒩𝒜𝒦).

𝒫𝒤𝒩ℰ𝒜𝒦: A DZOS, with

connectives: $\vee$ (2-place), $\wedge$ (2-place), $\supset$ (2-place), $\equiv$ (2-place), $\sim$ (1-place)

rules:
1. $A, A \supset B \vdash B$ — MP
2. $\alpha, A \vdash B \Rightarrow \alpha \vdash A \supset B$ — C

3. $A \wedge B \vdash A$	LS
4. $A \wedge B \vdash B$	RS
5. $A, B \vdash A \wedge B$	A
6. $A \vdash A \vee B$	AR
7. $B \vdash A \vee B$	AL
8. $(\alpha, A \vdash C$ and $\alpha, B \vdash C) \Rightarrow \alpha, A \vee B \vdash C$	D
9. $\alpha, A \vdash \sim B \Rightarrow \alpha, B \vdash \sim A$	Con
10. $A \equiv B, A \vdash B$	Bi-MP
11. $A \equiv B, B \vdash A$	Bi-MP
12. $(\alpha, A \vdash B$ and $\alpha, B \vdash A) \Rightarrow \alpha \vdash A \equiv B$	Bi-C

Bi-MP indicates **biconditional modus ponens** and Bi-C indicates **biconditionalization**.

PINEAK-1M. Every D- and T-theorem of PIN is a theorem of PINEAK.

Proof: This is obvious, because PINEAK R-includes PIN.

PINEAK-2M. $\alpha, A \vdash \sim A \Rightarrow \alpha \vdash \sim A$

Proof: 1. $\alpha, A \vdash \sim A$	Hypothesis
2. $\alpha, A \vdash A$	Premise
3. $\alpha, A \vdash \sim(A \supset A)$	1,2, PINEAK-1M, PIN-7D
4. $\alpha \vdash A \supset \sim(A \supset A)$	3, C
5. $\alpha \vdash \sim A$	4, PINEAK-1M, PIN-8D

PINEAK-3M. Every D- and T-theorem of MAN and MKN is a theorem of PINEAK.

Proof: This follows by rules 3-12 and PINEAK-2M.

PINEAK-4D. $A \supset B \vdash (A \vee C) \supset (B \vee C)$

Proof: 1. $A \supset B, A \vdash B$	MP
2. $A \supset B, A \vdash B \vee C$	1, AR
3. $A \supset B, C \vdash B \vee C$	AL

4. $A \supset B, A \vee C \vdash B \vee C$ 2, 3, D
5. $A \supset B \vdash (A \vee C) \supset (B \vee C)$ 4, C

𝔓𝔏𝔑𝔈𝔄𝔎-4T. $\vdash (A \supset B) \supset [(A \vee C) \supset (B \vee C)]$

𝔓𝔏𝔑𝔈𝔄𝔎-5D. $A \supset B \vdash (C \vee A) \supset (C \vee A)$ Exercise
𝔓𝔏𝔑𝔈𝔄𝔎-5T. $\vdash (A \supset B) \supset [(C \vee A) \supset (C \vee B)]$

𝔓𝔏𝔑𝔈𝔄𝔎-6D. $A \supset B \vdash (A \wedge C) \supset (B \wedge C)$

Proof: 1. $A \supset B, A \wedge C \vdash A$ LS
2. $A \supset B, A \wedge C \vdash A \supset B$ Premise
3. $A \supset B, A \wedge C \vdash B$ 1, 2, MP
4. $A \supset B, A \wedge C \vdash C$ RS
5. $A \supset B, A \wedge C \vdash B \supset C$ 3, 4, A

𝔓𝔏𝔑𝔈𝔄𝔎-6T. $\vdash (A \supset B) \supset [(A \wedge C) \supset (B \wedge C)]$

𝔓𝔏𝔑𝔈𝔄𝔎-7D. $A \supset B \vdash (C \wedge A) \supset (C \wedge A)$ Exercise
𝔓𝔏𝔑𝔈𝔄𝔎-7T. $\vdash (A \supset B) \supset [(C \wedge A) \supset (C \wedge B)]$

𝔓𝔏𝔑𝔈𝔄𝔎-8D. $A \supset B, B \supset A \vdash (A \equiv C) \supset (B \equiv C)$

Proof: 1. $A \supset B, B \supset A, A \equiv C, B \vdash A$ MP
2. $A \supset B, B \supset A, A \equiv C, B \vdash A \equiv C$ Premise
3. $A \supset B, B \supset A, A \equiv C, B \vdash C$ 1,2, Bi-MP
4. $A \supset B, B \supset A, A \equiv C, C \vdash A$ Bi-MP
5. $A \supset B, B \supset A, A \equiv C, C \vdash A \supset B$ Premise
6. $A \supset B, B \supset A, A \equiv C, C \vdash B$ 4, 5, MP
7. $A \supset B, B \supset A, A \equiv C \vdash B \equiv C$ 3, 6, Bi-C
8. $A \supset B, B \supset A \vdash (A \equiv C) \supset (C \equiv A)$ 7, C

𝔓𝔏𝔑𝔈𝔄𝔎-9D. $A \supset B, B \supset A \vdash (C \equiv A) \supset (C \equiv B)$ Exercise

𝔓𝔏𝔑𝔈𝔄𝔎-10M. The equivalence theorem holds unrestrictedly in 𝔓𝔏𝔑𝔈𝔄𝔎 (and 𝔓𝔏𝔑𝔈𝔄𝔎 is an E-logic).

Proof: This follows by 𝔓𝔏-14M and 2-17, utilizing 𝔓𝔏𝔑-4D and

PINEAK-4D through PINEAK-9D.

PINEAK-11D. $A \supset B, B \supset A \vdash A \equiv B$

Proof:	1. $A \supset B, B \supset A, A \vdash B$	MP
	2. $A \supset B, B \supset A, B \vdash A$	MP
	3. $A \supset B, B \supset A \vdash A \equiv B$	1,2, Bi-C

PINEAK-12D. $A \equiv B \vdash A \supset B$

Proof:	1. $A \equiv B, A \vdash B$	Bi-MP
	2. $A \equiv B \vdash A \supset B$	1, C

PINEAK-13D. $A \equiv B \vdash B \supset A$ Exercise

PINEAK-11D through PINEAK-13D allows one to substitute $A \equiv B$ for $A \supset B$ and $B \supset A$ in the equivalence theorem (see PI-14M). This formulation has the advantage of clarifying the nature of that theorem.

The variety of connectives in PINEAK allows establishment of relations between them. We will first establish some relations between implication and conjunction.

PINEAK-14D. $(A \wedge B) \supset C \vdash A \supset (B \supset C)$

Proof:	1. $(A \wedge B) \supset C, A, B \vdash A \wedge B$	A
	2. $(A \wedge B) \supset C, A, B \vdash (A \wedge B) \supset C$	Premise
	3. $(A \wedge B) \supset C, A, B \vdash C$	1, 2, MP
	4. $(A \wedge B) \supset C, A \vdash B \supset C$	3, C
	5. $(A \wedge B) \supset C \vdash A \supset (B \supset C)$	4, C

PINEAK-14T. $\vdash [(A \wedge B) \supset C] \supset [A \supset (B \supset C)]$

PINEAK-15D. $A \supset (B \supset C) \vdash (A \wedge B) \supset C$ Exercise

PINEAK-15T. $\vdash [A \supset (B \supset C)] \supset [(A \wedge B) \supset C]$

PINEAK-16T. $\vdash [(A \wedge B) \supset C] \equiv [A \supset (B \supset C)]$

Proof: This follows by Bi-C, utilizing $\mathcal{PINEAK}$-14D and $\mathcal{PINEAK}$-15D.

$\mathcal{PINEAK}$-17T. $\vdash(A \supset \sim B) \equiv \sim(A \wedge B)$

Proof:
1. $A \supset \sim B, A \wedge B \vdash A$	LS
2. $A \supset \sim B, A \wedge B \vdash A \supset \sim B$	Premise
3. $A \supset \sim B, A \wedge B \vdash \sim B$	1, 2, MP
4. $A \supset \sim B, A \wedge B \vdash B$	RS
5. $A \supset \sim B, A \wedge B \vdash \sim(A \supset A)$	3,4,$\mathcal{PIN}$-7D$\mathcal{PINEAK}$-1M
6. $A \supset \sim B \vdash (A \wedge B) \supset \sim(A \supset A)$	5, C
7. $A \supset \sim B \vdash \sim(A \wedge B)$	6,$\mathcal{PIN}$-8D,$\mathcal{PINEAK}$-1M
8. $\sim(A \wedge B), A \vdash \sim B$	$\mathcal{MKN}$-11D
9. $\sim(A \wedge B) \vdash A \supset \sim B$	8, C
10. $\vdash (A \supset \sim B) \equiv \sim(A \wedge B)$	7, 9, Bi-C

$\mathcal{PINEAK}$-17T represents the strongest equivalence between implication and conjunction provable in $\mathcal{PINEAK}$. It is to be noted that it is not strong enough to allow the elimination of either of the connectives in favor of the other, since each side contains a negation. Other, one-directional implications, can be shown; for example:

$\mathcal{PINEAK}$-18D. $A \supset B \vdash \sim(A \wedge \sim B)$

Proof:
1. $A \supset B, A \wedge \sim B \vdash A \supset B$	Premise
2. $A \supset B, A \wedge \sim B \vdash A$	LS
3. $A \supset B, A \wedge \sim B \vdash B$	1, 2, MP
4. $A \supset B, A \wedge \sim B \vdash \sim B$	RS
5. $A \supset B, A \wedge \sim B \vdash \sim(A \supset A)$	3,4,$\mathcal{PINEAK}$-1M$\mathcal{PIN}$-7D
6. $A \supset B \vdash A \wedge \sim B \supset \sim(A \supset A)$	5, C
7. $A \supset B \vdash \sim(A \wedge \sim B)$	6,$\mathcal{PINEAK}$-1M,$\mathcal{PIN}$-8D

$\mathcal{PINEAK}$-18T. $\vdash (A \supset B) \supset \sim(A \wedge \sim B)$

$\mathcal{PINEAK}$-19D. $A \wedge \sim B \vdash \sim(A \supset B)$ Exercise

$\mathcal{PINEAK}$-19T. $\vdash (A \wedge \sim B) \supset \sim(A \supset B)$

Similarly, relations between conjunction and disjunction are derivable.

PLNEAK-20T. ⊦ ~(A ∨ B) ≡ (~A ∧ ~B)

Proof: 1. ~(A ∨ B) ⊦ ~A	PLNEAK-3M, MAN-6D
2. A ∨ B ⊦ B ∨ A	PLNEAK-3M, SA-5D
3. B ∨ A ⊦ A ∨ B	PLNEAK-3M, SA-5D
4. ~(B ∨ A) ⊦ ~B	PLNEAK-3M, MAN-6D
5. ~(A ∨ B) ⊦ ~B	2,3, PLNEAK-10M
6. ~(A ∨ B) ⊦ ~A ∧ ~B	1, 5, A
7. ~A ∧ ~B, A ⊦ A	Premise
8. ~A ∧ ~B, A ⊦ ~A	LS
9. ~A ∧ ~B, A ⊦ ~(A ⊃ A)	7,8, PLNEAK-1MPLN-7D
10. ~A ∧ ~B, B ⊦ B	Premise
11. ~A ∧ ~B, B ⊦ ~B	RS
12. ~A ∧ ~B, B ⊦ ~(A ⊃ A)	10,11 PLNEAK-1MPLN-7D
13. ~A ∧ ~B, A ∨ B ⊦ ~(A ⊃ A)	9,12, D
14. ~A ∧ ~B ⊦ (A ∨ B) ⊃ ~(A ⊃ A)	13, C
15. ~A ∧ ~B ⊦ ~(A ∨ B)	14 PLNEAK-1MPLN-8D
16. ⊦ ~(A ∨ B) ≡ (~A ∧ ~B)	6, 15, Bi-C

PLNEAK-21D. ~A ∨ ~ B ⊦ ~(A ∧ B)

Proof: 1. ~A, A ∧ B ⊦ ~A	Premise
2. ~A, A ∧ B ⊦ A	LS
3. ~A, A ∧ B ⊦ ~(A ⊃ A)	1,2, PLNEAK-1MPLN-7D
4. ~A ⊦ (A ∧ B) ⊃ ~(A ⊃ A)	3, C
5. ~B, A ∧ B ⊦ ~B	Premise
6. ~B, A ∧ B ⊦ B	RS
7. ~B, A ∧ B ⊦ ~(A ⊃ A)	5,6, PLNEAK-1MPLN-7D
8. ~B ⊦ (A ∧ B) ⊃ ~(A ⊃ A)	7, C
9. ~A ∨ ~B ⊦ (A ∧ B) ⊃ ~(A ⊃ A)	4, 8, D
10. ~A ∨ ~B ⊦ ~(A ∧ B)	9 PLNEAK-1MPLN-8D

Additional proofs, to be supplied by the student, will establish the following:

PINEAK-22D. $A \wedge B \vdash \sim(\sim A \vee \sim B)$ Exercise

PINEAK-23D. $A \vee B \vdash \sim(\sim A \wedge \sim B)$ Exercise

PINEAK-24D. $\vdash [(A \vee B) \supset C] \equiv [(A \supset C) \wedge (B \supset C)]$ Exercise

PINEAK-25D. $(A \supset C) \vee (B \supset C) \vdash (A \wedge B) \supset C$ Exercise

PINEAK-26D. $\sim A \vee \sim B \vdash A \supset \sim B$ Exercise

PINEAK-27D. $\sim(\sim A \vee B \vdash \sim(A \supset B)$

Proof:

1.	$\sim(\sim A \vee B), A \supset B \vdash \sim\sim A \wedge \sim B$	PINEAK-20T, PINEAK-10M
2.	$\sim(\sim A \vee B), A \supset B \vdash A \supset B$	Premise
3.	$\sim(\sim A \vee B), A \supset B \vdash \sim B$	1, RS
4.	$\sim(\sim A \vee B), A \supset B \vdash \sim A$	3,4, PIN-4Da PINEAK-1M
5.	$\sim(\sim A \vee B), A \supset B \vdash \sim\sim A$	1, LS
6.	$\sim(\sim A \vee B), A \supset B \vdash \sim(A \supset B)$	4,5, PIN-15D, PINEAK-1M
7.	$\sim(\sim A \vee B) \vdash (A \supset B) \supset \sim(A \supset B)$	6, C
8.	$\sim(\sim A \vee B) \vdash \sim(A \supset B)$	7, PIN-16D PINEAK-1M

In addition to these, essentially transformational theorems, a number of "theses"–i.e. derivations from the null set– hold, the most familiar being inherited from the partial systems PIN, MAN, and MKN, e.g., MAN-14T $\vdash \sim\sim(A \vee \sim A)$ and MKN-7T $\vdash \sim(A \wedge \sim A)$. As we shall see, the double negation on MAN-14T is not dispensable and A and $\sim\sim A$ are in general not equivalent.

For the next significant general result, it will be useful to prove a few theorems, some of which hold in partial systems. To emphasize this, but still allow easy reference, we will give them two names: one as a PINEAK theorem and one as a theorem of the partial system.

PINEAK-28D. If **R** is two - valued logic, $\alpha \vdash_{PINEAK} A \Rightarrow \alpha \models_{R} A$.

Proof: This follows by the argument of INC-13M, INC-13M, SA-12M and SK-9M, extended to the biconditional.

PINEAK-29D. (=**PIN-20D**). $\sim\sim(A \supset B), \sim\sim A \vdash \sim\sim B$

Proof:
1. $\sim\sim A, \sim\sim(A \supset B) \vdash \sim B \supset \sim(A \supset B)$ — PIN-13Da
2. $\sim\sim A, \sim\sim(A \supset B) \vdash \sim\sim(A \supset B)$ — Premise
3. $\sim\sim A, \sim\sim(A \supset B) \vdash \sim\sim B$ — 1, 2, PIN-4Da

PINEAK-30D. $C \supset \sim A, D \supset \sim A, \sim\sim(C \vee D) \vdash \sim A$

Proof:
1. $C \supset \sim A, D \supset \sim A, \sim\sim(C \vee D), A \vdash \sim C$ — PIN-2D,PINEAK-1D
2. $C \supset \sim A, D \supset \sim A, \sim\sim(C \vee D), A \vdash \sim D$ — PIN-2D
3. $C \supset \sim A, D \supset \sim A, \sim\sim(C \vee D), A \vdash \sim(C \vee D)$ — MAN-8D,PINEAK-3M
4. $C \supset \sim A, D \supset \sim A, \sim\sim(C \vee D), A \vdash \sim\sim(C \vee D)$ — Premise
5. $C \supset \sim A, D \supset \sim A, \sim\sim(C \vee D), A \vdash \sim A$ — PIN-15D, PINEAK-1M
6. $C \supset \sim A, D \supset \sim A, \sim\sim(C \vee D) \vdash \sim A$ — 5,PINEAK-2M

PINEAK-31D(PIN-21D). $\sim A \supset \sim B, \sim\sim A \supset \sim B \vdash \sim B$

Proof:
1. $\sim A \supset \sim B, \sim\sim A \supset \sim B, B \vdash \sim\sim A$ — PIN-2DPINEAK-1M
2. $\sim A \supset \sim B, \sim\sim A \supset \sim B, B \vdash \sim\sim\sim A$ — PIN-2DPINEAK-1M
3. $\sim A \supset \sim B, \sim\sim A \supset \sim B, B \vdash \sim B$ — PIN-15DPINEAK-1M

PINEAK-32D. $A, \sim\sim(A \equiv \sim B) \vdash \sim B$

Proof:
1. $A, B, A \equiv \sim B \vdash B$ — Premise
2. $A, B, A \equiv \sim B \vdash \sim B$ — Bi-MP
3. $A, B, A \equiv \sim B \vdash \sim(A \equiv \sim B)$ — 1,2,PIN-15D, PINEAK-1M
4. $A, B \vdash \sim(A \equiv \sim B)$ — 3, PINEAK-2M
5. $A, B \vdash \sim\sim\sim(A \equiv \sim B)$ — 4PIN-2DPINEAK-1M
6. $A, \sim\sim(A \equiv \sim B) \vdash \sim B$ — 5, Con

These theorems allow us to prove an interesting relation between PINEAK and a somewhat stronger system which, as we shall see later, is complete. Let us use the term CINEAK for the system that results from PINEAK if one replaces **Con** with **RA** and **NgC** (see the discussion of INC, Chapter 6). We then get the following theorem:

PINEAK-33M. Let $g(v) = \sim\sim v$ for all variables v,

$g(A \supset B) = \sim\sim(g(A) \supset g(B))$, $g(A \wedge B) = \sim\sim(g(A) \wedge g(B))$, $g(A \vee B) = \sim\sim(g(A) \vee g(B))$, $g(\sim A) = \sim g(A)$, $g(A \equiv B) = \sim\sim(g(A) \equiv g(B))$. If α is a set of wffs, $g(\alpha) = \{g(A): A \subset \alpha\}$. Then

$\alpha \vdash_{CLNEAK} A \Rightarrow g(\alpha) \vdash_{PLNEAK} g(A)$.

Proof: Let $\alpha \vdash_{CLNEAK} A$. By induction on the number k of lines in the Y-derivation of $\alpha \vdash A$, we get:

(α) k=1. Then $\alpha \vdash A$. Hence $g(A) \in g(\alpha)$ and $g(\alpha) \vdash_{PLNEAK} g(A)$.

(β) Assume that the theorem is true for k < m. We will prove it true for an arbitrary derivation of length m. Then the k_0th line of the Y-derivation (in CLNEAK) is $\alpha_m \vdash A_m$ and follows by one of the 13 rules of CLNEAK or $A_m \in \alpha_m$. Throughout the argument we will use PLNEAK-1M and PLNEAK-3M without specific mention.

Case 1. $A_m \in \alpha_m$. We use the same argument as in the (α) case.

Case 2. The mth step is MP. Hence there exist i < m and j < m such that $\alpha_i = \alpha_j = \alpha_m$ and $A_j = A_i \supset A_m$. By the hypothesis of induction, we have $g(\alpha_m) \vdash_{PLNEAK} g(A_i)$ and $g(\alpha_m) \vdash_{PLNEAK} g(A_i \supset A_m)$. Hence $g(\alpha_m) \vdash \sim\sim(g(A_i) \supset g(A_m))$ (in PLNEAK of course). $g(A_i) \vdash \sim g(A_m) \supset \sim(g(A_i) \supset g(A_m))$, by PLN-12Da; by PLN-4D, $g(A_i) \vdash \sim\sim(g(A_i) \supset g(A_m)) \supset \sim\sim g(A_m)$. Hence, by MP, $g(\alpha_m) \vdash \sim\sim g(A_m)$. For every A, $g(A)$ equals $\sim C$ for some wff C, let $g(A_m) = \sim C_m$. Then we have $g(\alpha_m) \vdash \sim\sim\sim C_m$ and by MLN-3M, $g(\alpha_m) \vdash \sim C_m$ i.e., $g(\alpha_m) \vdash g(A_m)$.

Case 3. The mth step is C. There is a j < m such that $\alpha_j = \alpha_m \cup \{B\}$, $A_m = B \supset A_j$ for some wff B. By the hypothesis of induction, $g(\alpha_m)$, $g(B) \vdash g(A_j)$. By C, $g(\alpha_m) \vdash g(B) \supset g(A_j)$ and hence by PLN-2D, $g(\alpha_m) \vdash \sim\sim(g(B) \supset g(A_j))$, i.e., $g(\alpha_m) \vdash g(A_m)$.

Case 4. The mth step is LS. There is a = j < m such that $\alpha_j = \alpha_m$ and a B such that $A_j = A_m \wedge B$. Hence by the hypothesis of

induction, $g(\alpha_m) \vdash \sim\sim(g(A_m) \wedge g(B))$. Let $g(A_m) = \sim C_m$. By $\mathcal{MKN}$-12D, $g(\alpha_m) \vdash \sim\sim g(A_m) \wedge \sim\sim g(B)$ and hence by LS, $g(\alpha_m) \vdash \sim\sim\sim C_m$, and by $\mathcal{MN}$-3M, $g(\alpha_m) \vdash \sim C_m$ i.e. $g(\alpha_m) \vdash g(A_m)$.
Case 5. The mth step is **RS**. This is analogous to case 4.
Case 6. The mth step is **A**. There is an $i < m$ and a $j < m$ such that $\alpha_i = \alpha_j = \alpha_m$ and $A_m = A_i \wedge A_j$. By the hypothesis of induction, we have $g(\alpha_m) \vdash g(A_i)$ and $g(\alpha_m) \vdash g(A_j)$. By A, $g(\alpha_m) \vdash g(A_i) \wedge g(A_j)$; by $\mathcal{PIN}$-3D, $g(\alpha_m) \vdash \sim\sim(g(A_i) \wedge g(A_j))$ i.e. $g(\alpha_m) \vdash g(A_m)$.
Case 7. The mth step is **AR**. There is an $i < m$ and a wff B such that $\alpha_i = \alpha_m$ and $A_m = A_i \vee B$. By the hypothesis of induction, $g(\alpha_m) \vdash g(A_i)$. By **AR**, $g(\alpha_m) \vdash g(A_i) \vee g(B)$ and hence by $\mathcal{PIN}$-3D, $g(\alpha_m) \vdash \sim\sim(g(A_i) \vee g(B))$ i.e. $g(\alpha_m) \vdash g(A_m)$.
Case 8. The mth step is **AL**. This is analogous to case 7.
Case 9. The mth step is **D**. There is an $i < m$ and a $j < m$ such that there exists a set of wffs α and wffs B and C such that $\alpha_i = \alpha \cup \{B\}$, $\alpha_j = \alpha \cup \{C\}$, $\alpha_m = \alpha \cup \{B \vee C\}$ and $A_i = A_j = A_m$. By the hypothesis of induction, $g(\alpha), g(A) \vdash g(A_m)$ and $g(\alpha), g(B) \vdash g(A_m)$. There exists a C_m such that $A_m = \sim C_m$. By **C**, $g(\alpha) \vdash g(A) \supset g(A_m)$ and $g(\alpha) \vdash g(B) \supset g(A_m)$. Hence we have $g(\alpha), g(A \vee B) \vdash \sim\sim(g(A) \vee g(B))$. Hence by $\mathcal{PINEAK}$-30D, we have $g(\alpha), g(A \vee B) \vdash \sim C_m$, i.e. $g(\alpha), g(A \vee B) \vdash g(A_m)$.
Case 10. The mth step is **Bi-MP** left to right. There is an $i < m$ and a $j < m$ such that $\alpha_i = \alpha_j = \alpha_m$ and $A_j = A_i \equiv A_m$. By the hypothesis of induction, $g(\alpha_m) \vdash g(A_i)$ and $g(\alpha_m) \vdash g(A_i \equiv A_m)$, i.e. $g(\alpha_m) \vdash \sim\sim(g(A_i) \equiv g(A_m))$. Let $A_m = \sim C_m$. Hence by $\mathcal{PINEAK}$-32D, $g(\alpha_m) \vdash \sim C_m$, i.e., $g(\alpha_m) \vdash g(A_m)$.
Case 11. The mth step is **Bi-MP** right to left. By $\mathcal{PINEAK}$-11D through $\mathcal{PINEAK}$-13D, the proof is reducible to case 10.
Case 12. The mth step is **Bi-C**. There exists an $i < m$ and $j < m$ such that $\alpha_i = \alpha_m \cup \{A_j\}$, $\alpha_j = \alpha_m \cup \{A_i\}$, and $A_m = A_i \equiv A_j$. By the hypothesis of induction, $g(\alpha_m), g(A_j) \vdash g(A_i)$ and $g(\alpha_m), g(A_i) \vdash g(A_j)$ and by **Bi-C**, $g(\alpha_m) \vdash g(A_i) \equiv g(A_j)$. Hence, by $\mathcal{PIN}$-3D, $g(\alpha_m) \vdash \sim\sim[g(A_i) \equiv g(A_j)]$, i.e.,

$g(\alpha_m) \vdash g(A_m)$.

Case 13. The mth step is **RA**. There exists an $i < m$ and $j < m$ such that $\alpha_i = \alpha_j = \alpha_m$ and $\sim A_i \equiv A_j$. Let $g(A_m) = \sim C_m$. By the hypothesis of induction, $g(\alpha_m) \vdash g(A_i)$ and $g(\alpha_m) \vdash \sim g(A_i)$. Hence, by PIN-15D, $g(\alpha_m) \vdash \sim C_m$ i.e. $g(\alpha_m) \vdash g(A_m)$.

Case 14. The mth step is **NgC**. There is an $i < m$ and a $j < m$ and a wff B such that $\alpha_i = \alpha_m \cup \{B\}$, $\alpha_j = \alpha_m \cup \{\sim B\}$ and $A_i = A_j = A_m$. By the hypothesis of induction, $g(\alpha_m), g(A) \vdash g(A_m)$ and $g(\alpha_m), \sim g(A) \vdash g(A_m)$. Let $g(A_m) = \sim C_m$. By **Con**, we have $g(\alpha_m), \sim C_m \vdash \sim g(A)$. Hence $g(\alpha_m), C_m \vdash \sim C_m$. By PINEAK-2M, $g(\alpha_m) \vdash \sim C_m$, i.e. $g(\alpha_m) \vdash g(A_m)$.

By virtue of the fact that PINEAK is an E-logic and by PIN-3D, PINEAK-33M shows that the addition of $\sim\sim A \vdash A$ would make PINEAK equivalent to CINEAK. Since, as we shall see, CINEAK is complete, that would result in PINEAK being complete as well. It is, however, easy to see that $\sim\sim A \vdash A$ does not hold in PINEAK.

PINEAK-34M. PINEAK is model theoretically incomplete (with the usual two-valued interpretation) and hence is also deductively incomplete.

Proof: If all of the two-place connectives take their usual interpretations, but $g(\sim)$ is the constant function 1, all the rules remain validity preserving. But if A takes the value 0, $\sim\sim A \models A$ obviously fails.Since however all rules are valid with the usual interpretations, adding $\sim\sim A \vdash A$ will not make it deductively inconsistent.

Before turning to a new system, we shall prove a few theorems that will prove useful in connection with later systems.

PINEAK-35M.(=MAN-16D). $\sim\sim A \vdash \sim\sim(A \vee B)$

Proof:	1. $\sim(A \vee B) \vdash \sim A$	MAN-6D
	2. $\sim(A \vee B) \vdash \sim\sim\sim A$	1, MN-1D

Since however all rules are valid with the usual interpretations, adding $\sim\sim A \vdash A$ will not make it inconsistent. Adding $\sim\sim A \vdash A$ will not make it deductively inconsistent.

Before turning to a new system, we shall prove a few theorems that will prove useful in connection with later systems.

PLNEAK-35D. (=**MAN**-16D). $\sim\sim A \vdash \sim\sim(A \vee B)$

Proof:

1.	$\sim(A \vee B) \vdash \sim A$	MAN-6D
2.	$\sim(A \vee B) \vdash \sim\sim\sim A$	1, MN-1D
3.	$\sim\sim A \vdash \sim\sim(A \vee B)$	2, Con

PLNEAK-36D. (=**MAN**-17D). $\sim\sim A \vdash \sim\sim(A \vee B)$ Exercise

PLNEAK-37D. $\sim\sim A, \sim\sim(A \equiv B) \vdash \sim\sim B$

Proof:

1.	$A, \sim B, A \equiv B \vdash B$	Bi-MP
2.	$A, \sim B, A \equiv B \vdash \sim B$	Premise
3.	$A, \sim B, A \equiv B \vdash \sim(A \equiv B)$	1, 2, PLN-15D
4.	$A, \sim B \vdash \sim(A \equiv B)$	3, PLNEAK-2M
5.	$A, \sim B \vdash \sim\sim\sim(A \equiv B)$	4, PLN-3D
6.	$\sim B, \sim\sim(A \equiv B) \vdash \sim A$	5, Con
7.	$\sim B, \sim\sim(A \equiv B) \vdash \sim\sim\sim A$	6, PLN-3D
8.	$\sim\sim A, \sim\sim(A \equiv B) \vdash \sim\sim B$	7, Con

PLNEAK-37Da. $\sim\sim B, \sim\sim(A \equiv B) \vdash \sim\sim A$ Exercise

PLNEAK-38D. $\sim\sim(A \supset B), \sim\sim(B \supset A) \vdash \sim\sim(A \equiv B)$

Proof:

1.	$A \supset B, B \supset A \vdash A \equiv B$	PLNEAK-11D
2.	$A \supset B, B \supset A \vdash \sim\sim(A \equiv B)$	1, PLN-3D
3.	$\sim(A \equiv B), B \supset A \vdash \sim(A \supset B)$	2, Con
4.	$\sim(A \equiv B), B \supset A \vdash \sim\sim\sim(A \supset B)$	3, PLN-3D
5.	$\sim(A \equiv B), \sim\sim(A \supset B) \vdash \sim(B \supset A)$	4, Con
6.	$\sim(A \equiv B), \sim\sim(A \supset B) \vdash \sim\sim\sim(B \supset A)$	5, PLN-3D
7.	$\sim\sim(A \supset B), \sim\sim(B \supset A) \vdash \sim\sim(A \equiv B)$	6, Con

The desirability of excluding peculiar interpretations of ~, such as the one appearing in **PINEAK**-34M leads, as it did in the implication-negation systems, to the addition of a principle strong enough to exclude them. The result is the system suggested by intuitionistic mathematicians. We shall call this system **WINEAK** (for "weak implication, negation, equivalence, alternation, conjunction").

WINEAK: A DZOS, with

Connectives: $\supset$ (two-place), $\vee$ (two-place), $\wedge$ (two-place), $\equiv$ (two- place), ~ (one-place)

rules: 1. $A, A \supset B \vdash B$	MP
2. $\alpha, A \vdash B \Rightarrow \alpha \vdash A \supset B$	C
3. $A \wedge B \vdash A$	LS
4. $A \wedge B \vdash B$	RS
5. $A, B \vdash A \wedge B$	A
6. $A \vdash A \vee B$	AR
7. $B \vdash A \vee B$	AL
8. $(\alpha, A \vdash C$ and $\alpha, B \vdash C) \Rightarrow \alpha, B \vee C \vdash C$	D
9. $\alpha, A \vdash \sim B \Rightarrow \alpha, B \vdash \sim A$	Con
10. $A, \sim A \vdash B$	RA
11. $A \equiv B, A \vdash B$	Bi-MP
12. $A \equiv B, B \vdash A$	Bi-MP
13. $(\alpha, A \vdash B$ and $\alpha, B \vdash A) \Rightarrow \alpha \vdash A \equiv B$	Bi-C

WINEAK-1M. All T- and D- theorems of **PINEAK**, **WIN**, **WAN** and **WKN** are theorems of **WINEAK**.

Proof: This is trivial, since **WINEAK** clearly includes all rules of **PINEAK**, **WIN**, **WAN**, and **WKN**.

There are however some theorems not provable in weaker systems. One of these is the inference scheme generally known as tollendo ponens.

WINEAK-2D. $A \vee B, \sim A \vdash B$

Proof: 1. $A, \sim A \vdash B$	RA
2. $B, \sim A \vdash B$	Premise
3. $A \vee B, \sim A \vdash B$	1, 2, D

WINEAK-2Da. A ∨ B ⊢ ~A ⊃ B
WINEAK-2T. ⊢ (A ∨ B) ⊃ (~A ⊃ B)

WINEAK-3D. ~A ∨ B, A ⊢ B — Exercise
WINEAK-3Da. ~A ∨ B ⊢ A ⊃ B
WINEAK-3T. ⊢ (~A ∨ B) ⊃ (A ⊃ B)

WINEAK-4D. A ∨ ~A ⊢ ~~A ⊃ A

Proof:

1.	A ∨ ~A, ~~A ⊢ ~A ∨ A	**SA**-5D
2.	A ∨ ~A, ~~A ⊢ ~~A	**Premise**
3.	A ∨ ~A, ~~A ⊢ A	1,2, **WINEAK**-2D
4.	A ∨ ~A ⊢ ~~A ⊃ A	3, C

WINEAK-5M. The equivalence theorem holds unrestrictedly in **WINEAK** and hence **WINEAK** is an E-logic.

Proof: This follows by the argument of **PINEAK**-10M.

WINEAK-5M, together with **PINEAK**-32M, show that for **WINEAK** as well, the addition of ~~A ⊃ A would yield a system as strong as **CINEAK** (as will be seen, it is equivalent to **CINEAK**). **WINEAK**-4D shows the role of A ∨ ~A , the so-called "law of the excluded middle." It would be more accurate perhaps to call that formula the object-language or syntactical correlate of that law. While acceptance of the principle that every sentence is true or false would incline one to accept A ∨ ~A (assuming disjunction and negation to be reasonably normal), one might conceivably deny the former and still espouse a logic for which the latter was a theorem. As an example, consider the three-valued logic with the following tables:

	p ∨ q			~p
p\q	0	1	2	
0	0	1	2	2
1	1	1	2	1
2	2	2	2	0

where both 1 and 2 are designated values. Theorem **WINEAK**- 4D shows that if A ∨ ~A were added as an axiom, we would also get a system equivalent to **CINEAK**.

WINEAK-6D. (α, A $\vdash$ ~~B and α B $\vdash$ ~~A) $\Rightarrow$ $\alpha \vdash$ ~~(A $\equiv$ B)

Proof: 1. α, A $\vdash$ ~~B	Hypothesis
2. α, B $\vdash$ ~~A	Hypothesis
3. $\alpha \vdash$ A $\supset$ ~~B	1, C
4. $\alpha \vdash$ B $\supset$ ~~A	2, C
5. $\alpha \vdash$ ~~(A $\supset$ B)	3, **WIN**-9D
6. $\alpha \vdash$ ~~(B $\supset$ A)	4, **WIN**-9D
7. $\alpha \vdash$ ~~(A $\equiv$ B)	5,6, **PINEAK**-38D

We can thus strengthen **PINEAK**-33M as it applies to **WINEAK**.

WINEAK-7M. $\alpha \vdash_{CINEAK} A$ $\Rightarrow$ $\alpha \vdash_{WINEAK}$ ~~A

Proof: Let $\alpha \vdash_{CINEAK} A$. Then there is a Y-derivation $\alpha_1 \vdash A_1, \cdots, \alpha_n \vdash A_n$ in **CINEAK** such that $\alpha_n = \alpha$ and $A_n = A$ and for each i either $A_i \in \alpha_i$ or $\alpha_i \vdash A_i$ follows by one of MP, C, LS, RS, A, AR, AL, D, Bi-C, Bi-MP, RA or NgC. By induction on i:

(α) i = 1. Then $A_1 \in \alpha_1$ and $\alpha_1 \vdash A_1$ and by **PIN**-3D, $\alpha_1 \vdash$ ~~A_1.

(β) Assume the theorem is true for i < m.

Case 1. $A_m \in \alpha_m$. This follows the same argument as case (α).

Case 2. The mth step is MP. There is an i < m and a j < m such that $\alpha_i = \alpha_j = \alpha_m$ and $A_j = A_i \supset A_m$. By the hypothesis of induction, $\alpha_m \vdash_{WINEAK}$ ~~A_i and $\alpha_m \vdash_{WINEAK}$ ~~$(A_i \supset A_m)$. Hence by **PINEAK**-29D, $\alpha_m \vdash_{WINEAK}$ ~~A_m.

Case 3. The mth step is C. There is an i < m and a wff B such that $\alpha_i = \alpha_m \cup \{B\}$ and $A_m = B \supset A_i$. By the hypothesis of induction, α_m, B $\vdash_{WINEAK}$ ~~A_i. By C, $\alpha_m \vdash_{WINEAK} B \supset$ ~~A_i, by C. Hence, by **WIN**-9D, $\alpha_m \vdash_{WINEAK}$ ~~$(B \supset A_i)$, i.e., $\alpha_m \vdash_{WINEAK}$ ~~A_m.

Case 4. The mth step is LS. Then there is an i < m and a wff B such that $\alpha_i = \alpha_m$ and $A_i = A_m \wedge B$. By the hypothesis of induction, $\alpha_m \vdash_{WINEAK}$ ~~$(A_m \wedge B)$. Hence, by **MKN**-12D and

LS, $\alpha_m \vdash_{WINEAK} {\sim}{\sim}A_m$.

Case 5. The mth step is **RS**. This is analogous to case 4.

Case 6. The mth step is **A**. There is an $i < m$ and a $j < m$ such that $\alpha_i = \alpha_j = \alpha_m$ and $A_m = A_i \wedge A_j$. By the hypothesis of induction, $\alpha_m \vdash_{WINEAK} {\sim}{\sim}A_i$ and $\alpha_m \vdash_{WINEAK} {\sim}{\sim}A_j$. By **A** and *MKN*-13D, $\alpha_m \vdash_{WINEAK} {\sim}{\sim}A_i \wedge {\sim}{\sim}A_j$, i.e., $\alpha_m \vdash_{WINEAK} {\sim}{\sim}A_m$.

Case 7. The mth step is **AL**. There is an $i < m$ and a wff B such that $\alpha_i = \alpha_m$ and $A_m = A_i \vee B$. By the hypothesis of induction, $\alpha_m \vdash_{WINEAK} {\sim}{\sim}A_i$. Then, $\alpha_m \vdash_{WINEAK} {\sim}{\sim}(A_i \vee B)$ by *PINEAK*-35D, i.e., $\alpha_m \vdash_{WINEAK} {\sim}{\sim}A_m$.

Case 8. The mth step is **AR**. This is analogous to case 7.

Case 9. The mth step is **D**. There is an $i < m$ and c a $j < m$ and wffs B and C and a set of wffs β such that $\alpha_i = \beta \cup \{B\}$, $\alpha_j = \beta \cup \{C\}$, $\alpha_m = \beta \cup \{B \vee C\}$, $A_i = A_j = A_m$. By the hypothesis of induction, $\beta, B \vdash_{WINEAK} {\sim}{\sim}A_m$ and $\beta, C \vdash_{WINEAK} {\sim}{\sim}A_m$. Hence by **D**, $\beta, B \vee C \vdash_{WINEAK} {\sim}{\sim}A_m$, i.e. $\alpha_m \vdash_{WINEAK} {\sim}{\sim}A_m$.

Case 10. The mth step is **Bi–C**. There is an $i < m$ and a $j < m$ such that $\alpha_i = \alpha_m \cup A_j$ and $\alpha_j = \alpha_m \cup A_i$ and $A_m = A_i \equiv A_j$. By the hypothesis of induction, $\alpha_m, A_j \vdash_{WINEAK} {\sim}{\sim}A_i$ and $\alpha_m, A_i \vdash_{WINEAK} {\sim}{\sim}A_j$. By *WINEAK*-6D, $\alpha_m \vdash_{WINEAK} {\sim}{\sim}(A_i \equiv A_j)$ i.e. $\alpha_m \vdash_{WINEAK} {\sim}{\sim}A_m$.

Case 11. The mth step is **Bi–MP** (left to right). There is an $i < m$ and a $j < m$ such that $\alpha_i = \alpha_j = \alpha_m$ and $A_j = A_i \equiv A_m$. By the hypothesis of induction, $\alpha_m \vdash_{WINEAK} {\sim}{\sim}A_i$ and $\alpha_m \vdash_{WINEAK} {\sim}{\sim}(A_i \equiv A_m)$. Hence by *PINEAK*-37D, $\alpha_m \vdash_{WINEAK} {\sim}{\sim}A_m$.

Case 12. The mth step is **Bi–MP** (right to left). This is analogous to case 11.

Case 13. The mth step is **RA**. There is an $i < m$ and a $j < m$ such that $\alpha_i = \alpha_j = \alpha_m$ and $A_j = {\sim}A_i$. By the hypothesis of induction, $\alpha_m \vdash_{WINEAK} {\sim}{\sim}A_i$ and $\alpha_m \vdash_{WINEAK} {\sim}{\sim}{\sim}A_i$. By RA, $\alpha_m \vdash_{WINEAK} {\sim}{\sim}A_m$.

Case 14. The mth step is **NgC**. There is an $i < m$ and a $j < m$ and a wff B such that $\alpha_i = \alpha_m \cup \{B\}$, $\alpha_j = \alpha_m \cup \{\sim B\}$, and $A_i = A_j = A_m$. By the hypothesis of induction, $\alpha_m, B \vdash_{\mathcal{W1NEAK}} \sim\sim A_m$ and $\alpha_m, \sim B \vdash_{\mathcal{W1NEAK}} \sim\sim A_m$. By **Con**, $\alpha_m, \sim A_m \vdash_{\mathcal{W1NEAK}} \sim B$ and $\alpha_m, \sim A_m \vdash_{\mathcal{W1NEAK}} \sim\sim A_m$; hence by $\mathcal{P1NEAK}$-2M, $\alpha_m \vdash_{\mathcal{W1NEAK}} \sim\sim A_m$.

In order to show incompleteness, we will find it convenient to introduce an equivalent DZOS of which, considering what we know of the relation between $\mathcal{P1}$ and $\mathcal{P12}$, we can reasonably say that it differs only trivially from $\mathcal{W1NEAK}$. We will call it $\mathcal{W1NEAK2}$.

$\mathcal{W1NEAK2}$: A DZOS, with:

Connectives: $\supset$ (2-place), $\vee$ (2-place), $\wedge$ (2-place), $\equiv$ (2- place), $\sim$ (1-place)

Rules: 1. $A, A \supset B \vdash B$ **MP**

Axiom Schemata:

1. $\vdash A \supset (B \supset A)$
2. $\vdash [A \supset (B \supset C)] \supset [(A \supset B) \supset (A \supset C)]$
3. $\vdash (A \wedge B) \supset A$
4. $\vdash (A \wedge B) \supset B$
5. $\vdash A \supset [B \supset (A \wedge B)]$
6. $\vdash A \supset (A \vee B)$
7. $\vdash B \supset (A \vee B)$
8. $\vdash (A \supset C) \supset [(B \supset C) \supset ([A \vee B] \supset C)]$
9. $\vdash (A \supset \sim B) \supset (B \supset \sim A)$
10. $\vdash A \supset (\sim A \supset B)$
11. $\vdash (A \equiv B) \supset (A \supset B)$
12. $\vdash (A \equiv B) \supset (B \supset A)$
13. $\vdash (A \supset B) \supset [(B \supset A) \supset (A \equiv B)]$

$\mathcal{W1NEAK2}$-1M. $\alpha, A \vdash B \Rightarrow \alpha \vdash A \supset B$

Proof: Since $\mathcal{W1NEAK2}$ R-includes $\mathcal{P12}$, the conditions on $\mathcal{P12}$-2M are obviously satisfied.

WINEAK2-2M. WINEAK and WINEAK2 are equivalent.

Proof: Rules 1 and 2 of WINEAK follow in WINEAK2 by the equivalence of P1 and P12; the other rules follow from corresponding axiom schemes by WINEAK2-1M and MP. Similarly, Axioms 1 and 2 follow by the equivalence of P1 and P12 and the other axiom schemes follow by use of MP and C.

WINEAK2-3M. WINEAK2 (and consequently also WINEAK) is model-theoretically incomplete (with the usual two-valued interpretation) and also deductively incomplete.

Proof: Consider the three-valued logic defined by the following conditions: $g_r(\sim)$ is the function $f(X)$ such that $f(0) = 2$, $f(1) = f(2) = 0$, $g_r(\supset)$ is the function $g(x,y)$ such that $g(x,y) = 2$ if $x \leq y$ and $g(x,y) = y$ otherwise, $g_r(\vee)$ is $max(x,y)$, $g_r(\wedge)$ is $min(x,y)$ and $g_r(\equiv)$ is the function $h(x,y)$ such that $h(x,x) = 2$ and $h(x,y)$ equals $min(x,y)$ otherwise. We note that $g(x,y) = 1$ if and only if $x = 2$ and $y=1$, while $g(x,y) = 0$ if and only if $0 = y < x$. Hence obviously MP preserves the property of taking the value 2. We consider the axioms:

1. $\vdash A \supset (B \supset A)$

If $g'_r(A \supset (B \supset A)) = 1$, then $g'_r(A) = 2$ and $g'_r(B \supset A) = 1$, and hence $g'_r(A) = 1$, which is impossible. If $g'_r(A \supset (B \supset A)) = 0$, $g'_r(A) > g'_r(B \supset A) = 0$. Hence $g'_r(A) = 0$, which is impossible. Hence $g'_r(A \supset (B \supset A)) = 2$.

2. $\vdash [A \supset (B \supset C)] \supset [(A \supset B) \supset (A \supset C)]$

If $g'_r([A \supset (B \supset C)] \supset [(A \supset B) \supset (A \supset C)]) = 1$, $g'_r(A \supset (B \supset C)) = 2$ and $g'_r((A \supset B) \supset (A \supset C)) = 1$ Hence $g'_r((A \supset B)) = 2$ and $g'_r(A \supset C) = 1$.Then $g'_r(A) =2$ and $g'_r(C) = 1$. Thus $g'_r(B) = 2$. Therefore $g'_r(B \supset C))= 1$.But then $g'_r(A \supset (B \supset C)) = 1$, which is impossible. If $g'_r([A \supset (B \supset C)] \supset [(A \supset B) \supset (A \supset C)]) = 0$, then $g'_r(A \supset (B \supset C)) > g'_r((A \supset B) \supset (A \supset C)) = 0$. Hence

$g'_r(A \supset B) > g'_r(A \supset C) = 0$. Thus $g'_r(A) > g'_r(C) = 0$. Then $g'_r(A \supset (B \supset C)) = 2$ (since it couldn't take 1 unless C did). If $g'_r(A) = 1$, then $g'_r(B) = 0$, since otherwise $g'_r(A \supset (B \supset C)) = 0$. But then $g'_r(A \supset B) = 0$ which is impossible. If however $g'_r(A) = 2$, again $g'_r(B \supset C) = 2$ and $g'_r(B) = 0$, but then $g'_r(A \supset B) = 0$, which is impossible.

3. $\vdash (A \wedge B) \supset A$

Since $\min(g'_r(A), g'_r(B)) \leq g'_r(A)$, then $g'_r((A \wedge B) \supset A) = 2$.

4. $\vdash (A \wedge B) \supset B$

The proof for case 4 is analogous.

5. $\vdash A \supset [B \supset (A \wedge B)]$

If $g'_r(A \supset [B \supset (A \wedge B)]) = 1$, then $g'_r(A) = 2$ and $g'_r(A \wedge B) = 1$. Hence $g'_r(B) = 1$ and $g'_r(B \supset (A \wedge B)) = 1$, which is impossible. If however $g'_r(A \supset [B \supset (A \wedge B)]) = 0$, $g'_r(A) > g'_r(B \supset (A \wedge B)) = 0$, but then $g'_r(B) > \min(g'_r(A), g'_r(B)) = 0$, which is impossible.

6. $\vdash A \supset (A \vee B)$

Since $g'_r(A) \leq \max(g'_r(A), g'_r(B))$, then $g'_r(A \supset (A \vee B)) = 2$.

7. $\vdash B \supset (A \vee B)$

The proof for case 7 is analogous.

8. $\vdash (A \supset C) \supset [(B \supset C) \supset ([A \vee B] \supset C)]$

If $g'_r((A \supset C) \supset [(B \supset C) \supset ([A \vee B] \supset C)]) = 1$, then $g'_r(A \supset C) = 2$ and $g'_r((B \supset C) \supset ([A \vee B] \supset C)) = 1$. Hence $g'_r(B \supset C) = 2$ and $g'_r([A \vee B] \supset C) = 1$, and thus $g'_r(A \vee B) = \max(g'_r(A), g'_r(B)) = 2$ and $g'_r(C) = 1$. Then $g'_r(B) < 2$, since otherwise $g'_r(B \supset C) = 1$. But then the same holds for A, which is impossible. If $g'_r((A \supset C) \supset [(B \supset C) \supset ([A \vee B] \supset C)]) = 0$, then $g'_r(A \supset C) > g'_r((B \supset C) \supset ([A \vee B] \supset C)) = 0$. Hence $g'_r(B \supset C) > g'_r([A \vee B] \supset C) = 0$. Thus $g'_r(A \vee B) = \max(g'_r(A), g'_r(B)) > g'_r(C) = 0$. Then either $g'_r(A)$ or $g'_r(B)$ is positive. Suppose $g'_r(A) > 0$, then $g'_r(A \supset C) = 0$, which is impossible. But then $g'_r(B) > 0$, and $g'_r(B \supset C) = 0$, which is also impossible.

9. $\vdash (A \supset {\sim}B) \supset (B \supset {\sim}A)$

If $g'_r((A \supset {\sim}B) \supset (B \supset {\sim}A)) = 1$.Then $g'_r(A \supset {\sim}B) = 2$ and $g'_r(B \supset {\sim}A) = 1$. Thus $g'_r(B) = 2$ and $g'_r({\sim}A) = 1$, which is not possible. If $g'_r((A \supset {\sim}B) \supset (B \supset {\sim}A)) = 0$, then $g'_r(A \supset {\sim}B) > g'_r(B \supset {\sim}A) = 0$. Hence $g'_r(B) > g'_r({\sim}A) = 0$ Then $g'_r({\sim}B) = 0$ and $g'_r(A) > 0$ and therefore $g'_r(A \supset {\sim}B) = 0$, which is impossible.

10. $\vdash A \supset ({\sim}A \supset B)$

If $g'_r(A \supset ({\sim}A \supset B)) = 1$, then $g'_r(A) = 2$ and $g'_r({\sim}A \supset B) = 1$. Hence $g'_r({\sim}A) = 2$ which is impossible. If $g'_r(A \supset ({\sim}A \supset B)) = 0$, then $g'_r(A) > g'_r({\sim}A \supset B) = 0$. Hence $g'_r({\sim}A) > g'_r(B) = 0$. But if $g'_r({\sim}A) > 0$, then $g'_r(A) = 0$.

11. $\vdash (A \equiv B) \supset (A \supset B)$

If $g'_r((A \equiv B) \supset (A \supset B)) = 1$, then $g'_r(A \equiv B) = 2$ and $g'_r(A \supset B) = 1$. Hence $g'_r(A) = g'_r(B)$ and $g'_r(A \supset B) = 2$, which is impossible. If $g'_r((A \equiv B) \supset (A \supset B)) = 0$, then $g'_r(A \equiv B) > g'_r(A \supset B) = 0$. But then $g'_r(A) \neq g'_r(B)$ and $g'_r(A \equiv B) = \min(g'_r(A), g'_r(B)) = 0$,which is impossible.

12. $\vdash (A \equiv B) \supset (B \supset A)$

The proof for case 12 is analogous.

13. $\vdash (A \supset B) \supset [(B \supset A) \supset (A \equiv B)]$

If $g'_r((A \supset B) \supset [(B \supset A) \supset (A \equiv B)]) = 1$, then $g'_r(A \supset B) = 2$ and $g'_r((B \supset A) \supset (A \equiv B)) = 1$. Hence $g'_r(B \supset A) = 2$ and $g'_r(A \equiv B) = 1$. Then $g'_r(A) = g'_r(B)$ and $\min(g'_r(A), g'_r(B)) = 1$. But then either $g'_r(A \supset B)$ or $g'_r(B \supset A)$ equals 1. If $g'_r((A \supset B) \supset [(B \supset A) \supset (A \equiv B)]) = 0$, then $g'_r(A \supset B) > g'_r((B \supset A) \supset (A \equiv B)) = 0$. Hence $g'_r(B \supset A) > g'_r(A \equiv B) = 0$. Thus $g'_r(A) \neq g'_r(B)$ and $\min(g'_r(A), g'_r(B)) = 0$. Then either $g'_r(A \supset B)$ or $g'_r(B \supset A)$ equals 0.

From this it follows that every T- theorem of WINEAK2 – and hence of WINEAK--always takes the value 2. But if $g'_r(A) = 1$ and $g'_r(B) = 0$, then $g'_r(A \supset B) = 0$ and hence $g'_r((A \supset B) \supset A) = 2$. Consequently, $g'_r([(A \supset B) \supset A] \supset A) = 1$. Therefore, Peirce's law is not a theorem of WINEAK and since it is L-true in two valued logic, and all rules of WINEAK are 2-valued valid, our result follows.

In connection with WINEAK2-3M, notice :

WINEAK-8T. $\vdash\ \sim\sim([(A \supset B) \supset A] \supset A)$

Proof: 1. $\sim([(A \supset B) \supset A] \supset A) \vdash\ \sim A$	PIN-14D
2. $\sim([(A \supset B) \supset A] \supset A) \vdash\ \sim\sim[(A \supset B) \supset A]$	WIN-5D
3. $\sim\sim[(A \supset B) \supset A], \sim\sim(A \supset B) \vdash\ \sim\sim A$	PINEAK-28D
4. $\sim\sim[(A \supset B) \supset A], \sim A \vdash\ \sim\sim\sim(A \supset B)$	3, Con
5. $\sim\sim[(A \supset B) \supset A], \sim A \vdash\ \sim(A \supset B)$	4,MN-2D
6. $\sim([(A \supset B) \supset A] \supset A) \vdash\ \sim(A \supset B)$	1,2,5,closure
7. $\sim([(A \supset B) \supset A] \supset A) \vdash\ \sim\sim A$	6, WIN-5D
8. $\sim([(A \supset B) \supset A] \supset A) \vdash\ \sim(B \supset B)$	1, 7, RA
9. $\vdash\ \sim\sim([(A \supset B) \supset A] \supset A)$	8,PI1-4T,Con

From WINEAK-8T and the unprovability of Peirce's law, the unprovability of $\sim\sim A \vdash A$ follows and by WINEAK-2Da, the unprovability of $\vdash\ \sim A \vee A$ also. Furthermore, two interesting equivalences hold.

WINEAK-9T. $\vdash\ \sim(A \supset B) \equiv (\sim\sim A \wedge \sim B)$

Proof: 1. $\sim(A \supset B) \vdash\ \sim\sim A$	WIN-5D
2. $\sim(A \supset B) \vdash\ \sim B$	PIN-14D
3. $\sim(A \supset B) \vdash\ \sim\sim A \wedge \sim B$	1, 2, A
4. $A \supset B, \sim\sim A \wedge \sim B \vdash\ \sim B$	RS
5. $A \supset B, \sim\sim A \wedge \sim B \vdash A \supset B$	Premise
6. $A \supset B, \sim\sim A \wedge \sim B \vdash\ \sim A$	4, 5, PIN-4Da
7. $A \supset B, \sim\sim A \wedge \sim B \vdash\ \sim\sim A$	LS
8. $A \supset B, \sim\sim A \wedge \sim B \vdash\ \sim(A \supset B)$	6, 7, RA
9. $\sim\sim A \wedge \sim B \vdash\ \sim(A \supset B)$	8, PINEAK-2M
10. $\vdash\ \sim(A \supset B) \equiv (\sim\sim A \wedge \sim B)$	3, 9, Bi-C

WINEAK-10T. $\vdash\ \sim(A \equiv B) \equiv (\sim\sim A \equiv \sim B)$

Proof: 1. $\sim(A \equiv B), A, A \supset B \vdash B \supset A$	PI1-5D
2. $\sim(A \equiv B), A, A \supset B \vdash A \supset B$	Premise
3. $\sim(A \equiv B), A, A \supset B \vdash A \equiv B$	1,2,PINEAK-11D

4.	$\sim(A \equiv B),\ A, A \supset B \vdash \sim(A \equiv B)$	Premise
5.	$\sim(A \equiv B),\ A, A \supset B \vdash \sim(A \supset B)$	3, 4, RA
6.	$\sim(A \equiv B),\ A \vdash \sim(A \supset B)$	5, PINEAK-2M
7.	$\sim(A \equiv B),\ A \vdash \sim B$	6, PIN-14D
8.	$\sim(A \equiv B),\ B \vdash \sim A$	7, Con
9.	$\sim(A \equiv B),\ B \vdash \sim\sim\sim A$	8, PIN-3D
10.	$\sim(A \equiv B),\ \sim\sim A \vdash \sim B$	9, Con
11.	$\sim(A \equiv B),\ \sim B, A \supset B \vdash A \supset B$	Premise
12.	$\sim(A \equiv B),\ \sim B, A \supset B \vdash B \supset A$	WIN-4Da
13.	$\sim(A \equiv B),\ \sim B, A \supset B \vdash A \equiv B$	11,12, PINEAK-11D
14.	$\sim(A \equiv B),\ \sim B, A \supset B \vdash \sim(A \equiv B)$	Premise
15.	$\sim(A \equiv B),\ \sim B, A \supset B \vdash \sim(A \supset B)$	13,14, RA
16.	$\sim(A \equiv B),\ \sim B \vdash \sim(A \supset B)$	15, PINEAK-2M
17.	$\sim(A \equiv B),\ \sim B \vdash \sim\sim A$	16, WIN-5D
18.	$\sim(A \equiv B) \vdash \sim\sim A \equiv \sim B$	10, 17, Bi-C
19.	$A \equiv B,\ \sim\sim A \equiv \sim B, A \vdash B$	Bi-MP
20.	$A \equiv B,\ \sim\sim A \equiv \sim B, A \vdash \sim\sim A$	PIN-3D
21.	$A \equiv B,\ \sim\sim A \equiv \sim B, A \vdash \sim\sim A \equiv \sim B$	Premise
22.	$A \equiv B,\ \sim\sim A \equiv \sim B, A \vdash \sim B$	20, 21, Bi-MP
23.	$A \equiv B,\ \sim\sim A \equiv \sim B, A \vdash \sim A$	19, 22, RA
24.	$A \equiv B,\ \sim\sim A \equiv \sim B \vdash \sim A$	23, PINEAK-2M
25.	$A \equiv B,\ \sim\sim A \equiv \sim B \vdash B \supset A$	PINEAK-13D
26.	$A \equiv B,\ \sim\sim A \equiv \sim B \vdash \sim B$	24, 25, PIN-4Da
27.	$A \equiv B,\ \sim\sim A \equiv \sim B \vdash \sim\sim A \equiv \sim B$	Premise
28.	$A \equiv B,\ \sim\sim A \equiv \sim B \vdash \sim\sim A$	26, 27, Bi-MP
29.	$A \equiv B,\ \sim\sim A \equiv \sim B \vdash \sim(A \equiv B)$	24,28, RA
30.	$\sim\sim A \equiv \sim B \vdash \sim(A \equiv B)$	29, PINEAK-2M
31.	$\vdash \sim(A \equiv B) \equiv (\sim\sim A \equiv \sim B)$	18,30, Bi-C

Note that although PINEAK-2M is, strictly speaking, not a D-theorem, its proof holds in WINEAK or indeed any R-extension of PINEAK. This result together with PINEAK-17T and PINEAK-20T defines a procedure for eliminating negations which have two-place connectives in their scope:

For	Substitute
$\sim(A \supset B)$	$\sim\sim A \wedge \sim B$
$\sim(A \wedge B)$	$A \supset \sim B$
$\sim(A \vee B)$	$\sim A \wedge \sim B$
$\sim(A \equiv B)$	$\sim\sim A \equiv \sim B$

WINEAK-11M. If **R** is the standard two-valued interpretation, $\alpha \vdash_{\mathbf{WINEAK}} A \Rightarrow \alpha \vDash_{\mathbf{R}} A$.

Proof: This is left as an exercise for the student.

As we noted in the discussion of **PINEAK**-33M, replacing **Con** by **NgC** in **WINEAK** will yield a system we called **CINEAK**. Since this is the same substitution by which we obtained **INC** from **WIN**, it may come as no surprise that we discover **CINEAK** to be complete.

CINEAK: A DZOS, with

connectives: $\vee$ (2-place), $\wedge$ (2-place), $\supset$ (2-place), $\equiv$ (2-place), $\sim$ (1-place)

rules:

1.	$A, A \supset B \vdash B$	MP
2.	$\alpha, A \vdash B \Rightarrow \alpha \vdash A \supset B$	C
3.	$A \wedge B \vdash A$	LS
4.	$A \wedge B \vdash B$	RS
5.	$A, B \vdash A \wedge B$	A
6.	$A \vdash A \vee B$	AR
7.	$B \vdash A \vee B$	AL
8.	$(\alpha, A \vdash C$ and $\alpha, B \vdash C) \Rightarrow \alpha, A \vee B \vdash C$	D
9.	$A, \sim A \vdash B$	RA
10.	$(\alpha, A \vdash B$ and $\alpha, \sim A \vdash B) \Rightarrow \alpha \vdash B$	NgC
11.	$A \equiv B, A \vdash B$	Bi-MP
12.	$A \equiv B, B \vdash A$	Bi-MP
13.	$\alpha, A \vdash B \Rightarrow \alpha$ and $\alpha, B \vdash A) \Rightarrow \alpha \vdash A \equiv B$	Bi-C

CINEAK-1M. All T- and D-theorems of **INC** and **WINEAK** are theorems of **CINEAK**.

Proof: **CINEAK** **R**-includes **INC** since it has MP, C, and NgC. Hence it also R-includes WIN, and since it contains all of the rules of WINEAK which are not primitive rules of INC, it contains WINEAK.

CINEAK-2M. The equivalence theorem holds unrestrictedly in CINEAK and hence CINEAK is an E-logic.

Proof: The equivalence theorem follows from CINEAK-1M and the fact that all connectives of CINEAK are also in WINEAK. Hence, by virtue of MP and C, CINEAK is an E-logic.

CINEAK-3T. $\vdash (A \wedge B) \equiv \sim(A \supset \sim B)$

Proof:		
1.	$A \wedge B \vdash \sim\sim(A \wedge B)$	PIN-3D
2.	$\sim\sim(A \wedge B) \vdash A \wedge B$	INC-6D
3.	$\vdash (A \wedge B) \equiv \sim\sim(A \wedge B)$	1, 2, Bi-C
4.	$\vdash (A \wedge B) \equiv \sim(A \supset \sim B)$	3, PINEAK-17T, CINEAK-2M

CINEAK-4T. $\vdash (A \vee B) \equiv (\sim A \supset B)$

Proof:		
1.	$B \vdash \sim A \supset B$	PI-5D
2.	$A \vdash \sim A \supset B$	WIN-4D
3.	$A \vee B \vdash \sim A \supset B$	1, 2, D
4.	$\sim A \supset B, A \vdash A \vee B$	AR
5.	$\sim A \supset B, \sim A \vdash B$	MP
6.	$\sim A \supset B, \sim A \vdash A \vee B$	5, AL
7.	$\sim A \supset B \vdash A \vee B$	4, 6, NgC
8.	$\vdash (A \vee B) \equiv (\sim A \supset B)$	4, 7, Bi-C

CINEAK-5T. $\vdash (A \equiv B) \equiv [(A \supset B) \wedge (B \supset A)]$

Proof:		
1.	$A \equiv B \vdash A \supset B$	PINEAK-12D
2.	$A \equiv B \vdash B \supset A$	PINEAK-13D
3.	$A \equiv B \vdash (A \supset B) \wedge (B \supset A)$	1, 2, A
4.	$(A \supset B) \wedge (B \supset A), A \vdash A \supset B$	LS
5.	$(A \supset B) \wedge (B \supset A), A \vdash A$	Premise
6.	$(A \supset B) \wedge (B \supset A), A \vdash B$	4, 5, MP

7. $(A \supset B) \wedge (B \supset A), B \vdash B \supset A$	RS
8. $(A \supset B) \wedge (B \supset A), B \vdash B$	Premise
9. $(A \supset B) \wedge (B \supset A), B \vdash A$	7, 8, MP
10. $(A \supset B) \wedge (B \supset A) \vdash A \equiv B$	6, 9, Bi-C
11. $\vdash (A \equiv B) \equiv [(A \supset B) \wedge (B \supset A)]$	3, 10, Bi-C

CINEAK-6M. If **R** is the standard two-valued interpretation, $\alpha \vdash_{\mathrm{CINEAK}} A \Rightarrow \alpha \models_{\mathbf{R}} A$.

Proof: The details are left to the student. Refer to INC-13M and PINEAK-28M for the general technique.

CINEAK-7M. CINEAK is deductively (and, with the usual two-valued interpretations, model-theoretically) consistent.

Proof: This follows immediately from CINEAK-6M since not-$(p \models_{\mathbf{R}} p \wedge \sim p)$.

CINEAK-8M. CINEAK is deductively (with the usual two-valued interpretations, model-theoretically) complete.

Proof: This follows by INC-26M, utilizing CINEAK-2M, CINEAK-3T, CINEAK-4T, CINEAK-5T and CINEAK-6M.

10
Strict Implications: Introduction

We have now completed our examination of deductive zero-order systems which include **PI**. We do not mean to suggest that no other variants can be defined; indeed, we mentioned a few of them in passing in the last chapter. Before leaving the subject of zero-order systems, we point out that there are some which have been suggested which contain connectives that are generally of implication type, but are not positive implications in the sense we have defined. The motivation for having these connectives has varied: one group of authors has felt that the concept of "implication," as it is used in mathematics and logic, and presumably also in the natural sciences, has an element of necessary connection lacking in the complete logics such as **INC**, **ANC**, **NKC** and **CINEAK**. They feel this requires the rejection, not of principles not provable in **WINEAK** such as $\sim\sim A \vdash A$ or $\vdash A \vee \sim A$, but instead, of some which hold even in **PI** such as $\vdash A \supset (B \supset A)$ (which as you will recall, is **PI**1-5T). The objective of this first group of authors (e.g., of C.I.Lewis), then, is to define an implicational connective which could be the basis of a theory of modality (and hence of necessary connection).

A second group of authors objects to some of the theorems deducible in **PI** or **PIN** on other philosophical grounds, or on the basis of one or more of the principles sometimes called "material fallacies." In general, these attempt to interpret some of these fallacies in a way that some suggested forms of inference can be rejected on their basis, as is admittedly the case for those fallacies traditionally called formal (such as "undistributed middle"). Clearly, not all material fallacies can be readily used in this way: for example, "bégging the question" would seem to rule out simplification, addition and $\vdash A \supset A$ (and probably even modus ponens). On the other hand "irrelevant premise" does seem to be taken seriously in this sense. At least in some cases the stance seems due to reasons other than the wish to be faithful to logical tradition. A related but somewhat different motivation is a desire to formulate a logical system which will be as weak as possible, but still adequate for representing as many logical systems as possible by specialization. This device consists of appending the axioms of those systems as universally quantified antecedents in conditionals whose consequents are the universal quantification of their T-theorems. Actually developing this would involve systems expressively richer than what we have termed DZOSs. We will not in this book include a discussion of this class of system, which might perhaps be called **quantified zero-order systems**. However this motivation, which was apparently also involved in the first development of systems equivalent to **P1**, will interest us enough to cause us to examine a system inspired by it.

Considerations of space, if nothing else, will prevent us from examining more than a few of these systems. It is hoped that the reader will forgive us if the system or systems he finds most entrancing are thereby left unexamined and we will refer to a considerably greater number in the bibliographical notes in Appendix I.

The first group of systems we will examine were invented by the American philosopher C.I. Lewis. It consists of a group of DZOSs customarily referred to as **S1** through **S5**. Actually we will consider two forms for each of these systems. Our reason for this is that one of the rules Lewis used in his description of the systems is somewhat ambiguous. We will be considering two versions, which, at least in some cases, are of different strength, dependent on which interpretation of the rule is adopted. The rule in question reads: "Either of two equivalent expressions may be substituted for the other. Thus if an expression of the form p = q [i.e. (p ⥽ q)∧(q ⥽ p)] has been assumed, or subsequently established, what precedes the sign of equivalence in this expression may be substituted for what follows it, and vice versa." We will specify two rules below, one of which (SHE) appears to us to follow Lewis' formulation more closely, while another (SE) has been used by the greater number of writers who have discussed these systems. We will thus consider two groups of five systems, where the groups differ in this one rule.

For all of these (and for an additional two groups of five systems each which we will specify a bit later) the connectives will be: ⥽ (2-place), ∧ (2-place) and ~ (1-place). **S1**-**S5** will have 3 rules:

1. A, A ⥽ B ⊢ B — MMP
2. A, B ⊢ A ∧ B — A
3. (⊢ (A ⥽ B) ∧ (B ⥽ A) and ⊢ $\check{S}_{A}$C) ⇒ ⊢$\check{S}_{B}$C — SE (Substitution of Equivalents)

S1*-S5* differ from S1-S5 in that instead of SE they have, the following rule:

3*. (A ⥽ B) ∧ (B ⥽ A), $\mathbf{S}^{\cup}{}_{A}C \vdash \mathbf{S}^{\cup}{}_{B}C$ SHE
(Substitution of Hypothetical Equivalents)

Notational abbreviation: ◇A for ~(A ⥽ ~A).

S1 (and S1*) have in addition the following axiom schemata:

1. ⊢ (A ⥽ B) ⥽ ~◇(A ∧ ~B)
2. ⊢ ~◇(A ∧ ~B) ⥽ (A ⥽ B)
3. ⊢ (A ∧ B) ⥽ (B ∧ A)
4. ⊢ (A ∧ B) ⥽ A
5. ⊢ A ⥽ (A ∧ A)
6. ⊢ [(A ∧ B) ∧ C] ⥽ [A ∧ (B ∧ C)]
7. ⊢ A ⥽~~A
8. ⊢ [(A ⥽ B) ∧ (B ⥽ C)] ⥽(A ⥽ C)
9. ⊢ [A ∧ (A ⥽ B)] ⥽ B

S2 and S2* add:

10. ⊢ ◇(A ∧ B) ⥽ ◇A

S3 and S3* drop axioms 9 and 10 and substitute:

9'. ⊢ ~◇A ⥽ ~A

10'. ⊢ (A ⥽ B) ⥽ (~◇B ⥽ ~◇A)

S4 and S4* have axioms 1- 10 and add:

11. ⊢ ~◇~A ⥽ ~◇~~◇~A

Finally, S5 and S5*drops axiom 11 and substitutes:

11'. ⊢ ◇A ⥽ ~◇~◇A

We will now proceed to prove a number of theorems concerning S1:

S1-1D. A ∧ B ⊢ A Exercise

S1-2D. A ∧ B ⊢ B

Proof:

1.	A ∧ B ⊢ (A ∧ B) ⥽ (B ∧ A)	Ax3
2.	A ∧ B ⊢ (A ∧ B)	Premise
3.	A ∧ B ⊢ B ∧ A	1, 2, MMP
4.	A ∧ B ⊢ (B ∧ A) ⥽ B	Ax4
5.	A ∧ B ⊢ B	3, 4, MMP

S1-3M. Every T- and D- theorem of SK is a theorem of S1. Exercise

S1-4T. $\vdash A \prec A$

Proof:
1. $\vdash (A \wedge A) \prec A$ — Ax4
2. $\vdash A \prec (A \wedge A)$ — Ax5
3. $\vdash [(A \wedge A) \prec A] \wedge [A \prec (A \wedge A)]$ — 1,2, A
4. $\vdash ([(A \wedge A) \prec A] \wedge [A \prec (A \wedge A)]) \prec (A \prec A)$ — Ax8
5. $\vdash A \prec A$ — 3,4, MMP

S1-5T. $\vdash {\sim}{\sim}A \prec A$

Proof:
1. $\vdash {\sim}A \prec {\sim}A$ — S1-4T
2. $\vdash ({\sim}A \prec {\sim}A) \prec {\sim}\Diamond({\sim}A \wedge {\sim}{\sim}A)$ — Ax1
3. $\vdash {\sim}\Diamond\Diamond({\sim}A \wedge {\sim}{\sim}A)$ — 1, 2, MMP
4. $\vdash ({\sim}A \wedge {\sim}{\sim}A) \prec ({\sim}{\sim}A \wedge {\sim}A)$ — Ax3
5. $\vdash ({\sim}{\sim}A \wedge {\sim}A) \prec ({\sim}A \wedge {\sim}{\sim}A)$ — Ax3
6. $\vdash {\sim}\Diamond({\sim}{\sim}A \wedge {\sim}A)$ — 4,5, A,3, SE
7. $\vdash [{\sim}\Diamond({\sim}{\sim}A \wedge {\sim}A)] \prec ({\sim}{\sim}A \prec A)$ — Ax2
8. $\vdash {\sim}{\sim}A \prec A$ — 6,7, MMP

S1-6D. $A \prec B, B \prec C \vdash A \prec C$ — Exercise

S1-7T. $\vdash ({\sim}A \prec B) \prec ({\sim}B \prec A)$

Proof:
1. $\vdash ({\sim}A \prec B) \prec {\sim}\Diamond({\sim}A \wedge {\sim}B)$ — Ax1
2. $\vdash ({\sim}A \wedge {\sim}B) \prec ({\sim}B \wedge {\sim}A)$ — Ax3
3. $\vdash ({\sim}B \wedge {\sim}A) \prec ({\sim}A \wedge {\sim}B)$ — Ax3
4. $\vdash ({\sim}A \prec B) \prec {\sim}\Diamond({\sim}B \wedge {\sim}A)$ — 1,2,3, A, SE
5. $\vdash {\sim}\Diamond({\sim}B \wedge {\sim}A) \prec ({\sim}B \prec A)$ — Ax2
6. $\vdash ({\sim}A \prec B) \prec ({\sim}B \prec A)$ — 4,5, S1-6D

S1-7D. ${\sim}A \prec B \vdash {\sim}B \prec A$

S1-8T. $\vdash B \prec {\sim}(A \wedge {\sim}B)$

Proof:
1. $\vdash (A \wedge {\sim}B) \prec ({\sim}B \wedge A)$ — Ax3
2. $\vdash ({\sim}B \wedge A) \prec {\sim}B$ — Ax4
3. $\vdash (A \wedge {\sim}B) \prec {\sim}B$ — 1,2, S1-6D

4. $\vdash \sim\sim(A \wedge \sim B) \prec \sim B$	S1,5T, Ax7 ,3, S E
5. $\vdash \sim\sim B \prec \sim(A \wedge \sim B)$	4, S1-7D
6. $\vdash B \prec \sim(A \wedge \sim B)$	S1-5T, Ax7 ,5, S E

S1-9M. If A and B are conjunctions of the same elements, $\vdash_{S1} A \prec B$.

Proof: This follows by the argument of theorems 7-1 and 7-2, using **Ax3**, **Ax6**, S1-3T, S1-6D and **SE**.

S1-10T. $\vdash [(A \wedge B) \prec C] \prec [(A \wedge \sim C) \prec \sim B]$

Proof: 1. $\vdash [(A \wedge B) \prec C] \prec \sim\Diamond[(A \wedge B) \wedge \sim C]$	Ax1
2. $\vdash [(A \wedge B) \wedge \sim C] \prec [(A \wedge \sim C) \wedge B]$	S1-9M
3. $\vdash [(A \wedge \sim C) \wedge B] \prec [(A \wedge B) \wedge \sim C]$	S1-9M
4. $\vdash [(A \wedge B) \prec C] \prec \sim\Diamond [(A \wedge \sim C) \wedge B]$	1, S E ,2,3
5. $\vdash [(A \wedge B) \prec C] \prec \sim\Diamond[(A \wedge \sim C) \wedge \sim\sim B]$	4, S E , Ax7, S1-5T
6. $\vdash \sim\Diamond[(A \wedge \sim C) \wedge \sim\sim B] \prec [(A \wedge \sim C) \prec \sim B)]$	Ax2
7. $\vdash [(A \wedge B) \prec C] \prec [(A \wedge \sim C) \prec \sim B)]$	5,6, S1-6D

S1-10D. $(A \wedge B) \prec C \vdash (A \wedge \sim C) \prec \sim B$

S1-11M. The following pairs of wffs are equivalent in the sense required by **SE** (and hence also **SHE**) in S1, and therefore also in S2 - S5 and S1*-S5*: A and $\sim\sim A$, $A \wedge B$ and $B \wedge A$, $A \wedge (B \wedge C)$ and $(A \wedge B) \wedge C$, and A and $A \wedge A$.

Proof: For A and $\sim\sim A$, this follows by **Ax-7** and S1-5T; for $A \wedge B$ and $B \wedge A$, by **Ax-3**; for $A \wedge (B \wedge C)$ and $(A \wedge B) \wedge C$, by S1-9M; for A and $A \wedge A$, by **Ax-4** and **Ax-5**.

S1-12T. $\vdash (A \wedge \sim B) \prec \sim(A \prec B)$

Proof: 1. $\vdash [A \wedge (A \prec B)] \prec B$	Ax9
2. $\vdash (A \wedge \sim B) \prec \sim(A \prec B)$	1, S1-10D

S1-13T. $\vdash \sim(A \wedge \sim A)$

Proof:	1. ⊢ A ⥽ A	S1-4T
	2. ⊢ (A ∧ ~A) ⥽ ~(A ⥽ A)	S1-12T
	3. ⊢ ~~(A ∧ ~A) ⥽ ~(A ⥽ A)	2,S1-11M
	4. ⊢ ~~(A ⥽ A) ⥽ ~ (A ∧ ~A)	3,S1-7D
	5. ⊢ ~~(A ⥽ A)	4,S1-11M
	6. ⊢ ~ (A ∧ ~A)	4,5, MMP

S1-14T. ⊢ (A ⥽ B) ⥽ ~(A ∧ ~B)

Proof:	1. ⊢ (A ∧ ~B) ⥽ ~(A ⥽ B)	S1-12T
	2. ⊢ ~~(A ∧ ~B) ⥽ ~(A ⥽ B)	1,S1-11M
	3. ⊢ ~~(A ⥽ B) ⥽ ~(A ∧ ~B)	2,S1-7D
	4. ⊢ (A ⥽ B) ⥽ ~(A ∧ ~B)	3, S1-11M

S1-14D. (A ⥽ B) ⊢ ~(A ∧ ~B)

S1-15T. ⊢ (A ⥽ B) ⥽ (~B ⥽ ~A)

Proof:	1. ⊢ (~~A ⥽ B) ⥽ (~B ⥽ ~A)	2,S1-7T
	2. ⊢ (A ⥽ B) ⥽ (~B ⥽ ~A)	1,S1-11M

S1-15D. A ⥽ B ⊢ ~B ⥽ ~ A

S1-16T. ⊢ [A ∧ ~(A ∧ B)] ⥽ ~B

Proof:	1. ⊢ (A ∧ B) ⥽ (A ∧ B)	S1-4T
	2. ⊢ [A ∧ ~(A ∧ B)] ⥽ ~B	1, S1-10D

S1-16D. A, ~(A ∧ B) ⊢ ~B

S1-17D. ~(A ∧ ~B), ~(A ∧ B) ⊢ ~A

Proof:	1. ~(A ∧ ~B), ~(A ∧ B) ⊢ [A ∧ ~(A ∧ B)] ⥽ ~B	S1-16T
	2. ~(A ∧ ~B), ~(A ∧ B) ⊢ [A ∧ ~(A ∧ ~B)] ⥽ ~~B	S1-16T
	3. ~(A ∧ ~B), ~(A ∧ B) ⊢ [A ∧ ~(A ∧ ~B)] ⥽ B	2,S E S1-11M
	4. ~(A ∧ ~B), ~(A ∧ B) ⊢ ~~[A ∧ ~(A ∧ ~B)] ⥽ B	3,S E S1-11M
	5. ~(A ∧ ~B), ~(A ∧ B) ⊢ ~B ⥽ ~ [A ∧ ~(A ∧ ~B)]	4,S1-7D

6. $\sim(A \wedge \sim B), \sim(A \wedge B) \vdash [A \wedge \sim(A \wedge B)] \prec \sim[A \wedge \sim(A \wedge \sim B)]$ — 1,5, S1-6D

7. $\sim(A \wedge \sim B), \sim(A \wedge B) \vdash (A \wedge \sim\sim[A \wedge \sim(A \wedge \sim B)]) \prec \sim\sim(A \wedge B)$ — 6, S1-10D

8. $\sim(A \wedge \sim B), \sim(A \wedge B) \vdash \llbracket A \wedge [A \wedge \sim(A \wedge \sim B)]\rrbracket \prec (A \wedge B)$ — 7,SE,S1-11M

9. $\sim(A \wedge \sim B), \sim(A \wedge B) \vdash [(A \wedge A) \wedge \sim(A \wedge \sim B)] \prec (A \wedge B)$ — 8,SE,S1-11M

10. $\sim(A \wedge \sim B), \sim(A \wedge B) \vdash [A \wedge \sim(A \wedge \sim B)] \prec (A \wedge B)$ — 9,SE,S1-11M

11. $\sim(A \wedge \sim B), \sim(A \wedge B) \vdash [\sim(A \wedge \sim B) \wedge A] \prec [A \wedge \sim(A \wedge \sim B)]$ — 10, Ax-3

12. $\sim(A \wedge \sim B), \sim(A \wedge B) \vdash [\sim(A \wedge \sim B) \wedge A] \prec (A \wedge B)$ — 10,11,S1-6D

13. $\sim(A \wedge \sim B), \sim(A \wedge B) \vdash [\sim(A \wedge \sim B) \wedge \sim(A \wedge B)] \prec \sim A$ — 12,S1-10D

14. $\sim(A \wedge \sim B), \sim(A \wedge B) \vdash \sim(A \wedge \sim B) \wedge \sim(A \wedge B)$ — Premise

15. $\sim(A \wedge \sim B), \sim(A \wedge B) \vdash \sim A$ — 13,14,MMP

S1-18T. $\vdash \sim A \prec \sim(A \wedge B)$ — Exercise

Proof: 1. $\vdash (A \wedge B) \prec A$ — Ax-4

2. $\vdash \sim\sim(A \wedge B) \prec A$ — 1, S1-11M

3. $\vdash \sim A \prec \sim(A \wedge B)$ — 2, S1-7D

S1-19T. $\vdash \sim[A \wedge \sim\sim(B \wedge \sim A)]$

Proof: 1. $\vdash \sim(A \wedge \sim A)$ — S1-13T

2. $\vdash \sim(A \wedge \sim A) \prec [(A \wedge \sim A) \wedge B]$ — S1-18T

3. $\vdash \sim[(A \wedge \sim A) \wedge B]$ — 2, MMP

4. $\vdash \sim[A \wedge (\sim A \wedge B)]$ — 3,S1-11M

5. $\vdash \sim[A \wedge (B \wedge \sim A)]$ — 4,S1-11M

6. $\vdash \sim[A \wedge \sim\sim(B \wedge \sim A)]$ — 5,S1-11M

S1-20T. $\vdash \sim\llbracket\sim[A \wedge \sim\sim(B \wedge \sim C)] \wedge \sim\sim[\sim(A \wedge \sim B) \wedge \sim\sim(A \wedge \sim C)]\rrbracket$

Proof:

1.	⊢ ⟦[~(A ∧~B) ∧ (A ∧ ~C)] ∧ ~[A ∧ (B ∧ ~C)]⟧ ⥽ [~(A ∧ ~B) ∧ (A ∧ ~C)]	Ax4
2.	⊢ ⟦[~(A∧~B)∧~~(A∧~C)] ∧ ~[A ∧ ~~(B ∧ ~C)]⟧ ⥽ [~(A ∧ ~B) ∧ (A ∧ ~C)]	1,SE,S1-11M
3.	⊢ ⟦~[A∧~~(B∧~C)]∧~~[~(A∧~B)∧~~(A∧~C)]⟧ ⥽ [~(A ∧ ~B) ∧ (A ∧ ~C)]	2,SE,S1-11M
4.	⊢ ⟦~[A∧~~(B∧~C)] ∧~~[~(A∧~B)∧~~(A∧~C)] ⥽ ⟦[~(A ∧ ~B) ∧ A] ∧ ~C⟧	3,SE,S1-11M
5.	⊢ ⟦[~(A ∧ ~B) ∧ A] ∧ ~C⟧ ⥽ [~(A ∧ ~B) ∧ A]	Ax4
6.	⊢ ⟦~[A∧~~(B∧~C)]∧~~[~(A∧~B)∧~~(A∧~C)]⟧ ⥽ [~(A ∧ ~B) ∧ A]	4,5,S1-6D
7.	⊢ ⟦~[A∧~~(B∧~C)]∧~~[~(A∧~B)∧~~(A∧~C)]⟧ ⥽ [A ∧ ~(A ∧ ~B)]	6,SE,S1-11M
8.	⊢ [A ∧ ~(A ∧ ~B)] ⥽ ~~B	S1-16T
9.	⊢ ⟦~[A ∧ ~~(B ∧ ~C)] ∧ ~~[~(A ∧ ~B) ∧ ~~(A ∧ ~C)]⟧ ⥽ ~~B	7,8,S1-6D
10.	⊢ [⟦~[(~C ∧ A) ∧ B] ∧ (~C ∧ A)⟧ ∧ ~(A ∧ ~B)] ⥽ ⟦~[(~C ∧ A) ∧ B] ∧ (~C ∧ A)⟧	Ax4
11.	⊢ ⟦~[(~C ∧ A) ∧ B] ∧ (~C ∧ A)⟧ ⥽ ~B	S1-16T
12.	⊢ [⟦~[(~C ∧ A) ∧ B] ∧ (~C ∧ A)⟧ ∧ ~(A ∧ ~B)] ⥽ ~B	10,11,S1-6D
13.	⊢ {⟦~[A ∧ (B ∧ ~C)] ∧ (A ∧ ~C)⟧ ∧ ~(A ∧ ~B)} ⥽ ~B	12,SE,S1-9M
14.	⊢ ⟦~[A ∧ (B ∧ ~C)] ∧ [~(A ∧ ~B) ∧ (A ∧ ~C)]⟧ ⥽ ~B	13,SE,S1-9M
15.	⊢ ~~⟦~[A ∧ (B ∧ ~C)] ∧ [~(A ∧ ~B) ∧ (A ∧ ~C)]⟧ ⥽ ~B	14,SE,S1-9M
16.	⊢ ~~B ⥽ ~⟦~[A ∧ (B ∧ ~C)] ∧ [~(A ∧ ~B) ∧ (A ∧ ~C)]⟧	15,S1-7D
17.	⊢ ⟦~[A∧ ~~(B∧~C)] ∧ ~~[~(A∧~B) ∧ ~~(A∧~C)]⟧ ⥽ ~⟦~[A ∧ (B ∧ ~C)] ∧ [~(A ∧ ~B) ∧ (A ∧ ~C)]⟧	9,16,S1-6D
18.	⊢ ~{⟦~[A∧ ~~(B∧~C)] ∧ ~~[~(A∧~B) ∧ ~~(A∧~C)]⟧ ∧ ~~⟦~[A∧~~(B∧~C)] ∧ ~~[~(A∧~B)∧~~(A∧~C)]}	17,S1-14D
19.	⊢ ~{⟦~[A ∧ ~~(B ∧ ~C)] ∧ ~~[~(A∧~B) ∧~~(A∧~C]⟧ ∧ ⟦~[A∧~~(B∧~C)] ∧ ~~[~(A∧~B)∧ ~~(A∧~C)]⟧}	18,S1-11M
20.	⊢~⟦~[A∧~~(B∧~C)] ∧ ~~[~(A∧ ~B) ∧ ~~(A∧ ~C)]⟧	19,S1-11M

S1-21T. ⊢ ~[(A ∧ B) ∧ ~A]

Proof: 1. ⊢ (A ∧ B) ⥽ A	Ax4
2. ⊢ ~[(A ∧ B) ∧ ~A]	1, S1-14D

S1-22T. ⊢ ~[(A ∧ B) ∧ ~B] Exercise

S1-23T. ⊢ ~⟦A ∧ ~~[B ∧ ~(A ∧ B)]⟧

Proof: 1. ⊢ ~[(A ∧ B) ∧ ~(A ∧ B)]	S1-13T
2. ⊢ ~⟦A ∧ [B ∧ ~(A ∧ B)]⟧	1, SE, S1-9M
3. ⊢ ~⟦A ∧ ~~[B ∧ ~(A ∧ B)]⟧	2, SE, S1-11M

S1-24T. ⊢ ~[A ∧ ~~(~A ∧ ~B)]

Proof: 1. ⊢ ~(A ∧ ~A)	S1-13T
2. ⊢ ~(A ∧ ~A) ⥽ ~[(A ∧ ~A) ∧ ~B]	S1-19T
3. ⊢ ~[(A ∧ ~A) ∧ ~B]	1,2, MMP
4. ⊢ ~[A ∧ (~A ∧ ~B)]	3, S1-11M
5. ⊢ ~[A ∧ ~~(~A ∧ ~B)]	3, S1-11M

S1-25T. ⊢ ~⟦~(A ∧ ~B) ∧ ~~[~(~A ∧ ~B) ∧ ~B]⟧

Proof: 1. ⊢ ⟦[~(~A ∧ ~B) ∧ ~B] ∧ ~(A ∧ ~B) ⟧ ⥽ [~(~A ∧ ~B) ∧ ~B]	Ax4
2. ⊢ ⟦ ~(A ∧ ~B) ∧ [~(~A ∧ ~B) ∧ ~B]⟧ ⥽ [~(~A ∧ ~B) ∧ ~B]	1, S1-11M
3. ⊢ ⟦ ~(A ∧ ~B) ∧ [~(~A ∧ ~B) ∧ ~B]⟧ ⥽ [~B ∧ ~(~A ∧ ~B)]	2, S1-11M
4. ⊢ [~B ∧ ~(~A ∧ ~B)] ⥽ ~~A	S1-16T
5. ⊢ ⟦ ~(A ∧ ~B) ∧ [~(~A ∧ ~B) ∧ ~B]⟧ ⥽ ~~A	3,4, S1-6D
6. ⊢ ~~⟦ ~(A ∧ ~B) ∧ [~(~A ∧ ~B) ∧ ~B]⟧ ⥽ A	5, S1-11M
7. ⊢ ~A ⥽ ~⟦ ~(A ∧ ~B) ∧ [~(~A ∧ ~B) ∧ ~B]⟧	6, S1-7D
8. ⊢ ⟦[~B ∧ ~(~B ∧ A)] ∧ ~(~A ∧ ~B)⟧ ⥽ [~B ∧ ~(~B ∧ A)]	Ax4
9. ⊢ [~B ∧ ~(~B ∧ A)] ⥽ ~A	S1-16T
10. ⊢ ⟦[~B ∧ ~(~B ∧ A)] ∧ ~(~A ∧ ~B)⟧ ⥽ ~A	8,9, S1-6D

11. ⊢ ⟦[~B ∧ ~(A ∧ ~B)] ∧ ~(~A ∧ ~B)⟧ ⥽ ~A	10,S1-11M
12. ⊢ ⟦ ~(A ∧ ~B) ∧ [~(~A ∧ ~B) ∧ ~B]⟧ ⥽ ~A	11,S1-11M
13. ⊢ ~~⟦ ~(A ∧ ~B) ∧ [~(~A ∧ ~B) ∧ ~B]⟧ ⥽ ~A	12,S1-11M
14. ⊢~~A ⥽ ~⟦ ~(A ∧ ~B) ∧ [~(~A ∧ ~B) ∧ ~B]⟧	13,S1-7D
15. ⊢ ⟦~(A ∧ ~B) ∧ [~(~A ∧ ~B) ∧ ~B]⟧ ⥽ ~⟦ ~(A ∧ ~B) ∧ [~(~A ∧ ~B) ∧ ~B]	5,14,S1-6D
16. ⊢ ⟦ ~(A ∧ ~B) ∧ [~(~A ∧ ~B) ∧ ~B]⟧ ∧ ~~⟦ ~(A ∧ ~B) ∧ [~(~A ∧ ~B) ∧ ~B]⟧	15, S1-14T
17. ⊢ ⟦ ~(A ∧ ~B) ∧ [~(~A ∧ ~B) ∧ ~B]⟧ ∧ ⟦~(A ∧ ~B) ∧ [~(~A ∧ ~B) ∧ ~B]⟧	16,S1-11M
18. ⊢ ⟦~(A ∧ ~B) ∧ [~(~A ∧ ~B) ∧ ~B]⟧	17, S1-11M
19. ⊢ ⟦ ~(A ∧ ~B) ∧ ~~[~(~A ∧ ~B) ∧ ~B]⟧	18, S1-11M

S1-26M. Every T- and D-theorem of NKC1 (and hence of NKC) is a theorem of S1 (and hence of S2- S5 and S1*- S5*).

Proof: By S1-19T through S1-25T and S1-16D, S1 R-includes NKC1.

S1-26M shows that S1 can be considered an extension of the complete logic NKC. Since all of our other S systems are extensions of S1, the same will hold for them as well. But since all the axioms are tautological (i.e. L-true in two-valued logic), if ⥽ were interpreted as material implication, C1NEAK (which is also a complete logic and thus in an important sense equivalent to NKC) would be an extension of S1. Despite this, S1 (and the other S systems) are not equivalent to NKC and C1NEAK because the sense in which S1 is an extension of NKC requires that ⥽ be considered an additional connective and although ⊃ is definable in NKC, it cannot be identified with ⥽. In other words, the somewhat broad sense of "equivalence," whereby one can speak of the equivalence of P1A and P1N, or of NKC and C1NEAK, only preserves R-inclusion properties subject to the transformations. While we can, with the help of definition (i.e., notational abbreviation), reproduce C1NEAK in NKC, the resulting implication introduced by this abbreviation cannot be identified with ⥽.

Note in passing that although S1* is a proper extension of S1, no T-theorem is provable in S1* which is not provable in S1. This is clear because no primitive rule allows the elimination of premises and hence if ⊢A holds at all, there is a derivation of A which never introduces any premise. It might be thought that this means that S1 and S1* are equivalent, but as we shall subsequently see, this is not the case.

S1 (and S1*) has a certain odd characteristic, namely, the presence of theorems of the form ⊢ (A ∧ B) ⥽ C where we also have ⊢ B but nevertheless, we do not have ⊢ A ⥽ C. An example follows:

S1-27T. ⊢ ⟦[(B ∧ C) ⥽ (B ∧ C)] ∧ (A ⥽ B)⟧ ⥽ [(A ∧ C) ⥽ (B ∧ C)]

Proof:

1.	⊢ {⟦[C ∧ ~(B ∧ C)] ⥽ ~B⟧∧(~B ⥽ ~A)} ⥽ ⟦[C ∧ ~(B ∧ C)] ⥽ ~A⟧	Ax8
2.	⊢ [(C ∧ B) ⥽ (B ∧ C)] ⥽ ⟦[C ∧ ~(B ∧ C)] ⥽ ~B⟧	S1-10T
3.	⊢ [(B ∧ C) ⥽ (B ∧ C)] ⥽ ⟦[C ∧ ~(B ∧ C)] ⥽ ~B⟧	2,S1-11M
4.	⊢ ⟦[C ∧ ~(B ∧ C)] ⥽ ~B⟧ ⥽ [(C ∧ ~~B) ⥽ ~~(B ∧ C)]	S1-10T
5.	⊢ ⟦[C ∧~(B ∧ C)] ⥽ ~B⟧ ⥽ [(C ∧ B) ⥽ (B ∧ C)]	4,S1-11M
6.	⊢ ⟦[C ∧ ~(B ∧ C)] ⥽ ~B⟧ ⥽ [(B ∧ C) ⥽ (B ∧ C)]	5,S1-11M
7.	⊢ ⟦[(B ∧ C) ⥽ (B ∧ C)] ∧ (~B ⥽ ~A)⟧ ⥽ ⟦[C ∧ ~(B ∧ C)] ⥽ ~A⟧	1,SE,3,6
8.	⊢ (A ⥽ B) ⥽ (~B ⥽ ~A)	S1-7T
9.	⊢ (~B ⥽ ~A) ⥽ (~~A ⥽ ~~B)	S1-7T
10.	⊢ (~B ⥽ ~A) ⥽ (A ⥽ B)	9,S1-11M
11.	⊢ ⟦[(B ∧ C) ⥽ (B ∧ C)] ∧ (A ⥽ B)⟧ ⥽ ⟦[C ∧ ~(B ∧ C)] ⥽ ~A⟧	7,SE,8,10
12.	⊢ ⟦[C ∧ ~(B ∧ C)] ⥽ ~A⟧ ⥽ [(C ∧ ~~A) ⥽ ~~(B ∧ C)]	S1-7T
13.	⊢ ⟦[C ∧ ~(B ∧ C)] ⥽ ~A⟧ ⥽ [(C ∧ A) ⥽ (B ∧ C)]	12,S1-11M
14.	⊢ ⟦[C ∧ ~(B ∧ C)] ⥽ ~A⟧ ⥽ [(A ∧ C) ⥽ (B ∧ C)]]	13,S1-11M
15.	⊢ [(C ∧ A) ⥽ (B ∧ C)] ⥽ ⟦[C ∧ ~(B ∧ C)] ⥽ ~A⟧	S1-7T
16.	⊢ [(A ∧ C) ⥽ (B ∧ C)] ⥽ ⟦[C ∧ ~(B ∧ C)] ⥽ ~A⟧	15,S1-11M
17.	⊢ ⟦[(B ∧ C) ⥽ (B ∧ C)] ∧ (A ⥽ B)⟧ ⥽ [(A ∧ C) ⥽ (B ∧ C)]	11,SE,14,16

S1-27D. A ⥽ B ⊢ (A ∧ C) ⥽ (B ∧ C)

Proof:

1.	A ⥽ B ⊢ ⟦[(B ∧ C) ⥽ (B ∧ C)] ∧ (A ⥽ B)⟧ ⥽ [(A ∧ C) ⥽ (B ∧ C)]	S1-27D

2. A ⥽ B ⊢ A ⥽ B	Premise
3. A ⥽ B ⊢ (B ∧ C) ⥽ (B ∧ C)	S1-4T
4. A ⥽ B ⊢ [(B ∧ C) ⥽ (B ∧ C)] ∧ (A ⥽ B)	2,3, A
5. A ⥽ B ⊢ (A ∧ C) ⥽ (B ∧ C)	1,4, MMP

S1-28M. The following do not hold in **S**1:

⊢ (A ⥽ B) ⥽ [(A ∧ C) ⥽(B ∧ C)] and ⊢ ◇(A ∧ B) ⥽ ◇A.

Proof: Consider the following four-valued logic **R** with 2 and 3 designated:

q	∧				~p	⥽				p ⥽ ~p	◇p	p ∧ ~q				~◇(p ∧ ~q)			
p	0	1	2	3		0	1	2	3			0	1	2	3	0	1	2	3
0	0	0	0	0	3	2	2	2	2	2	1	0	0	0	0	2	2	2	2
1	0	1	0	1	2	0	2	0	2	0	3	1	0	1	0	0	2	0	2
2	0	0	2	2	1	1	1	2	2	1	2	2	2	0	0	1	1	2	2
3	0	1	2	3	0	0	1	0	2	0	3	3	2	1	0	0	1	0	2

We will call a property P **conjunction-stable** provided A ∧ B has P iff both A and B do. We will call a property P **preserved under implication** provided if A has P and A ⥽ B takes a designated value, B also has P. We note from the above tables that the following properties are both conjunction-stable and preserved under implication: (1) taking the value 3, (2) taking a designated value, (3) taking an odd value. We also note that A ⥽ B takes a non-designated value iff for one of the above 3 properties A has that property and B lacks it. It follows immediately that if A and B take the same value, A ⥽ B takes only designated values. Each of the following pairs of expressions always take the same values (as can be verified with the above table): A ∧ B and B ∧ A ; A and A ∧ A ; A and ~~A ; A ⥽ B and ~◇(A ∧ ~B) Hence axioms 1, 2, 3, 5, and 7 take only designated values. Similarly because each of the three properties are conjunction-stable and preserved under implication, axioms 4 and 6 can take only designated values, since the antecedent must take one of the three properties and hence the consequent cannot lack that property. For the remaining two axioms, we note that A ⥽ B cannot take the value 3. Hence if it takes a designated value, that value is

2, and if it takes an odd value, that value is 1. Also if $A \prec B$ takes 1, A takes a designated value and takes a non-designated value. Hence if axiom 8 takes a non-designated value, either (1) $(A \prec B) \wedge (B \prec C)$ takes 1 and hence both take 1 (since they cannot take 3), and therefore B takes a value which is both designated and undesignated; or (2)$(A \prec B) \wedge (B \prec C)$ takes 2 and so do both $A \prec B$ and $B \prec C$, while $A \prec C$ does not. But then A must have one of the three properties which C lacks and hence, since they are conjunction- stable and preserved under implication, C must have that property. Consequently axiom 8 can take only designated values. Finally, if axiom 9 takes a non-designated value, either (1) $A \wedge (A \prec B)$ takes an odd value and B does not or (2) $A \wedge (A \prec B)$ takes a designated value and B does not. If (1) both A and $A \prec B$ take odd values and hence $A \prec B$ take 1 and thus A must take 3 and therefore B takes 1, which is an odd value. If (2), both A and $A \prec B$ take designated values and hence so does B. Consequently, all axioms take only designated values.

Since taking a designated value is both conjunction-stable and preserved under implication, **MMP** and **A** preserve taking only designated values. Also $\models A \prec B$ and $\models B \prec A$ imply A and B always take the same value and hence SE (and trivially SHE) also preserves taking only designated values. Hence $\vdash_{\mathbf{S1}} A$ implies $\models_{\mathbf{R}} A$.

If A takes 3 and both B and C take 1, $A \prec B$ takes 1, $A \wedge C$ takes 1, $B \wedge C$ takes 1, hence $(A \wedge C) \prec (B \wedge C)$ takes 2 and $(A \prec B) \prec [(A \wedge C) \prec (B \wedge C)]$ takes 0, and hence is not provable in **S1**. If A takes 2 and B takes 0, $A \wedge B$ takes 0, hence $\Diamond(A \wedge B)$ takes 1. Similarly, $\Diamond A$ takes 2 and hence $\Diamond(A \wedge B) \prec \Diamond A$ takes 0 and hence is not provable in **S1**.

Since Lewis' stated purpose is "to develop a calculus based upon a meaning of implies such that 'p implies q' will be synonymous with 'q is deducible from p' ", this result is odd indeed since $(A \wedge C) \prec (B \wedge C)$ is deducible from $A \prec B$ by **S1**-27D, but $(A \prec B) \prec [(A \wedge C) \prec (B \wedge C)]$ is not provable. The easiest way to guarantee that this kind of anomaly will not happen is to add a weak form of conditionalization (which we will call **WFC**) $A \vdash B \Rightarrow \vdash A \rightarrow B$ to our systems, S1-S5, and S1*-S5*, calling the resulting DZOSs S1'-S5' and S1*'-S5*'. We then obtain:

S1'-1M. All D- and T-theorems of S1 (S2, S3, S4, S5) are theorems of S1' (S2', S3', S4', S5').

Proof: This is trivial.

S1'-2T. $\vdash \Diamond(A \wedge B) \rightarrow \Diamond A$

Proof:

1. $\sim\Diamond A \vdash \sim\sim(A \rightarrow \sim A)$	S1-4T, SE, ◇Df
2. $\sim\Diamond A \vdash A \rightarrow \sim A$	1, SE, S1-11M
3. $\sim\Diamond A \vdash (A \wedge B) \rightarrow A$	Ax4
4. $\sim\Diamond A \vdash (A \wedge B) \rightarrow \sim A$	2,3, S1-6D
5. $\sim\Diamond A \vdash \sim A \rightarrow \sim(A \wedge B)$	3, S1-15D
6. $\sim\Diamond A \vdash (A \wedge B) \rightarrow \sim(A \wedge B)$	4,5, S1-6D
7. $\vdash \sim\Diamond A \rightarrow [(A \wedge B) \rightarrow \sim(A \wedge B)]$	6, WFC
8. $\vdash \sim[(A \wedge B) \rightarrow \sim(A \wedge B)] \rightarrow \Diamond A$	7, S1-7D
9. $\vdash \Diamond(A \wedge B) \rightarrow \Diamond A$	8, ◇Df

S1'-3M. S1' and S2' (and hence also S1*' and S2*') are equivalent.

Proof: S2' obviously R-includes S1'. The converse holds by S1'-2T.

S1'-4T. $\vdash (A \rightarrow B) \rightarrow [[\sim B \rightarrow (\sim B \wedge \sim A)] \wedge [(\sim B \wedge \sim A) \rightarrow \sim B]]$

Proof:

1. $\sim B \wedge \sim\sim A \vdash \sim\sim A$	S1-2D
2. $\sim B \wedge \sim\sim A \vdash \sim\sim A \rightarrow \sim(\sim B \wedge \sim A)$	S1-8T
3. $\sim B \wedge \sim\sim A \vdash \sim(\sim B \wedge \sim A)$	1,2, MMP
4. $\sim B \wedge \sim\sim A \vdash \sim\sim B$	S1-1D
5. $\sim B \wedge \sim\sim A \vdash \sim B \wedge \sim(\sim B \wedge \sim A)$	3,4, A
6. $\vdash (\sim B \wedge \sim\sim A) \rightarrow [\sim B \wedge \sim(\sim B \wedge \sim A)]$	5, WFC
7. $\sim B \wedge \sim(\sim B \wedge \sim A) \vdash \sim B$	S1-1D
8. $\sim B \wedge \sim(\sim B \wedge \sim A) \vdash \sim(\sim B \wedge \sim A)$	S1-2D
9. $\sim B \wedge \sim(\sim B \wedge \sim A) \vdash A$	7,8, NKC-2D
10. $\sim B \wedge \sim(\sim B \wedge \sim A) \vdash \sim\sim A$	9, S1-11M

11. ~B ∧ ~(~B ∧ ~A) ⊢ ~B ∧ ~~A	7,10, A
12. ⊢ [~B ∧ ~(~B ∧ ~A)] ⥽ (~B ∧ ~~A)	11, WFC
13. A ⥽ B ⊢ ~B ⥽ ~A	𝐒1-15D
14. A ⥽ B ⊢ (~B ⥽ ~A) ⥽ ~◇(~B ∧ ~~A)	Ax1
15. A ⥽ B ⊢ ~◇(~B ∧ ~~A)	13,14, MMP
16. A ⥽ B ⊢ ~◇[~B ∧ ~(~B ∧ ~A)]	15, SE, 6,12
17. A ⥽ B ⊢ ~◇[~B ∧ ~(~B ∧ ~A)] ⥽ [~B ⥽ (~B ∧ ~A)]	Ax2
18. A ⥽ B ⊢ ~B ⥽ (~B ∧ ~A)	16,17, MMP
19. A ⥽ B ⊢ (~B ∧ ~A) ⥽ ~B	Ax4
20. A ⥽ B ⊢ [~B ⥽ (~B ∧ ~A)] ∧ [(~B ∧ ~A) ⥽ ~B]	18,19, A
21. ⊢ (A ⥽ B) ⥽ [~B ⥽ (~B ∧ ~A)] ∧ [(~B ∧ ~A) ⥽ ~B]	20, WFC

𝐒1′-5T. ⊢ (A ⥽ B) ⥽ [(A ∧ C) ⥽ (B ∧ C)]

Proof:

1. A ⥽ B ⊢ (A ∧ C) ⥽ (B ∧ C)	𝐒1-27D
2. ⊢ (A ⥽ B) ⥽ [(A ∧ C) ⥽ (B ∧ C)]	1, WFC

𝐒1′-6T. ⊢ [(A ⥽ B) ∧ (A ⥽ C)] ⥽ [A ⥽ (B ∧ C)]

Proof:

1. (A ⥽ B) ∧ (A ⥽ C) ⊢ A ⥽ B	𝐒1-1D
2. (A ⥽ B) ∧ (A ⥽ C) ⊢ (A ∧ C) ⥽ (B ∧ C)	1, 𝐒1′-5T
3. (A ⥽ B) ∧ (A ⥽ C) ⊢ A ⥽ C	𝐒1-2D
4. (A ⥽ B) ∧ (A ⥽ C) ⊢ (A ∧ A) ⥽ (C ∧ A)	3, 𝐒1′-5T
5. (A ⥽ B) ∧ (A ⥽ C) ⊢ A ⥽ (A ∧ C)	4, 𝐒1-11M
6. (A ⥽ B) ∧ (A ⥽ C) ⊢ A ⥽ (B ∧ C)	5,2, 𝐒1-6D
7. ⊢ [(A ⥽ B) ∧ (A ⥽ C)] ⥽ [A ⥽ (B ∧ C)]	6, WFC

𝐒1′-7T. ⊢ (~◇~A ∧ ~◇~B) ⥽ ~◇~(A ∧ B)

Proof:

1. ~◇~A ∧ ~◇~B ⊢ ~◇~A	𝐒1-1D
2. ~◇~A ∧ ~◇~B ⊢ ~◇~B	𝐒1-2D
3. ~◇~A ∧ ~◇~B ⊢ ◇[~A ∧ ~(A ∧ B)] ⥽ ◇~A	𝐒1′-2T
4. ~◇~A ∧ ~◇~B ⊢ ~◇~A ⥽ ~◇ [~A ∧ ~(A ∧ B)]	3, 𝐒1′-2T
5. ~◇~A ∧ ~◇~B ⊢ ~◇ [~A ∧ ~(A ∧ B)]	1,4, MMP
6. ~◇~A ∧ ~◇~B ⊢ ~◇[~(A ∧ B)] ∧ ~A]	5, 𝐒1-11

7. ~◇~A ∧ ~◇~B ⊢ ~◇[~(A ∧ B)] ∧ ~A] ⥽ [~(A ∧ B) ⥽ A] — Ax2
8. ~◇~A ∧ ~◇~B ⊢ ~(A ∧ B) ⥽ A — 6,7, MMP
9. ~◇~A ∧ ~◇~B ⊢ ◇[~B ∧ ~(B ∧ A)] ⥽ ◇~B — S1'-2T
10. ~◇~A ∧ ~◇~B ⊢ ◇[~(A ∧ B) ∧ ~B] ⥽ ◇~B — 9, S1-11M
11. ~◇~A ∧ ~◇~B ⊢ ~◇~B ⥽ ~◇[~(A ∧ B) ∧ ~B] — 10, S1-15D
12. ~◇~A ∧ ~◇~B ⊢ ~◇[~(A ∧ B) ∧ ~B] — 2,11, MMP
13. ~◇~A ∧ ~◇~B ⊢ ~◇[~(A ∧ B)] ∧ ~B] ⥽ [~(A ∧ B) ⥽ B] — Ax2
14. ~◇~A ∧ ~◇~B ⊢ ~(A ∧ B) ⥽ B — 12,13, MMP
15. ~◇~A ∧ ~◇~B ⊢ ⟦[~(A ∧ B) ⥽ A] ∧ [~(A ∧ B) ⥽ B] ⥽ [~(A ∧ B) ⥽ (A ∧ B)] — S1'-6T
16. ~◇~A ∧ ~◇~B ⊢ [~(A ∧ B) ⥽ A] ∧ [~(A ∧ B) ⥽ B] — 8,14, A
17. ~◇~A ∧ ~◇~B ⊢ ~(A ∧ B) ⥽ (A ∧ B) — 15,16, MMP
18. ~◇~A ∧ ~◇~B ⊢ ~~[~(A ∧ B) ⥽ ~~(A ∧ B)] — 17, S1-11M
19. ~◇~A ∧ ~◇~B ⊢ ~◇~(A ∧ B) — 18, ◇ df
20. ⊢ (~◇~A ∧ ~◇~B) ⥽ ~◇~(A ∧ B) — 19, WFC

S1'-8T. ⊢ ~◇~(A ∧ B) ⥽ ~◇~A

Proof:
1. ⊢ ◇[~(A ∧ B) ∧ ~A] ⥽ ◇~(A ∧ B) — S1'-2T
2. ⊢ ~◇~(A ∧ B) ⥽ ~◇[~(A ∧ B) ∧ ~A] — 1, S1-15T
3. A ∧ B ⊢ A — S1-1D
4. A ∧ B ⊢ ~~A — 3, S1-11M
5. ~A ⊢ ~(A ∧ B) — 4, NKC-11D
6. ~A ⊢ ~A — Premise
7. ~A ⊢ ~(A ∧ B) ∧ ~A — 5,6, A
8. ⊢ ~A ⥽ [~(A ∧ B) ∧ ~A] — 7, WFC
9. ~(A ∧ B) ∧ ~A ⊢ ~A — S1-2D
10. ⊢ [~(A ∧ B) ∧ ~A] ⥽ ~A — 9, WFC
11. ⊢ ~◇~(A ∧ B) ⥽ ~◇~A — 2, SE, 8, 10

S1'-9T. ⊢ ~◇~(A ∧ B) ⥽ (~◇~A ∧ ~◇~B)

Proof:
1. ⊢ ~◇~(A ∧ B) ⥽ ~◇~A — S1'-9T
2. ⊢ ~◇~(B ∧ A) ⥽ ~◇~B — S1'-9T

3. ⊢ ∼◇∼(A ∧ B) ⥽ ∼◇∼B	2,S1-11M
4. ⊢ [[∼◇∼(A ∧ B) ⥽ ∼◇∼A] ∧ [∼◇∼(A ∧ B) ⥽ ∼◇∼B]] ⥽ [∼◇∼(A∧B)⥽(∼◇∼A∧∼∼B)]	S1'-9T
5. ⊢ [∼◇∼(A ∧ B) ⥽ ∼◇∼A] ∧ [∼◇∼(B ∧ A) ⥽ ∼◇∼B]	1,3, A
6. ⊢ ∼◇∼(A∧B) ⥽ (∼◇∼A∧∼∼B)	4,5, MMP

S1*'-1T. ⊢ (A ⥽ B) ⥽ (∼◇B ⥽ ∼◇A)

Proof:

1. A⥽B⊢(A⥽B) ⥽ [[∼B⥽(∼B∧∼A)]∧[(∼B∧∼A)⥽∼B]]	S1'-4T
2. A ⥽ B ⊢ A ⥽ B	Premise
3. A ⥽ B ⊢ [∼B ⥽ (∼B ∧ ∼A)] ∧ [(∼B ∧ ∼A) ⥽ ∼B]	1,2, MMP
4. A ⥽ B ⊢ ∼B ⥽ (∼B ∧ ∼A)	3, S1-1D
5. A ⥽ B ⊢ (∼B ∧ ∼A) ⥽ ∼B	4, S1-2D
6. A ⥽ B ⊢ ∼◇∼∼B ⥽ ∼◇∼∼B	S1-4T
7. A ⥽ B ⊢ ∼◇∼∼B ⥽ ∼◇∼(∼B ∧ ∼A)	6, SHE,4,5
8. A ⥽ B ⊢ ∼◇B ⥽ ∼◇∼(∼B ∧ ∼A)	7,S1-11M
9. A ⥽ B ⊢ ∼◇∼(∼B ∧ ∼A)⥽ (∼◇∼∼B ∧ ∼◇∼∼A)	S1'-9T
10. A ⥽ B ⊢ ∼◇B ⥽ (∼◇∼∼B ∧ ∼◇∼∼A)	8,9, S1-6D
11. A ⥽ B ⊢ ∼◇B ⥽ (∼◇B ∧ ∼◇A)	10,S1-11M
12. A ⥽ B ⊢ (∼◇A ∧ ∼◇B) ⥽ ∼◇A	Ax4
13. A ⥽ B ⊢ (∼◇B ∧ ∼◇A) ⥽ ∼◇A	12,S1-11M
14. A ⥽ B ⊢ ∼◇B ⥽ ∼◇A	11,13, S1-6D
15. ⊢ (A ⥽ B) ⥽ (∼◇B ⥽ ∼◇A)	14, WFC

S1'-10T. ⊢ ∼◇A ⥽ ∼A

Proof:

1. ∼◇A ⊢ ∼∼(A ⥽ ∼A)	◇df
2. ∼◇A ⊢ A ⥽ ∼A	1,S1-11M
3. ∼◇A ⊢ ∼(A ∧ ∼∼A)	2, S1-14D
4. ∼◇A ⊢ ∼(A ∧ A)	3,S1-11M
5. ∼◇A ⊢ ∼A	4,S1-11M
6. ⊢ ∼◇A ⥽ ∼A	5, WFC

S1*'-2M. S1*' and S3*' are equivalent.

Proof: S3*' obviously R-includes S1*'. Since S1*' R-includes S1', which is equivalent to S2' by S1'-3M, S1*' R-includes S2' and hence by S1'-3M, S1*' R-includes S2*' and therefore by S1*'-1T and S1'-10T, also S3*'.

S3-1M. Theorems numbered S1-1 through S1-10, S1-15 and S1-16 hold in S3.

Proof: The proofs of these theorems do not involve Ax9.

S3-2T. $\vdash (A \prec B) \prec [(A \land C) \prec (B \land C)]$

Proof:

1.	$\vdash [C \land \sim(C \land B)] \prec \sim B$	S1-16T
2.	$\vdash (A \land \sim B) \prec (A \land \sim B)$	S1-4T
3.	$\vdash \{[[A \land \sim(A \land \sim B)] \prec B] \land [B \prec \sim[C \land \sim(B \land C)]]\} \prec [[A \land \sim(A \land \sim B)] \prec \sim[C \land \sim(B \land C)]]$	Ax8
4.	$\vdash [A \land \sim(A \land \sim B)] \prec B$	2,S1-10D
5.	$\vdash \sim\sim B \prec \sim[C \land \sim(C \land B)]$	1,S1-15D
6.	$\vdash B \prec \sim[C \land \sim(C \land B)]$	5,S1-11M
7.	$\vdash [[A \land \sim(A \land \sim B)] \prec B] \land [B \prec \sim[C \land \sim(C \land B)]]$	4,6, A
8.	$\vdash [[A \land \sim(A \land \sim B)] \prec \sim[C \land \sim(B \land C)]]$	3,7, MMP
9.	$\vdash [A \land \sim\sim[C \land \sim(B \land C)]] \prec \sim\sim(A \land \sim B)$	8,S1-10D
10.	$\vdash [A \land [C \land \sim(B \land C)]] \prec (A \land \sim B)$	9,S1-11M
11.	$\vdash [(A \land C) \land \sim(B \land C)] \prec (A \land \sim B)$	10,S1-9M
12.	$\vdash [[(A \land C) \land \sim(B \land C)] \prec (A \land \sim B)] \prec [\sim\Diamond (A \land \sim B) \prec \sim\Diamond[(A \land C) \land \sim(B \land C)]]$	Ax10'
13.	$\vdash \sim\Diamond (A \land \sim B) \prec \sim\Diamond[(A \land C) \land \sim(B \land C)]$	11,12, MMP
14.	$\vdash (A \prec B) \prec \sim\Diamond(A \land \sim B)$	Ax1
15.	$\vdash (A \prec B) \prec \sim\Diamond[(A \land C) \land \sim(B \land C)]$	13,14,S1-6D
16.	$\vdash \sim\Diamond[(A \land C) \land \sim(B \land C)] \prec [(A \land C) \prec (B \land C)]$	Ax2
17.	$\vdash (A \prec B) \prec [(A \land C) \prec (B \land C)]$	15,16, S1-6D

S3-2D. $A \prec B \vdash (A \land C) \prec (B \land C)$

S3-3T. $\vdash [A \land (A \prec B)] \prec B$

Proof:

1.	$\vdash (A \land \sim B) \prec (A \land \sim B)$	S1-4T

2. ⊢ [A ∧ ~(A ∧ ~B)] ⥽ ~~B	1,S1-10D
3. ⊢ [A ∧ ~(A ∧ ~B)] ⥽ B	2,S1-11M
4. ⊢ ~◇(A ∧ ~B) ⥽ ~(A ∧ ~B)	Ax9′
5. ⊢ (A ⥽ B) ⥽ ~◇(A ∧ ~B)	Ax1
6. ⊢ (A ⥽ B) ⥽ ~(A ∧ ~B)	4,5,S1-6D
7. ⊢ [(A ⥽ B) ∧ A] ⥽ [~(A ∧ ~B) ∧ A]	6,S3-2D
8. ⊢ [A ∧ (A ⥽ B)] ⥽ [A ∧ ~(A ∧ ~B)]	7,S1-11M
9. ⊢ [A ∧ (A ⥽ B)] ⥽ B	3,8,S1-6D

S3-4T. ⊢ ◇(A ∧ B) ⥽ ◇A

Proof:	
1. ⊢ (A ∧ B) ⥽ A	Ax4
2. ⊢ [(A ∧ B) ⥽ A] ⥽ [~◇A ⥽ ~◇(A ∧ B)]	Ax10′
3. ⊢ ~◇A ⥽ ~◇(A ∧ B)	1,2,S1-6D
4. ⊢ ~~◇(A ∧ B) ⥽ ◇A	3,S1-7D
5. ⊢ ◇(A ∧ B) ⥽ ◇A	4,S1-11M

S3-5M. S3 R-includes S2.

Proof: This follows by Ax-1 to Ax-8, S3-3T and S3-4T.

S3-6T. ⊢ (A ⥽ B) ⥽ [(B ⥽ C) ⥽ (A ⥽ C)]

Proof:	
1. ⊢ (A ⥽ B) ⥽ [(A ∧ ~C) ⥽ (B ∧ ~C)]	S3-2T
2. ⊢ [(A∧~C) ⥽ (B∧~C)] ⥽ [~◇(B∧~C) ⥽ ~◇(A∧~C)]	Ax10′
3. ⊢ (B ⥽ C) ⥽ ~◇(B∧~C)	Ax1
4. ⊢ (A ⥽ C) ⥽ ~◇(A∧~C)	Ax1
5. ⊢ ~◇(B∧~C) ⥽ (B ⥽ C)	Ax2
6. ⊢ ~◇(A∧~C) ⥽ (A ⥽ C)	Ax2
7. ⊢ [(A∧~C) ⥽ (B∧~C)] ⥽ [(B ⥽ C) ⥽ (A ⥽ C)]	2,SE,3,4,5,6
8. ⊢ (A ⥽ B) ⥽ [(B ⥽ C) ⥽ (A ⥽ C)]	7,S1-6D

S3-7T. ⊢ (A ⥽ B) ⥽ [(C ⥽ A) ⥽ (C ⥽ B)]

Proof:	
1. ⊢ (~B ⥽ ~A) ⥽ [(~B ∧ C) ⥽ (~A ∧ C)]	S3-2T
2. ⊢ (A ⥽ B) ⥽ (~B ⥽ ~A)	S1-15D
3. ⊢ (A ⥽ B) ⥽ [(~B ∧ C) ⥽ (~A ∧ C)]	1,2,S1-6D

4. $\vdash [(\sim B \wedge C) \prec (\sim A \wedge C)] \prec [\sim \Diamond(\sim A \wedge C) \prec \sim \Diamond(\sim B \wedge C)]$ Ax10′
5. $\vdash [(\sim B \wedge C) \prec (\sim A \wedge C)] \prec [\sim \Diamond(C \wedge \sim A) \prec \sim \Diamond(C \wedge \sim B)]$ 3,S1-11M
6. $\vdash (C \prec A) \prec \sim \Diamond(C \wedge \sim A)$ Ax1
7. $\vdash (C \prec B) \prec \sim \Diamond(C \wedge \sim B)$ Ax1
8. $\vdash \sim \Diamond(C \wedge \sim A) \prec (C \prec A)$ Ax2
9. $\vdash \sim \Diamond(C \wedge \sim B) \prec (C \prec B)$ Ax2
10. $\vdash (A \prec B) \prec [\sim \Diamond(C \wedge \sim A) \prec \sim \Diamond(C \wedge \sim B)]$ 3,5,S1-6D
11. $\vdash (A \prec B) \prec [(C \prec A) \prec (C \prec B)]$ 10,SE,6,7,8,9

S3-8M. S3 and S3* (and consequently starred and unstarred pairs of S-systems R-including it) are equivalent.

Proof: By the argument if PL-14M, utilizing S3-6T, S3-7T, and S3-2T, SHE holds in S3, so that S3 R-includes S3*. Since the converse is trivial, because SHE implies SE, the converse holds.

S1*′-3T. $\vdash \sim \Diamond \sim A \prec \sim \Diamond \sim \sim \Diamond \sim A$

Proof: 1. $\sim \Diamond \sim A \vdash \sim \sim (\sim A \prec \sim \sim A)$ $\Diamond$ df
2. $\sim \Diamond \sim A \vdash \sim A \prec A$ 1,S1-11M
3. $\sim \Diamond \sim A \vdash (\sim A \wedge \sim A) \prec (\sim A \wedge A)$ 2,S1-27D
4. $A \wedge \sim A \vdash \sim (A \prec A)$ MKN-6D
5. $\vdash (A \wedge \sim A) \prec \sim (A \prec A)$ 4, WFC
6. $\sim \Diamond \sim A \vdash (\sim A \wedge \sim A) \prec \sim (A \prec A)$ 3,5,S1-6D
7. $\sim \Diamond \sim A \vdash \sim A \prec \sim (A \prec A)$ 6,S1-11M
8. $\sim \Diamond \sim A \vdash [\sim A \prec \sim (A \prec A)] \prec [\sim \Diamond \sim (A \prec A) \prec \sim \Diamond \sim A]$ Ax10′
9. $\sim \Diamond \sim A \vdash \sim \Diamond \sim (A \prec A) \prec \sim \Diamond \sim A$ 7,8, MMP
10. $\sim \Diamond \sim A \vdash \sim \sim \Diamond \sim A \prec \Diamond \sim (A \prec A)$ 9,S1-7D
11. $\sim \Diamond \sim A \vdash \Diamond \sim A \prec \Diamond \sim (A \prec A)$ 10,S1-11M
12. $\sim \Diamond \sim A \vdash [\Diamond \sim A \prec \Diamond \sim (A \prec A)] \prec$
$[\sim \Diamond \Diamond \sim (A \prec A) \prec \sim \Diamond \Diamond \sim A]$ Ax10′
13. $\sim \Diamond \sim A \vdash \sim \Diamond \Diamond \sim (A \prec A) \prec \sim \Diamond \Diamond \sim A$ 11,12,MMP
14. $\sim (A \prec A) \vdash A \prec A$ S1-4T
15. $\vdash \sim (A \prec A) \prec (A \prec A)$ 14,WFC
16. $\vdash \sim (A \prec A) \prec \sim \sim (A \prec A)$ 15,S1-11M

17. $\Diamond\sim(A \prec A) \vdash \sim\Diamond\sim(A \prec A)$	16, $\Diamond$df
18. $\vdash \Diamond\sim(A \prec A) \prec \sim\Diamond\sim(A \prec A)$	17,WFC
19. $\vdash \sim\Diamond\Diamond\sim(A \prec A)$	18, $\Diamond$df
20. $\sim\Diamond\sim A \vdash \sim\Diamond\Diamond\sim A$	13,19,MMP
21. $\vdash \sim\Diamond\sim A \prec \sim\Diamond\Diamond\sim A$	20,WFC
22. $\vdash \sim\Diamond\sim A \prec \sim\Diamond\sim\sim\Diamond\sim A$	21,S1-11M

S1*' accordingly R-includes even S4. To show the converse, we must establish the equivalent in S4 of the cases of P12-2M (excluding the case where w_i is an element of α and adding cases for the modal connectives). We hence turn to the appropriate lemmas.

S3-9T. $\vdash [(A \prec B) \wedge (A \prec C)] \prec [A \prec (B \wedge C)]$

Proof:

1. $\vdash [(A \prec B) \wedge (A \prec C)] \prec (A \prec B)$	Ax4
2. $\vdash (A \prec B) \prec [(A \wedge C) \prec (B \wedge C)]$	S3-2T
3. $\vdash [(A \prec B) \wedge (A \prec C)] \prec [(A \wedge C) \prec (B \wedge C)]$	1,2, S1-6D
4. $\vdash [(A \prec C) \wedge (A \prec B)] \prec (A \prec C)$	Ax4
5. $\vdash [(A \prec B) \wedge (A \prec C)] \prec (A \prec C)$	4,S1-11
6. $\vdash (A \prec C) \prec [(A \wedge A) \prec (A \wedge C)]$	S3-2T
7. $\vdash [(A \prec B) \wedge (A \prec C)] \prec [(A \wedge A) \prec (A \wedge C)]$	5,6, S1-6D
8. $\vdash [(A \prec B) \wedge (A \prec C)] \prec [A \prec (A \wedge C)]$	7,S1-11M
9. $\vdash [\![[(A \prec B) \wedge (A \prec C)] \wedge [(A \prec B) \wedge (A \prec C)]]\!] \prec [\![[(A \wedge C) \prec (B \wedge C)] \wedge [(A \prec B) \wedge (A \prec C)]]\!]$	3,S3-2D
10. $\vdash [(A \prec B) \wedge (A \prec C)] \prec [\![[(A \prec B) \wedge (A \prec C)] \wedge [(A \wedge C) \prec (B \wedge C)]]\!]$	9,S1-11M
11. $\vdash [\![[(A \prec B) \wedge (A \prec C)] \wedge [(A \wedge C) \prec (B \wedge C)]]\!] \prec [\![[A \prec (A \wedge C)] \wedge [(A \wedge C) \prec (B \wedge C)]]\!]$	8,S3-2D
12. $\vdash [(A \prec B) \wedge (A \prec C)] \prec [\![[A \prec (A \wedge C)] \wedge [(A \wedge C) \prec (B \wedge C)]]\!]$	10,11,S1-6D
13. $\vdash [\![[A \prec (A \wedge C)] \wedge [(A \wedge C) \prec (B \wedge C)]]\!] \prec [A \prec (B \wedge C)]$	Ax8
14. $\vdash [(A \prec B) \wedge (A \prec C)] \prec [A \prec (B \wedge C)]$	12,13,S1-6D

S3-9D. $A \prec B, A \prec C \vdash A \prec (B \wedge C)$

S3-10D. A ⥽ B, A ⥽ (B ⥽ C) ⊢ A ⥽ C

Proof: 1. A ⥽ B, A ⥽ (B ⥽ C) ⊢ A ⥽ [B ∧ (B ⥽ C)] S3-9D
2. A ⥽ B, A ⥽ (B ⥽ C) ⊢ [B ∧ (B ⥽ C)] ⥽ C S3-3T
3. A ⥽ B, A ⥽ (B ⥽ C) ⊢ A ⥽ C 1,2, S1-6D

For convenience, we will introduce a number of notational abbreviations, indicating their use in proofs by the notation Df throughout; specifically:

Defined term	**Definition**
A ⥼ B	(A ⥽ B) ∧ (B ⥽ A)
A ∨ B	~(~A ∧ ~B)
A ⊃ B	~(A ∧ ~B)

Note that by virtue of these abbreviations A ⥼ B ⊢ A ⥽ B is an instance of left simplification.

S3-11T. ⊢ (A ⥼ B) ⥽ (C ⥽ C)

Proof: 1. ⊢ (A ⥼ B) ⥽ (A ⥽ B) Ax4
2. ⊢ [C ∧ ~(A ∧ ~B)] ⥽ C Ax4
3. ⊢ (C ∧ ~C) ⥽ ~~(A ∧ ~B) 2, S1-10D
4. ⊢ (C ∧ ~C) ⥽ (A ∧ ~B) 3, S1-11M
5. ⊢ [(C∧~C) ⥽ (A∧~B)] ⥽
[~◇(A ∧ ~B) ⥽ ~◇ (C ∧ ~C)] Ax10'
6. ⊢ ~◇(A ∧ ~B) ⥽ ~◇ (C ∧ ~C) 4,5,MMP
7. ⊢ (A ⥽ B) ⥽ ~◇(A ∧ ~B) Ax1
8. ⊢ (A ⥽ B) ⥽ ~◇ (C ∧ ~C) 6,7, S1-6D
9. ⊢ ~◇ (C ∧ ~C) ⥽ (C ⥽ C) Ax2
10. ⊢ (A ⥽ B) ⥽ (C ⥽ C) 8,9, S1-6D
11. ⊢ (A ⥼ B) ⥽ (C ⥽ C) 1,10, S1-6D

S3-12M. If v is a variable, $\vdash_{S3}$(A ⥼ B) ⥽ (S^{v}_{A}C ⥽ S^{v}_{B}C).

Proof: This is proved by induction on the number of connectives, in a manner analogous to PL-14M, utilizing S3-6T, S3-7T, S3-2T and S3-11T.

S3-13M. If v is a variable, D ⥽ (A ⥽⥼ B) ⊢ D ⥽ ($\mathbf{S}^{v}_{A}$C ⥽ $\mathbf{S}^{v}_{B}$C).

Proof: By S3-12M and S1-6D, the result follows immediately.

S4-1T. ⊢ ~◇~(A ⥽ A)

Proof:

1.	⊢ A ⥽ A	S1-4T
2.	⊢ (A ⥽ A) ⥽ ~◇(A ∧ ~A)	Ax1
3.	⊢ ~◇(A ∧ ~A)	1,2, MMP
4.	⊢ ~◇~~(A ∧ ~A)	3,S1-11M
5.	⊢ ~◇~~(A ∧ ~A) ⥽ ~◇~~◇~~(A ∧ ~A)	Ax11
6..	⊢ ~◇~~◇ ~~ (A ∧ ~A)	4,5, MMP
7.	⊢ ~◇~~◇(A ∧ ~A)	6,S1-11M
8.	⊢ ~◇(A ∧ ~A) ⥽ (A ⥽ A)	Ax2
9.	⊢ ~◇~(A ⥽ A)	8,SE,2,8

S4-2T. ⊢ ~◇A ⥽ ~A

Proof:

1.	⊢ (A ⥽ ~A) ⥽ ~(A ∧ ~~A)	S1-14T
2.	⊢ (A ⥽ ~A) ⥽ ~(A ∧ A)	1,S1-11M
3.	⊢ ~~(A ⥽ ~A) ⥽ ~A	2,S1-11M
4.	⊢ ~◇A ⥽ ~A	3,Df

S1-29T. ⊢ ⟦(A ⥽ B) ∧ [(B ⥽ C) ∧ (C ⥽ D)]⟧ ⥽ (A ⥽ D)

Proof:

1.	⊢ [(B ⥽ C) ∧ (C ⥽ D)] ⥽ (B ⥽ D)	Ax8
2.	⊢ [(A ⥽ B) ∧ (B ⥽ D)] ⥽ (A ⥽ D)	Ax8
3.	⊢ [(A ⥽ B) ∧ ~(A ⥽ D)] ⥽ ~(B ⥽ D)	2,S1-10D
4.	⊢ ~(B ⥽ D) ⥽~[(B ⥽ C) ∧ (C ⥽ D)]	1,S1-15D
5.	⊢ [(A ⥽ B) ∧ ~(A ⥽ D)] ⥽ ~[(B ⥽ C) ∧ (C ⥽ D)]	3,4, S1-6D
6.	⊢ ⟦(A ⥽ B) ∧ ~~[(B ⥽ C) ∧ (C ⥽ D)]⟧ ⥽ (A ⥽ D)	5,S1-7D
7.	⊢ ⟦(A ⥽ B) ∧ [(B ⥽ C) ∧ (C ⥽ D)]⟧ ⥽ (A ⥽ D)	6,S1-11M

S1-30T. ⊢ [(A ⥽ B) ∧ ~◇B] ⥽ ~◇A

Proof:

1.	⊢ [(A ⥽ B) ∧ ~◇B] ⥽ [(A ⥽ B) ∧ ~◇B]	S1-4T
2.	⊢ [(A⥽B) ∧~◇B] ⥽ ⟦[(A⥽B) ∧(A⥽B)] ∧~◇(B ∧~~B)⟧	1,S1-11M

3. ⊢ [(A⥽B) ∧ ~◇B] ⥽ ⟦[(A⥽B) ∧ (A⥽B)] ∧ (B⥽~B)⟧	2, Df
4. ⊢ [(A⥽B) ∧ ~◇B] ⥽ ⟦(A⥽B) ∧ [(B⥽~B) ∧ (A⥽B)]⟧	1, S1-9M
5. ⊢ (A⥽B) ⥽ (~B ⥽ ~A)	S1-15T
6. ⊢ (~B ⥽ ~A) ⥽ (~~A ⥽ B)	S1-7T
7. ⊢ (~B ⥽ ~A) ⥽ (A ⥽ B)	6, S1-11M
8. ⊢ [(A⥽B) ∧ ~◇B] ⥽ ⟦(A⥽B) ∧ [(B⥽~B) ∧ (~B⥽~A)]⟧	7, SE, 5,7
9. ⊢ ⟦(A⥽B) ∧ [(B⥽~B) ∧ (~B⥽~A)]⟧ ⥽ (A⥽~A)	S1-29T
10. ⊢ [(A ⥽ B) ∧ ~◇B] ⥽ (A ⥽ ~A)	8,9, S1-6D
11. ⊢ [(A ⥽ B) ∧ ~◇B] ⥽ ~◇A	10, Df

S4-3T. ⊢ (A ⥽ B) ⥽ (~◇B ⥽ ~◇A)

Proof: 1. ⊢ [(A ⥽ B) ∧ ~◇B] ⥽ ~◇A	S1-31T
2. ⊢ [~◇B ∧ (A ⥽ B)] ⥽ ~◇A	1, S1-9M
3. ⊢ [~◇B ∧ ~~◇A] ⥽ ~(A ⥽ B)	2, S1-10D
4. ⊢ [(~◇B ∧ ~~◇A) ∧ (~◇B ∧ ~~◇A)] ⥽ [~(A⥽B) ∧ (~◇B ∧ ~~◇A)]	3, S1-27D
5. ⊢ (~◇B ∧ ~~◇A) ⥽ [~(A⥽B) ∧ (~◇B ∧ ~~◇A)]	4, S1-11M
6. ⊢ [(~◇B ∧ ~~◇A) ∧ ~(A⥽B)] ⥽ (~◇B ∧ ~~◇A)	Ax4
7. ⊢ [~(A⥽B) ∧ (~◇B ∧ ~~◇A)] ⥽ (~◇B ∧ ~~◇A)	6, S1-11M
8. ⊢ ◇[~(A ⥽ B) ∧ (~◇B ∧ ~~◇A)] ⥽ ◇[~(A ⥽B)]	Ax10
9. ⊢ ◇(~◇B ∧ ~~◇A) ⥽ ◇[~(A ⥽B)]	8, SE, 5,7
10. ⊢ ~◇~(A ⥽B) ⥽ ~◇(~◇B ∧ ~~◇A)	9, S1-15D
11. ⊢ (A ⥽ B) ⥽ ~◇(A ∧ ~B)	Ax1
12. ⊢ ~◇(A ∧ ~B) ⥽ (A ⥽ B)	Ax2
13. ⊢ ~◇~~◇(A ∧ ~B) ⥽ ~◇(~◇B ∧ ~~◇A)	10, SE, 11,12
14. ⊢ ~◇(~◇B ∧ ~~◇A) ⥽ (~◇B ⥽ ~◇A)	Ax2
15. ⊢ ~◇~~◇(A ∧ ~B) ⥽ (~◇B ⥽ ~◇A)	13,14, S1-6D
16. ⊢ ~◇~~(A ∧ ~B) ⥽ ~◇~~◇~~(A ∧ ~B)	Ax11
17. ⊢ ~◇~~(A ∧ ~B) ⥽ (~◇B ⥽ ~◇A)	15,16, S1-6D
18. ⊢ ~◇(A ∧ ~B) ⥽ (~◇B ⥽ ~◇A)	17, S1-11M
19. ⊢ (A ⥽ B) ⥽ ~◇(A ∧ ~B)	Ax1
20. ⊢ (A ⥽ B) ⥽ (~◇B ⥽ ~◇A)	18,19, S1-6D

S4-4M. S4 R-includes S3.

Proof: This follows by S4-2T and S4-3T.

S4-5M. $A \vdash_{S4} B \Rightarrow \ \vdash_{S4} A \prec B$

Proof: Let $A \vdash_{S4} B$. Then there exists a Y-derivation $\alpha_1 \vdash A_1, \cdots, \alpha_n \vdash A_n$ such that for each i, either $A_i \subset \alpha_i$, A_i is an axiom or $\alpha_i \vdash A_i$ follows from earlier steps by the rules of S4. Since no rule of S4 allows the elimination of a premise, we can without loss of generality require that $\alpha_i = \varnothing$ or $\alpha_i = \{A\}$. By induction on the length n of the Y-derivation, we will prove that $\vdash_{S4} A \prec A_n$.

(α) n = 1. Then either $A = A_n$ or A_n is an axiom.

Case 1: $\alpha_n \vdash A_n$ is $A \vdash A$. By S1-4T, $\vdash_{S4} A \prec A$.

Case 2: A_n is an axiom. But each axiom is of the form $B_n \prec C_n$. Hence by **Ax1** and **MMP**, $\vdash_{S4} \sim\Diamond(B_n \wedge \sim C_n)$. Hence by **Ax11** and **MMP**, $\vdash_{S4} \sim\Diamond\sim\sim\Diamond(B_n \wedge \sim C_n)$ and by **SE**, **Ax1** and **Ax2**, $\vdash_{S4} \sim\Diamond\sim A_n$. By **Ax10**, $\vdash_{S4} \Diamond(\sim A_n \wedge A) \prec \Diamond\sim A_n$. Hence, by S1-15D $\vdash_{S4} \sim\Diamond\sim A_n \prec \sim\Diamond(\sim A_n \wedge A)$ and by **MMP**, $\vdash_{S4} \sim\Diamond(\sim A_n \wedge A)$ and by S1-11M, Ax-2 and MMP, $\vdash_{S4} A \prec A_n$.

(β) Suppose the assertion is true for m< k. We will prove it for m = k.

Case 1: A_k is A or A_k is an axiom. The proof is the same as in (α) above.

Case 2. There exist i < k and j < k such that $\alpha_i = \alpha_j = \alpha_k$ and $A_j = A_i \prec A_k$. By the hypothesis of induction, $\vdash_{S4} A \prec A_i$ and $\vdash_{S4} A \prec (A_i \prec A_k)$. By S3-10D, $\vdash_{S4} A \prec A_k$.

Case 3. There exist i < k and j < k such that $\alpha_i = \alpha_j = \alpha_k$ and $A_k = A_i \wedge A_j$. By the hypothesis of induction, $\vdash_{S4} A \prec A_i$ and $\vdash_{S4} A \prec A_j$. Hence, $\vdash_{S4} A \prec (A_i \wedge A_j)$, i.e., $\vdash_{S4} A \prec A_k$, by S3-9D.

Case 4. There exist i < k and j < k such that $\alpha_i = \varnothing$, $\alpha_j = \alpha_k$, $A_i = B \leftrightarrow C$, $A_j = \check{S}_B D$ and $A_k = \check{S}_C D$. By the hypothesis of induction, $\vdash_{S4} A \prec (B \leftrightarrow C)$ and $\vdash_{S4} A \prec \check{S}_B D$. Then,

$\vdash_{S4} A \mathrel{-\!\!3} (S^{\vee}{}_{B}D \mathrel{-\!\!3} S^{\vee}{}_{C}D)$, by S3-13M. Hence $\vdash_{S4} A \mathrel{-\!\!3} [S^{\vee}{}_{B}D \wedge (S^{\vee}{}_{B}D \mathrel{-\!\!3} S^{\vee}{}_{C}D)]$, by S3-9D. Thus, by Ax9, $\vdash_{S4}[S^{\vee}{}_{B}D \wedge (S^{\vee}{}_{B}D \mathrel{-\!\!3} S^{\vee}{}_{C}D)] \mathrel{-\!\!3} S^{\vee}{}_{C}D$. Therefore by S1-6D, $\vdash_{S4} A \mathrel{-\!\!3} S^{\vee}{}_{C}D$.

S4-6M. S4 and S1*' are equivalent (and hence also S4*, S4' and S4*').

Proof: S4 R-includes S1. Since S4 R-includes S3 and contains no additional alphabet and SHE holds in S3 by S3-8M, SHE holds also in S4. By S4-5M, WFC holds in S4. Hence S4 R-includes S1*'. But by S1'-2T and S1*'-1T, S1*' R-includes S4 and S4*' and hence the theorem follows.

From the equivalence of the four S4 systems, it is obvious that the equivalence of the corresponding S5 systems follows.

11
Strict Implications: Additional Results

To understand systems like **S1'** further, it is desirable to define a version of model theory appropriate to modal zero-order logics. The type of structures involved are frequently called **Kripke models**. In the following, we will use A, B, C, and D as metalogical variables taking wffs as values, α, β, γ and δ as variables taking sets of wffs, $\mathbf{v}, \mathbf{w}, \mathbf{x}, \mathbf{y}$, and $\mathbf{z}$ as variables taking assignments, $\mathfrak{A}$, $\mathfrak{B}$, $\mathfrak{C}$, $\mathfrak{D}$ as variables taking modal assignment sets and $\mathbf{f}, \mathbf{g}$, and $\mathbf{h}$ as variables taking functions. We start with a number of definitions:

A **proper assignment** $\mathbf{f}$ (in a zero-order logic $\mathbf{L}$) is a function $\mathbf{f}: S_0 \rightarrow \{0,1\}$. An **assignment** $\mathbf{x}$ is an ordered couple $<\mathbf{f}, n>$ where n is a real number and $\mathbf{f}$ is a proper assignment.

A **modal assignment set** (MAS) $\mathfrak{A}$ is an ordered couple $<\mathfrak{G}, \mathbf{g}>$ where $\mathfrak{G}$ is a set of assignments such that if w_0 is a constant and $<\mathbf{f_1}, n>$ and $<\mathbf{f_2}, m>$ are both elements of $\mathfrak{G}$, then $\mathbf{f_1}(w_0) = \mathbf{f_2}(w_0)$ and $\mathbf{g}$ is a function whose domain is $\mathfrak{G}$ and whose range is the power set of $\mathfrak{G}$. In other words, values of constants are fixed and $\mathbf{g}$ ranges over the assignments which are members of $\mathfrak{G}$ and take as values subsets of $\mathfrak{G}$ (including possibly the null set). Associated with each modal assignment set $<\mathfrak{G}, \mathbf{g}>$ is the relation $\mathbf{R_g}$ which holds between two assignments $\mathbf{x}$ and $\mathbf{y}$ iff $\mathbf{x}, \mathbf{y} \in \mathfrak{G}$ and $\mathbf{y} \in \mathbf{g}(\mathbf{x})$.

If $\mathfrak{A} = <\mathfrak{G}, \mathbf{g}>$ is a modal assignment set, the value is a function $\mathbf{V}_{\mathfrak{A}}: \mathfrak{G} \times \mathbf{W} \rightarrow \{0,1\}$, satisfying the following conditions:

(1) If A is a zero-place connective (i.e. a variable or constant) and $\mathbf{x} = <\mathbf{f}, n>$, $\mathbf{V}_{\mathfrak{A}}(\mathbf{x}, A) = \mathbf{f}(A)$.

(2) $\mathbf{V}_{\mathfrak{A}}(\mathbf{x}, A \wedge B) = \mathbf{V}_{\mathfrak{A}}(\mathbf{x}, A) \cdot \mathbf{V}_{\mathfrak{A}}(\mathbf{x}, B)$

(3) $\mathbf{V}_{\mathfrak{A}}(\mathbf{x}, A \vee B) = 1$ iff $\mathbf{V}_{\mathfrak{A}}(\mathbf{x}, A) = 1$ or $\mathbf{V}_{\mathfrak{A}}(\mathbf{x}, B) = 1$

(4) $\mathbf{V}_{\mathfrak{A}}(\mathbf{x}, A \supset B) = 1$ iff $\mathbf{V}_{\mathfrak{A}}(\mathbf{x}, A) = 0$ or $\mathbf{V}_{\mathfrak{A}}(\mathbf{x}, B) = 1$

(5) $\mathbf{V}_{\mathfrak{A}}(\mathbf{x}, \sim A) = 1$ iff $\mathbf{V}_{\mathfrak{A}}(\mathbf{x}, A) = 0$

(6) $\mathbf{V}_{\mathfrak{A}}(\mathbf{x}, A \equiv B) = 1$ iff $\mathbf{V}_{\mathfrak{A}}(\mathbf{x}, A) = \mathbf{V}_{\mathfrak{A}}(\mathbf{x}, B)$

(7) $\mathbf{V}_{\mathfrak{A}}(\mathbf{x}, A \prec B) = 1$ iff $(\mathbf{y} \in \mathbf{g}(\mathbf{x})$ and $\mathbf{V}_{\mathfrak{A}}(\mathbf{y}, A) = 1) \Rightarrow \mathbf{V}_{\mathfrak{A}}(\mathbf{y}, B) = 1)$.

(8) $\mathbf{V}_{\mathfrak{A}}(\mathbf{x}, \Diamond A) = 1$ iff there exists $\mathbf{y} \in \mathbf{g}(\mathbf{x})$ such that $\mathbf{V}_{\mathfrak{A}}(\mathbf{y}, A) = 1$.

(9) $\mathbf{V}_{\mathfrak{A}}(\mathbf{x}, \Box A) = 1$ if $\mathbf{y} \in \mathbf{g}(\mathbf{x}) \Rightarrow \mathbf{V}_{\mathfrak{A}}(\mathbf{y}, A) = 1$.

An assignment $\mathbf{x}$ is a **model** of a wff A in a MAS $\mathfrak{A}$ (symbolized $\mathbf{x}_{\mathfrak{A}} \Vdash A$ or $\mathbf{x} \Vdash A$) iff $\mathbf{V}_{\mathfrak{A}}(\mathbf{x}, A) = 1$. An assignment $\mathbf{x}$ is a **model** of a set of wffs α in a MAS $\mathfrak{A}$ (symbolized $\mathbf{x}_{\mathfrak{A}} \Vdash \alpha$ or $\mathbf{x} \Vdash \alpha$) iff $A \in \alpha \Rightarrow \mathbf{x} \Vdash_{\mathfrak{A}} A$ (i.e. $\mathbf{x}$ is a model of every element of α).

α is (model theoretically) **consistent** (or **satisfiable**): α has a model in some MAS. α is **contradictory** (or **inconsistent**): α has no models. α **entails** A (symbolically $\alpha \vDash A$): Every model of α is a model of A.

An assignment $\mathbf{x}$ is a **$\mathfrak{Y}$-model** of a wff A in a MAS $\mathfrak{A}$ (symbolized $\mathbf{x}_{\mathfrak{A}} \Vdash_{\mathfrak{Y}} A$ or $\mathbf{x} \Vdash_{\mathfrak{Y}} A$) iff $\mathbf{x}$ is a model of A and $\mathfrak{A}$ is an $\mathfrak{Y}$ MAS. An assignment $\mathbf{x}$ is a **$\mathfrak{Y}$-model** of a set of wffs α in a MAS $\mathfrak{A}$ (symbolized $\mathbf{x}_{\mathfrak{A}} \Vdash_{\mathfrak{Y}} \alpha$ or $\mathbf{x} \Vdash_{\mathfrak{Y}} \alpha$) iff $\mathbf{x}$ is a model of α and $\mathfrak{A}$ is an $\mathfrak{Y}$ MAS. α is **$\mathfrak{Y}$-consistent** (or **$\mathfrak{Y}$-satisfiable**): α has a $\mathfrak{Y}$-model in some MAS. α is **$\mathfrak{Y}$-contradictory** (or **$\mathfrak{Y}$-inconsistent**): α has no $\mathfrak{Y}$-models. α **$\mathfrak{Y}$-entails** A (symbolically $\alpha \vDash_{\mathfrak{Y}} A$): Every $\mathfrak{Y}$-model of α is a $\mathfrak{Y}$-model of A.

A wff A is **modal-free** iff there is no wffs A and B such that neither $\Diamond A$, $\Box A$, nor $A \prec B$ occurs in A. A set α is **modal-free** iff every element of α is modal-free.

Every MAS is $\mathfrak{K}$.

A logic $\mathfrak{L}$ is $\mathfrak{K}$ iff

1. $\mathfrak{L}$ $\mathbf{R}$-includes $\mathfrak{CLNEAK}$ (or equivalent).
2. $A \prec B, \Box A \vdash_{\mathfrak{L}} \Box B$
3. $\vdash_{\mathfrak{L}} A \equiv B \Rightarrow \check{\mathbf{S}}_{A}C \vdash_{\mathfrak{L}} \check{\mathbf{S}}_{B}C$
4. $\vdash_{\mathfrak{L}} A \Rightarrow \vdash_{\mathfrak{L}} \Box A$
5. $\vdash_{\mathfrak{L}} \Box A \equiv \sim\Diamond\sim A$
6. $\vdash_{\mathfrak{L}} (A \prec B) \equiv \sim\Diamond(A \wedge \sim B)$

An MAS $\mathfrak{A}$ is $\mathbf{D}$ iff for every $x \in \mathfrak{A}$, $g(x) \neq \varnothing$. A logic $\mathcal{L}$ is $\mathbf{D}$ iff it is $\mathcal{K}$ and $\Box A \vdash_{\mathcal{L}} \Diamond A$.

An MAS $\mathfrak{A}$ is $\mathbf{T}$ iff for every $x \in \mathfrak{A}$, $x \in g(x)$. A logic $\mathcal{L}$ is $\mathbf{T}$ iff it is $\mathcal{K}$ and $A \vdash_{\mathcal{L}} \Diamond A$.

An MAS $\mathfrak{A}$ is **S4** iff it is $\mathbf{T}$ and for every x,y and $z \in \mathfrak{A}$, $(x \in g(y)$ and $y \in g(z)) \Rightarrow x \in g(z)$. A logic $\mathcal{L}$ is **S4** iff it is $\mathbf{T}$ and $\Diamond\Diamond A \vdash_{\mathcal{L}} \Diamond A$.

An MAS $\mathfrak{A}$ is **S5** iff it is S4 and for every $x,y \in \mathfrak{A}$, $x \in g(y) \Rightarrow y \in g(x)$. A logic $\mathcal{L}$ is **S5** iff it is S4 and $\Diamond A \vdash_{\mathcal{L}} \Box\Diamond A$.

A logic $\mathcal{L}$ is minimally **$\mathcal{K}$ ($\mathbf{D}$, $\mathbf{T}$, S4, S5)** iff it is $\mathcal{K}$ ($\mathbf{D}$, $\mathbf{T}$, S4, S5) and for every $\mathcal{K}$ ($\mathbf{D}$, $\mathbf{T}$, S4, S5) logic $\mathcal{L}'$, $\alpha \vdash_{\mathcal{L}} A \Rightarrow \alpha \vdash_{\mathcal{L}'} A$.

α is **A-$\mathcal{L}$-inconsistent** iff $\alpha \vdash_{\mathcal{L}} A$. α is **A-$\mathcal{L}$-consistent** iff it is not A-$\mathcal{L}$-inconsistent. α is **A-$\mathcal{L}$-complete** iff for every wff B, either $B \in \alpha$ or $B \supset A \in \alpha$.

When no ambiguity will occur, we will abbreviate $\mathsf{v}_{\mathfrak{A}}(x,A)$ as $\mathsf{v}_x(A)$.

A set of wffs α is **$\mathcal{L}$-Lewis regular** iff

(1) α is deductively consistent in $\mathcal{L}$

(2) α is **deductively closed** (i.e. $\alpha \vdash_{\mathcal{L}} A \Rightarrow A \in \alpha$)

(3) α is **disjunctive** (i.e. $A \vee B \in \alpha \Leftrightarrow [A \in \alpha$ or $B \in \alpha]$)

(4) α is **negation-complete** (i.e. $\sim A \in \alpha \Leftrightarrow A \notin \alpha$)

Let α be $\mathcal{L}$-Lewis regular. Then $\mathbf{f}_\alpha: W_0 \to \{0,1\}$ is **the proper assignment associated with** α provided $\mathbf{f}_\alpha(A) = 1$ iff $A \in \alpha$. Let $\{w_1, w_2, \cdots\}$ be the infinite sequence of all wffs (in some particular order). We define r_α as **the real number associated with** α provided (1) $0 < r_\alpha < 1$, (2) for every i, $w_i \in \alpha \Rightarrow$ the ith digit of the decimal expansion of r_α is 7, (3) for every i, $w_i \notin \alpha \Rightarrow$ the ith digit of the decimal expansion of r_α is 3. Note that these definitions imply that if α and β are $\mathcal{L}$-Lewis regular (for the same $\mathcal{L}$), $\langle \mathbf{f}_\alpha, r_\alpha \rangle = \langle \mathbf{f}_\beta, r_\beta \rangle \Leftrightarrow \alpha = \beta$.

Let α be $\mathcal{L}$-Lewis regular. Then $x_\alpha = \langle \mathbf{f}_\alpha, r_\alpha \rangle$ is **the assignment correlated with** α. For this assignment, we will use

$\mathsf{V}_\alpha(A)$ as an alternative notation for $\mathsf{V}_{x_\alpha}(A)$.

$<\mathfrak{G}, \mathsf{g}>$ is the $\mathfrak{K}$ ($\mathfrak{D}$, $\mathfrak{T}$, $\mathfrak{S}4$, $\mathfrak{S}5$) - **regular** MAS provided:

(1) $\mathfrak{G}$ is the set of assignments correlated with the $\mathfrak{L}$-Lewis-regular sets of wffs, for some minimally $\mathfrak{K}$ ($\mathfrak{D}$, $\mathfrak{T}$, $\mathfrak{S}4$, $\mathfrak{S}5$) logic $\mathfrak{L}$.

(2) $x_\beta \in \mathsf{g}(x_\alpha)$ iff (a) $\sim\Diamond A \in \alpha \Rightarrow \sim A \in \beta$, and (b) there exists a B such that $\Diamond B \in \alpha$ and $B \in \beta$.

Having burdened the reader with such a long series of definitions, let us prove a number of elementary properties before proceeding to more significant results.

$\mathfrak{K}$-1. If $\mathfrak{A}$ is $\mathfrak{K}$, $\mathsf{V}_{\mathfrak{A}}(x,\sim\Diamond\sim A) = \mathsf{V}_{\mathfrak{A}}(x,\Box A)$.

Proof: Let $\mathsf{V}_{\mathfrak{A}}(x,\sim\Diamond\sim A) = 1$. Then $\mathsf{V}_{\mathfrak{A}}(x,\Diamond\sim A) = 0$. Hence there is no assignment y in $\mathsf{g}(x)$ such that $\mathsf{V}_{\mathfrak{A}}(y,\sim A) = 0$. Thus, $y \in \mathsf{g}(x) \Rightarrow \mathsf{V}_{\mathfrak{A}}(y,A) = 1$. Therefore, $\mathsf{V}_{\mathfrak{A}}(x,\Box A) = 1$. The converse follows by the same steps in reverse order.

$\mathfrak{K}$-2. If $\mathfrak{A}$ is $\mathfrak{K}$, $\mathsf{V}_{\mathfrak{A}}(x,\sim\Diamond(A \wedge \sim B)) = \mathsf{V}_{\mathfrak{A}}(x,A \dashv B)$.

Proof: Let $\mathsf{V}_{\mathfrak{A}}(x, \sim\Diamond(A \wedge \sim B)) = 1$. Then $\mathsf{V}_{\mathfrak{A}}(x,\Diamond(A \wedge \sim B)) = 0$. Hence there is no assigment y in $\mathsf{g}(x)$ such that $\mathsf{V}_{\mathfrak{A}}(y,A \wedge \sim B) = 0$. Hence, $[y \in \mathsf{g}(x)$ and $\mathsf{V}_{\mathfrak{A}}(y,A) = 1] \Rightarrow \mathsf{V}_{\mathfrak{A}}(y,B) = 1$. Therefore, $\mathsf{V}_{\mathfrak{A}}(x,A \dashv B) = 1$. The converse follows by the same steps in reverse order.

$\mathfrak{K}$-3. If α and A are modal-free, $\alpha \vdash_{\mathfrak{CLNEAK}} A \Leftrightarrow \alpha \vDash_{\mathfrak{K}} A$.

Proof: This follows by the definition of value and the soundness and completeness of $\mathfrak{CLNEAK}$.

$\mathfrak{K}$-4. $A \dashv B, \Box A \vDash_{\mathfrak{K}} \Box B$

Proof: Let $\mathfrak{A}$ be a $\mathfrak{K}$ MAS. Let x be an assignment of $\mathfrak{A}$ and $\mathsf{V}_{\mathfrak{A}}(x,A \dashv B) = \mathsf{V}_{\mathfrak{A}}(x,\Box A) = 1$. Suppose $y \in \mathsf{g}(x)$. Then we have $\mathsf{V}_{\mathfrak{A}}(y,A \supset B) = \mathsf{V}_{\mathfrak{A}}(y,A) = 1$ and hence by the ordinary two-valued validity of MP, $\mathsf{V}_{\mathfrak{A}}(y,B) = 1$. Since this holds for arbitrary $y \in g(x)$, $V_{\mathfrak{A}}(x,\Box B) = 1$.

$\mathcal{K}$-5. Every wff of a $\mathcal{K}$ logic is equivalent to one containing no connectives other than $\sim$, $\Diamond$ and $\wedge$.

Proof: This is an immediate result of the equivalence theorem for CINEAK and conditions 3, 5 and 6 in the definition of $\mathcal{K}$ logic.

$\mathcal{K}$-6. $\vDash_{\mathcal{K}} A \equiv B \Rightarrow \overset{v}{S}_A C \vDash_{\mathcal{K}} \overset{v}{S}_B C$.

Proof: Assume $\vDash_{\mathcal{K}} A \equiv B$. Then for any assignment x in any MAS $\mathfrak{A}$ $V_{\mathfrak{A}}(x, A \equiv B) = 1$. Hence $V_{\mathfrak{A}}(x,A) = V_{\mathfrak{A}}(x,B)$. By induction on $\ell(C)$, we will show that $V_{\mathfrak{A}}(x, \overset{v}{S}_A C) = 1$ implies $V_{\mathfrak{A}}(x, \overset{v}{S}_B C) = 1$:

(α) $\ell(C) = 1$. Then C is a variable.

Case 1. $C = v$. Then $\overset{v}{S}_A C = A$ and $\overset{v}{S}_B C = B$. Hence $1 = V_{\mathfrak{A}}(x, \overset{v}{S}_A C) = V_{\mathfrak{A}}(x,A) = V_{\mathfrak{A}}(x,B) = V_{\mathfrak{A}}(x, \overset{v}{S}_B C)$.

Case 2. $C \neq v$. Then $\overset{v}{S}_A C = \overset{v}{S}_B C = C$ and $1 = V_{\mathfrak{A}}(x, \overset{v}{S}_A C) = V_{\mathfrak{A}}(x,C) = V_{\mathfrak{A}}(x, \overset{v}{S}_B C)$.

(β) Assume the assertion is true for all D with $\ell(D) < k$. We will prove it for $\ell(C) = k$. Without loss of generality, we may assume that all wffs contain only the connectives $\sim$, $\Diamond$ and $\wedge$, by $\mathcal{K}$-5.

Case 1. $C = \sim E$. Then $\ell(E) = k-1$. By the hypothesis of induction, since $V_{\mathfrak{A}}(x, A \equiv B) = 1$, $V_{\mathfrak{A}}(x, B \equiv A) = 1$. Hence $V_{\mathfrak{A}}(x, \overset{v}{S}_B E) = 1$ implies $V_{\mathfrak{A}}(x, \overset{v}{S}_A E) = 1$. If $V_{\mathfrak{A}}(x, \sim\overset{v}{S}_A E) = 1$, $V_{\mathfrak{A}}(x, \overset{v}{S}_A E) = 0$. Hence $V_{\mathfrak{A}}(x, \overset{v}{S}_B E) = 0$ and $V_{\mathfrak{A}}(x, \sim\overset{v}{S}_B E) = 1$. But since $\overset{v}{S}_A C = \sim\overset{v}{S}_A E$ and $\overset{v}{S}_B C = \sim\overset{v}{S}_B E$, the result follows.

Case 2. $C = \Diamond E$. Then $\ell(E) = k-1$. By the hypothesis of induction, since $V_{\mathfrak{A}}(x, A \equiv B) = 1$ for all assignments y, $V_{\mathfrak{A}}(y, \overset{v}{S}_A E) = 1 \Leftrightarrow V_{\mathfrak{A}}(y, \overset{v}{S}_B E) = 1$. Let $V_{\mathfrak{A}}(x, \Diamond\overset{v}{S}_A E) = 1$. Then there exists a $z \in g(x)$ such that $v_{\mathfrak{A}}(z, \mathbf{S}^{\vee}_{A}E) = 1$. Hence $v_{\mathfrak{A}}(z, \mathbf{S}^{\vee}_{B}E) = 1$ and thus $v_{\mathfrak{A}}(x, \Diamond\mathbf{S}^{\vee}_{B}E) = 1$. But $\mathbf{S}^{\vee}_{A}C = \Diamond\mathbf{S}^{\vee}_{A}E$ and $\mathbf{S}^{\vee}_{B}C = \Diamond\mathbf{S}^{\vee}_{B}E$; Reversing the direction of the bi-conditional, the result follows.

Case 3. $C = E \wedge F$. Then $\ell(E) < k$ and then $\ell(F) < k$. By the hypothesis of induction, since $v_{\mathfrak{A}}(x, A \equiv B) = 1$, $v_{\mathfrak{A}}(x, \mathbf{S}^{\vee}_{A}E) = 1$ implies $v_{\mathfrak{A}}(x, \mathbf{S}^{\vee}_{B}E) = 1$ and also $v_{\mathfrak{A}}(x, \mathbf{S}^{\vee}_{A}F) = 1$ implies $v_{\mathfrak{A}}(x, \mathbf{S}^{\vee}_{B}F) = 1$. Now let $v_{\mathfrak{A}}(x, \mathbf{S}^{\vee}_{A}(E \wedge F)) = 1$. Hence $1 = v_{\mathfrak{A}}(x, \mathbf{S}^{\vee}_{A}(E \wedge F)) = v_{\mathfrak{A}}(x, \mathbf{S}^{\vee}_{A}E \wedge \mathbf{S}^{\vee}_{A}F) = v_{\mathfrak{A}}(x, \mathbf{S}^{\vee}_{A}E) = v_{\mathfrak{A}}(x, \mathbf{S}^{\vee}_{A}F) = v_{\mathfrak{A}}(x,\mathbf{S}^{\vee}_{B}E) = v_{\mathfrak{A}}(x,\mathbf{S}^{\vee}_{B}F) = v_{\mathfrak{A}}(x, \mathbf{S}^{\vee}_{B}E \wedge \mathbf{S}^{\vee}_{B}F) = v_{\mathfrak{A}}(x, \mathbf{S}^{\vee}_{B}(E \wedge F))$, and conversely.

$\mathcal{K}$-7. $\models_{\mathcal{K}} A \Rightarrow \models_{\mathcal{K}} \Box A$

Proof: $v_{\mathfrak{A}}(x, A) = 1$ for all x and $\mathfrak{A}$. Then for arbitrary $\mathfrak{B}$ and y, if $z \in g(y)$, $v_{\mathfrak{B}}(z, A) = 1$ and hence $v_{\mathfrak{B}}(y, \Box A) = 1$.

$\mathcal{K}$-8. Let $\mathcal{L}$ R-contain $\mathcal{CINEAK}$ and have as additional rules, the exact conditions 2-6 of the definition of $\mathcal{K}$. Then $\alpha \vdash_{\mathcal{L}} A \Rightarrow \alpha \models_{\mathcal{K}} A$.

Proof: Assume $\alpha \vdash_{\mathcal{L}} A$. Then there exists a Y-derivation $\alpha_1 \vdash A_1, \cdots, \alpha_n \vdash A_n$ in $\mathcal{L}$. By induction on n and $\mathcal{K}$-1 through $\mathcal{K}$-7, the rules preserve entailment.

K-9. Let $\mathcal{L}$ be a minimal $\mathcal{K}$ ($\mathcal{D}$, $\mathcal{T}$, $\mathcal{S}4$, $\mathcal{S}5$) logic. Then if α is A-$\mathcal{L}$-consistent, there exists a set of wffs β such that $\alpha \subset \beta$, β is A-$\mathcal{L}$-consistent and A-$\mathcal{L}$-complete.

Proof: Let $w_1, w_2, \cdots$ be the wffs of $\mathcal{L}$. Suppose α is A-$\mathcal{L}$-consistent. Let $\beta_0 = \alpha$ and $\beta_{n+1} = \beta_n$ if $\beta_n, w_{n+1} \vdash_{\mathcal{L}} A$, and $\beta_{n+1} = \beta_n \cup \{w_{n+1}\}$

otherwise. Let $\beta = \bigcup_n(\beta_n)$. Then β_0 is A-$\mathcal{L}$-consistent and if β_n is A-$\mathcal{L}$-consistent and β_{n+1} is not, then $\beta_{n+1} = \beta_n \cup \{w_{n+1}\}$ and $\beta_n, w_{n+1} \vdash_{\mathcal{L}} A$, (i.e. $\beta_{n+1} \vdash_{\mathcal{L}} A$) is false, and therefore β_{n+1} is A-$\mathcal{L}$-consistent. Hence β_n is A-$\mathcal{L}$-consistent for all n. Suppose β were A-$\mathcal{L}$-inconsistent. Then $\beta \vdash_{\mathcal{L}} A$ and hence there is a derivation of A from β in $\mathcal{L}$. If β' is the intersection of β with the set of wffs which occur in any element of that derivation, it is finite and $\beta' \vdash_{\mathcal{L}} A$. Hence there exists an n such that $\beta' \subset \beta_n$ and hence $\beta_n \vdash_{\mathcal{L}} A$ contrary to our last result. Hence β is A-$\mathcal{L}$-consistent. Suppose that for some n, $w_{n+1} \notin \beta$. Then $w_{n+1} \notin \beta_{n+1}$ and $\beta_n, w_{n+1} \vdash_{\mathcal{L}} A$. Hence, by **C**, $\beta_n \vdash_{\mathcal{L}} w_{n+1} \supset A$. Then there is an m such that $w_{m+1} = w_{n+1} \supset A$. Suppose $w_{m+1} \notin \beta_{m+1}$. Then $\beta_m, w_{n+1} \supset A \vdash_{\mathcal{L}} A$ and hence $\beta, w_{n+1} \supset A \vdash_{\mathcal{L}} A$. Thus $\beta \vdash_{\mathcal{L}} A$, contrary to our result that β is A-$\mathcal{L}$-complete.

K-10. Let $\mathcal{L}$ be minimally $\mathcal{K}$ ($\mathcal{D}$,$\mathcal{T}$,$\mathcal{S}4$,$\mathcal{S}5$). Then if α is A-$\mathcal{L}$-consistent and A-$\mathcal{L}$-complete, it is $\mathcal{L}$-Lewis regular.

Proof: Let α be A-$\mathcal{L}$-consistent and A-$\mathcal{L}$-complete, for some wff A. Then since $\alpha \vdash_{\mathcal{L}} A$ is false, α is deductively consistent. Suppose $\alpha \vdash_{\mathcal{L}} B$. Since α is A-complete, if $B \notin \alpha$, $B \supset A \in \alpha$. Hence $\alpha \vdash_{\mathcal{L}} B \supset A$ and, by **MP**, $\alpha \vdash_{\mathcal{L}} A$, which we know is false. Then, $B \in \alpha$. Thus, α is deductively closed. Suppose $B \vee C \in \alpha$. Then $\alpha \vdash_{\mathcal{L}} B \vee C$. Since α is A-$\mathcal{L}$-complete, either $B \in \alpha$ or $C \in \alpha$ or else both $B \supset A \in \alpha$ and $C \supset A \in \alpha$. Hence, by **MP**, $\alpha, B \vdash_{\mathcal{L}} A$ or $\alpha, C \vdash_{\mathcal{L}} A$. Therefore, by **D**, $\alpha, B \vee C \vdash_{\mathcal{L}} A$. Then $\alpha \vdash_{\mathcal{L}} A$, which contradicts α's A-$\mathcal{L}$-consistency. Thus, $B \in \alpha$ or $C \in \alpha$. Suppose $B \in \alpha$ or $C \in \alpha$. Then $\alpha \vdash_{\mathcal{L}} B$ or $\alpha \vdash_{\mathcal{L}} C$. Thus $\alpha \vdash_{\mathcal{L}} B \vee C$ and $B \vee C \in \alpha$, by deductive closure, and α is disjunctive. Suppose that (for some B), $B \notin \alpha$ and $\sim B \notin \alpha$. Then $B \supset A \in \alpha$ and $\sim B \supset A \in \alpha$. Hence by MP, $\alpha, B \vdash_{\mathcal{L}} A$ and $\alpha, \sim B \vdash_{\mathcal{L}} A$, and by **D**, $\alpha, B \vee \sim B \vdash_{\mathcal{L}} A$. But since $\alpha \vdash_{\mathcal{L}} B \vee \sim B$ and thus $\alpha \vdash_{\mathcal{L}} A$, which contradicts α's A-$\mathcal{L}$-consistency. Therefore, α is negation-complete.

$\mathcal{K}$-11. There exist minimally $\mathcal{K}$ ($\mathcal{D}, \mathcal{T}, \mathcal{S}4$ and $\mathcal{S}5$) logics.

Proof: This is trivial since any DZOS with the rules of a complete (non-modal) logic (e.g. CLNEAK) with the special rules indicated for $\mathcal{K}$, $\mathcal{D}$, $\mathcal{T}$. $\mathcal{S}4$ and $\mathcal{S}5$ would have to be minimal.

$\mathcal{K}$-12. Let $\mathcal{L}$ be a $\mathcal{K}$ logic. Then $A_1,\cdots,A_n \vdash_{\mathcal{L}} B$ implies $\Box A_1,\cdots,\Box A_n \vdash_{\mathcal{L}} \Box B$.

Proof: We will prove by induction on n:

(α) $n = 1$. Let $A_1 \vdash_{\mathcal{L}} B$. Then $\vdash_{\mathcal{L}} A_1 \supset B$ by C. Hence $\vdash_{\mathcal{L}} \Box(A_1 \supset B)$. Then $\vdash_{\mathcal{L}} A_1 \prec B$. Since $A_1 \prec B, \Box A_1 \vdash_{\mathcal{L}} \Box B$, we get by closure $\Box A_1 \vdash_{\mathcal{L}} \Box B$.

(β) Assume this is true for $n < k$. We will prove it for $n = k$. Assume $A_1,\cdots,A_k \vdash_{\mathcal{L}} B$. Hence by C, $A_1,\cdots, A_{k-1} \vdash_{\mathcal{L}} A_k \supset B$. By the hypothesis of induction, $\Box A_1,\cdots, \Box A_{k-1} \vdash_{\mathcal{L}} \Box(A_k \supset B)$, i. e.

$\Box A_1,\cdots, \Box A_{k-1} \vdash_{\mathcal{L}} A_k \prec B$, and since

$\Box A_1,\cdots, \Box A_{k-1}, \Box A_k, A_k \prec B \vdash_{\mathcal{L}} \Box B$, therefore

$\Box A_1,\cdots,\Box A_k \vdash_{\mathcal{L}} \Box B$.

$\mathcal{K}$-13. Let $\mathcal{L}$ be a minimal $\mathcal{K}(\mathcal{D}, \mathcal{T}, \mathcal{S}4, \mathcal{S}5)$ logic. Then if $\mathfrak{A} = \langle \mathfrak{G}, \mathbf{g} \rangle$ is the $\mathcal{K}(\mathcal{D}, \mathcal{T}, \mathcal{S}4, \mathcal{S}5)$ regular MAS and α is $\mathcal{L}$-Lewis-regular, then $A \in \alpha$ iff $\mathbf{V}_\alpha(A) = 1$ in $\mathfrak{A}$.

Proof: Without loss of generality we can assume that the only connectives are $\sim$, $\vee$, $\wedge$, and $\Diamond$, since all assignments assign the values to equivalent wffs. By induction on $\ell(A)$:

(α) $\ell(A) = 1$. Then A is a variable or constant and $A \in \alpha$ iff $\mathbf{f}_\alpha(A) = 1$. Then $\mathbf{V}_\alpha(A) = \mathbf{f}_\alpha(A)$ and $\mathbf{V}_\alpha(A) = 1$ iff $A \in \alpha$.

(β) Suppose the assertion is true for all wffs B such that $\ell(B) < k$. We will prove it true if $\ell(A) = k$:

Case 1. $A = C \wedge D$. (left-right) Let $A \in \alpha$. Hence $\alpha \vdash_{\mathcal{L}} C \wedge D$. By **LS** and **RS**, $\alpha \vdash_{\mathcal{L}} C$ and $\alpha \vdash_{\mathcal{L}} D$. Then, by the hypothesis of induction, $\mathbf{V}_{\alpha}(C) = \mathbf{V}_{\alpha}(D) = 1$. Therefore $\mathbf{V}_{\alpha}(C \wedge D) = \mathbf{V}_{\alpha}(A) = 1$. (right-left) Let $\mathbf{V}_{\alpha}(A) = \mathbf{V}_{\alpha}(C \wedge D) = 1$. Hence $\mathbf{V}_{\alpha}(C) = \mathbf{V}_{\alpha}(D) = 1$. By the hypothesis of induction, $C \in \alpha$ and $D \in \alpha$. Thus $\alpha \vdash_{\mathcal{L}} C$ and $\alpha \vdash_{\mathcal{L}} D$, and therefore, by A, $\alpha \vdash_{\mathcal{L}} C \wedge D$, i.e. $\alpha \vdash_{\mathcal{L}} A$ and since α is $\mathcal{L}$ - Lewis-regular, $A \in \alpha$.

Case 2. $A = C \vee D$. (left-right) Let $A \in \alpha$, i.e., $C \vee D \in \alpha$. Since α is disjunctive, $C \in \alpha$ or $D \in \alpha$. Since $\ell(C) < k$ and $\ell(D) < k$, $\mathbf{V}_{\alpha}(C) = 1$ or $\mathbf{V}_{\alpha}(D) = 1$, and hence, $\mathbf{V}_{\alpha}(C \vee D) = \mathbf{V}_{\alpha}(A) = 1$. (right-left) Let $\mathbf{V}_{\alpha}(A) = \mathbf{V}_{\alpha}(C \vee D) = 1$. Then $\mathbf{V}_{\alpha}(C) = 1$ or $\mathbf{V}_{\alpha}(D) = 1$. By the hypothesis of induction, $C \in \alpha$ or $D \in \alpha$. Hence $\alpha \vdash_{\mathcal{L}} C$ or $\alpha \vdash_{\mathcal{L}} D$, and by AR and AL, $\alpha \vdash_{\mathcal{L}} C \vee D$, i.e. $\alpha \vdash_{\mathcal{L}} A$. Since α is $\mathcal{L}$-Lewis -regular,

Case 3. $A = {\sim}C$. Then $\ell(C) < k$. (left-right) Let $A \in \alpha$, i.e., ${\sim}C \in \alpha$. Since α is deductively consistent and $\mathcal{L}$ $\mathbf{R}$-includes $\mathfrak{CINEAK}$, $C \notin \alpha$. By the hypothesis of induction, $\mathbf{V}_{\alpha}(C) = 0$ and $\mathbf{V}_{\alpha}({\sim}C) = \mathbf{V}_{\alpha}(A) = 1$. (right-left) Let $\mathbf{V}_{\alpha}(\alpha) = \mathbf{V}_{\alpha}({\sim}C) = 1$. Hence $\mathbf{V}_{\alpha}(C) = 0$ and by the hypothesis of induction, $C \notin \alpha$, and since α is negation complete, ${\sim}C$ (which is A) $\in \alpha$.

Case 4. $A = \Diamond C$. Then $\ell(C) < k$. (left-right) Let $A \in \alpha$, i.e. $\Diamond C \in \alpha$. Let $\beta = \{{\sim}D : {\sim}\Diamond D \in \alpha\}$ and suppose $\beta \cup \{C\}$ were deductively inconsistent in $\mathcal{L}$. Then $\beta, C \vdash {\sim}C$, and hence $\beta \vdash {\sim}C$. Thus there exists a finite subset of β, $\beta' = \{{\sim}D_1, \ldots, {\sim}D_n\}$ such that $\beta' \vdash {\sim}C$, i.e., ${\sim}D_1, \ldots, {\sim}D_n \vdash {\sim}C$ and hence by $\mathcal{K}$-12, $\Box{\sim}D_1, \ldots, \Box{\sim}D_n \vdash \Box{\sim}C$. By the logical equivalence of $\Box{\sim}B$ with ${\sim}\Diamond B$, we obtain ${\sim}\Diamond D_1, \ldots, {\sim}\Diamond D_n \vdash {\sim}\Diamond C$. Hence we would have $\alpha \vdash {\sim}\Diamond C$ and $\alpha \vdash \Diamond C$ and α would be deductively inconsistent. Thus $\beta \cup \{C\}$ is deductively consistent in $\mathcal{L}$ and β is ${\sim}C$-$\mathcal{L}$-consistent. Hence there exists a ${\sim}C$-$\mathcal{L}$-consistent and ${\sim}C$-complete set δ with $\beta \subset \delta$, by $\mathcal{K}$-9, and δ is $\mathcal{L}$-Lewis-regular by $\mathcal{K}$-10. Then ${\sim}\Diamond D \in \alpha$ implies ${\sim}D \in \delta$ and $\Diamond C \in \alpha$, while $C \in \delta$.

Hence $x_\delta \in g(x_\alpha)$ and by the hypothesis of induction, $V_\delta(C) = 1$. Therefore $V_\alpha(\Diamond C) = 1$. (right-left) Let $V_\alpha(A) = V_\alpha(\Diamond C) = 1$. Then there exists an $x_\gamma \in g(x_\alpha)$ such that $V_\gamma(C) = 1$. Since $x_\gamma \in g(x_\alpha)$, $\sim\Diamond C \in \alpha$ implies $\sim C \in \gamma$. But since γ is deductively consistent in $\mathcal{L}$, $\sim C \notin \gamma$. Hence $\sim\Diamond C \notin \alpha$ and by negation-completeness, $\Diamond C \in \alpha$, i.e., $A \in \alpha$.

D-1. Let $\mathcal{L}$ be minimally **D**. Then $\alpha \vdash_{\mathcal{L}} A \Rightarrow \alpha \models_{\mathbf{D}} A$.

Proof : Any minimal **D**-logic is equivalent to a minimal **K**-logic with an added rule $\Box A \vdash \Diamond A$. By **K**-8, all rules of a minimal **K**-logic will be validity preserving. Suppose x is an assignment in a **D** MAS $\langle \mathfrak{G}, g \rangle$ such that $x \Vdash \Box A$ but not $x \Vdash \Diamond A$. Since $\langle \mathfrak{G}, g \rangle$ is **D**, there exists a $y \in g(x)$, with $y \Vdash A$ and $y \Vdash \sim A$, which is impossible.

T-1. Let $\mathcal{L}$ be minimally **T**. Then $\alpha \vdash_{\mathcal{L}} A \Rightarrow \alpha \models_{\mathbf{T}} A$.

Proof: Any minimal **T**-logic is equivalent to a minimal **D**-logic with an added rule $A \vdash \Diamond A$. By **D**−1, all rules of a minimal **D**-logic will be validity preserving. Suppose x is an assignment in a **T** MAS $\langle \mathfrak{G}, g \rangle$ such that $x \Vdash A$. Since $\langle \mathfrak{G}, g \rangle$ is **T**, $x \in g(x)$, and hence $x \Vdash \Diamond A$.

S4-7. Let $\mathcal{L}$ be minimally **S4**. Then $\alpha \vdash_{\mathcal{L}} A \Rightarrow \alpha \models_{\mathbf{S4}} A$.

Proof: Any minimal **S4**-logic is equivalent to a minimal **T**-logic with an added rule $\Diamond\Diamond A \vdash \Diamond A$. By **T**−1, all rules of α minimal **T**-logic will be validity preserving. Suppose x is an assignment in a **S4** MAS, $\langle \mathfrak{G}, g \rangle$ such that $x \Vdash \Diamond\Diamond A$. Hence there is a $y \in g(x)$ such that $y \Vdash \Diamond A$ and thus there is a $z \in g(y)$ such that $z \Vdash A$. But since $\langle \mathfrak{G}, g \rangle$ is **S4**, $z \in g(x)$ and hence $x \Vdash \Diamond A$.

S5-1. Let $\mathcal{L}$ be minimally **S5**. Then $\alpha \vdash_{\mathcal{L}} A \Rightarrow \alpha \models_{\mathbf{S5}} A$.

Proof: Any minimal S5-logic is equivalent to a minimal S4-logic with an added rule $\Diamond A \vdash \Box\Diamond A$. By S4-7, all rules of a minimal S4-logic will be validity preserving. Suppose x is an assignment in a S5 MAS $<\mathfrak{G},g>$ such that $x \Vdash \Diamond A$. Then there is a $y \in g(x)$ such that $y \Vdash A$. Now suppose $z \in g(x)$. Since $<\mathfrak{G},g>$ is S5, $x \in g(z)$ and hence since it is also S4, $y \in g(z)$ and therefore $z \Vdash \Diamond A$. Thus, since $z \in g(x)$ implies $z \Vdash \Diamond A$, $x \Vdash \Box\Diamond A$.

$\mathfrak{D}$-2. The $\mathfrak{D}$ regular MAS is $\mathfrak{D}$.

Proof: Let $<\mathfrak{G},g>$ be the $\mathfrak{D}$ regular MAS and let $\mathcal{L}$ be a minimal $\mathfrak{D}$ logic. Let $x \in \mathfrak{T}$. Then there is an $\mathcal{L}$-Lewis-regular set α such that $x = x_\alpha$. Let $\beta = \{A : \Box A \in \alpha\}$. Since $\mathcal{L}$ R-includes CLNEAK, $\vdash_{\mathcal{L}} A \supset A$ and hence $\vdash_{\mathcal{L}} \Box(A \supset A)$. Thus $\vdash_{\mathcal{L}} \Diamond(A \supset A)$. Therefore $\Diamond(A \supset A) \in \alpha$. Then β is $(A \wedge {\sim}A)$-$\mathcal{L}$-consistent. Since $\gamma \vdash_{\mathcal{L}} C$ implies $\Box\gamma \vdash_{\mathcal{L}} \Box C$, if α is $(A \wedge {\sim}A)$-$\mathcal{L}$-consistent (as it is), so is β. Hence there exists an $(A \wedge {\sim}A)$-$\mathcal{L}$- consistent and $(A \wedge {\sim}A)$-$\mathcal{L}$-complete δ with $\beta \subset \delta$. Then δ is $\mathcal{L}$-Lewis-regular and ${\sim}\Diamond A \in \alpha$ implies ${\sim}A \in \delta$. Since $\Diamond(A \supset A) \in \alpha$ and $A \supset A \in \delta$, $x_\delta \in g(x_\alpha)$ and hence $g(x) \neq \varnothing$.

$\mathfrak{T}$-2. The $\mathfrak{T}$-regular MAS is $\mathfrak{T}$.

Proof: Let $<\mathfrak{G},g>$ be the $\mathfrak{T}$ regular MAS and let $\mathcal{L}$ be a minimal $\mathfrak{T}$ logic. Let $x \in \mathfrak{T}$. Then there is an $\mathcal{L}$-Lewis-regular set α such that $x = x_\alpha$. Suppose $\Box A \in \alpha$. Hence $\alpha \vdash_{\mathcal{L}} \Box A$ and $\alpha \vdash_{\mathcal{L}} A$, and, since α is closed, $A \in \alpha$. Since $\Diamond(A \supset A) \in \alpha$ and $A \supset A \in \alpha$, $x_\alpha \in g(x_\alpha)$ and $<\mathfrak{S},g>$ is $\mathfrak{T}$.

S4-8. The S4 regular MAS is S4.

Proof: Let $<\mathfrak{G},g>$ be the S4 regular MAS and let $\mathcal{L}$ be a minimal S4 logic. For each $\mathcal{L}$-Lewis-regular set α, let x_α be the assignment associated with α. Let $x_\beta \in g(x_\alpha)$ and $x_\gamma \in g(x_\beta)$.

Suppose $\Box A \in \alpha$. Then $\alpha \vdash_{\mathcal{L}} \Box A$ and hence $\alpha \vdash_{\mathcal{L}} \Box\Box A$. Thus $\Box\Box A \in \alpha$. Therefore $\Box A \in \beta$ and $A \in \gamma$. Since $\Diamond(A \supset A) \in \alpha$ and $A \supset A \in \gamma$, $x_\gamma \in g(x_\alpha)$ and the $\mathcal{S}4$ regular MAS is $\mathcal{S}4$.

$\mathcal{S}5$-2. The $\mathcal{S}5$ regular MAS is $\mathcal{S}5$.

Proof: Let $\langle \mathcal{G}, g \rangle$ be the $\mathcal{S}5$ regular MAS and $\mathcal{L}$ be a minimal $\mathcal{S}5$ logic. Let x_α be the assignment associated with α where α is $\mathcal{L}$-Lewis-regular and $x_\beta \in g(x_\alpha)$. Suppose $\Box A \in \beta$ and $A \notin \alpha$. Since α is negation-complete, $\sim A \in \alpha$. Then $\alpha \vdash_{\mathcal{L}} \sim A$ and $\alpha \vdash_{\mathcal{L}} \Diamond\sim A$. Then $\alpha \vdash_{\mathcal{L}} \Box\Diamond\sim A$. Since α is deductively closed, $\Box\Diamond\sim A \in \alpha$ and $\Diamond\sim A \in \beta$. Hence $\sim\Box A \in \beta$. But this cannot be. Thus $\Box A \in \beta$ implies $A \in \alpha$. Since $A \supset A \in \beta$ and $\Diamond(A \supset A) \in \alpha$, $x_\alpha \in g(x_\beta)$.

$\mathcal{K}$-14. If $\mathcal{L}$ is minimally $\mathcal{K}$, $\alpha \vDash_{\mathcal{K}} A$ implies $\alpha \vdash_{\mathcal{L}} A$.

Proof: Suppose $\alpha \vDash_{\mathcal{K}} A$. For any assignment x and MAS, if $x \Vdash \alpha$, then $x \Vdash A$. Hence this holds for the $\mathcal{K}$-regular MAS and any $\mathcal{L}$-Lewis-regular set β such that $\alpha \subset \beta$ contains A. But if $\alpha \vdash_{\mathcal{L}} A$ were false, α would be $\sim A$-$\mathcal{L}$-consistent and hence is contained in a set which is $\sim A$-$\mathcal{L}$-consistent and $\sim A$-complete and hence $\mathcal{L}$-Lewis-regular, which is impossible.

$\mathcal{D}$-3. If $\mathcal{L}$ is minimally $\mathcal{D}$ ($\mathcal{T}$, $\mathcal{S}4$, $\mathcal{S}5$), $\alpha \vDash_{\mathcal{D}(\mathcal{T}, \mathcal{S}4, \mathcal{S}5)} A$ implies $\alpha \vdash_{\mathcal{L}} A$.

Proof: This follows by the argument of $\mathcal{K}$-14, restricted respectively to $\mathcal{D}$, $\mathcal{T}$, $\mathcal{S}4$, or $\mathcal{S}5$ MAS's. The counterexample is taken analogously from the $\mathcal{D}$, $\mathcal{T}$, $\mathcal{S}4$, $\mathcal{S}5$ regular MAS. (Note that for this purpose it was necessary to prove in each case that the regular MAS was the proper kind of MAS.)

$\mathcal{S}1'$-11T. $\vdash A \dashv\!\!\!\!\!\!\prec \Diamond A$ Exercise

$\mathcal{S}1'$-12D. $A \dashv\!\!\!\!\!\!\prec B, \Box A \vdash \Box B$

Proof: 1. $(A \supset B) \wedge A \vdash (A \supset B) \wedge A$	Premise
2. $(A \supset B) \wedge A \vdash A \supset B$	LS
3. $(A \supset B) \wedge A \vdash A$	RS
4. $(A \supset B) \wedge A \vdash B$	2,3, $\mathcal{NKC}$-3D
5. $(A \supset B) \wedge A \vdash [(A \supset B) \wedge A] \wedge B$	1, 4, A
6. $\vdash [(A \supset B) \wedge A] \strictif \llbracket [(A \supset B) \wedge A] \wedge B \rrbracket$	5, WFC
7. $\vdash \llbracket [(A \supset B) \wedge A] \wedge B \rrbracket \strictif [(A \supset B) \wedge A]$	6, Ax4
8. $\vdash [(A \supset B) \wedge A] \strictiff \llbracket [(A \supset B) \wedge A] \wedge B \rrbracket$	6,7, A, Df
9. $\vdash \Box[(A \supset B) \wedge A] \strictiff \Box\llbracket [A \supset B) \wedge A] \wedge B \rrbracket$	$\mathcal{S}$1-4T, SE, 8
10. $\vdash [(A \strictif B) \wedge \Box A] \strictiff$ $\llbracket \Box[(A \supset B) \wedge A] \wedge \Box B \rrbracket$	9, SE, $\mathcal{S}$1'-7T, $\mathcal{S}$1'-9T
11. $\vdash [(A \strictif B) \wedge \Box A] \strictiff$ $\llbracket [(A \strictif B) \wedge \Box A] \wedge \Box B \rrbracket$	10, SE, $\mathcal{S}$1'-7T, $\mathcal{S}$1'-9T
12. $\vdash \llbracket [(A \strictif B) \wedge \Box A] \wedge \Box B \rrbracket \strictif$ $\llbracket \Box B \wedge [(A \strictif B) \wedge \Box A] \rrbracket$	Ax3
13. $\vdash \llbracket \Box B \wedge [(A \strictif B) \wedge \Box A] \rrbracket \strictif \Box B$	Ax4
14. $\vdash \llbracket [(A \strictif B) \wedge \Box A] \wedge \Box B \rrbracket \strictif \Box B$	12,13, $\mathcal{S}$1-6D
15. $\vdash [(A \strictif B) \wedge \Box A] \strictif \Box B$	14, SE, 11

Theorem 11-1M. Let $\mathcal{L}$ satisfy $\mathbf{Equiv}_{\mathcal{L}}(\Box(A \supset B), A \strictif B)$, $\mathbf{Equiv}_{\mathcal{L}}(\Box A, \sim A \strictif A)$, and C (for $\supset$). Then $\vdash_{\mathcal{L}} A \Rightarrow \vdash_{\mathcal{L}} \Box A$ iff $A \vdash_{\mathcal{L}} B \Rightarrow \vdash_{\mathcal{L}} A \strictif B$.

Proof: Suppose $\vdash_{\mathcal{L}} A \Rightarrow \vdash_{\mathcal{L}} \Box A$. Let $C \vdash_{\mathcal{L}} B$. By C, $\vdash_{\mathcal{L}} A \supset B$. Hence $\vdash_{\mathcal{L}} \Box(A \supset B)$. Therefore, $\vdash_{\mathcal{L}} A \strictif B$. Suppose $A \vdash_{\mathcal{L}} B \Rightarrow \vdash_{\mathcal{L}} A \strictif B$. Let $\vdash_{\mathcal{L}} C$. Then $\sim C \vdash_{\mathcal{L}} C$. Hence $\vdash_{\mathcal{L}} \sim C \strictif C$. Therefore, $\vdash_{\mathcal{L}} \Box C$.

The completeness results of our modal model theory together with theorems from many-valued logic will allow us to compare modal systems. In doing this, we frequently prove that a system is valid or invalid relative to some system of models. One proof of that type, using many-valued logic, was presented in S1-28M. We will give one complete validity proof in modal model theory, and thereafter prove only the additional detailed results required for the particular comparison.

S1′-13M. All rules of S1′ are $\mathcal{T}$ valid.

Proof: Suppose x is an assignment in a $\mathcal{T}$ MAS. (1) Let $0 = V(x, (A \prec B) \prec \sim\Diamond(A \wedge \sim B))$. Then there is a $y \in g(x)$ such that $V(y, (A \prec B)) = 1$ and $V(y, \sim\Diamond(A \wedge \sim B)) = 0$. Hence $V(y, \Diamond(A \wedge \sim B)) = 1$. Thus, there is a $z \in g(y)$ such that $V(z, (A \wedge \sim B)) = 1$. Then $V(z, A) = V(z, \sim B) = 1$ and $V(y, (A \prec B)) = 0$. (2). Let $V(x, \sim\Diamond(A \wedge \sim B) \prec (A \prec B)) = 0$. Then there is a $y \in g(x)$ such that $V(y, \sim\Diamond(A \wedge \sim B)) = 1$ and $V(y, (A \prec B)) = 0$. Hence there is a $z \in g(y)$ such that $V(z, A) = V(z, \sim B) = 1$ and therefore $V(z, A \wedge \sim B) = 1$ and $V(y, \Diamond(A \wedge \sim B)) = 1$ and $V(y, \sim\Diamond(A \wedge \sim B)) = 0$. (3). Let $V(x, (A \wedge B) \prec (B \wedge A)) = 0$. But then there is a $y \in g(x)$ such that $V(y, (A \wedge B)) = 1$ while $V(y, (B \wedge A)) = 0$, which is impossible. (4) Let $V(x, (A \wedge B) \prec A) = 0$. Then there is a $y \in g(x)$ such that $V(y, (A \wedge B)) = 1$ (and hence $V(y, A) = 1$), but $V(y, A) = 0$, which is impossible. (5) Let $V(x, (A \prec (A \wedge A)) = 0$. Then there is a $y \in g(x)$ such that $V(y, A) = 1$, but $V(y, A \wedge A) = 0$, but then $V(y, A) = 0$. (6) Let $V(x, [A \wedge (B \wedge C)] \prec [(A \wedge B) \wedge C]) = 0$. Hence there is a $z \in g(y)$ such that $V(y, A \wedge (B \wedge C)) = 1$, but $V(y, (A \wedge B) \wedge C) = 0$. But then $V(y, A) = V(y, B) = V(y, C) = 1$ and $V(y, (A \wedge B) \wedge C) = 1$. (7) Let $V(x, (A \prec \sim\sim A) = 0$. Then there is a $y \in g(x)$ such that $V(y, A) = 1$ and $V(y, \sim\sim A) = 0$. But then $V(y, A) = 0$. (8) Suppose $V(X, [(A \prec B) \wedge (B \prec C)] \prec (A \prec C)) = 0$. Then there is a $y \in g(x)$ such that $V(y, [(A \prec B) \wedge (B \prec C)]) = 1$, but $V(y, A \prec C) = 0$. But then $z \in g(y)$, $V(z, A) = 1$ and $V(z, C) = 0$. Then $V(y, A \prec B) = V(y, B \prec C) = 1$. Therefore $V(z, B) = 1$ and $V(z, B) = 0$. (9) Suppose $V(x, [A \wedge (A \prec B)] \prec B) = 0$. Then there is a $y \in g(x)$ such that $V(y, A \wedge (A \prec B)) = 1$, but $V(y, B) = 0$. Then $V(y, A) = 1 = V(y, A \prec B)$. However, $y \in g(y)$ and $V(y, A \prec B) = 0$. (10) Suppose $V(x, \Diamond(A \wedge B) \prec \Diamond A) = 0$. Then there is a $y \in g(x)$ such that $V(y, \Diamond(A \wedge B)) = 1$ and $V(y, \Diamond A) = 0$. Hence there is a $z \in g(y)$, such that $V(z,A) = V(z,B) = 1$, but then $V(y, \Diamond A) = 1$. Obviously A is 1-preserving, while $V(x,A) = 1$ and $V(x, A \prec B) = 1$. Since $x \in g(x)$, $V(x,A)$ cannot be 0 and MMP preserves validity. Since $\models A \leftrightarrow B$ implies $V(y,A) = V(y,B)$, SE preserves validity. Finally if $x \Vdash A$ for all assignments x, it does so for all assignments in the range of g and hence $\models A$ implies $\models \Box A$.

S1'-14M. S1' is a minimal $\mathcal{T}$ logic.

Proof: By the R-inclusion of NKC, S E , S1'-11T, S1'-12D and 11-1M, S1' is a $\mathcal{T}$ logic. By S1'-13M, it is minimal.

$\mathcal{K}$-15. $\vdash \Diamond(A \vee \sim A)$ is not provable in a minimal $\mathcal{K}$ logic.

Proof: Let $\mathfrak{A} = \langle \mathfrak{G}, g \rangle$ be the following MAS: $\mathfrak{G} = \{x\}$, $g(x) = \varnothing$. Hence $V(x, \Diamond(A \vee \sim A)) = 0$.

$\mathcal{K}$-16. $\Box A \vdash \Diamond A$ is not provable in a minimal $\mathcal{K}$ logic.

Proof: $\vdash A \vee \sim A$ and hence $\vdash \Box(A \vee \sim A)$. But by $\mathcal{K}$-15, not-$\vdash \Diamond(A \vee \sim A)$ and $\Box(A \vee \sim A) \vdash \Diamond(A \vee \sim A)$ does not hold.

$\mathfrak{D}$-4. $A \vdash \Diamond A$ is not provable in a minimal $\mathfrak{D}$ logic.

Proof: Let $\mathfrak{A} = \langle \mathfrak{G}, g \rangle$ be the following MAS: $\mathfrak{G} = \{x,y\}$, $g(x) = g(y) = \{y\}$. Then clearly $\mathfrak{A}$ is $\mathfrak{D}$. Let $V(x,p) = 1$ and $V(y,p) = 0$. Then $V(x, \Diamond p) = 0$.

$\mathcal{T}$-3. $\Diamond\Diamond A \vdash \Diamond A$ is not provable in a minimal $\mathcal{T}$ logic.

Proof: Let $\mathfrak{A} = \langle \mathfrak{G}, g \rangle$ be the following MAS: $\mathfrak{G} = \{x,y,z\}$, $g(x) = \{x,y\}$, $g(y) = \{y,z\}$ and $g(z) = \{z\}$. Then clearly $\mathfrak{A}$ is $\mathcal{T}$. Let $V(x,p) = V(y,p) = 0$ and $V(z,p) = 1$. Then $V(y, \Diamond p) = 1$, $V(x, \Diamond\Diamond p) = 1$, but $V(x, \Diamond p) = 0$.

S4-8. $\Diamond A \vdash \Box\Diamond A$ is not provable in a minimal **S4** logic.

Proof: Let $\mathfrak{A} = \langle \mathfrak{G}, g \rangle$ be the following MAS: $\mathfrak{G} = \{x, y,\}$, $g(x) = \{x, y\}$ and $g(y) = \{y\}$. Then clearly $\mathfrak{A}$ is **S4**. Let $V(x,p) = 1$ and $V(y,p) = 0$. Hence $V(x,\Diamond p) = 1$ and $V(y,\Diamond p) = 0$. Hence $V(x, \Box\Diamond p) = 0$.

S3-14M. $\vdash \Diamond\Diamond A \supset \Diamond A$ is not provable in **S3**.

Proof: Consider the following 4-valued logic **R** with 2 and 3 as designated values:

p\q	∧ 0	1	2	3	~p	⥽ 0	1	2	3	p ⥽ ~p	◇p	◇◇p	◇◇p ⥽ ◇p
0	0	0	0	0	3	2	2	2	2	2	1	3	0
1	0	1	0	1	2	0	2	0	2	0	3	3	2
2	0	0	2	2	1	0	0	2	2	0	3	3	2
3	0	1	2	3	0	0	0	0	2	0	3	3	2

By the argument of **S1**-28M, the rules of **S3** preserve validity in this model. As can be seen above, $\Diamond\Diamond p \prec \Diamond p$ takes an undesignated value when p takes 0.

S1′-15M. $\vdash (A \prec B) \prec (\sim\Diamond B \prec \sim\Diamond A)$ is not provable in **S1'** (or other minimal $\mathcal{T}$ logics).

Proof: Let $\mathfrak{A} = \langle \mathfrak{G}, g \rangle$ be the following MAS: $\mathfrak{G} = \{x, y, z\}$, $g(x) = \{x, y\}$, $g(y) = \{y, z\}$ and $g(z) = \{z\}$. Then clearly $\mathfrak{A}$ is $\mathcal{T}$. Let $V(x,p) = V(x,q) = V(z,p) = 1$ and $V(y,p) = V(y,q) = V(z,q) = 0$. Then $V(x,\Diamond p) = V(x,\Diamond q) = V(y,\Diamond p) = V(z,\Diamond p) = 1$ and $V(y,\Diamond q) = V(z,\Diamond q) = 0$. $V(x, p \supset q) = V(y, p \supset q) = 1$. Hence $V(x, p \prec q) = 1$, but $V(x, \sim\Diamond q \supset \sim\Diamond p) = 1$, and $V(y, \sim\Diamond q \supset \sim\Diamond p) = 0$. Hence $V(x, \sim\Diamond q \prec \sim\Diamond p) = 0$, so that $V(x, (p \prec q) \prec (\sim\Diamond q \prec \sim\Diamond p)) = 0$.

S1-31T. $\vdash \sim\Diamond A \prec \sim A$

Proof:	1. $\vdash (A \mathbin{-\!\!\!3} {\sim}A) \mathbin{-\!\!\!3} (A \mathbin{-\!\!\!3} {\sim}A)$	S1-4T
	2. $\vdash {\sim}\Diamond(A \wedge {\sim}{\sim}A) \mathbin{-\!\!\!3} (A \mathbin{-\!\!\!3} A)$	1, SE, Ax-1, Ax-2
	3. $\vdash {\sim}\Diamond A \mathbin{-\!\!\!3} (A \mathbin{-\!\!\!3} A)$	2, S1-11M
	4. $\vdash (A \mathbin{-\!\!\!3} {\sim}A) \mathbin{-\!\!\!3} {\sim}(A \wedge {\sim}{\sim}A)$	S1-14T
	5. $\vdash (A \mathbin{-\!\!\!3} {\sim}A) \mathbin{-\!\!\!3} {\sim}A$	4, S1-11M
	6. $\vdash {\sim}\Diamond A \mathbin{-\!\!\!3} {\sim}A$	3, 5, S1-6D

S5-3T. $\vdash \Diamond A \mathbin{E\!\!\!3} \Box\Diamond A$

Proof:	1. $\vdash {\sim}\Diamond{\sim}\Diamond A \mathbin{-\!\!\!3} {\sim}{\sim}\Diamond A$	S1-31T
	2. $\vdash {\sim}\Diamond{\sim}\Diamond A \mathbin{-\!\!\!3} \Diamond A$	1, S1-11M
	3. $\vdash \Box\Diamond A \mathbin{-\!\!\!3} \Diamond A$	2, Df
	4. $\vdash \Diamond A \mathbin{-\!\!\!3} {\sim}\Diamond{\sim}\Diamond A$	Ax-11'
	5. $\vdash \Diamond A \mathbin{-\!\!\!3} \Box\Diamond A$	4, Df
	6. $\vdash \Diamond A \mathbin{E\!\!\!3} \Box\Diamond A$	3, 5, A, Df

S5-4T. $\vdash \Diamond\Diamond A \mathbin{E\!\!\!3} \Diamond A$

Proof:	1. $\vdash {\sim}\Diamond\Diamond A \mathbin{-\!\!\!3} {\sim}\Diamond A$	S1-31T
	2. $\vdash \Diamond A \mathbin{-\!\!\!3} \Diamond\Diamond A$	1, S1-11M
	3. $\vdash \Diamond\Diamond A \mathbin{-\!\!\!3} \Diamond\Diamond A$	S1-4T
	4. $\vdash \Diamond\Diamond A \mathbin{-\!\!\!3} \Diamond\Box\Diamond A$	3, S5-3T
	5. $\vdash \Diamond\Diamond A \mathbin{-\!\!\!3} \Diamond{\sim}\Diamond{\sim}\Diamond A$	4, Df
	6. $\vdash \Diamond\Diamond A \mathbin{-\!\!\!3} {\sim}{\sim}\Diamond{\sim}\Diamond{\sim}\Diamond A$	5, S1-11M
	7. $\vdash \Diamond\Diamond A \mathbin{-\!\!\!3} {\sim}\Box\Diamond{\sim}\Diamond A$	6, Df
	8. $\vdash \Diamond\Diamond A \mathbin{-\!\!\!3} {\sim}\Diamond{\sim}\Diamond A$	7, SE, S5-3T
	9. $\vdash {\sim}\Diamond{\sim}\Diamond A \mathbin{-\!\!\!3} {\sim}{\sim}\Diamond A$	S1-31T
	10. $\vdash \Diamond\Diamond A \mathbin{-\!\!\!3} {\sim}{\sim}\Diamond A$	8, 9, S1-6T
	11. $\vdash \Diamond\Diamond A \mathbin{-\!\!\!3} \Diamond A$	10, S1-11M
	12. $\vdash \Diamond A \mathbin{E\!\!\!3} \Diamond\Diamond A$	2, 11, A, Df

S5-5T. $\vdash \Box A \mathbin{-\!\!\!3} \Box\Box A$

Proof:	1. $\vdash {\sim}\Diamond{\sim}A \mathbin{-\!\!\!3} {\sim}\Diamond{\sim}A$	S1-3T
	2. $\vdash {\sim}\Diamond{\sim}A \mathbin{-\!\!\!3} {\sim}\Diamond\Diamond{\sim}A$	1, S5-4T
	3. $\vdash {\sim}\Diamond{\sim}A \mathbin{-\!\!\!3} {\sim}\Diamond{\sim}{\sim}\Diamond{\sim}A$	2, S1-11M
	4. $\vdash \Box A \mathbin{-\!\!\!3} \Box\Box A$	3, Df

We are now able to fully summarize the relative strengths of the systems we have been discussing by means of a partial ordering in which < represents proper R-inclusion:

S1 < S2, S1 < S1*, S2 < S2*, S1* < S2*, K < D, S2 < T, D < T,
S2* < S3, S3 < S4, T < S4, S4 < S5.

If we classify the systems according to whether **SHE** and **WFC** hold in them, indicating equivalent systems in parenthesis, we get:

Neither **SHE** nor **WFC**: S1; S2
SHE, not **WFC**: S1*; S2*; S3(S3*)
WFC, not **SHE**: K; D; T (S1', S2')
SHE and **WFC**: S4 (S1*', S2*', S3', S3*', S4*, S4', S5*'); S5 (S5*, S5', S5*')

The equivalence of the four S4 systems follows from the equivalence of S1*' to both S4 and S4*', while that of the four S5 systems follows from the fact that each can be generated by adding axiom 11' to the corresponding S4 system. The non-equivalence of S1 and S1*, and of S2 and S2* follows from that of S2' and S2*', and similarly the non-equivalence of S2 and S3 follows from that of S2' and S3'.

The failure of **WFC** to hold in the weaker systems creates a certain implausibility given Lewis' stated intentions, as we have earlier mentioned. This implausibility is perhaps most clearly marked by the non-equivalence of S1 and S1*, despite the clear fact that they have the same set of T-theorems. If we restrict ourselves to the stronger systems S1', S4 and S5, we can point out the most significant differences. At least one of them is that S4 is S1' with the less restricted substitution rule **SHE** instead of **SE**. We can more clearly express the difference by proving a result which expresses this equivalence rule in a form most closely approaching that in S4. We recall that in S4, $A \Leftrightarrow B$ or equivalently $\Box(A \equiv B)$ provides a sufficient basis for the substitution of A for B even when it is a premise (or follows from one), while this does not hold in S1' . Let us now define a special operator: $\Box^0 A = A$ and $\Box^{k+1} A = \Box\,\Box^k A$.

S1'-16T. $\vdash_{S1'}\ \Box^k(A \equiv B) ⥽ (\Box^k A \equiv \Box^k B)$

Proof: By induction on k:

(α) $k = 0$. $\Box^0(A \equiv B) = (A \equiv B)$, $\Box^0 A = A$ and $\Box^0 B = B$.
$\vdash (A \equiv B) ⥽ (A \equiv B)$, by S1-4T.

(β) Assume k = m. Prove for k = m + 1.

1.	$\vdash \Box^m(A \equiv B) \prec (\Box^m A \equiv \Box^m B)$	Hyp.induction
2.	$\Box^{m+1}(A \equiv B) \vdash \Box(\Box^m A \equiv \Box^m B)$	1,S1-12D
3.	$\Box^{m+1}(A \equiv B) \vdash \Box[(\Box^m A \supset \Box^m B) \wedge (\Box^m B \supset \Box^m A)]$	2,SE,Df
4.	$\vdash \Box[(\Box^m A \supset \Box^m B) \wedge (\Box^m B \supset \Box^m A)] \prec \Box(\Box^m A \supset \Box^m B) \wedge \Box(\Box^m B \supset \Box^m A)$	S1'-9T
5.	$\Box^{m+1}(A \equiv B) \vdash \Box(\Box^m A \supset \Box^m B) \wedge \Box(\Box^m B \supset \Box^m A)$	3,4,MMP
6.	$\Box^{m+1}(A \equiv B) \vdash \Box(\Box^m A \supset \Box^m B)$	5, LS
7.	$\Box^{m+1}(A \equiv B) \vdash \Box^m A \prec \Box^m B$	6,S1-11M,Df
8.	$\Box^{m+1}(A \equiv B),\ \Box^{m+1} A \vdash \Box^{m+1} B$	7, S1-12D
9.	$\Box^{m+1}(A \equiv B) \vdash \Box(\Box^m B \supset \Box^m A)$	5, RS
10.	$\Box^{m+1}(A \equiv B) \vdash \Box^m B \prec \Box^m A$	9,S1-11M,Df
11.	$\Box^{m+1}(A \equiv B),\ \Box^{m+1} B \vdash \Box^{m+1} A$	7,S1-12D
12.	$\Box^{m+1}(A \equiv B) \vdash \Box^{m+1} A \equiv \Box^{m+1} B$	8,11,Bi-C
13.	$\vdash \Box^{m+1}(A \equiv B) \prec \Box^{m+1} A \equiv \Box^{m+1} B$	12,WFC

We can express S1'-16T by saying that one can indeed substitute on the basis of assumed necessary (or strict) equivalence in S1', but only if the context is not of a higher modal degree than the equivalence is. When two wffs are **proved** necessarily equivalent, they are so in **all** degrees of necessity and hence can be substituted without restriction. Since, in S4 and S5, all degrees of necessity are equivalent, the result collapses to universal substitutivity on the basis of necessary equivalence.

The principal difference between S4 and S5 is that S5 reduces the modalities to the classic triple of necessity, contingency and impossibility so that all that can be consistently asserted of a single wff A is $\Box A$, $A \wedge \Diamond{\sim}A$, A, $\Diamond A$, $\Diamond A \wedge \Diamond{\sim}A$, $\Diamond{\sim}A$, ${\sim}A$, ${\sim}A \wedge \Diamond A$, ${\sim}\Diamond A$.

An interesting result that follows is that one can define a family of 2^n-valued logics as follows: The values are 1, ⋯ , 2^n with 1 as the only designated value. For each value j there exists a unique sequence of 0s and 1s $c_1, \cdots, c_n$ such that j = $1 + \sum_{i=1}^{n+1} (c_i * 2^i)$. Then if $\mathbf{V}(A) = 1 + \sum_{i=1}^{n+1} (a_i * 2^i)$ and $\mathbf{V}(B) = 1 + \sum_{i=1}^{n+1} (b_i * 2^i)$,

$\mathbf{V}(A \wedge B) = 1 + \sum_{i=1}^{n+1} (c_i * 2^i)$ such that $c_i = \max(a_i, b_i)$. Furthermore, $\mathbf{V}(\sim A) = \mathbf{V}(\Diamond A) = 2^n$ if $\mathbf{V}(A) = 2^n$, and $\mathbf{V}(\Diamond A) = 1$, otherwise. It follows that **NKC** is **R**-included and (with the standard definitions) each of these logics **R**-includes **S**5. Since we can show that every wff of **S**5 is equivalent to one with no modalities of level greater than 1, it follows by an argument similar to the one we used with Kripke models, that only wffs that hold in all these logics are provable in **S**5. Since the coefficients are isomorphic to a Boolean algebra, this family of models could be considered as Boolean algebras with ◇ as a special operator. This operator can be interpreted as a closure in the degenerate topological space in which only the null set and the entire space are closed. Interestingly enough (we shall have to refrain from proving it for reasons of space), **S**4 can be interpreted in the same way but with **all** the topological spaces definable over finite Boolean algebras as models (and not only the degenerate ones). Interested readers are referred to the bibliography.

Another type of **weak implication** has been suggested by Church. This system has the interesting property of avoiding those theorems that result from applying conditionalization to irrelevant premises (or at least very obviously irrelevant ones; it is not clear that this can be achieved for all such cases); consequently it has some attractiveness for those who feel that such results of **P1** like A ⊢ B ⊃ A are odd or paradoxical. We shall call this system **WI** (the mnemonic is obvious).

WI : A DZOS with:

Connectives: ⊃ (two-place)

Axiom schemata:

1. ⊢ [A ⊃ (A ⊃ B)] ⊃ (A ⊃ B)
2. ⊢ (A ⊃ B)] ⊃ [(C ⊃ A) ⊃ (C ⊃ B)]
3. ⊢ [A ⊃ (B ⊃ C)] ⊃ [B ⊃ (A ⊃ C)]
4. ⊢A ⊃ A

Rule: 1. A, A ⊃ B ⊢ B MP

WI-1D. A ⊃ B, B ⊃ C ⊢A ⊃ C **Ax2,MP**

WI-2T. ⊢ [A ⊃ (B ⊃ C)] ⊃ [(A ⊃ B) ⊃ (A ⊃ C)]

Proof: 1. $\vdash (B \supset C) \supset [(A \supset B) \supset (A \supset C)]$ Ax2

2. $\vdash [\![(B \supset C) \supset [(A \supset B) \supset (A \supset C)]]\!] \supset$
$\{[A \supset (B \supset C) \supset [\![A \supset [(A \supset B) \supset (A \supset C)]]\!]\}$ Ax2

3. $\vdash [A \supset (B \supset C)] \supset [\![A \supset [(A \supset B) \supset (A \supset C)]]\!]$ 1,2, MP

4. $\vdash [\![A \supset [(A \supset B) \supset (A \supset C)]]\!] \supset$
$[\![(A \supset B) \supset [A \supset (A \supset C)]]\!]$ Ax3

5. $\vdash [A \supset (B \supset C)] \supset [\![(A \supset B) \supset [A \supset (A \supset C)]]\!]$ 3,4, **W1**-1D

6. $\vdash [\![[A \supset (A \supset C)] \supset (A \supset C)]\!] \supset$
$\{[\![(A \supset B) \supset [A \supset (A \supset C)]]\!] \supset [(A \supset B) \supset (A \supset C)]\}$ Ax2

7. $\vdash [A \supset (A \supset C)] \supset (A \supset C)$ Ax1

8. $\vdash [\![(A \supset B) \supset [A \supset (A \supset C)]]\!] \supset [(A \supset B) \supset (A \supset C)]$ 6,7, MP

9. $\vdash [A \supset (B \supset C)] \supset [(A \supset B) \supset (A \supset C)]$ 5,8, **W1**-1D

We can now prove a slightly weaker form of conditionalization than C. It may be argued that this form covers the immense majority of cases in which conditionalization is actually used in non-mathematical contexts.

W1-3M. $\alpha, A \vdash_{W1} B \Rightarrow (\alpha \vdash_{W1} A \supset B$ or $\alpha \vdash_{W1} B)$

Proof: Let $\alpha, A \vdash_{W1} B$. Then there is a sequence $A_1, \cdots, A_n$ such that each A_i is either (1) an element of α, (2)A, (3) an axiom, or (4) follows from earlier steps by **MP**, and A_n is B. By induction on the number of steps k:

(α) $k = 1$.

Case 1. $A_1 \subset \alpha$. Then $\alpha \vdash A_1$

Case 2. A_1 is A. Then $\alpha \vdash A \supset A_1$

Case 3. A_1 is an axiom. Then $\alpha \vdash A_1$

(β) Let us assume the theorem is true for $k < m$. We will prove it for $k = m$.

Case 1 to 3. This is the same as for (α).

Case 4. There is an $i < m$ and $j < m$ such that $A_j = A_i \supset A_m$. By the hypothesis of induction, $\alpha \vdash A \supset A_i$ or $\alpha \vdash A_i$, and $\alpha \vdash A \supset (A_i \supset A_m)$ or $\alpha \vdash A_i \supset A_m$.

Case 4a. $\alpha \vdash A \supset A_i$ and $\alpha \vdash A \supset (A_i \supset A_m)$. By **W1**-2T, $\vdash [A \supset (A_i \supset A_m)] \supset [(A \supset A_i) \supset (A \supset A_m)]$ and hence by **MP** twice, $\alpha \vdash A \supset A_m$.

Case 4b. $\alpha \vdash A \supset A_i$ and $\alpha \vdash A_i \supset A_m$. Then by $\mathfrak{W1}$-1D, $\alpha \vdash A \supset A_i$.

Case 4c. $\alpha \vdash A_i$ and $\alpha \vdash A \supset (A_i \supset A_m)$. By Ax-3, $\alpha \vdash [A \supset (A_i \supset A_m)] \supset [A_i \supset (A \supset A_m)]$, and by two applications of MP, $\alpha \vdash A \supset A_m$.

Case 4d. $\alpha \vdash A_i$ and $\alpha \vdash A_i \supset A_m$. Hence, by MP, $\alpha \vdash A_m$.

The relation between $\mathfrak{P1}$ and $\mathfrak{W1}$ can perhaps be made more clear if we formulate $\mathfrak{W1}$ in an equivalent form (which is however not a DZOS in our sense, though it is almost one).

$\mathfrak{W1}$1: A zero-order system with:

Connective: $\supset$ (two-place)

Rules: 1. $A, A \supset B \vdash B$ MP

2. If ($\alpha, A \vdash_{\mathfrak{W1}} B$ and not $\alpha \vdash_{\mathfrak{1C}} B$) $\Rightarrow$

$$S^{v_1}_{A_1}, \ldots, {}^{v_n}_{A_n}\alpha \vdash_{\mathfrak{W1}} S^{v_1}_{A_1}, \ldots, {}^{v_n}_{A_n}B \qquad \text{RC}$$

Of course any logic which is complete relative to two-valued logic could be used instead of $\mathfrak{1C}$. More significantly, one can use our completeness results to establish the failure of derivability in $\mathfrak{1C}$.

$\mathfrak{W1}$1-1T. $\vdash [A \supset (A \supset B)] \supset (A \supset B)$

Proof: 1. $A \supset (A \supset B), A \vdash_{\mathfrak{W1}} A \supset B$ MP

2. $A \supset (A \supset B), A \vdash_{\mathfrak{W1}} A$ Premise

3. $A \supset (A \supset B), A \vdash_{\mathfrak{W1}} B$ 1, 2, MP

4. not $A \supset (A \supset B) \vdash_{\mathfrak{1C}} B$ $\mathrm{V}(A) = \mathrm{V}(B) = 0$

5. $A \supset (A \supset B) \vdash_{\mathfrak{W1}} A \supset B$ 3, 4, RC

6. not $\vdash_{\mathfrak{1C}} A \supset B$ $\mathrm{V}(A) = 1, \mathrm{V}(B) = 0$

7. $\vdash_{\mathfrak{W1}} [A \supset (A \supset B)] \supset (A \supset B)$ 5, 6, RC

$\mathfrak{W1}$1-2T. $\vdash (A \supset B) \supset [(C \supset A) \supset (C \supset B)]$

Proof: 1. $A \supset B, C \supset A, C \vdash_{\mathfrak{W1}} A$ MP

2. $A \supset B, C \supset A, C \vdash_{\mathfrak{W1}} A \supset B$ Premise

3. $A \supset B, C \supset A, C \vdash_{\mathfrak{wl}} B$	1, 2, MP
4. not $A \supset B, C \supset A \vdash_{\mathfrak{lc}} B$	$\mathfrak{V}(A) = \mathfrak{V}(B) = \mathfrak{V}(C) = 0$
5. $A \supset B, C \supset A \vdash_{\mathfrak{wl}} C \supset B$	3, 4, RC
6. not $A \supset B \vdash_{\mathfrak{lc}} C \supset B$	$\mathfrak{V}(A) = \mathfrak{V}(B) = 0, \mathfrak{V}(C) = 1$
7. $A \supset B \vdash_{\mathfrak{wl}} (C \supset A) \supset (C \supset B)$	5, 6, RC
8. not $\vdash_{\mathfrak{lc}} (C \supset A) \supset (C \supset B)$	$\mathfrak{V}(A) = \mathfrak{V}(C) = 1, \mathfrak{V}(B) = 0$
9. $\vdash_{\mathfrak{wl}} (A \supset B) \supset [(C \supset A) \supset (C \supset B)]$	7, 8, RC

$\mathfrak{wl}$1-3T. $\vdash [A \supset (B \supset C)] \supset [B \supset (A \supset C)]$

Proof:

1. $A \supset (B \supset C), A, B \vdash_{\mathfrak{wl}} B \supset C$	MP
2. $A \supset (B \supset C), A, B \vdash_{\mathfrak{wl}} B$	Premise
3. $A \supset (B \supset C), A, B \vdash_{\mathfrak{wl}} C$	1, 2, MP
4. not $A \supset (B \supset C), B \vdash_{\mathfrak{lc}} C$	$\mathfrak{V}(A) = \mathfrak{V}(C) = 0, \mathfrak{V}(B) = 1$
5. $A \supset (B \supset C), B \vdash_{\mathfrak{wl}} A \supset C$	3, 4, RC
6. $A \supset (B \supset C) \vdash_{\mathfrak{lc}} A \supset C$	$\mathfrak{V}(A) = 1, \mathfrak{V}(B) = \mathfrak{V}(C) = 0$
7. $A \supset (B \supset C) \vdash_{\mathfrak{wl}} B \supset (A \supset C)$	5, 6, RC
8. not $\vdash_{\mathfrak{lc}} B \supset (A \supset C)$	$\mathfrak{V}(A) = \mathfrak{V}(B) = 1, \mathfrak{V}(C) = 0$
9. $\vdash_{\mathfrak{wl}} [A \supset (B \supset C)] \supset [B \supset (A \supset C)]$	7, 8, RC

$\mathfrak{wl}$1-4T. $\vdash A \supset A$

Proof:

1. $A \vdash_{\mathfrak{wl}} A$	Premise
2. not $\vdash_{\mathfrak{lc}} A$	$\mathfrak{V}(A) = 0$
3. $\vdash_{\mathfrak{wl}} A \supset A$	1, 2, RC

$\mathfrak{wl}$1-5M. $\mathfrak{wl}$ and $\mathfrak{wl}$1 are equivalent.

Proof: It is clear that $\mathfrak{wl}$ R-includes $\mathfrak{wl}$1 since MP is a rule of $\mathfrak{wl}$ and $\alpha \vdash_{\mathfrak{wl}} A$ implies $\alpha \vdash_{\mathfrak{lc}} A$, since $\mathfrak{lc}$ R-includes $\mathfrak{wl}$. Hence if α, $A \vdash_{\mathfrak{wl}} B$ and not- $\alpha \vdash_{\mathfrak{lc}} B$, then not- $\alpha \vdash_{\mathfrak{wl}} B$ and by $\mathfrak{wl}$-4M, $\alpha \vdash_{\mathfrak{wl}} A \supset B$ (and all its instances). The converse holds by $\mathfrak{wl}$-1T through $\mathfrak{wl}$-4T and the fact that MP is also a rule of $\mathfrak{wl}$1.

Accordingly we see that $\mathfrak{W1}$ is like $\mathfrak{P1}$ except that conditionalization is restricted to cases in which the premise which is eliminated would not be redundant in two-valued logic, and to substitution instances of these cases. (The complexity represented by the last clause is unavoidable, since redundancy is not preserved under instantiation.)

$\mathfrak{W1}$ can be extended by adding a constant $\mathfrak{F}$ (as we did to get $\mathfrak{P1A}$ from $\mathfrak{P1}$) and still have a system non-equivalent to $\mathfrak{P1A}$. Perhaps even more interesting is the fact that if we change the negation to intuitionistic strength, by adding a rule like $\mathfrak{F} \vdash A$, the resulting system will be non-equivalent to $\mathfrak{W1N}$, as the following tables show:

	$\supset$			$\mathfrak{F}$
p\q	0	1	2	
0	1	1	1	0
1	0	1	0	0
2	0	1	2	0

Designated values: 1 and 2.

The situation alters drastically if we add normal conjunction or disjunction. Let us consider a DZOS incorporating $\mathfrak{W1}$ and $\mathfrak{SK}$ (with the rules conditionalized):

$\mathfrak{W1SK}$: A DZOS with:

Connectives: $\supset$ (two-place) $\wedge$ (two-place)

Axiom schemata:

1. $\vdash [A \supset (A \supset B)] \supset (A \supset B)$
2. $\vdash (A \supset B) \supset [(C \supset A) \supset (C \supset B)]$
3. $\vdash [A \supset (B \supset C)] \supset [B \supset (A \supset C)]$
4. $\vdash A \supset A$
5. $\vdash (A \wedge B) \supset A$
6. $\vdash (A \wedge B) \supset B$
7. $\vdash A \supset [B \supset (A \wedge B)]$

Rule: 1. $A, A \supset B \vdash B$ MP

$\mathfrak{W1SK}$-1T. $\vdash [A \supset (A \wedge B)] \supset (A \supset B)$

Proof: 1. $\vdash [(A \wedge B) \supset B)] \supset [\![[A \supset (A \wedge B)] \supset (A \supset B)]\!]$ Ax2

2. $\vdash (A \wedge B) \supset B$ Ax6
3. $\vdash [A \supset (A \wedge B)] \supset (A \supset B)$ 1, 2, MP

WISK-2T. $\vdash B \supset (A \supset B)$

Proof: 1. $\vdash A \supset [B \supset (A \wedge B)]$ Ax7
2. $\vdash \llbracket A \supset [B \supset (A \wedge B)]\rrbracket \supset \llbracket B \supset [A \supset (A \wedge B)]\rrbracket$ Ax3
3. $\vdash B \supset [A \supset (A \wedge B)]$ 1, 2, MP
4. $\vdash [A \supset (A \wedge B)] \supset (A \supset B)$ WISK-1T
5. $\vdash \llbracket [A \supset (A \wedge B)] \supset (A \supset B)\rrbracket \supset$
$\{\llbracket B \supset [A \supset (A \wedge B)]\rrbracket \supset [B \supset (A \supset B)]\}$ Ax2
6. $\vdash \llbracket B \supset [A \supset (A \wedge B)]\rrbracket \supset [B \supset (A \supset B)]$ 4, 5, MP
7. $\vdash B \supset (A \supset B)$ 3, 6, MP

A similar result holds for disjunction.

WISA: A DZOS with
Connectives: $\supset$ (two-place), $\vee$ (two-place)
Axiom schemata:
1. $\vdash [A \supset (A \supset B)] \supset (A \supset B)$
2. $\vdash (A \supset B) \supset [(C \supset A) \supset (C \supset B)]$
3. $\vdash [A \supset (B \supset C)] \supset [B \supset (A \supset C)]$
4. $\vdash A \supset A$
5. $\vdash A \supset (A \vee B)$
6. $\vdash A \supset (B \vee A)$
7. $\vdash (A \supset C) \supset \llbracket (B \supset C) \supset [(A \vee B) \supset C]\rrbracket$

Rule: 1. $A,\ A \supset B \vdash B$ MP

WISA-1M. Every T and D theorem of **WI** and **SA** is a theorem of **WISA**.

Proof: This is trivial.

WISA-2D. $[A \supset (B \supset C)] \vdash [B \supset (A \supset C)]$ Ax 3 and MP

WISA-3D. $A \supset B,\ B \supset C \vdash A \supset C$ Ax 2 and MP

WISA-4T. ⊢ B ⊃ (A ⊃ B)

Proof:

1. ⊢ (A ⊃ B) ⊃ (A ⊃ B)	Ax4
2. ⊢ A ⊃ [(A ⊃ B) ⊃ B]	1, WISA-2D
3. ⊢ ⟦[(A ⊃ B) ⊃ B] ⊃ B⟧ ⊃ {⟦A ⊃ [(A ⊃ B) ⊃ B]⟧ ⊃ (A ⊃ B)}	Ax2
4. ⊢ ⟦A ⊃ [(A⊃B) ⊃ B]⟧ ⊃ {⟦[(A⊃B) ⊃ B] ⊃ B⟧ ⊃ (A⊃B)}	3, WISA-2D
5. ⊢ ⟦[(A ⊃ B) ⊃ B] ⊃ B⟧ ⊃ (A ⊃ B)	2, 4, MP
6. ⊢ [(A ⊃ B) ⊃ B] ⊃ {(B ⊃ B) ⊃ ⟦[(A ⊃ B) ∨ B] ⊃ B⟧}	Ax7
7. ⊢ (B ⊃ B) ⊃ {[(A ⊃ B) ⊃ B] ⊃ ⟦[(A ⊃ B) ∨ B] ⊃ B⟧}	6, WISA-2D
8. ⊢ B ⊃ B	Ax4
9. ⊢ [(A ⊃ B) ⊃ B] ⊃ ⟦[(A ⊃ B) ∨ B] ⊃ B⟧	7, 8, MP
10. ⊢ [(A ⊃ B) ∨ B] ⊃ ⟦ [(A ⊃ B) ⊃ B] ⊃ B⟧	9, WISA-2D
11. ⊢ B ⊃ [(A ⊃ B) ∨ B]	Ax6
12. ⊢ [(A ⊃ B) ∨ B] ⊃ (A ⊃ B)	5, 10, WISA-3D
13. ⊢ B ⊃ (A ⊃ B)	11, 12, WISA-3D

This result does not depend on any assumption concerning ~. It follows that this kind of weakening of implication is without effect unless any "and" and "or" expressible is weaker than what we have termed "normal."

Even though we are, strictly speaking, departing from the topic of strict implications, the type of model theory we found useful in modal logic can be applied to systems of the strength of PINEAK and WINEAK. For convenience, we will use versions related to these systems as PIAN was related to PIN, i.e. with the additional 0-place connective $\mathfrak{F}$ and the additional rules **R** (i.e. A, ~A ⊢ $\mathfrak{F}$) and **N** (i.e., A ⊃ $\mathfrak{F}$ ⊢ ~A). We can now define: $\mathbf{V_x}$ is the M-valuation associated with the assignment **x** in the MAS $\mathfrak{A}$ = <$\mathfrak{G}$,**g**>, provided **x**=<**f**,**r**>, **x** ∈ $\mathfrak{G}$ and

1. If A is 0-place, $\mathbf{V_x}$(A) = **f**(A).
2. If A = B ∧ C, $\mathbf{V_x}$ (A) = $\mathbf{V_x}$(B) · $\mathbf{V_x}$(C).
3. If A = B ∨ C, $\mathbf{V_x}$(A) = 1 iff $\mathbf{V_x}$(B) = 1 or $\mathbf{V_x}$(C) = 1.
4. If A = B ⊃ C, $\mathbf{V_x}$(A) = 1 iff **y** ∈ **g**(x) implies $\mathbf{V_y}$(B) = 0 or $\mathbf{V_y}$(C) = 1.

5. If A = ~B, $V_x(A) = 1$ iff $y \in g(x)$ implies $V_y(B) = 0$ or or $V_y(\mathcal{F}) = 1$.

6. If A = B ≡ C, $V_x(A) = 1$ iff $y \in g(x)$ implies $V_y(B) = V_y(C)$.

An MAS <𝔊,,g> is M provided (1) <𝔊,g> is S4, (2) [$y \in g(x)$ and $V_x(A) = 1$] implies $V_y(A) = 1$ (where of course V_x is the M-valuation associated with the assignment x). An MAS <𝔊,g> is I provided (1) <𝔊,g> is M and (2) $x \in 𝔊$ implies $f(\mathcal{F}) = 0$.

In order to carry out the analogue of the argument we used with the modal systems, it will be necessary to redefine the regularity concept, as follows: α is **M-regular** provided (1) α is deductively consistent in PLANEAK, (2) α is deductively closed, i.e. $\alpha \vdash_{PLANEAK} A \Rightarrow A \in \alpha$, (3) α is disjunctive, i.e., A ∨ B ∈ α ⇒ (A ∈ α or B ∈ α). α is **I-regular** under the same conditions, but applied to WLANEAK instead of PLANEAK.

<𝔊,g> is the **regular M-MAS** provided (1) x_α = <f,r> iff α is M-regular and (2) $x_\alpha \in g(x_\beta)$ iff β ⊂ α. <𝔊,g> is the **regular I-MAS** under the same conditions with "I" subtituted for "M."

PLANEAK-1. If α is A-M-consistent there exists an A-M-consistent and A-M-complete set β with α ⊂ β.

Proof: This follows by the argument of K−9.

WLANEAK-1. If α is A-I-consistent there exists an A-I-consistent and A-I-complete set β with α ⊂ β.

Proof:This follows by the same argument, mutatis mutandis.

PLANEAK-2. If α is A-M-consistent and A-M-complete, it is M-regular.

Proof: Let α be A-M-consistent and A-M-complete. Then (1) Since $\alpha \vdash_{PLANEAK} A$, α is deductively consistent in PLANEAK. (2) Let $\alpha \vdash_{PLANEAK} B$. Suppose B ⊃ A ∈ α. Then $\alpha \vdash_{PLANEAK} B \supset A$. Hence $\alpha \vdash_{PLANEAK} A$, by MP and α is A-M-inconsistent. Since either $B \in \alpha$ or $B \supset A \in \alpha$, $B \in \alpha$. (3) Let $B \vee C \in \alpha$, $B \notin \alpha$ and $C \notin \alpha$. Then $B \supset A \in \alpha$ and $C \supset A \in \alpha$. Hence $\alpha \vdash_{\mathbf{PLANEAK}} B \vee C$, $\alpha \vdash_{\mathbf{PLANEAK}} B \supset A$ and $\alpha \vdash_{\mathbf{PLANEAK}} C \supset A$. Therefore, $\alpha \vdash_{\mathbf{PLANEAK}} A$ and α is A-M-inconsistent.

WLANEAK-2. If α is A-I-consistent and A-I-complete, it is I-regular.

Proof: This follows by the same argument as **PLANEAK**-2 mutatis mutandis.

PLANEAK-3. If α is A-M-regular, then $\mathbf{V}_{\alpha}(A) = 1$ (in the M-regular MAS) iff $A \in \alpha$.

Proof: By induction on the number of connectives, we get:

(1) If A is 0-place, $\mathbf{V}_{\alpha}(A) = \mathbf{f}_{\alpha}(A) = 1$ iff $A \in \alpha$.

(2) Let $A = B \wedge C$ and $\mathbf{V}_{\alpha}(A) = 1$. Then $\mathbf{V}_{\alpha}(B \wedge C) = 1$ and $\mathbf{V}_{\alpha}(B) = \mathbf{V}_{\alpha}(C) = 1$ and by the hypothesis of induction $B \in \alpha$ and $C \in \alpha$. Then $\alpha \vdash_{\mathbf{PLANEAK}} B$ and $\alpha \vdash_{\mathbf{PLANEAK}} C$. Thus $\alpha \vdash_{\mathbf{PLANEAK}} B \wedge C$ (i.e. $\alpha \vdash_{\mathbf{PLANEAK}} A$), by A. Hence $A \in \alpha$. Suppose $A \in \alpha$. Then $\alpha \vdash_{\mathbf{PLANEAK}} B \wedge C$. By LS and RS, $\alpha \vdash_{\mathbf{PLANEAK}} B$ and $\alpha \vdash_{\mathbf{PLANEAK}} C$, hence $B \in \alpha$ and $C \in \alpha$, and by the hypothesis of induction, $\mathbf{V}_{\alpha}(B) = \mathbf{V}_{\alpha}(C) = 1$, i.e. $\mathbf{V}_{\alpha}(A) = 1$.

(3) Let $A = B \vee C$. Suppose $\mathbf{V}_{\alpha}(B \vee C) = 1$. Then either $\mathbf{V}_{\alpha}(B) = 1$ or $\mathbf{V}_{\alpha}(C) = 1$. By the hypothesis of induction, either $B \in \alpha$ or $C \in \alpha$. Hence $\alpha \vdash_{\mathbf{PLANEAK}} B$ or $\alpha \vdash_{\mathbf{PLANEAK}} C$. By AL or AR, as the case may be $\alpha \vdash_{\mathbf{PLANEAK}} B \vee C$. Hence $A \in \alpha$. Suppose $A \in \alpha$. Since α is disjunctive, $B \in \alpha$ or $C \in \alpha$. By the hypothesis of induction, $\mathbf{V}_{\alpha}(B) = 1$ or $\mathbf{V}_{\alpha}(C) = 1$, and hence $\mathbf{V}_{\alpha}(A) = 1$.

(4) Let $A = B \supset C$. Suppose $\mathbf{V}_{\alpha}(A) = 1$. Then $\mathbf{V}_{\alpha}(B \supset C) = 1$. Then $\mathbf{x}_{\beta} \in \mathbf{g}(\mathbf{x}_{\alpha})$ implies $\mathbf{V}_{\beta}(B) = 0$ or $\mathbf{V}_{\beta}(C) = 1$. By the hypothesis of induction, $B \notin \beta$ or $C \in \beta$. Hence $\beta \subset \alpha$ and β M-regular

imply $B \notin \beta$ or $C \in \beta$. Suppose $B \supset C \notin \alpha$. Then not-($\alpha \vdash_{\mathbf{PLANEAK}} B \supset C$), since α is M-regular. Therefore there exists a $(B \supset C)$-M-consistent and $B \supset C$-M-complete set δ with $\alpha \subset \delta$. Then by **PLANEAK**-2, δ is M-regular. Since δ is $(B \supset C)$-M-consistent, we do not have $\delta \vdash_{\mathbf{PLANEAK}} B \supset C$. Since δ is $(B \supset C)$-M-complete, $\delta \vdash_{\mathbf{PLANEAK}} B$ or $\delta \vdash_{\mathbf{PLANEAK}} B \supset (B \supset C)$. If the latter, $\delta, B \vdash_{\mathbf{PLANEAK}} C$ by MP applied twice and hence we would have $\delta \vdash_{\mathbf{PLANEAK}} B \supset C$. Therefore, $\delta \vdash_{\mathbf{PLANEAK}} B$. But δ is M- regular and contains α. Hence $\mathbf{x}_\delta \in \mathbf{g}(\mathbf{x}_\alpha)$ and $\mathbf{V}_\delta(B) = 0$ or $\mathbf{V}_\delta(C) = 1$. By the hypothesis of induction, $B \notin \delta$ or $C \in \delta$ and, by M-regularity, $B \in \delta$. Hence $C \in \delta$ and $\delta \vdash_{\mathbf{PLANEAK}} C$ and thus $\delta \vdash_{\mathbf{PLANEAK}} B \supset C$, which is impossible. Therefore $B \supset C \in \alpha$, i.e. $A \in \alpha$. Let $B \supset C \in \alpha$, β be M-regular and $\alpha \subset \beta$. Then $B \supset C \in \beta$ and $\beta \vdash_{\mathbf{PLANEAK}} B \supset C$. Thus if $B \in \beta$, $\beta \vdash_{\mathbf{PLANEAK}} B$ and by MP, $\beta \vdash_{\mathbf{PLANEAK}} C$. Hence by the hypothesis of induction, $\mathbf{V}_\beta(B) = 0$ or $\mathbf{V}_\beta(C) = 1$. Therefore $\mathbf{V}_\alpha(B \supset C) = 1$, i.e., $\mathbf{V}_\alpha(A) = 1$.

(5) $A = B \equiv C$. This follows immediately from parts (2) and (4) above, in view of the equivalence between $B \equiv C$ and $(B \supset C) \wedge (C \supset B)$.

(6) $A = \sim B$. Suppose $\mathbf{V}_\alpha(\sim B) = 1$. Then $\mathbf{x}_\beta \in \mathbf{g}(\mathbf{x}_\alpha)$ implies $\mathbf{V}_\beta(B) = 0$ or $\mathbf{V}_\beta(\mathcal{F}) = 1$. By the hypothesis of induction, $\mathcal{F} \in \beta$ or $B \notin \beta$. Suppose $\sim B \notin \alpha$. Then α is $\sim B$-M-consistent. There is a $\sim B$-M-consistent and $\sim B$-M-complete set δ with $\alpha \subset \delta$. Thus δ is also M-regular. Since δ is $\sim B$-M-complete, $B \in \delta$ or $B \supset \sim B \in \delta$. Since $B \supset \sim B \vdash_{\mathbf{PLANEAK}} \sim B$, either $B \in \delta$ or $\sim B \in \delta$. Hence $B \in \delta$. Then $\mathcal{F} \in \delta$. Since $\mathcal{F} \vdash_{\mathbf{PLANEAK}} B \supset \mathcal{F}$ and $B \supset \mathcal{F} \vdash_{\mathbf{PLANEAK}} \sim B$, $\delta \vdash_{\mathbf{PLANEAK}} \sim B$, which is contradictory. Hence $\sim B \in \alpha$. Suppose $\sim B \in \alpha$. Then $\delta \vdash_{\mathbf{PLANEAK}} \sim B$ and $\delta \vdash_{\mathbf{PLANEAK}} B \supset \mathcal{F}$. Thus, by (4), $\mathbf{x}_\beta \in \mathbf{g}(\mathbf{x}_\alpha)$ implies $\mathbf{V}_\beta(B) = 0$ or $\mathbf{V}_\beta(\mathcal{F}) = 1$, and hence $\mathbf{V}_\alpha(A) = 1$.

WLANEAK-3. If α is I-regular, then $\mathbf{V}_\alpha(A) = 1$ (in the I-regular

MAS) iff $A \in \alpha$.

Proof: (1)-(5). As in PLANEAK-3.

(6). Suppose $V_\alpha(\sim B) = 1$. Then $x_\beta \in g(x_\alpha)$ implies $V_\beta(B) = 0$. By the hypothesis of induction, $B \notin \beta$. Hence $\alpha \subset \beta$ and β I-regular implies $B \in \beta$. Suppose $\sim B \notin \alpha$. Then α is $\sim B$-I-consistent. There is a $\sim B$-I-consistent and $\sim B$-I-complete set δ with $\alpha \subset \delta$. Thus δ is I-regular. Hence $B \in \delta$ or $\sim B \in \delta$. But then $B \in \delta$, which is impossible. Hence $\sim B \in \alpha$. Now suppose $\sim B \in \alpha$. Then $\alpha \vdash_{WLANEAK} \sim B$. Since $B, \sim B \vdash_{WLANEAK} C$, $\alpha \subset \beta$ and β I-regular imply $B \in \beta$. Hence $x_\beta \in g(x_\alpha)$ implies $V_\beta(B) = 0$, by the hypothesis of induction. Therefore, $V_\alpha(\sim B) = 1$, i.e, $V_\alpha(A) = 1$.

PLANEAK-4. $\alpha \vdash_{PLANEAK} A \Rightarrow \alpha \models_M A$.

Proof: (1) All rules with $\wedge$ and $\vee$ are clearly validity preserving by the normal two-valued arguments.

(2) Let $x \Vdash A$ and $x \Vdash A \supset B$. Since the M-regular MAS is S4, $x \in g(x)$. Hence $V_x(A) = 0$ or $V_x(B) = 1$. Since $V_x(A) = 1$, $V_x(B) = 1$. Therefore **MP** preserves validity.

(3) Suppose $\alpha, A \models_M B$. Let $x_\beta \Vdash \alpha$. Suppose $V_\beta(A \supset B) = 0$. There exists a x_δ in the M-regular MAS with $x_\delta \in g(x_\beta)$ and $V_\delta(A) = 1$ while $V_\delta(B) = 0$. But then by PLANEAK-3, $x_\delta \Vdash \alpha$ and hence $x_\delta \Vdash B$, which contradicts the assumption. Therefore **C** preserves validity.

(4) Let $x \Vdash A$ and $x \Vdash A \in B$. Since the M-regular MAS is S4, $x \in g(x)$. Hence $V_x(A) = V_x(B)$. Hence $x \Vdash B$. The same argument is applicable in the opposite direction. Therefore **Bi-MP** preserves validity.

(5) Suppose $\alpha, A \models B$ and $\alpha, B \models A$. Hence by (3), $x \Vdash \alpha$ implies that $y \in g(x) \Rightarrow$ [(either $V_y(A) = 0$ or $V_y(B) = 1$) and ($V_y(A) = 1$ or $V_y(B) = 0$)]. But the consequent is equivalent to $V_y(A) = V_y(B)$. Therefore **Bi-C** preserves validity.

(6) Let $\alpha, A \models \sim B$. Let $x_\beta \Vdash \alpha$ and $x_\beta \Vdash B$. Suppose $V_\beta(\sim A) = 0$.

There is $x_\delta \in g(x_\beta)$ and $V_\delta(\mathcal{F}) = 0$ and $V_\delta(A) = 1$. But then $x_\delta \Vdash A$. Then $\alpha \subset \beta$ and $A \in \delta$. But $\beta \subset \delta$ and hence $V_\delta(\sim B) = 1$. Hence $V_\delta(\mathcal{F}) = 1$ or $V_\delta(B) = 0$, contrary to the previous result. Therefore **Imm** preserves validity.

(7) Let α, $A \models \sim A$. Suppose $x \Vdash \alpha$ and $V_x(\sim A) = 0$. There is a $y \in g(x)$ such that $V_y(\mathcal{F}) = 0$ and $V_y(A) = 1$. But then by the definition of the MAS, $y \Vdash \alpha$ and $y \Vdash A$, hence by the entailment, $V_y(\sim A) = 1$. Since however the MAS is S4, $y \in g(y)$ and we thereby contradict our previous result. Therefore **CM** preserves validity.

(8) Suppose $x \Vdash A$ and $x \Vdash \sim A$. Since the MAS is S4, $x \in g(x)$ and $V_x(\mathcal{F}) = 1$ or $V_x(A) = 0$. Therefore $V_x(\mathcal{F}) = 1$ and R preserves validity.

(9) Suppose $x \Vdash A \supset \mathcal{F}$. Then $y \in g(x)$ implies $V_y(A) = 0$ or $V_y(\mathcal{F}) = 1$. Therefore $x \Vdash \sim A$.

WLANEAK-4. $\alpha \vdash_{\text{WLANEAK}} A \Rightarrow \alpha \models_I A$.

Proof: All the rules except those concerning negation, as well as case (6) and (9) are validated in the same manner as in the proof of PLANEAK-4. RA and R follow trivially since no assignment can assign 1 both to A and $\sim$A.

PLANEAK-5. $\alpha \models_M A \Rightarrow \alpha \vdash_{\text{PLANEAK}} A$.

Proof: Suppose $\alpha \models_M A$ and not ($\alpha \vdash_{\text{PLANEAK}} A$). Then α is A-M-consistent. By PLANEAK-1 and 2, it is included in an A-M-consistent and M-regular set which by PLANEAK-3 has a model. Hence α has a model which is not a model of A and this contradicts our assumptions.

WLANEAK-5. $\alpha \models_I A \Rightarrow \alpha \vdash_{\text{WLANEAK}} A$.

Proof: This follows by the argument of PLANEAK-5, mutatis mutandis.

Note that the corresponding theorems for PLNEAK and WLNEAK

follow from the argument of **PLN**-9M. Notice also that, unlike the situation in two-valued logic, the regular sets are generally **not** maximally consistent.

Here we finally take our leave of zero-order logic. We hope that our presentation has displayed some of the techniques of dealing with these elementary formal systems, while also displaying a variety of interesting systems with regard to the possibility of interpretation. We do not assume that we have exhausted our subject, but rather at best that we have helped prepare the interested student for further study. A short list of additional books on the subject is included in the bibliography.

We now turn to a class of systems of an intrinsically stronger character, the so-called first-order logics. Lack of space will prevent us from giving as thorough a presentation of them as we did of zero-order logics. We will, however, give an indication of the formal character of these systems and examine a few of the more significant of them in greater detail.

Exercises
Chapters 10 and 11

1. Prove $\vdash_{\mathbf{S1}} (A \dashv \sim B) \dashv (B \dashv \sim A)$.

2. If **SHE** is a rule of a DZOS $\mathfrak{D}$, then **SE** is a rule of $\mathfrak{D}$.

12
Quantification and First-Order Logic

Before starting our discussion of first-order systems, we want to point out that the expressive means provided in zero-order logic (variables and connectives), though simple, essentially exhaust what can be said on a single level (with a partial exception soon to be noted). Connectives provide in principle the means of expressing any transformation – provided the property in question holds of all wffs, a restriction implied by saying that we are talking about logic. From this point of view connectives can be considered the structural correlate of transformations from wffs to wffs that we have called wff functions.

The most basic feature of our generalization is that we provide two levels of well-formed expressions, called respectively **terms** and **well-formed formulae (wffs)**. We will in addition want to extend the expressive means in two directions. The first of these generalizations consists of allowing operators whose character ("value") and arguments are allowed to vary over the elements of either of the levels, though each argument position of these operators will be restricted to one level or the other. The second extension involves a kind of indexed operator of which the familiar universal and existential quantifiers are the best known examples.

Accordingly, our formal presentation is generalized so that our infinite family of sets $\{S_\alpha\}$ runs over an index set such that α decomposes into a natural number i and a sequence of i+1 0's and 1's. Since the latter is structured like the binary representation of the numbers $0,1,\cdots, 2^{i+1}-1$, the index could be regarded as an ordered pair of natural numbers, the first of which is i and the second a natural number between 0 and $2^{i+1}-1$. As before $S = \cup S_\alpha$ (over all α). The two additional conditions specified in chapter 1 for elements of S remain unchanged. Similarly, we insist as before that there should be a decision procedure for the elements of each S_α. In addition, the S_α's are subdivided as follows:

1. S_{00} and S_{01} have subsets (called V_T and V_F, respectively,-- for **term variables** and **formula variables**).

2. All the other S_α's are divided into a subset $S_{\alpha 0}$ of elements not further indexed and $S_{\alpha\beta}$ where β in turn decomposes into a first element j and a sequence of j 0's and 1's. As before, some or all of the S_α's or the $S_{\alpha\beta}$'s may be finite or indeed empty. We call such an S a **first-order system.**

Likewise we define the property $\mathcal{T}_{S\cap}$ and $\sigma_{S\cap}$ as we did in chapter 1 (with S_α replacing S_i) with conditions F1-F5 still required as applying to "follows" ($\cap$).

We then define properties D and E applicable to elements of $\sigma_{S\cap}$, as follows:

1. If $x \in S_{00}$, $x \in D$
2. If $x \in S_{01}$, $x \in E$
3. If $f \in S_{\alpha 0}$, (i) α decomposes into k and $n_1,\cdots,n_k$ and n_{k+1}, (ii) $x_i \in D$ iff $n_i=0$ and $x_i \in E$ iff $n_i=1$ (for $1 \leq i \leq k$), and (iii) $n_{k+1}=0$, then $fx_1\cdots x_k \in D$.
4. If $f \in S_{\alpha 1}$, (i) α decomposes into k and $n_1,\cdots,n_k$ and n_{k+1}, (ii) $x_i \in D$ iff $n_i=0$ and $x_i \in E$ iff $n_i=1$ (for $1 \leq i \leq k$), and (iii) $n_{k+1}=1$, then $fx_1\cdots x_k \in E$.
5. If $f \in S_{\alpha\beta}$, (i) α decomposes into j and $m_1,\cdots,m_j$ and m_{j+1}, β decomposes into k and $m_1,\cdots,m_k$, (ii) $x_i \in D$ iff $m_i=0$ and $x_i \in E$ iff $m_i=1$ (for $1 \leq i \leq j$), (iii) $v_i \in V_T$ iff $n_i=0$ and $v_i \in V_F$ iff $n_i=1$ (for $1 \leq i \leq k$) and (iv) $n_{j+1}=0$, then $fv_1\cdots v_k x_1\cdots x_j \in D$.
6. If $f \in S_{\alpha\beta}$, (i) α decomposes into j and $m_1,\cdots,m_j$ and m_{j+1},β decomposes into k and $m_1,\cdots,m_k$, (ii) $x_i \in D$ iff $m_i=0$ and $x_i \in E$ iff $m_i=1$ (for $1 \leq i \leq j$), (iii) $v_i \in V_T$ iff $n_i=0$ and $v_i \in V_F$ iff $n_i=1$ (for $1 \leq i \leq k$), and (iv) $n_{j+1}=1$, then $fv_1\cdots v_k x_1\cdots x_j \in E$.

Then we define T_S as the intersection of all sets having property D relative to the system S, and W_S as the intersection of all sets having property E relative to S.

In accordance with customary practice, the elements of T_S are called **terms** and those of W_S are called **well-formed formulae.** As in zero-order logic, the reader is warned that the words are used in a "denatured" sense.

As an aside, notice that the extra complexity of the indices provides no special problem since indices of the kind in question can readily be mapped (one-to-one) into (decidable) subsets of the natural numbers.

If $x \in W_S \cup T_S$, we will, when convenient, call x a **well-formed expression (wfe)**. If $x \in S_{00}$, S_{01}, $S_{\alpha 0}$ or $S_{\alpha 1}$, we will say x is a **functor**. If x is a functor, $x \in S_\alpha$ and the last element of the decomposition of α is 0, we will call x an **F-functor**, and if this is not the case, a **T-functor**. If x is a functor, $x \in S_\alpha$ and the first element of the decomposition of α is k, we will call x a **k-place functor**. If $x \in S_\alpha$ and is not a functor we will term it a **quantifier**. If the quantifier x is an element of $S_{\alpha\beta}$ and the first component of α is j, while the first component of β is k, we call x a **k-variable,j-argument quantifier**. The reader will note that the ordinary universal and existential quantifiers are one-variable, one-argument quantifiers.

To explain some of the conditions needed for calculi to be considered logics, as well as to specify the rules of the systems, it will be desirable to define a number of substitution concepts. The first of these is a slight generalization of a concept defined in chapter 1.

We define $\mathbf{S}^A{}_B C$ (to be read "the result of uniformly substituting B for A in C") as follows:

1. $\mathbf{S}^A{}_B A = B$ provided A and B are both terms or both wffs.

2. If $A \neq C$ and either $C \in S_{00}$ or $C \in S_{01}$, $\mathbf{S}^A{}_B C = C$.

3. If $A \neq C$, f is an n-place functor and $x_1,\cdots,x_n$ and $fx_1\cdots x_n$ are well-formed then $\mathbf{S}^A{}_B fx_1\cdots x_n = f\,\mathbf{S}^A{}_B x_1\cdots \mathbf{S}^A{}_B x_n$.

4. If $A \neq C$, f is an m-variable, n-argument quantifier, $v_1,\cdots,v_m$ are variables and $x_1,\cdots,x_n$ and $fv_1\cdots v_m x_1\cdots x_n$ are well-formed, then $\mathbf{S}^A{}_B fv_1\cdots v_m x_1\cdots x_n = f\mathbf{S}^A{}_B v_1\cdots\mathbf{S}^A{}_B v_m \mathbf{S}^A{}_B x_1\cdots \mathbf{S}^A{}_B x_n$.

5. If any of A,B or C are not well-formed expressions or if one of A and B is a wff and the other a term, $\mathbf{S}^A{}_B C$ is not defined.

As before, if A and B are well-formed expressions we say A **occurs in** B provided there is a wfe C such that $\mathbf{S}^A{}_C B \neq B$. If f is a functor or quantifier and A is a wfe, f **occurs in** A provided there exists a sequence B such that fB is well-formed and occurs in A. The reader will note that all of the theorems of chapter 1 (1-1 through 1-10) hold without change.

A second important substitution operator called **free substitution** (and indicated by $\mathbf{F}$) can be defined as follows: if $v \in V_F \cup V_T$, either $v, A \in W_S$ or $v, A \in T_S$ and B is well-formed

1. $\mathbf{F}^{v}_{A}v = A$

2. If $v \neq B$ and $B \in S_{00}$ or S_{01}, $\mathbf{F}^{v}_{A}B = B$.

3. If f is an n-place functor, $x_1,\cdots,x_n$ and $fx_1\cdots x_n$ are well-formed, $\mathbf{F}^{v}_{A}fx_1\cdots x_n = f\,\mathbf{F}^{v}_{A}x_1\cdots\,\mathbf{F}^{v}_{A}x_n$.

4. If f is an m-place, n-argument quantifier, $v_1,\cdots,v_m$ variables, $x_1,\cdots,x_n$ and $fv_1\cdots v_m x_1\cdots x_n$ are well- formed and for every i $(1 \leq i \leq m)$, $v \neq v_i$, then $\mathbf{F}^{v}_{A}fv_1\cdots v_m x_1\cdots x_n = fv_1\cdots v_m\,\mathbf{F}^{v}_{A}x_1\cdots\,\mathbf{F}^{v}_{A}x_n$.

5. If f is an m-place, n-argument quantifier, $v_1,\cdots,v_m$ variables, $x_1,\cdots,x_n$ and $fv_1\cdots v_m x_1\cdots x_n$ are well-formed and for some i $(1 \leq i \leq m)$, $v = v_i$, then $\mathbf{F}^{v}_{A}fv_1\cdots v_m x_1\cdots x_n = fv_1\cdots v_m x_1\cdots x_n$.

A variable v **occurs free** in a wfe A provided there is a wfe B such that $\mathbf{F}^{v}_{B}A \neq A$. A variable v **occurs bound** in a wfe A iff there is an m-variable n-argument quantifier f, variables $v_1, \cdots, v_m$ and wfes $x_1, \cdots, x_n$ such that $fv_1\cdots v_m x_1\cdots x_n$ occurs in A, for some i $(1 \leq i \leq n)$, v occurs free in x_i, and for some j $(1 \leq j \leq m)$, $v = v_j$. Two wfes are **of the same type** if either both are terms or both are wffs. A variable v_1 **is free for** the variable v_2 in a wfe A, if v_1 and v_2 are of the same type, and for every variable v which does not occur in A, $v \neq v_1$, $v \neq v_2$ imply $\mathbf{F}^{v_1}_{v}\mathbf{F}^{v_2}_{v}A = \mathbf{F}^{v_1}_{v}\mathbf{F}^{v_2}_{v_1}A$. A well-formed expression x **is free for** a variable v in A provided every variable free in x is free for v in A. Multiple and simultaneous substitution are defined analogous to the way they are defined for zero-order logic, as are numbered occurrences. Consequently one can even deal with such clumsy characterizations as "the third occurrence of v in A is free, but the fifth is bound." We define A to be a

free substitution instance of B provided there exist distinct variables $v_1,\cdots,v_n$ and wfes $x_1,\cdots,x_n$ such that $A = \mathbf{F}^{v_1}{}_{x_1}{}^{\cdots\cdots}{}^{v_n}{}_{x_n}B$ with each x_i free for v_i in B.

Another type of substitution, useful in distinguishing theories that might be regarded as logics per se, as opposed to those which might be regarded as the logic of some particular subject matter, may be termed "analogous case." We will use the letter A to represent it. Specifically, if $v_1, \cdots, v_m$ are variables, $E_1,\cdots,E_n$ well-formed expressions such that for every i and j $(1 \leq i,j \leq n)$, $(v_i = v_j$ implies $i = j)$, v_i and E_i are of the same type, D and E are well-formed expressions, f an n-place functor and $fv_1\cdots v_n$ a wfe, then:

1. $\mathbf{A}^{fv_1\cdots v_n}{}_E fE_1\cdots E_n = \mathbf{F}^{v_1}{}_{E_1}{}^{\cdots}{}^{v_n}{}_{E_n}E$ provided v_i does not occur bound in E and no variable occurs both bound and free in E.

2. If D is a zero-place functor, $\mathbf{A}^{fv_1\cdots v_n}{}_E D = D$.

3. If $f \neq g$ and g is an n-place functor (not a quantifier), $E_1, \cdots, E_m$ and $gE_1\cdots E_m$ are well-formed expressions, then $\mathbf{A}^{fv_1\cdots v_n}{}_E gE_1\cdots E_m = g\mathbf{A}^{fv_1\cdots v_n}{}_E E_1\cdots \mathbf{A}^{fv_1\cdots v_n}{}_E E_m$.

4. If g is a k-variable m-place quantifier, $w_1,\cdots,w_k$ are variables and $E_1, \cdots,E_m$ and $gw_1\cdots w_kE_1\cdots E_m$ are well-formed expressions, then $\mathbf{A}^{fv_1\cdots v_n}{}_E gw_1\cdots w_kE_1\cdots E_m = gw_1\cdots w_k \mathbf{A}^{fv_1\cdots v_n}{}_E E_1\cdots \mathbf{A}^{fv_1\cdots v_n}{}_E E_m$.

We say that G is an **immediate analogous case** of H relative to a set of functors β provided there exists a functor f in β such that f is n-place, $v_1,\cdots,v_n$ are variables, $E_1,\cdots,E_n$ are wfe's and a wfe E such that $\mathbf{A}^{fv_1\cdots v_n}{}_E H = G$ if $\mathbf{A}^{fv_1\cdots v_n}{}_E H$ is defined and, furthermore, no variable that occurs free in E occurs bound in G.

For any well-formed expression E and set of functors β, let us define the property $A_{E\sigma}$ as a property possessed by any set α of wfe's such that

1. $E \in \alpha$

2. If $A \in \alpha$ and B is an immediate analogous case of A relative to β, $B \in \alpha$.

3. If $v_1,\cdots,v_n$ are variables, $E_1,\cdots,E_n$ well-formed expressions such that for every i $(1 \leq i \leq n)$ v_i and E_i are of the same type and $A \in \alpha$, then

$\mathbf{S}^{v_1 \cdots v_n}_{E_1 \cdots E_n}A \in \alpha$ and $\mathbf{F}^{v_1 \cdots v_n}_{E_1 \cdots E_n}A \in \alpha$, provided no variable that occurs free in $E_1, \cdots, E_n$ occurs bound in $\mathbf{S}^{v_1 \cdots v_n}_{E_1 \cdots E_n}A$ or $\mathbf{F}^{v_1 \cdots v_n}_{E_1 \cdots E_n}A$, respectively.

G is an **analogous case** of H relative to β provided G is an element of the intersection of all sets having property $A_{E\sigma}$.

We are now in a position to define conditions which in general a first order system may possess and which are relevant to whether it should be considered a logic. Derivation, proof and related concepts can be defined in the same way as they were for zero-order logic, mutatis mutandis. To ensure that the system is a logic, certain normality conditions must be be satisfied. We shall now turn to these.

A zero-place functor g, is an **abstract variable** (F- or T-, as the case may be) provided:

1. For every zero-place functor g′ of the same kind as g, every wff A and set of wffs α such that g′ does not occur in A nor in any element of α, $\alpha \vdash A \Rightarrow \mathbf{S}^{g}_{g'}\alpha \vdash \mathbf{S}^{g}_{g'}A$, and

2. For any wfe E of the same kind as g which satisfies the conditions: if (i) $C \in \alpha$ implies $\mathbf{F}^{g}_{E}C$ is a free substitution instance of C and (ii) $\mathbf{F}^{g}_{E}A$ is a free substitution instance, then $\alpha \vdash A \Rightarrow \mathbf{F}^{g}_{E}\alpha \vdash \mathbf{F}^{g}_{E}A$.

A quantifier q is a **normal quantifier** provided for each wff A, if $G = qv_1 \cdots v_m E_1 \cdots E_n$ and $G^* = \mathbf{S}^{w}_{v}G$, where w is a v_i $(1 \leq i \leq m)$ which occurs only free (if at all), and v is a variable that does not occur at all, in any of $E_1, \cdots, E_n$, and for each variable g of the same type as G such that G and G^* are free for g in A, then $\mathbf{F}^{g}_{G}A$ is deductively equivalent to $\mathbf{F}^{g}_{G^*}A$. A first-order logical calculus is a **first-order logic** provided all its variables are abstract variables and all its quantifiers are normal. We call an n-place functor f **representative** provided it is neither a quantifier nor a connective (i.e. an F-functor with only F-arguments) and $\beta \vdash B \Rightarrow \mathbf{A}^{D}_{E}\beta \vdash \mathbf{A}^{D}_{E}B$ where $D = fv_1 \cdots v_n$ whenever $\mathbf{A}^{D}_{E}B$ is an immediate analogous case of B and $\mathbf{A}^{D}_{E}C$ is an immediate analogous case of C for $C \in \beta$.

A first order logic is called **pure** provided all functors (other than variables, quantifiers, and connectives) are representative. A logic is called the **logic of the set of functors** α iff every functor not in α is representative (with the same exceptions) .

Let α be a set of wffs of the same type as the variable v and let β be a set of wfe's. Then $\mathbf{R}^{v}_{\alpha}\beta$ is the set of all elements $\mathbf{S}^{v}_{x}C$ for all $C \in \beta$ and $x \in \alpha$ (i.e. $\mathbf{R}^{v}_{\alpha}\beta = \{\mathbf{S}^{v}_{x}C : C \in \beta \text{ and } x \in \alpha\}$). [Important note: taken literally, the above definition and those that depend on it would be applicable only to first-order logics that have F-variables. Actually, the correct force is obtained if, when these definitions are to be applied to logics without F-variables, the logic is embedded in a system which has the requisite variables.] A **deductive formula description** is either a wff or the result of applying the $\mathbf{R}$ operation to the singleton containing the wff x, but only if we apply it to variables that occur in x and at most once to each variable. A rule is a function from a finite set of ordered couples $\langle\alpha_1,A_1\rangle,\cdots,\langle\alpha_n,A_n\rangle$ into the set {0,1}. A **basic deductive sequence** is a sequence of ordered pairs $\langle x_1, y_1\rangle,\cdots,\langle x_n, y_n\rangle$, where each x_i is a finite sequence of deductive formula descriptions and each y_i is a wff.

A first-order logic L is a **deductive first order system** if it has a finite number of rules $\mathbf{R}_i$ such that for each rule there is a basic deductive sequence $\langle x_1, y_1\rangle,\cdots,\langle x_n, y_n\rangle$ and $\mathbf{R}_i(\langle\alpha_1,A_1\rangle,\cdots,\langle\alpha_n,A_n\rangle) = 1$ iff $\langle\alpha_1,A_1\rangle,\cdots,\langle\alpha_n,A_n\rangle$ is a substitution instance of $\langle x_1, y_1\rangle,\cdots,\langle x_n, y_n\rangle$, in which each α_i is finite.

In zero-order logic we used structures based on values and functions on values to characterize assignments in extensional model theory. In constructing an extensional model theory for first order logics, ewe will use the same principle that we used in the zero-order case: viz., we will assign values and functions which agree in domain, range, and arity with the structure theoretic items they "interpret." Playing the analogous role here to the values and functions of zero-order model theory is a more complicated collection of things, namely:

1. A well-ordered set $\mathcal{V}$ whose members are called values and which without loss of generality might be considered ordinals (when the set is denumerable, they can indeed be considered to be the naturals).

2. A subset $\mathfrak{D}$ of $\mathcal{V}$. Usually this can be specified by naming the largest element of $\mathcal{V}$ which is in $\mathfrak{D}$. When we do this, we will sometimes refer to that element as d. The elements of $\mathfrak{D}$ are called designated values.

3.A set $\mathfrak{I}$ whose elements are called "individuals."

4. A set $\mathfrak{G}$ of functions $\mathfrak{g}: \times\mathcal{A}_i \rightarrow \mathcal{A}$ (i = 1 to n) such that $\mathcal{A}$ and

each $\mathcal{A}_i$ are either $\mathcal{V}$ or $\mathcal{I}$.

5. The set $\mathcal{H}$ of functions $h: \mathcal{P}(\times \mathcal{B}_i) \rightarrow \mathcal{B}$ where $\mathcal{P}(X)$ is the power set of X (i.e. the set of subsets of X) and, as before, $\mathcal{B}$ and each $\mathcal{B}_i$ is either $\mathcal{V}$ or $\mathcal{I}$.

We now define an **assignment** of $\mathcal{L}$ on the structure $(\mathcal{V}, D, \mathcal{I}, \mathcal{G}, \mathcal{H})$ to be a function $f: V_F \cup V_T \rightarrow \mathcal{V} \cup \mathcal{I}$ such that $f(V_F) \subset \mathcal{V}$ and $f(V_T) \subset \mathcal{I}$ where V_F is the set of formula variables and V_T is the set of term variables. If $v_1, \cdots, v_n$ are distinct variables and $w_1, \cdots, w_n$ are elements of $\mathcal{V} \cup \mathcal{I}$ such that v_i is a formula variable iff $w_i \in \mathcal{V}$ and f is an assignment of $\mathcal{L}$ on $(\mathcal{V}, D, \mathcal{I}, \mathcal{G}, \mathcal{H})$ then $B^{v_1 \cdots v_n}_{w_1 \cdots w_n}(f)$ is the assignment f' such that $f'(v_i) = w_i$ for $1 \leq i \leq n$ and $f'(v) = f(v)$ otherwise. An **interpretation** of $\mathcal{L}$ on the structure $(\mathcal{V}, D, \mathcal{I}, \mathcal{G}, \mathcal{H})$ is a function P from the set of non-variable functors, including quantifiers, into particular parts of the structure $(\mathcal{V}, D, \mathcal{I}, \mathcal{G}, \mathcal{H})$ such that:

1. If x is a non-quantifier functor whose (argument) indices are $i_1, \cdots, i_n, i$, $P(x) \in \mathcal{G}$, $P(x)$ has n arguments, $\mathcal{A}_j = \mathcal{V}$ iff $i_j = 0$, and $\mathcal{A} = \mathcal{V}$ iff $i = 0$.

2. If x is an m-variable n-place quantifier with quantifier indices $q_1, \cdots, q_m$ and argument indices $i_1, \cdots, i_n$, i, $P(x) \in \mathcal{H} \times \mathcal{G}$ such that g is an n-place function, h a function on the power set of m+1-tuples, and $\mathcal{A}_j = \mathcal{V}$ iff $i_j = 0$ (for $1 \leq j \leq n$), $\mathcal{B}_j = \mathcal{V}$ iff $q_j = 0$ $(1 \leq j \leq m)$, $\mathcal{B}_{m+1} = \mathcal{A}$ and $\mathcal{B} = \mathcal{V}$ iff $i = 0$.

An assignment is called **compatible** with an interpretation provided they are of the same calculus and on the same structure.

A **valuation** relative to an interpretation P and a compatible assignment f is a function V_f from the set of well-formed expressions into $\mathcal{V} \cup \mathcal{I}$ such that:

1. If x is a variable, $\mathrm{V}_f(x) = f(x)$

2. If f is an n place non-quantifier functor and $w_1, \cdots, w_n$ are wfe's (all agreeing with the index of f), $\mathrm{V}_f(f w_1 \cdots w_n) =$

$P(f)(\mathbf{V}_{\mathbf{f}}(w_1),\cdots,\mathbf{V}_{\mathbf{f}}(w_n))$

3. If f is an m-variable n-place quantifier, $v_1,\cdots,v_m$ (distinct) variables and $w_1,\cdots,w_n$ are wfe's (all agreeing with the index of f), $\mathbf{V}_{\mathbf{f}}(fv_1\cdots v_m w_1\cdots w_n) =$

$d_1(P(f))\Big(\{a_1,\cdots,a_m,d_2(P(f))\big[\mathbf{B}_{v_1 a_1\cdots v_m a_m}\mathbf{V}\mathbf{f}(w_1),\cdots,\mathbf{B}_{v_1 a_1\cdots v_m a_m}\mathbf{V}\mathbf{f}(w_n)\big]\}\Big)$

for all combinations of $\alpha_i \in \mathbf{B}_i$ and where $d_1(<x,y>) = x$ and $d_2(<x,y>) = y$.

An assignment **f** relative to an interpretation **P** is called a **model** of a wff W (**f** ||- W) provided $\mathbf{V}_{\mathbf{f}}(W)$ is designated. Let α be a set of interpretations. Then **f** is an **α-model** of W provided there is a **P** ∈ α and an assignment **f**, compatible with **P**, which is a model of W. A wff is **α-L-true** (or **α-analytic**) iff every assignment in α is an α-model of the wff. A wff A is **α-L-false** (or **α-inconsistent**) if no assignment in α is an α-model of A. We will call **f** an **α-model of a set of wffs** β provided it is an α-model of every element of β.

Similarly we will call a set of wffs **α-L-false** (or **α-inconsistent**) iff it has no α-models. A set α of wffs **α-entails** a set of a set of wffs δ (in symbols, $\beta \models_{\alpha} \delta$) provided every α-model of α is an α-model of δ. If δ = {A} for a wff A we will usually write $\beta \models_{\alpha} A$.

A set of interpretations α is **compact** provided every α-inconsistent set contains an α-inconsistent finite set. A calculus $\mathcal{L}$ is called **α-sound** provided $\alpha \vdash_{\mathcal{L}} B$ implies $\beta \models_{\alpha} B$, and is called **α-complete** provided $\beta \models_{\alpha} B$ implies $\beta \vdash_{\mathcal{L}} B$. Note in passing that it follows from the definition of derivation that if $\mathcal{L}$ is α-sound and α-complete, it could not be a logic unless α is compact.

Theorem 12-1. Let $A = gv_1\cdots v_m w_1\cdots w_n$ and v be a variable that does not occur in A. Then for any interpretation **P** and any compatible assignment **f**, $\mathbf{V}_{\mathbf{f}}(A) = \mathbf{V}_{\mathbf{f}}(\mathbf{S}^{v_j}{}_{v}A)$, for any j ($1 \le j \le m$).

Proof: This is a trivial consequence of the definition of valuation, since the sets on which the values depend are identical.

Let A be a wfe and v_1 and v_2 be variables of the same type such that v_1 is either v_2 or else does not occur in A. Then $\mathbf{S}^{v_2}{}_{v_1}A$ is a **closed alphabetical variant** of A provided $\mathbf{F}^{v_1}{}_{v_2}\mathbf{S}^{v_2}{}_{v_1}A = \mathbf{S}^{v_2}{}_{v_1}A$. Theorem 12-1 clearly implies that if A and B are closed alphabetical variants, $\mathbf{V}_\mathbf{f}(A) = \mathbf{V}_\mathbf{f}(B)$, for all **f** and **P**.

We will say that a set of wfes **has the property** S relative to a wfe A provided (1) $A \in \alpha$, and (2) If B is a closed alphabetical variant of C, and v is a variable not in B or C and also $\mathbf{F}^{v}{}_{B}D \in \alpha$, then so is $\mathbf{F}^{v}{}_{B}D$.

The **S-equivalence class** of A is the intersection of all sets of wfes having property S relative to A. Two wfes are **S-equivalent** iff they are elements of the same S-equivalence class. Obviously the equivalence classes partition the set of wfes (i.e. every wfe is a member of one, but only one, S-equivalence class). Notice that the members of the same S-equivalence class are the wfes that can be obtained one from the other by a finite sequence of substitutions of closed alphabetical variant parts.

Theorem 12-2. If B is an element of the S-equivalence class of A, every model of A is a model of B (and, of course, conversely).

Proof: If B is an element of the S-equivalence class of A, there exists a sequence $A_1,\cdots,A_n$ such that $A_1 = A$, $A_n = B$ and A_{n+1} is the result of substituting a closed alphabetical variant for a well-formed part of A_n. Then by 12-1, $\mathbf{V}(A_{n+1}) = \mathbf{V}(A_n)$. Hence by induction, the theorem follows.

Theorem 12-3. If α and β are finite sets of wffs such that no element of α is S-equivalent to an element of β, then there exists an interpretation **P** and an assignment **f** such that **f** is a model of β but is not a model of any element of α.

Proof: Assume the hypotheses of the theorem; then there exists a finite set Ψ satisfying the following:

1. Every element of Ψ is a wfe occurring in an element of $\alpha \cup \beta$.
2. Every wfe occurring in $\alpha \cup \beta$ is S-equivalent to an element of Ψ.
3. No two elements of Ψ are S- equivalent.

That Ψ is finite is obvious because the set of well-formed parts is finite and Ψ is a pruning of it. Let m be the number of elements of Ψ. Let $\gamma = \Psi - \alpha - \beta$. Let Θ be a set satisfying the following:

1. Every element of Θ is a wfe B = QA occurring in an element of $\alpha \cup \beta$.
2. Every wfe B= QA occurring in $\alpha \cup \beta$ is S-equivalent to an element of Θ.
3. No two elements of Θ are S- equivalent.

Let δ be the set of n + 1-tuples $<B,x_1,\cdots,x_n>$ such that $B \in \Theta$ and $0 \le x_i \le m-1$. Then there exists a one-one function $\mathbf{k}$ from $\alpha \cup \beta \cup \gamma \cup \delta$ onto an initial sequence of natural numbers such that $A \in \alpha$, $B \in \beta$, $C \in \gamma$ and $D \in \delta$ implies $\mathbf{k}(A) < \mathbf{k}(B) < \mathbf{k}(C) < \mathbf{k}(D)$.

We define the following interpretation **P**:

1. If f is an n-place functor, **P**(f) is the function $\mathbf{g}$ such that if $fw_1\cdots w_n \in (\alpha \cup \beta \cup \gamma)$ then $\mathbf{g}(\mathbf{k}(w_1),\cdots, \mathbf{k}(w_n)) = \mathbf{k}(fw_1\cdots w_n)$ and otherwise $\mathbf{g}(x_1,\cdots,x_n) = 0$.

2. If Q is an m-variable, n-argument quantifier $\mathbf{P}(Q) = <\mathbf{h},\mathbf{g}>$ satisfying the conditions: if $Qv_1\cdots v_m w_1\cdots w_n \in \alpha \cup \beta \cup \gamma$, $<A,x_1,\cdots,x_n> \in \delta$, and for the assignment $\mathbf{m}$ with $\mathbf{m}(v) = \mathbf{k}(v)$ for every $v \in (\alpha \cup \beta \cup \gamma)$ and $\mathbf{m}(v) = 0$ otherwise, $\mathbf{g}(\mathbf{B}^{v_1}{}_{x_1}\cdots{}^{v_m}{}_{x_m}\mathbf{V_m}(w_1), \cdots, \mathbf{B}^{v_1}{}_{x_1}\cdots{}^{v_m}{}_{x_m}\mathbf{V_m}(w_n)) = \mathbf{k}(<A,x_1,\cdots,x_n>)$ and, if the conditions are not satisfied, $\mathbf{g}(x_1,\cdots,x_n) = 0$; while if for every A such that $A \in (\alpha \cup \beta \cup \gamma)$ and $A = Qy$, $\mathbf{h}(\{x_1,\cdots,x_m,\mathbf{k}(<A,x_1,\cdots,x_m>)\}) = \mathbf{k}(A)$, and $\mathbf{h}(\alpha) = 0$ otherwise. We now prove by induction on the formula length $\ell(A)$ that $\mathbf{V_m}(A) = \mathbf{k}(A)$ for all $A \in (\alpha \cup \beta \cup \gamma)$:

(α) $\ell(A) = 1$.

Case 1. A is a variable. Then $\mathbf{V_m}(A) = \mathbf{m}(A) = \mathbf{k}(A)$

Case 2. A is a (0-place) constant. Then $\mathbf{V_m}(A) = \mathbf{g}(A) = \mathbf{k}(A)$

(β) Assume it is true for $\ell(B) < k$. We will prove it for $\ell(A) = k$.

Case 1. $A = fw_1\cdots w_n$ for some functor f and wffs $w_1,\cdots,w_n$. Then $\ell(w_i) < k$, for each i. Hence, by hypothesis of induction, $\mathbf{V_m}(A_i) = \mathbf{k}(A_i)$. Therefore, $\mathbf{V_m}(fw_1\cdots w_n) = (\mathbf{g}(f))(\mathbf{V_m}(w_1),\cdots,\mathbf{V_m}(w_n)) = (\mathbf{g}(f))(\mathbf{k}(w_1),\cdots,\mathbf{k}(w_n)) = \mathbf{k}(fw_1\cdots w_n) = \mathbf{k}(A)$

Case 2. $A = Qv_1\cdots v_m w_1\cdots w_n$. Then $\mathbf{V_m}(Qv_1\cdots v_m w_1\cdots w_n) =$

$\mathfrak{h}(\{x_1,\cdot\cdot,x_m,\mathfrak{g}[\mathbf{B}^{v_1}{}_{x_1}\cdots{}^{v_m}{}_{x_m}\mathbf{v}_{\mathfrak{m}}(w_1),\cdots,\mathbf{B}^{v_1}{}_{x_1}\cdots{}^{v_m}{}_{x_m}\mathbf{v}_{\mathfrak{m}}(w_n)]\})$ $=$ $\mathfrak{h}(\{x_1,''',x_m,\mathfrak{k}(<A,x_1,\cdots,x_m>)\}) = \mathfrak{k}(Qv_1\cdots v_m w_1\cdots w_n)$. Hence we indeed have $\mathbf{v}_{\mathfrak{m}}(A) = \mathfrak{k}(A)$. Hence if d is set as the highest value y such that there is an $A \in \alpha$ with $\mathbf{v}_{\mathfrak{m}}(A) = y$, the theorem is satisfied.

Theorem 12-4. Let α be finite. Then $\alpha \models A$ holds without restrictions on the type of interpretation (except for being first-order) iff A is S-equivalent to an element of α.

Proof: Suppose $B \in \alpha$ and A S-equivalent to B. Then $\alpha \models B$ and since $B \models A$, $\alpha \models A$. By theorem 12-3, if A is not S-equivalent to any element of β, there is a model of β and not of A and therefore not $(\alpha \models A)$.

Theorem 12-5. Let $\mathfrak{G}$ be compact in a first-order logic $\mathfrak{L}$. If for every finite set of wffs β, there exists a set γ such that for every interpretation and assignment $\mathfrak{m}$, $\mathfrak{m}$ is a model of γ iff $\mathfrak{m}$ is not a model of β, then $\delta \models D$ iff D is S-equivalent to an element of δ.

Proof: (right-to-left) This is trivial. (left-to right) Assume $\delta \models D$. Let $\mathfrak{m}$ be a model of γ iff it is not a model of D, for every $\mathfrak{m}$. Then $\delta \cup \gamma$ has no models. By compactness, there is a finite subset of $\delta \cup \gamma$ which has no models. Hence there is a finite set $\beta \subset \delta$ such that $\beta \cup \gamma$ has no models. Then if $\mathfrak{m}$ is a model of β, it is not a model of γ and therefore is a model of δ, so that $\beta \models D$ and hence by theorem 12-4, D is S-equivalent to an element of β and hence of δ.

Let α and β be finite sets of wffs. Then for every wff A, we define the set $clos_{\alpha\beta}(A)$ to be the least set satisfying the following conditions:

1. $A, B \in \alpha \Rightarrow A \in clos_{\alpha\beta}(B)$.
2. $A, B \in \beta \Rightarrow A \in clos_{\alpha\beta}(B)$.
3. A is S-equivalent to $B \Rightarrow A \in clos_{\alpha\beta}(B)$.
4. $[A \in clos_{\alpha\beta}(B)$ and $\mathbf{F}^{v}{}_{A}C \in clos_{\alpha\beta}(D)] \Rightarrow \mathbf{F}^{v}{}_{B}C \in clos_{\alpha\beta}(D))$.

Theorem 12-6. For all wffs A and B and sets of wffs α and β, $A \in clos_{\alpha\beta}(B)$ is an equivalence relation on the set of wffs [and hence $clos_{\alpha\beta}(B)$ is the cell of a partition on the set of wffs].

Proof: Since S-equivalence is an equivalence relation on the set of wffs $A \in clos_{\alpha\beta}(A)$. Since the conditions are symmetric, $A \in clos_{\alpha\beta}(B)$ implies $B \in clos_{\alpha\beta}(A)$. Finally, suppose $A \in clos_{\alpha\beta}(B)$ and $B \in clos_{\alpha\beta}(C)$. Since $\mathbf{F}^{\upsilon}{}_{B}v = B$, we have, by symmetry, $B \in clos_{\alpha\beta}(A)$, and hence $\mathbf{F}^{\upsilon}{}_{A}v \in clos_{\alpha\beta}(C)$, i.e. $A \in clos_{\alpha\beta}(C)$.

Theorem 12-7. If there is a two-valued model of α that is not a model of any element of β, then there is an $A \in \alpha$ and $B \in \beta$ such that $clos_{\alpha\beta}(A) \cap clos_{\alpha\beta}(B) = \varnothing$.

Proof: Let $\mathfrak{m}$ be a model of α and not be a model of any element of β. If $A \in \alpha$, then $\mathbf{V}_{\mathfrak{m}}(A) = 1 = \mathbf{V}_{\mathfrak{m}}(B)$, for every $B \in \alpha$. Similarly if $A \in \beta$, $\mathbf{V}_{\mathfrak{m}}(A) = 0 = \mathbf{V}_{\mathfrak{m}}(B)$, for every $B \in \beta$. Since A is S-equivalent to B implies that every model of A is a model of B, condition 3 preserves truth values. Similarly if A and B have the same value, so will $\mathbf{F}^{\upsilon}{}_{A}C$ and $\mathbf{F}^{\upsilon}{}_{B}C$. Hence $A \in clos_{\alpha\beta}(B)$ implies $\mathbf{V}_{\mathfrak{m}}(A) = \mathbf{V}_{\mathfrak{m}}(B)$. But then if $\mathbf{V}_{\mathfrak{m}}(A) = 1$, all elements of $clos_{\alpha\beta}(A)$ take 1, and if $\mathbf{V}_{\mathfrak{m}}(B) = 0$, all elements of $clos_{\alpha\beta}(B)$ take 0 and hence $clos_{\alpha\beta}(A) \cap clos_{\alpha\beta}(B) = \varnothing$.

Let α and β be sets of wffs of a first-order system $\mathfrak{L}$. Let δ be a set of wfes such that there is an A such that $A \in \alpha \cup \beta$ and B occurs in A. Then $\gamma = \{\gamma_1, \gamma_2, \cdots\}$ is an extensional partition on $\alpha;\beta$ provided:

1. There is an i such that $\alpha \subset \gamma_i$.
2. There is an i such that $\beta \subset \gamma_i$.
3. If A is S-equivalent to B and $A \in \gamma_i$, $B \in \gamma_i$.
4. $\cup\gamma_i = \delta$
5. $i \neq j \Rightarrow \gamma_i \cap \gamma_j = \varnothing$
6. $(A \in \gamma_i, B \in \gamma_i, \mathbf{F}^{\upsilon}{}_{A}C \in \gamma_i) \Rightarrow \mathbf{F}^{\upsilon}{}_{A}C \in \gamma_i$
7. $(A \in \gamma_i, B \in \gamma_i, A \in W) \Rightarrow B \in W$

Note that if α and β are finite, every extensional partition on $\alpha;\beta$ is finite. Let $\gamma = \{\gamma_1, \gamma_2, \cdots\}$ be a set of sets of wffs such that (1) $\cup\gamma_i = \delta$, (2) A and B are elements of γ_i iff for every extensional partition γ^* on $\alpha;\beta$, there exists a j such that $A \in \gamma^*_j$ and $B \in \gamma^*_j$. Then γ is an extensional partition on $\alpha;\beta$. We will term this partition **the finest partition on** $\alpha;\beta$.

Theorem 12-8: Let α and β be finite sets of wffs of a first (or zero)-order system $\mathcal{L}$. Then there exists an interpretation **P** with an assignment $\mathfrak{m}$ which is a model of α and which is not a model of any element of β, iff there exists an extensional partition γ on $\alpha;\beta$, such that exactly two elements of γ are sets of wffs.

Proof: Assume there is an interpretation **P** and an assignment $\mathfrak{m}$ such that $\mathfrak{m}$ is a model of α and not of any element of β. Let γ_1 be the set of wffs A such that $A \in \delta$ and $\mathbf{V}_{\mathfrak{m}}(A) = 1$. Let γ_2 be the set of wffs A such that $A \in \delta$ and $\mathbf{V}_{\mathfrak{m}}(A) = 0$. Let $\{i_1, \cdots, i_n)$ be the set of elements of $\mathcal{I}$ such that there exists a term A such that $A \in \delta$ and $\mathbf{V}_{\mathfrak{m}}(A) = i_j$, for some j $(1 \le j \le n)$. Then let γ_{j+2} be the set of all elements of δ such that $\mathbf{V}_{\mathfrak{m}}(A) = i_j$. Then $\alpha \subset \gamma_1$, $\beta \subset \gamma_2$ and γ satisfies conditions (3) - (7).

Assume $\gamma = \{\gamma_1, \cdots, \gamma_p\}$ is an extensional partition on $\alpha;\beta$ such that exactly two elements of γ are sets of wffs (without loss of generality we may assume that these are γ_1 and γ_2 and that furthermore $\alpha \subset \gamma_1$ and $\beta \subset \gamma_2$). Let $\mathcal{P}$ be the set of elements of δ such that $A \in \mathcal{P}$ iff there is a quantifier Q and a sequence B such that A = QB. Let $\mathcal{R}$ be the set of finite sequences $\langle A, x_1, \cdots, x_{n(A)} \rangle$ where A = QB, $A \in \mathcal{P}$ and Q takes n(A) variable indices and for every i $(1 \le i \le n(A))$ there is a j $(3 \le j \le p)$.Then let $\{\gamma_1, \gamma_2\}$, $\mathcal{I} = \{\gamma_3, \cdots, \gamma_p\} \cup \mathcal{R}$. Let $\mathfrak{m}(v) = \gamma_i$ if $v \in \gamma_i$, and $\mathfrak{m}(v) = \gamma_1$ if $v \notin \delta$ and $v \in W$, and $\mathfrak{m}(v) = \gamma_3$ otherwise. Let **P** be the interpretation such that:

1. If f is an n-place functor, then P(f) is the function **f** such that if $A = fw_1 \cdots w_n \in \gamma_i$, $\mathbf{f}(\mathbf{V}_{\mathfrak{m}}(w_1), \cdots, \mathbf{V}_{\mathfrak{m}}(w_n)) = \gamma_i$, and $\mathbf{f}(x_1, \cdots, x_n)$ is γ_1 or γ_3 depending on whether f is a formula or term

functor.

2. If Q is an m-variable n-place quantifier, then $P(Q) = <h,g>$ such that if $A = Qv_1\cdots v_m w_1\cdots w_n$ and for every i $(1 \leq i \leq m)$, there is a j $(3 \leq j \leq p)$ such that $x_i = \gamma_j$, then

$$g[B^{\upsilon_1}{}_{x_1}\cdots{}^{\upsilon_m}{}_{x_m}U_m(w_1),\cdots,B^{\upsilon_1}{}_{x_1}\cdots{}^{\upsilon_m}{}_{x_m}U_m(w_n)] = <A,x_1,\cdots,x_n>$$

and $g(y_1,\cdots,y_n) = \gamma_3$ otherwise. Also, h is the function which satisfies the condition: if η is the set of m+1-tuples such that if $A \in \mathcal{P}$ and for every i $(1 \leq i \leq m)$ there is a j $(3 \leq j \leq p)$ such that $x_i = \gamma_j$, $<x_1,\cdots,x_m,<A,x_1,\cdots,x_m>> \in \eta$, and $<x_1,\cdots,x_m,\gamma_3> \in \eta$ for all other values of x_1, then $h(\eta) = \gamma_k$ if $A \in \gamma_k$; while $h(y) = \gamma_1$ or γ_3 for any other case, as it was for functors.

By induction on $\ell(A)$, if A is a wfe and $A \in \gamma_i$, $U_m(A) = \gamma_i$.

(α) $\ell(A) = 1$

Case 1. A is a variable. If $A \in \gamma_i$, then $U_m(A) = m(A) = \gamma_i$.

Case 2. A is not a variable. If $A \in \gamma_i$, then $U_m(A) = f(A) = \gamma_i$.

(β) Assume the assertion is true for all wfes B with $\ell(B) < k$. We will prove it for $\ell(A) = k$.

Case 1. Let $A = fw_1\cdots w_n \in \gamma_i$. Then for every i, $\ell(w_i) = k$. By the hypothesis of induction, $U_m(w_i) = \gamma_{j}(i)$ where $w_i \in \gamma_{j(i)}$. Then $U_m(fw_1\cdots w_n) = (P(f))(U_m(w_1),\cdots,U_m(w_n)) = (P(f))(\gamma_1,\cdots,\gamma_n) = \gamma_i$.

Case 2. Suppose $A = Qv_1\cdots v_m w_1\cdots w_n \in \gamma_i$. Then $U_m(A) = (d1(Q))[\{<x_1,\cdots,x_m, D>] $ where D is

$$<(d2(Q))(B^{\upsilon_1}{}_{x_1}\cdots{}^{\upsilon_m}{}_{x_m}Um(w_1),\cdots,B^{\upsilon_1}{}_{x_1}\cdots{}^{\upsilon_m}{}_{x_m}Um(w_n))>$$

The set of m+1-tuples which are the values of the expression on the right consists of: $<x_1\cdots,x_m,<A,x_1,\cdots,x_n>>$ if $A \in \gamma_i$ and of $<x_1\cdots,x_m,\gamma_3>$ otherwise. Hence $Um(A) = \gamma_i$.

Therefore, all elements of α are in γ_1 and all of β are in γ_2 and the theorem follows.

Theorem 12-9. If α is finite, $\alpha \vDash A$ for all two-valued interpretations iff there exist no extensional partition of $\alpha;\{A\}$ such that exactly two of its sets contain wffs.

Proof: This follows by theorem 12-8 taking $\beta = \{A\}$.

Note that if α and β are finite, the finest extensional partition on $\alpha;\beta$ can be determined in a finite number of steps by assigning each wfe which occurs in an element of $\alpha \cup \beta$ to an existing γ_i iff conditions (1) - (7) compel it. Then there will be a finite number of γ_i's whose members are wffs. If $\alpha \cup \beta$ is a subset of one of them there will be no two-valued models which "separate" the two. Otherwise there will be 2^{k-2} ways of choosing a subset γ^* of γ such that:

1. $\gamma_i \in \gamma^* \Rightarrow \gamma_i$ is a set of wffs.
2. $\alpha^* = \cup\gamma_i$ such that $\gamma_i \in \gamma^*$.
3. $\beta^* = \cup\gamma_i$ such that $\gamma_i \notin \gamma^*$ and $\gamma_i$is a set of wffs.
4. $\alpha \subset \alpha^*$
5. $\beta \subset \beta^*$

Then since α^* and β^* are finite and $\alpha^* \cup \beta^*$ equals the set of wffs which occur in $\alpha \cup \beta$, extensional partitions on $\alpha^*;\beta^*$ either have one or two elements whose members are wffs. If the latter is the case, it is also an extensional partition on $\alpha;\beta$. Hence there is a procedure for determining for every finite α and β whether there is a two-valued model of α which is not a model of any element of β.

It should be noted that the models generated by our theorems are not usually the simplest ones, and what is more important, that we have placed no conditions on the functors and quantifiers other than being two-valued, and as a result the interpretation generated may be non-standard. For example, consider $p, \sim p \models \sim q$ where p and q are formula variables. Since $\sim q = \mathbf{F}^{p}_{q}\sim p$, the fact that p and $\sim p$ are in the same set implies that q and $\sim q$ must be. Hence $\mathfrak{m}(\sim)$ has to be the identity function. Note that this result tells us that $p, \sim p, q \models \sim q$ will hold in any two-valued logic. That this is the case can be seen by a specific argument, since $\sim$ must be be a one-place two-valued function and hence must be one of the two constants, the identity function or standard two-valued negation. If it is the constant 0 or negation, p and $\sim p$ cannot both be satisfied, if it were the constant 1, $\sim q$ would have to be 1, and finally, if it is the identity function, q and $\sim q$ are equivalent.

Before we consider specific and more familiar quantifiers, let us note that we can define specific occurrences of expressions, and more specifically, variables. To do so, one must mention the expression that occurs, the expression in which it occurs, and exactly where it occurs. Accordingly, If A = BCD, we define <A,C,B> as an **occurrence triple** provided BC is an initial segment of A. If this condition is not satisfied, the triple is **not** an occurrence triple. (Of course, B or D or both may be null.) If the occurrence triple exists, we can use it to refer to a particular occurrence of C in A. One particularly useful application is in classification of occurrences of variables.

Specifically we will call <A,v,B> a **bound occurrence** if A is a wfe, v a variable, and (1) there is a quantifier Q such that A = $Qv_1 \cdots v_m w_1 \cdots w_n$, an i such that $v = v_i$, and a j such that w_j = CvD and B = $Qv_1 \cdots v_m w_1 \cdots w_{j-1}C$, or (2) there is a wfe C such that A = DCE and <C,v,F> is a bound occurrence and B = DF. We will call <A,v,B> an **quantifier occurrence** if A is a wfe, v a variable, and (1) there is a quantifier Q such that A = $Qv_1 \cdots v_m w_1 \cdots w_n$, an i such that $v = v_i$, and B = $Qv_1 \cdots v_{i-1}$, or (2) there is a wfe C such that A = DCE and <C,v,F> is a quantifier occurrence and B = DF. Finally, <A,v,B> is a **free occurrence** if A is a wfe, v a variable, and <A,v,B> is an occurrence which is neither a bound nor a quantifier occurrence.

In the sequel, we will consider (except in passing) only two of the many possible quantifiers. Both are one-variable one-place formula quantifiers. The first of these we will call the **universal quantifier** and symbolize by an inverted A (i.e. an A rotated 180^0). We can characterize it by two rules:

1. $\alpha, \mathbf{F}^{v}_{z}\beta \vdash \mathbf{F}^{v}_{z}A \Rightarrow \alpha, \forall v\beta \vdash \forall vA$, where α and β are sets of wffs, A is a wff, v is a term variable, z a term variable or constant, v does not occur in any element of α, z does not occur (free) in any element of $\alpha \cup \beta \cup \{A\}$, and z is free for v in every element of $\beta \cup \{A\}$. We will indicate this rule as **UT** (for universal typical instance).

2. $\forall vA \vdash \mathbf{F}^{v}_{t}A$, where A is a wff, v is a term variable, t a term free for v in A. We will indicate this rule as **US** (for universal specification).

The second quantifier, which we shall call the **existential quantifier**, will be symbolized by a backwards E (thus likewise with a 180^0 rotation) and can be characterized by the following three rules:

1. $\mathbf{F}^{v}_{t}A \vdash \exists vA$, where A is a wff, v is a term variable, t a term free for v in A. We will indicate this rule as **EG** (for existential generalization).

2. $\alpha, \mathbf{F}^{v}_{z}A \vdash \mathbf{F}^{v}_{z}B \Rightarrow \alpha, \exists vA \vdash \exists vB$, where α is a set of wffs, A and

B are wffs, v a term variable, z a term variable or constant, v does not occur free in any element of α, z does not occur (free) in A, B or in any element of α and z is free for v in A and B. We will indicate this rule as **ET** (for existential typical instance).

3. $\exists vA \vdash A$, if A is a wff and v is a term variable that does not occur free in A. We will indicate this rule as **ER** (for existential redundant).

The universal quantifier behaves much the same as expressions like "all" or "for every" in English; similarly, the existential quantifier behaves much like "some" and "there exists." Likewise the rules might be regarded as formal analogues of common inferential arguments. So, **US** can represent the principle "true for all, true for every," which allows us to conclude from the fact that if something holds for all cases, it holds for every particular case. Likewise, **EG** represents the inference from the fact that something holds in a particular case to the assertion that it holds for some case. **UT** and **ET** represent the common reasoning from arbitrary instances to universal and existential conclusions.

Theorem 12-10. If $\mathcal{L}$ contains UT, $\vdash_{\mathcal{L}} A \Rightarrow \vdash_{\mathcal{L}} \forall vA$.

Proof: This follows by UT, with $\alpha = \beta = \varnothing$.

Theorem 12-11. If $\mathcal{L}$ contains UT and R-includes $\mathcal{P1}$ and v does not occur free in A, $\vdash_{\mathcal{L}} \forall v(A \supset B) \supset (A \supset \forall vB)$.

Proof:

1.	$A, A \supset B \vdash B$	MP
2.	$A, \forall v(A \supset B) \vdash \forall vB$	1, UT ($\alpha = \{A\}$)
3.	$\vdash \forall v(A \supset B) \supset (A \supset \forall vB)$	2, C(2)

Theorem 12-12. If $\mathcal{L}$ contains US and $\mathcal{R}$-includes $\mathcal{P1}$,

$\vdash_{\mathcal{L}} \forall vA \supset \mathbf{F}^{v}{}_{t}A$.

Proof: This follows by US and one application of C.

Theorem 12-13. If $\mathcal{L}$ contains UT and $\mathcal{R}$-includes $\mathcal{P1}$, $\vdash_{\mathcal{L}} \forall v(A \supset B) \supset [\forall vA \supset \forall vB)$.

Proof:

1.	$A, A \supset B \vdash B$	MP
2.	$\forall vA, \forall v(A \supset B) \vdash \forall vB$	1, UT($\alpha=\{A, A\supset B\}$)

3. $\vdash \forall v(A \supset B) \supset [\forall vA \supset \forall vB)$	2, C(2)

Theorem 12-14. If $\mathcal{L}$ contains **US**, **ET** and $\mathcal{R}$-includes $\mathcal{P}1$, $\vdash_{\mathcal{L}} \forall v(A \supset B) \supset [\exists vA \supset \exists vB)$.

Proof:

1. $\forall v(A \supset B), A \vdash A \supset B$	US
2. $\forall v(A \supset B), A \vdash A$	**Premise**
3. $\forall v(A \supset B), A \vdash B$	1, 2, MP
4. $\forall v(A \supset B), \exists A \vdash \exists B$	3, ET
5. $\vdash \forall v(A \supset B) \supset (\exists vA \supset \exists vB)$	4, C(2)

Theorem 12-15. If $\mathcal{L}$ contains **US**, **ET**, and **ER** and $\mathcal{R}$-includes $\mathcal{P}1\mathcal{N}$, $\forall vA \vdash_{\mathcal{L}} \sim\exists v\sim A$.

Proof:

1. $\forall vA, \mathbf{F}^{v}{}_{v*}\sim A \vdash \mathbf{F}^{v}{}_{v*}A$	US
2. $\forall vA, \mathbf{F}^{v}{}_{v*}\sim A \vdash \sim\mathbf{F}^{v}{}_{v*}A$	**Premise** (df. of F)
3. $\forall vA, \mathbf{F}^{v}{}_{v*}\sim A \vdash \sim(B \supset B)$	1, 2, $\mathcal{P}1\mathcal{N}$-7D, with no free v or v* in B
4. $\forall vA, \exists v\sim A \vdash \exists v\sim(B \supset B)$	3, ET
5. $\forall vA, \exists v\sim A \vdash \sim(B \supset B)$	4, ER
6. $\forall vA \vdash B \supset B$	$\mathcal{P}1$-4T
7. $\forall vA, B \supset B \vdash \sim\exists v\sim A$	5, **Con**
8. $\forall vA \vdash \sim\exists v\sim A$	6, 7, **Clos**

The reader will note that $\mathcal{P}1\mathcal{N}$ is a trifle strong as a requirement; what is obviously really required is any system that $\mathcal{R}$-includes $\mathcal{M}\mathcal{N}$ and has at least one T-theorem.

Theorem 12-16. If $\mathcal{L}$ contains **US**, **ET**, and **ER** and R-includes $\mathcal{P}1\mathcal{N}$, $\exists vA \vdash_{\mathcal{L}} \sim\forall v\sim A$.

Proof: The proof is analogous to that of theorem 12-15.

Although in the succeeding chapters we will only use the universal and existential quantifiers, it should not be assumed that there are no other interesting ones. For example, one quantifier whose standard interpretation might be "there are at least two things satisfying A," can be characterized by the following three rules. We will symbolize the quantifier by the numeral 2.

T1. $\mathbf{F}^{v}{}_{x}A, \sim \mathbf{F}^{v}{}_{y}A, \mathbf{F}^{v}{}_{x}B, \mathbf{F}^{v}{}_{y}B \vdash 2vB$, where v is a term variable and x and y are terms free for v in both A and B.

T2. $\alpha, A \vdash B \Rightarrow \alpha, 2vA \vdash 2x\mathbf{F}^{v}{}_{x}B$, if v and x are term variables and v does not occur free in any element of α and x is free for v in B.

T3. $2vA \vdash \exists vA$

Theorem 12-17. If $\mathcal{L}$ contains UT and T1 and R-includes $\mathcal{LNC}$,
$\forall x{\sim}2yPxy, \forall xPxx \vdash_{\mathcal{L}} \forall x\forall y(Pxy \supset Pyx)$.

Proof:

1. $\sim 2yPxy, Pxx, Pxy, \sim Pyx \vdash_{\mathcal{L}} Pxx$ — Premise
2. $\sim 2yPxy, Pxx, Pxy, \sim Pyx \vdash_{\mathcal{L}} Pxy$ — Premise
3. $\sim 2yPxy, Pxx, Pxy, \sim Pyx \vdash_{\mathcal{L}} \sim Pyx$ — Premise

Hence, since $\mathbf{F}^{y}{}_{x}Pyx = Pxx$ and $\mathbf{F}^{y}{}_{x}Pxy = Pxx$,

4. $\sim 2yPxy, Pxx, Pxy, \sim Pyx \vdash_{\mathcal{L}} 2xPxy$ — 1, 2, 3, T1
5. $\sim 2yPxy, Pxx, Pxy, \sim Pyx \vdash_{\mathcal{L}} \sim 2xPxy$ — Premise
6. $\sim 2yPxy, Pxx, Pxy, \sim Pyx \vdash_{\mathcal{L}} Pyx$ — 4, 5, RA
7. $\sim 2yPxy, Pxx, Pxy \vdash_{\mathcal{L}} Pyx$ — 6, CM
8. $\sim 2yPxy, Pxx \vdash_{\mathcal{L}} Pxy \supset Pyx$ — 7, C
9. $\forall x{\sim}2yPxy, \forall xPxx \vdash_{\mathcal{L}} \forall x\forall y(Pxy \supset Pyx)$ — 8, UT (2)

Theorem 12-18. If $\mathcal{L}$ contains UT and T1 and R-includes $\mathcal{LNC}$,
$\forall x{\sim}2yPxy, \forall xPxx \vdash_{\mathcal{L}} \forall x\forall y\forall z[Pxy \supset (Pyz \supset Pxz)]$.

Proof:

1. $\sim 2yPxy, Pxx, Pxy, Pyz, \sim Pxz \vdash_{\mathcal{L}} Pxx$ — Premise
2. $\sim 2yPxy, Pxx, Pxy, Pyz, \sim Pxz \vdash_{\mathcal{L}} Pyz$ — Premise
3. $\sim 2yPxy, Pxx, Pxy, Pyz, \sim Pxz \vdash_{\mathcal{L}} \sim Pxz$ — Premise
4. $\sim 2yPxy, Pxx, Pxy, Pyz, \sim Pxz \vdash_{\mathcal{L}} Pxy$ — Premise

Since $\mathbf{F}^{y}{}_{x}Pyz = Pxz$ and $\mathbf{F}^{y}{}_{x}Pxy = Pxx$,

5. $\sim 2yPxy, Pxx, Pxy, Pyz, \sim Pxz \vdash_{\mathcal{L}} 2yPxy$ — 1, 2, 3, 4, T1
6. $\sim 2yPxy, Pxx, Pxy, Pyz, \sim Pxz \vdash_{\mathcal{L}} \sim 2yPxy$ — Premise
7. $\sim 2yPxy, Pxx, Pxy, Pyz, \sim Pxz \vdash_{\mathcal{L}} Pxz$ — 5, 6, RA
8. $\sim 2yPxy, Pxx, Pxy, Pyz \vdash_{\mathcal{L}} Pxz$ — 7, CM

9. ~2yPxy, Pxx $\vdash_{\mathcal{L}}$ Pxy ⊃ (Pyz ⊃ Pxz) 8, C(2)

10. ∀x~2yPxy, ∀xPxx $\vdash_{\mathcal{L}}$
∀x∀y∀z[Pxy ⊃ (Pyz ⊃ Pxz)] 9, UT(3)

Theorems 12-17 and 12-18 show that a relation which is reflexive and satisfies ∀x~2yPxy is an equivalence relation. It is even more interesting that these conditions create a formal representative of the identity relation. More specifically, any two relations satisfying these conditions are equivalent and if a relation satisfies these conditions, replacibility can be shown.

Theorem 12-19. If $\mathcal{L}$ contains UT and T1 and R-includes 1NC, ∀x~2yPxy, ∀xPxx, ∀x~2yRxy, ∀xRxx $\vdash_{\mathcal{L}}$ ∀x∀y(Pxy ⊃ Rxy).

Proof:	1. ~2yPxy, Pxx, ~2yRxy, Rxx, Pxy, ~Rxy $\vdash_{\mathcal{L}}$ 2yPxy	T1
	2. ~2yPxy, Pxx, ~2yRxy, Rxx, Pxy, ~Rxy $\vdash_{\mathcal{L}}$ ~2yPxy	Premise
	3. ~2yPxy, Pxx, ~2yRxy, Rxx, Pxy, ~Rxy $\vdash_{\mathcal{L}}$ Rxy	RA
	4. ~2yPxy, Pxx, ~2yRxy, Rxx, Pxy, Rxy $\vdash_{\mathcal{L}}$ Rxy	Premise
	5. ~2yPxy, Pxx, ~2yRxy, Rxx, Pxy $\vdash_{\mathcal{L}}$ Rxy	3,4, NgC
	6. ~2yPxy, Pxx, ~2yRxy, Rxx $\vdash_{\mathcal{L}}$ Pxy ⊃ Rxy	5, C
	7. ∀x~2yPxy, ∀xPxx, ∀x~2yRxy, ∀xRxx $\vdash_{\mathcal{L}}$ ∀x∀y(Pxy ⊃ Rxy)	6, UT(2)

Theorem 12-20. If $\mathcal{L}$ contains US, T1 and R-includes 1NC ∀x~2zPxz, ∀xPxx, Pyz, F^x_yA $\vdash_{\mathcal{L}}$ F^x_zA, provided x is a term variable and y and z are free for x in A.

Proof:	1. ∀x~2zPxz, ∀xPxx, Pyz, F^x_yA , F^x_z~A $\vdash_{\mathcal{L}}$ F^x_yA	Premise
	2. ∀x~2zPxz, ∀xPxx, Pyz, F^x_yA , F^x_z~A $\vdash_{\mathcal{L}}$ F^x_z~A	Premise
	3. ∀x~2zPxz, ∀xPxx, Pyz, F^x_yA , F^x_z~A $\vdash_{\mathcal{L}}$ Pyz	Premise
	4. ∀x~2zPxz, ∀xPxx, Pyz, F^x_yA , F^x_z~A $\vdash_{\mathcal{L}}$ Pyy	US
	5. ∀x~2zPxz, ∀xPxx, Pyz, F^x_yA , F^x_z~A $\vdash_{\mathcal{L}}$ 2zPyz	1,2,3,4, T1
	6. ∀x~2yPxy, ∀xPxx, Pyz, F^x_yA , F^x_z~A $\vdash_{\mathcal{L}}$ ~2zPyz	US
	7. ∀x~2yPxy, ∀xPxx, Pyz, F^x_yA , F^x_z~A $\vdash_{\mathcal{L}}$ F^x_zA	5,6, RA

8. $\forall x \sim 2yPxy, \forall xPxx, Pyz, \mathbf{F}^{x}{}_{y}A \vdash_{\mathcal{L}} \mathbf{F}^{x}{}_{z}A$ 7, CM

We will conclude this chapter by characterizing the types of systems that we will consider in the succeeding two chapters. These will be calculi using as primitive signs two kinds of variables, formula variables (p, q and r, with or without subscript) and term variables (x,y,z, with or without subscript), three types of functors: predicates (P,Q, R, with or without subscript), operations (M,N,R, with or without subscript) and connectives (as indicated) and finally quantifiers (existential and universal only). Each predicate and operation will have a superscript indicating the number of arguments. Except as otherwise indicated, these systems (first-order logics) will have **UT**, **US**, **ET**, **EG** and **ER** as rules. They will of course have other rules governing their connectives.

13
Quantification and Complete Logics

We will now consider some of the results that follow from appending standard quantification rules to those of zero-order logics. From our discussion of zero-order logics and our basic discussion of quantification, it is obvious that the variety of possible systems is considerable, especially with respect to those systems weaker than complete two-valued logic; note that we get a system from every zero-order system just by adding quantifiers. For systems weaker than complete logics, one frequently can obtain more than one non-equivalent system by adding appropriate quantificational conditions. In this book we will not do more than give a treatment of complete logics and a very brief look at a few others.

As to complete logics, we could if we wished, construct our system around $\mathcal{ANC}$, $\mathcal{INC}$ or $\mathcal{NKC}$, but since we have already explored their mutual relations, it seems appropriate to examine a system based on $\mathcal{CINEAK}$. We will call it $\mathcal{CFOL}$ (for complete first-order logic).

$\mathcal{CFOL}$: A deductive first-order system with:

Quantifiers: $\forall$, $\exists$ (both one-variable one-place)

Connectives: $\sim$ (1-place), $\vee$ (2-place), $\wedge$ (2-place), $\supset$ (2-place), $\equiv$ (2-place)

Axioms: none

Rules:		
	1. $A, A \supset B \vdash B$	MP
	2. $\alpha, A \vdash B \Rightarrow \alpha \vdash A \supset B$	C
	3. $A, \sim A \vdash B$	RA
	4. $(\alpha, A \vdash B$ and $\alpha, \sim A \vdash B) \Rightarrow \alpha \vdash B$	NgC
	5. $A \wedge B \vdash A$	LS
	6. $A \wedge B \vdash B$	RS
	7. $A, B \vdash A \wedge B$	A
	8. $A \vdash A \vee B$	AR
	9. $B \vdash A \vee B$	AL
	10. $(\alpha, A \vdash C$ and $\alpha, B \vdash C) \Rightarrow \alpha, A \vee B \vdash C$	D
	11. $A, A \equiv B \vdash B$	Bi-MP(L)

12. B, A ≡ B ⊢ A Bi-MP(R)

13. (α, A ⊢ B and α, B ⊢ A) ⇒ α ⊢ A ≡ B Bi-C

14. ∀vA ⊢ $\mathbf{F}^{v}{}_{t}$A US

where v is a (term) variable and t a term free for v in A.

15. α, $\mathbf{F}^{v}{}_{v'}\beta \vdash \mathbf{F}^{v}{}_{v'}$A ⇒ α, ∀vβ ⊢ ∀vA UT

where (1) v and v′ are (term) variables, (2) v′ = v or else v′ is not free in any element of α ∪ β ∪ {A}, (3) v is not free in any element of α and (4) v′ is free for v in every element of β ∪ {A}.

16. $\mathbf{F}^{v}{}_{t}$A ⊢ ∃v A EG

where v is a (term) variable and t a term free for v in A.

17. α, $\mathbf{F}^{v}{}_{v'}$A ⊢ $\mathbf{F}^{v}{}_{v'}$ B ⇒ α, ∃v A ⊢ ∃v B ET

where (1) v and v′ are (term) variables, (2) v′ = v or else v′ is not free in any element of α ∪ {A,B}, (3) v is not free in any element of α and (4) v′ is free for v in both A and B.

18. ∃vA ⊢ A ER

where v is not free in A.

CFOL-1M. Every T- and D-theorem of CINEAK is a theorem of CFOL.

Proof: This is trivial.

CFOL-2T. ⊢ ∃vA ≡ ~∀v~A

Proof:

1. ∃vA ⊢ ~∀v~A	12-16
2. A ⊢ ∃vA	EG
3. A ⊢ ~~∃vA	2, PIN-3D
4. ~∃vA ⊢ ~A	3, Con
5. ~∃vA ⊢ ∀v~A	4, UT
6. ~∃vA ⊢ ~~∀v~A	5, PIN-3D
7. ~∀v~A ⊢ ~~∃vA	6, Con
8. ~∀v~A ⊢ ∃vA	7, INC-6D
9. ⊢ ∃vA ≡ ~∀v~A	1, 8, Bi-C

CFOL-3T. ⊢ ∀vA ≡ ~∃v~A Exercise

CFOL-4D. ∀v(A ≡ B) ⊢ ∀vA ≡ ∀vB

Proof: 1. $A \equiv B, A \vdash B$ Bi-MP(L)

2. $\forall v(A \equiv B), \forall vA \vdash \forall vB$ 1, UT

3. $A \equiv B, B \vdash A$ Bi-MP(R)

4. $\forall v(A \equiv B), \forall vB \vdash \forall vA$ 3, UT

5. $\forall v(A \equiv B) \vdash \forall vA \equiv \forall vB$ 2, 4, Bi-C

CFOL-5D. $\forall v(A \equiv B) \vdash \exists vA \equiv \exists vB$

Proof: 1. $\forall v(A \equiv B), A \vdash A \equiv B$ US

2. $\forall v(A \equiv B), A \vdash A$ Premise

3. $\forall v(A \equiv B), A \vdash B$ 1, 2, Bi-MP(L)

4. $\forall v(A \equiv B), \exists vA \vdash \exists vB$ 3, ET

5. $\forall v(A \equiv B), B \vdash A \equiv B$ US

6. $\forall v(A \equiv B), B \vdash B$ Premise

7. $\forall v(A \equiv B), B \vdash A$ 5, 6, Bi-MP(R)

8. $\forall v(A \equiv B), \exists vB \vdash \exists vA$ 7, ET

9. $\forall v(A \equiv B) \vdash \exists vA \equiv \exists vB$ 4, 8, Bi-C

CFOL-6M. CFOL is an E-logic.

Proof: This follows by the argument of P1-14M and 2-17, utilizing PINEAK-10M, CFOL-4D and CFOL-5D.

CFOL-7D. $\forall x \forall y A \vdash \forall y \forall x A$

Proof: 1. $\forall yA \vdash A$ US

2. $\forall x \forall y A \vdash \forall x A$ 1, UT

3. $\forall x \forall y A \vdash \forall y \forall x A$ 2, UT

CFOL-8T. $\vdash \forall x \forall y A \equiv \forall y \forall x A$ Exercise

CFOL-9D. $\exists x \exists y A \vdash \exists y \exists x A$ Exercise

CFOL-10T. $\vdash \exists x \exists y A \equiv \exists y \exists x A$ Exercise

CFOL-11M. $\vdash \forall y \mathbf{F}^{\vee}{}_{y}A \equiv \forall z \mathbf{F}^{\vee}{}_{z}A$ (if y and z are free for x in A and neither occur free in A).

Proof: Since y and z do not occur free in A, $\mathbf{F}^{y}{}_{z}\mathbf{F}^{x}{}_{y}A = \mathbf{F}^{x}{}_{z}A$. Hence $\forall y\mathbf{F}^{x}{}_{y}A \vdash \mathbf{F}^{x}{}_{z}A$, by U S and $\forall y\mathbf{F}^{x}{}_{y}A \vdash \forall z\mathbf{F}^{x}{}_{z}A$, by UT, and vice versa, and the theorem follows by **Bi-C**.

CFOL-12D. $\forall v(A \wedge B) \vdash \forall vA$ Exercise

CFOL-13T. $\vdash \forall v(A \wedge B) \equiv (\forall vA \wedge \forall vB)$ Exercise

CFOL-14M. If $v_1,\cdots,v_n$ are term variables and $x_1,\cdots,x_n$ is a rearrangement of $v_1,\cdots,v_n$, $\vdash \forall v_1\cdots\forall v_nA \equiv \forall x_1\cdots\forall x_nA$.

Proof: By induction on n, we get:

(α) n = 0. Then $\forall v_1\cdots\forall v_nA = \forall x_1\cdots\forall x_nA = A$.

(β) Assume the theorem is true for n < k. We will prove it for n = k.

There is an i ($1 \leq i \leq k$) such that $v_k = x_i$.

Case 1. i = k. By the hypothesis of induction, $\vdash \forall v_1\cdots\forall v_{k-1}B \equiv \forall x_1\cdots\forall x_{k-1}B$. Let $B = \forall v_kA$. Then the result follows immediately.

Case 2. i < k. Let $B = \forall x_kA$. Let $y_1,\cdots,y_{k-1}$ be a reordering of $x_1,\cdots,x_{k-1}$ such that $y_{k-1} = v_k$. Then

$\vdash\forall y_1\cdots\forall y_{k-1}B \equiv \forall x_1\cdots\forall x_{k-1}B$, i.e. $\vdash\forall y_1\cdots\forall y_kA \equiv \forall x_1\cdots\forall x_kA$.

But then $\vdash \forall y_2\cdots\forall y_kA \equiv \forall y_2\cdots\forall y_{k-2}y_ky_{k-1}A$, which is $\vdash \forall y_2\cdots\forall y_kA \equiv \forall y_{\cdot}\cdots\forall y_{k-2}y_kv_kA$, hence, by **UT**,**Bi-MP** and **Bi-C** $\vdash \forall y_1\cdots\forall y_kA \equiv \forall y_1\cdots\forall y_{k-2}y_kv_kA$ and by the transitivity of the bi-conditional and case 1, the result follows.

If $v_1,\cdots,v_n$ are the free variables in A (the order is irrelevant as a result of CFOL-14M), we will call $\forall v_1\cdots\forall v_nA$ the **universal closure** of A. We will use the notation ( )A to symbolize it. Two simple results follow easily:

CFOL-15D. $(\,)A \vdash A$

CFOL-16M. $\vdash A \Rightarrow\ \vdash (\,)A$

In addition, it is convenient to modify the equivalence theorem to allow substitution under the widest possible context. Accordingly, we redefine the **equivalence theorem** to be:

$$()(A \equiv B) \vdash ()(\mathbf{F}^{w}{}_{A}C \equiv \mathbf{F}^{w}{}_{B}C)$$

where w is a formula variable (and any variable that occurs in C, is free in A iff it also is in B). In the absence of formula variables, we would state this as: if C were like D except for having an occurrence of A where D has one of B, $()(A \equiv B) \vdash ()(C \equiv D)$. We then readily get:

CFOL-17M. The equivalence theorem holds in CFOL.

Proof: The proof is basically the same as that of CFOL-6M, utilizing **UT** and **ET** to extend the result to the quantifiers. (The restriction is sufficient to ensure UT and ET.)

Note that the effect of **UT** is to give a quantified form of every D- and T-theorem of CINEAK and included systems so that for instance PI-1Da becomes

$$\forall v(Px \supset Qx), \forall x(Qx \supset Rx) \vdash \forall x(Px \supset Rx)$$

which is the familiar syllogism in Barbara. ET plays a similar role in generating existential inference forms.

As we turn to the interpretation of CFOL, we utilize the model theory explained in chapter 12 with the following limitations on the models (except when specifically stated to the contrary): 1) the members of the set of values are 0 and 1, with 1 as the (sole) designated value, 2) the connectives are given their standard two-valued interpretations, 3) $\mathfrak{V}_{\mathfrak{m}}(\forall vA) = 1$ iff: for every $\mathfrak{m}'$ such that $\mathfrak{m}'(x) = \mathfrak{m}(x)$ for $x \neq v$ and $\mathfrak{l}_{\mathfrak{m}} = \mathfrak{l}_{\mathfrak{m}'}$, $\mathfrak{V}_{\mathfrak{m}'}(A) = 1$, 4) $\mathfrak{V}_{\mathfrak{m}}(\exists vA) = 1$ iff for some $\mathfrak{m}'$ such that $\mathfrak{m}'(x) = \mathfrak{m}(x)$ for $x \neq v$ and $\mathfrak{l}_{\mathfrak{m}} = \mathfrak{l}_{\mathfrak{m}'}$ and $\mathfrak{V}_{\mathfrak{m}'}(A) = 1$. This class of interpretations will, when necessary, be referred to as **standard two-valued** and will be abbreviated as **2V**. Because of the special role of assignments which differ from a given assignment $\mathfrak{m}$ at most in the value assigned to the term variable v, we will call such an assignment a **$\mathfrak{m}$-v-variant assignment**.

CFOL-18M. If A contains no free v or x, $\mathfrak{V}_{\mathfrak{m}}(A) = \mathfrak{V}_{\mathfrak{m}}(\forall vA) =$

$\mathfrak{V}_{\mathfrak{m}}(\exists vA) = \mathfrak{V}_{\mathfrak{m}}(\forall x\mathbf{F}^{v}{}_{x}A) = \mathfrak{V}_{\mathfrak{m}}(\exists x\mathbf{F}^{v}{}_{x}A)$, for every standard two-valued $\mathfrak{m}$.

Proof: By induction on $\mathfrak{L}(A)$:

(α) $\mathfrak{L}(A) = 1$.

Case 1. $A = v$. This is not possible since neither $\forall vv$ nor $\exists vv$ is well formed in CFOL.

Case 2. $A \neq v$. Then if $\mathfrak{m}'$ is $\mathfrak{m}$–v-variant, $\mathfrak{V}_{\mathfrak{m}'}(A) = \mathfrak{m}'(A) = \mathfrak{m}(A) = \mathfrak{V}_{\mathfrak{m}}(A)$. Hence $\mathfrak{V}_{\mathfrak{m}}(A) = \mathfrak{V}_{\mathfrak{m}}(\forall vA)$. Since $\mathfrak{m}$ is $\mathfrak{m}$–v-variant, $\mathfrak{V}_{\mathfrak{m}}(A) = \mathfrak{V}_{\mathfrak{m}}(\exists vA)$. Since $\forall x\mathbf{F}^{v}{}_{x}A$ and $\forall vA$ (and likewise $\exists x\mathbf{F}^{v}{}_{x}A$ and $\exists vA$) are closed alphabetical variants, the result follows.

(β) Suppose the theorem is true for $\mathfrak{L}(B) < k$. We will prove it for $\mathfrak{L}(A) = k$:

Case 1. $A = Pt_1 \cdots t_n$, where P is a predicate (i.e. a functor with all its arguments terms and value a wff). Then for each i ($1 \leq i \leq n$), $t_i \neq v$, as in case $\alpha(2)$, $\mathfrak{V}_{\mathfrak{m}'}(t_i) = \mathfrak{V}_{\mathfrak{m}}(t_i)$. Hence $\mathfrak{V}_{\mathfrak{m}'}(A) = \mathfrak{V}_{\mathfrak{m}'}(Mt_1 \cdots t_n) = (\mathfrak{g}_{\mathfrak{m}'}(M))(\mathfrak{V}_{\mathfrak{m}'}(t_1),\cdots,\mathfrak{V}_{\mathfrak{m}'}(t_n)) = (\mathfrak{g}_{\mathfrak{m}}(M))(\mathfrak{V}_{\mathfrak{m}'}(t_1),\cdots,\mathfrak{V}_{\mathfrak{m}'}(t_n))$ (since $\mathfrak{m}'$ is $\mathfrak{m}$–v-variant) $= (\mathfrak{g}_{\mathfrak{m}}(M))(\mathfrak{V}_{\mathfrak{m}}(t_1),\cdots,\mathfrak{V}_{\mathfrak{m}}(t_n)) = \mathfrak{V}_{\mathfrak{m}'}(Mt_1 \cdots t_n) = \mathfrak{V}_{\mathfrak{m}'}(A)$.

Case 2. $A = ✿w_1 \cdots w_n$, where ✿ is a connective (of course, in CFOL all connectives are either 1- or 2-place). $\mathfrak{V}_{\mathfrak{m}'}(A) = \mathfrak{V}_{\mathfrak{m}'}(✿w_1 \cdots w_n) = (\mathfrak{g}_{\mathfrak{m}'}(✿))(\mathfrak{V}_{\mathfrak{m}'}(w_1),\cdots,\mathfrak{V}_{\mathfrak{m}'}(w_n))$. But then v is not free in any w_i, and hence by the hypothesis of induction, the argument of case 1 [and for the other cases, that of $\alpha(2)$, follows, mutatis mutandis].

Case 3. $A = \forall vB$. By the hypothesis of induction, $\mathfrak{V}_{\mathfrak{m}'}(\forall vB) = \mathfrak{V}_{\mathfrak{m}'}(B)$, $\mathfrak{V}_{\mathfrak{m}}(\forall vB) = \mathfrak{V}_{\mathfrak{m}}(B)$ and since $\mathfrak{m}'$ is $\mathfrak{m}$–v-variant, $\mathfrak{V}_{\mathfrak{m}}(\forall vB) = \mathfrak{V}_{\mathfrak{m}'}(\forall vB)$. Hence $\mathfrak{V}_{\mathfrak{m}'}(A) = \mathfrak{V}_{\mathfrak{m}}(A)$. The remainder of the cases follows from the fact that $\mathfrak{m}$ is $\mathfrak{m}$–v-variant and by alphabetical variance.

Case 4. $A = \exists vB$. This is analogous to case 3.

CFOL-19M. Let $\mathfrak{m}'$ be an $\mathfrak{m}$–v-variant and $\mathfrak{m}'(v) = \mathfrak{V}_{\mathfrak{m}}(A)$. Then for every wfe B, $\mathcal{V}_{\mathfrak{m}'}(B) = \mathcal{V}_{\mathfrak{m}}(\mathbf{F}^{v}{}_{A}B)$.

Proof: By induction on $\ell(B)$:

(α) $\ell(B) = 1$.

Case 1. $B = v$. Then $\mathcal{V}_{\mathfrak{m}'}(B) = \mathcal{V}_{\mathfrak{m}'}(v) = \mathfrak{m}'(v) = \mathcal{V}_{\mathfrak{m}}(A) = \mathcal{V}_{\mathfrak{m}}(\mathbf{F}^{v}{}_{A}v) = \mathcal{V}_{\mathfrak{m}}(\mathbf{F}^{v}{}_{A}B)$

Case 2. $B \neq v$. Then since $\mathbf{F}^{v}{}_{A}B = B$, $\mathcal{V}_{\mathfrak{m}'}(B) = \mathfrak{m}'(B) = \mathfrak{m}(B) = \mathcal{V}_{\mathfrak{m}}(B) = \mathcal{V}_{\mathfrak{m}}(\mathbf{F}^{v}{}_{A}B)$.

(β) Suppose the theorem is true for $\ell(C) < k$. We will prove it for $\ell(B) = k > 1$:

Case 1. $B = fx_1 \cdots x_n$, where f is a functor and $x_1, \cdots, x_n$ are appropriate wfes (i.e. wfes such that B is well-formed). By the hypothesis of induction, $\mathcal{V}_{\mathfrak{m}'}(x_i) = \mathcal{V}_{\mathfrak{m}}(\mathbf{F}^{v}{}_{A}x_i)$. Hence $\mathcal{V}_{\mathfrak{m}'}(B) = \mathcal{V}_{\mathfrak{m}'}(fx_1 \cdots x_n) = (g_{\mathfrak{m}'}(f))(\mathcal{V}_{\mathfrak{m}'}(x_1), \cdots, \mathcal{V}_{\mathfrak{m}'}(x_n)) = (g_{\mathfrak{m}}(f))(\mathcal{V}_{\mathfrak{m}}(\mathbf{F}^{v}{}_{A}x_1), \cdots, \mathcal{V}_{\mathfrak{m}}(\mathbf{F}^{v}{}_{A}x_n)) = \mathcal{V}_{\mathfrak{m}}(\mathbf{F}^{v}{}_{A}fx_1 \cdots x_n) = \mathcal{V}_{\mathfrak{m}}(\mathbf{F}^{v}{}_{A}B)$.

Case 2. $B = \forall xC$, $x \neq v$. Let $1 = \mathcal{V}_{\mathfrak{m}'}(B) = \mathcal{V}_{\mathfrak{m}'}(\forall xC)$. Then if $\mathfrak{m}'^*$ is an $\mathfrak{m}'$–x–variant $\mathcal{V}_{\mathfrak{m}'^*}(C) = 1$. Suppose $\mathcal{V}_{\mathfrak{m}}(\mathbf{F}^{v}{}_{A}B) = \mathcal{V}_{\mathfrak{m}}(\mathbf{F}^{v}{}_{A}\forall xC) = 0 = \mathcal{V}_{\mathfrak{m}}(\forall x\mathbf{F}^{v}{}_{A}C)$. Then there is an $\mathfrak{m}$–x–variant $\mathfrak{m}^*$ such that $\mathcal{V}_{\mathfrak{m}^*}(\mathbf{F}^{v}{}_{A}C) = 0$. Let $\mathfrak{m}^{**}$ be an $\mathfrak{m}^*$–v–variant such that $\mathfrak{m}^{**}(v) = \mathcal{V}_{\mathfrak{m}}(A)$. By the hypothesis of induction, $\mathcal{V}_{\mathfrak{m}^{**}}(C) = \mathcal{V}_{\mathfrak{m}^*}(\mathbf{F}^{v}{}_{A}C) = 0$. But $\mathfrak{m}^{**}$ is an $\mathfrak{m}'$–x–variant. Similarly if $0 = \mathcal{V}_{\mathfrak{m}'}(B) = \mathcal{V}_{\mathfrak{m}'}(\forall xC)$ then there is an $\mathfrak{m}'$–x–variant $\mathfrak{m}^*$ such that $\mathcal{V}_{\mathfrak{m}^*}(C) = 0$. Let $\mathfrak{m}^{**}(x) = m^*(x)$ and $\mathfrak{m}^{**}$ be an $\mathfrak{m}$-x-variant. Then $\mathfrak{m}^*$ is an $\mathfrak{m}^{**}$-v-variant and $\mathfrak{m}^*(v) = \mathcal{V}_{\mathfrak{m}^{**}}(A)$. Hence $0 = \mathcal{V}_{\mathfrak{m}^{**}}(C) = \mathcal{V}_{\mathfrak{m}}(\forall xC)$.

Case 3. $B = \forall vC$. Suppose $1 = \mathcal{V}_{\mathfrak{m}}'(B) = \mathcal{V}_{\mathfrak{m}}'(\forall vC)$. Then every $\mathfrak{m}'$-v-variant, including $\mathfrak{m}$, satisfies C and hence also B. But $F^{v}{}_{A}\forall vA = \forall vA$, since $\forall vA$ has no free v.

Cases 4 and 5. These are similar to 2 and 3, but with the existential quantifier; the proofs are analogous to those of cases 2 or 3.

CFOL-20M. If $\mathfrak{V}_{\mathfrak{m}'}(A) = \mathfrak{V}_{\mathfrak{m}^*}(B)$ and both are $\mathfrak{m}$-v-variants, $\mathfrak{V}_{\mathfrak{m}'}(\mathbf{F}^{v}{}_{A}C) = \mathfrak{V}_{\mathfrak{m}^*}(\mathbf{F}^{v}{}_{B}C)$.

Proof: This follows immediately from CFOL-19M.

CFOL-21M. $\alpha \vdash_{CFOL} A \Rightarrow \alpha \vDash_{2V} A$ **(Soundness theorem for first order logic).**

Proof: By induction on the number of steps n in the Y-derivation of $\alpha \vdash A$ (Cf. INC-13M) :

(α) $k = 1$.

Then since CFOL has no axioms, $A_1 \in \alpha_1$.

(β) Suppose true for $k < n$. Prove true for $k = n$.

Case 1. The nth step is a case of a rule other than rules 14-18. The result follows from the hypothesis of induction and CINEAK-6M.

Case 2. The nth step is a case of **US**. Then there is a $j < n$ such that $\alpha_j \vDash A_j$ and $\alpha_j = \alpha_n$ and there is a wff B such that $A_j = \forall vB$ and $A_n = \mathbf{F}^{v}{}_{t}B$. Assume $\mathfrak{m} \Vdash \alpha_n$. By the hypothesis of induction, $\mathfrak{V}_{\mathfrak{m}}(\forall vB) = 1$. Hence for any $\mathfrak{m}$-v-variant, $\mathfrak{m}'$, $\mathfrak{V}_{\mathfrak{m}'}(B) = 1$. Let $\mathfrak{m}^*$ be the $\mathfrak{m}$-v-variant such that $\mathfrak{m}^*(v) = \mathfrak{V}_{\mathfrak{m}}(t)$. Then by CFOL-19M, $\mathfrak{V}_{\mathfrak{m}}(\mathbf{F}^{v}{}_{t}B) = \mathfrak{V}_{\mathfrak{m}^*}(B) = 1$.

Case 3. The nth step is a case of **UT**. There is a $j < n$ such that there exist term variables v and x and sets of wffs β and δ such that $\alpha_j = \beta \cup \{\mathbf{F}^{v}{}_{x}C\colon C \in \delta\}$ and $\alpha_n = \beta \cup \{\forall vC\colon C \in \delta\}$, while $A_j = \mathbf{F}^{v}{}_{x}B$ and $A_n = \forall vB$, with no free x in any element of β or δ, no free x in B, and with x free for v in B and in every element of δ and also v not free in any element of β. Assume $\mathfrak{m} \Vdash \beta$ and $\mathfrak{m} \Vdash \forall vA$, but $\mathfrak{V}_{\mathfrak{m}}(\forall vB) = 0$. Since there is no free x in any element of β or δ nor in B, if $D \in \beta \cup \delta \cup \{B\}$, then if $\mathfrak{n}$ is an $\mathfrak{m}$-x-variant, $\mathfrak{n} \Vdash D$ iff $\mathfrak{m} \Vdash D$. Then there is an $\mathfrak{m}$-v-variant $\mathfrak{m}^*$ such that $\mathfrak{V}_{\mathfrak{m}^*}(B) = 0$. Let $\mathfrak{n}^*$ be the $\mathfrak{m}$-x-variant with $\mathfrak{n}^*(x) = \mathfrak{m}^*(v)$ and $\mathfrak{m}^{**}$ be the $\mathfrak{m}^*$-x-variant with $\mathfrak{m}^{**}(x) = \mathfrak{m}^*(v)$. Likewise since there is no free x in $\beta \cup \delta \cup \{B\}$, $\mathfrak{m}^* \Vdash D$ iff $\mathfrak{m}^{**} \Vdash D$ if $D \in (\beta \cup \delta \cup \{B\})$. Then $\mathfrak{m}^{**}$ is an $\mathfrak{n}^*$–v-variant with $\mathfrak{m}^{**}(v) = \mathfrak{m}^*(v) = \mathfrak{n}^*(x)$. Then by $\mathcal{CFOL}$-19M, for every wfe D, $\mathcal{V}_{\mathfrak{m}^{**}}(D) = \mathcal{V}_{\mathfrak{n}^*}(\mathbf{F}^{v}_{x}D)$. Hence since $\mathfrak{m}^*$ is an $\mathfrak{m}$–v-variant, $\mathfrak{m}^* \Vdash \beta$ and $\mathfrak{m}^* \Vdash \delta$ and therefore $\mathfrak{m}^{**} \Vdash \beta$ and $\mathfrak{m}^{**} \Vdash \delta$. Hence $\mathfrak{n}^* \Vdash \beta$ and $\mathfrak{n}^* \Vdash \mathbf{F}^{v}_{x}\delta$. By the hypothesis of induction, $\mathfrak{n}^* \Vdash \mathbf{F}^{v}_{x}B$. Hence $\mathfrak{m}^{**} \Vdash B$. But then, $\mathfrak{m}^* \Vdash B$, which is contradictory.

Case 4. The nth step is a case of EG. There is a $j < n$ such that $\alpha_j = \alpha_n$ and a wff B such that $A_j = \mathbf{F}^{v}_{t}B$ and $A_n = \exists vB$, where v is a term variable and t is a term free for v in B. Let $\mathfrak{m} \Vdash \alpha_n$. Then $\mathfrak{m} \Vdash \mathbf{F}^{v}_{t}B$. Let $\mathfrak{m}^*$ be the $\mathfrak{m}$–v-variant with $\mathfrak{m}^*(v) = \mathcal{V}_{\mathfrak{m}}(t)$. Then by $\mathcal{CFOL}$-19M, $\mathfrak{m}^* \Vdash B$ and hence $\mathfrak{m} \Vdash \exists vB$.

Case 5. The nth step is a case of ET. There is a $j < n$ such that $\alpha_j = \beta \cup \{\mathbf{F}^{v}_{x}B\}$, $\alpha_n = \beta \cup \{\exists vB\}$, $A_j = \mathbf{F}^{v}_{x}C$ and $A_n = \exists vC$, where v and x are term variables, no free x is in B, C or any element of β, no free v is in any element of β and x is free for v in B and in C. Suppose $\mathfrak{m} \Vdash \beta$ and $\mathfrak{m} \Vdash \exists vB$. Hence there exists an $\mathfrak{m}$–v-variant $\mathfrak{m}^*$ with $\mathfrak{m}^* \Vdash B$. Since x is not free in α, B or C, if $\mathfrak{n}$ is an $\mathfrak{m}$–x-variant and $D \in (\beta \cup \{B,C\})$, $\mathfrak{n} \Vdash D$ iff $\mathfrak{m} \Vdash D$. Let $\mathfrak{n}^*$ be the $\mathfrak{m}$–x-variant with $\mathfrak{n}^*(x) = \mathfrak{m}^*(v)$ and $\mathfrak{m}^{**}$ be the $\mathfrak{m}^*$–x-variant with $\mathfrak{m}^{**}(x) = \mathfrak{m}^*(v)$. Then for $D \in \beta \cup \{B,C\})$, $\mathfrak{m}^* \Vdash D$ iff $\mathfrak{m}^{**} \Vdash D$. Thus $\mathfrak{m}^{**}$ is an $\mathfrak{n}^*$–v-variant with $\mathfrak{m}^{**}(v) = \mathfrak{m}^*(v) = \mathfrak{n}^*(x)$ and hence by $\mathcal{CFOL}$-19M, $\mathcal{V}_{\mathfrak{m}^{**}}(B) = \mathcal{V}_{\mathfrak{n}^*}(\mathbf{F}^{v}_{x}B)$. Since $\mathfrak{m}^* \Vdash B$, $\mathfrak{m}^{**} \Vdash B$ and hence $\mathfrak{n}^* \Vdash \mathbf{F}^{v}_{x}B$. Since $\mathfrak{n}^*$ is an $\mathfrak{m}$–x-variant, $\mathfrak{n}^* \Vdash \beta$, and hence by the hypothesis of induction, $\mathfrak{n}^* \Vdash \mathbf{F}^{v}_{x}C$. Thus $\mathfrak{m}^{**} \Vdash C$ and $\mathfrak{m}^* \Vdash C$ and since $\mathfrak{m}^*$ is an $\mathfrak{m}$–v-variant, $\mathfrak{m} \Vdash \exists vC$.

Case 6. The nth step is a case of ER. There is a $j < n$ such that $\alpha_j = \alpha_n$ and $A_j = \exists vA_n$, where v does not occur free in A_n. Assume $\mathfrak{m} \Vdash \alpha_n$. Then $\mathfrak{m} \Vdash \exists vA_n$, by the hypothesis of induction; hence, by $\mathcal{CFOL}$-18M, $\mathfrak{m} \Vdash A_n$.

The soundness theorem shows that the "semantic system" of two-valued interpretations is satisfied by the rules of CFOL. As we shall see, the converse, the derivability of all two-valued first-order entailments (that are expressible) also holds. Exactly what this means beyond showing the equivalence of two systems is not completely beyond dispute. At least one philosophical tradition views truth in such a way as to make two-valued semantics a natural representation. On the other hand, the actual rules of CFOL are very well-known and "comfortable" types of inference. One might conceivably argue that the two-valued rules make the model theory plausible, rather than vice versa. Let us, however, continue with our formal results. Our next theorem is primarily a result that will show that a restriction we will use later is a mere matter of convenience.

CFOL-22M. Let $\{v_1, v_2, v_3, \cdots\}$ be the set of all term variables of CFOL. Let $\mathbf{Q}(v_i) = v_{2i}$. For any (0-place) constant and for any formula variables x, $\mathbf{Q}(x) = x$. For any n-place functor f, $\mathbf{Q}(fx_1\cdots x_n) = f\mathbf{Q}(x_1)\cdots\mathbf{Q}(x_n)$ and $\mathbf{Q}(\forall vA) = \forall\mathbf{Q}(v)\mathbf{Q}(A)$ and $\mathbf{Q}(\exists vA) = \exists\mathbf{Q}(v)\mathbf{Q}(A)$. Finally, $\mathbf{Q}(\alpha) = \{\mathbf{Q}(A) : A \in \alpha\}$. Then for any set of wffs α, α has a model iff $\mathbf{Q}(\alpha)$ has a model.

Proof: Assume $\mathfrak{m} \Vdash \alpha$. Let $\mathfrak{m}^*(v_{2i}) = \mathfrak{m}^*(v_{2i-1}) = \mathfrak{m}(v_i)$ and otherwise, $\mathfrak{m}^*(x) = \mathfrak{m}(x)$. We show that $A \in \alpha \Rightarrow \mathfrak{V}_{\mathfrak{m}^*}(\mathbf{Q}(A)) = \mathfrak{V}_{\mathfrak{m}}(A)$. By induction on $\mathfrak{L}(A)$:

(α) $\mathfrak{L}(A) = 1$.

Case 1. A is a term variable v_i. $\mathfrak{V}_{\mathfrak{m}^*}(\mathbf{Q}(A)) = \mathfrak{V}_{\mathfrak{m}^*}(\mathbf{Q}(v_i)) = \mathfrak{V}_{\mathfrak{m}^*}(v_{2i}) = \mathfrak{m}^*(v_{2i}) = \mathfrak{m}(v_i) = \mathfrak{V}_{\mathfrak{m}}(v_i) = \mathfrak{V}_{\mathfrak{m}}(A)$.

Case 2. A is not a term variable. $\mathfrak{V}_{\mathfrak{m}^*}(\mathbf{Q}(A)) = \mathfrak{V}_{\mathfrak{m}^*}(A) = \mathfrak{m}^*(A) = \mathfrak{m}(A) = \mathfrak{V}_{\mathfrak{m}}(A)$.

(β) We assume the assertion is true for $\mathfrak{L}(B) < k$. We will prove it for $\mathfrak{L}(A) = k > 1$:

Case 1. $A = fx_1\cdots x_n$, where A is a functor and $x_1, \cdots, x_n$ are wfes. Then $\mathfrak{V}_{\mathfrak{m}^*}(\mathbf{Q}(A)) = \mathfrak{V}_{\mathfrak{m}^*}(\mathbf{Q}(fx_1\cdots x_n)) =$
$\mathfrak{V}_{\mathfrak{m}^*}((\mathbf{Q}(f))(\mathbf{Q}(x_1)\cdots\mathbf{Q}(x_n)) = \mathfrak{V}_{\mathfrak{m}^*}(f\mathbf{Q}(x_1)\cdots\mathbf{Q}(x_n)) =$
$(\mathfrak{g}_{\mathfrak{m}^*}(f))(\mathfrak{V}_{\mathfrak{m}^*}(\mathbf{Q}(x_1)), \cdots, \mathfrak{V}_{\mathfrak{m}^*}(\mathbf{Q}(x_n))) =$
$(\mathfrak{g}_{\mathfrak{m}}(f))(\mathfrak{V}_{\mathfrak{m}}(x_1), \cdots, \mathfrak{V}_{\mathfrak{m}}(x_n)) = \mathfrak{V}_{\mathfrak{m}}(A)$

Case 2. $A = \forall vB$. Then $\mathbf{Q}(\forall vB)$ is a closed alphabetic variant of $\forall v\mathbf{Q}(B)$ and the result follows by the hypothesis of induction.

Case 3. $A = \exists vB$. This follows by the same argument as in case 2.

Let α be a consistent set of wffs of CFOL such that there are a denumerably infinite number of term variables not in α. Let $\{w_1, w_2, w_3, \cdots\}$ be the set of all wffs of CFOL and let $\{v_1, v_2, v_3, \cdots\}$ be the set of the term variables not in α. Now let:

$\alpha_0 = \alpha$

$\alpha_{k+1} = \alpha_k$ if $\alpha_k \vdash \sim w_{k+1}$

$\alpha_{k+1} = \alpha_k \cup \{w_{k+1}, \mathbf{F}^{v}_{v(k)} B_{k+1}\}$, if not ($\alpha_k \vdash \sim w_{k+1}$) and $w_{k+1} = \exists v B_{k+1}$, for some wff B_{k+1}, and $v(k)$ is the first variable in the v_i-ordering not in α_k or B_{k+1}.

$\alpha_{k+1} = \alpha_k \cup \{w_{k+1}\}$ otherwise.

CFOL-23M. For every i, α_i (as defined above), is deductively consistent.

Proof: By induction on i:

(α) i = 0. This is trivial since $\alpha_0 = \alpha$ which is by assumption consistent.

(β) Assume α_k is consistent, but α_{k+1} is not. Obviously $\alpha_{k+1} \neq \alpha_k$. Hence the first case above could not hold and not ($\alpha_k \vdash \sim w_{k+1}$). Case 1. w_{k+1} is not an existential wff. Then α_{k+1} is $\alpha_k \cup \{w_{k+1}\}$, hence $\alpha_k, w_{k+1} \vdash \sim w_{k+1}$ and by **CM**, $\alpha_k \vdash \sim w_{k+1}$, which is impossible.

Case 2. w_{k+1} is an existential wff, i.e. $\exists v B_{k+1}$. Then $\alpha_{k+1} = \alpha_k \cup \{\exists v B_{k+1}, \mathbf{F}^{v}_{v(k)} B_{k+1}\}$ is inconsistent. Hence $\alpha_k, \exists v B_{k+1}, \mathbf{F}^{v}_{v(k)} B_{k+1} \vdash \sim \mathbf{F}^{v}_{v(k)} B_{k+1}$. Then by **CM**, $\alpha_k, \exists v B_{k+1} \vdash \sim \mathbf{F}^{v}_{v(k)} B_{k+1}$. Thus by **UT**, $\alpha_k, \exists v B_{k+1} \vdash \forall v \sim B_{k+1}$. Therefore, by CFOL-3T, $\alpha_k, \exists v B_{k+1} \vdash \sim \exists v B_{k+1}$. Then by **CM**, $\alpha_k \vdash \sim \exists v B_{k+1}$, which is impossible. Note that the question of the presence of the variable v in α_k is not important. If one substitutes for B_{k+1} its alphabetical variant with a new variable, the inference would be the same; i.e. $\mathbf{F}^{v}_{v(k)} B_{k+1} = \mathbf{F}^{v*}_{v(k)} \mathbf{F}^{v}_{v*} B_{k+1}$ and $\exists v B_{k+1}$ is equivalent to $\exists v^* \mathbf{F}^{v}_{v*} B_{k+1}$, (provided of course v^*

does not occur in B_{k+1} or α_k).

CFOL-24M. $\cup_i\alpha_i$ is maximally (deductively) consistent.

Proof: Suppose $\cup_i\alpha_i$ were inconsistent. Then there is a derivation of $A \wedge \sim A$ from $\cup_i\alpha_i$. Let β be the set of wffs which occur in wffs of that derivation. Then $\beta \cap \cup_i\alpha_i$ is finite and inconsistent. Since every element of $\cup_i\alpha_i$ is a w_j, there exists a k such that $(\beta \cap \cup_i\alpha_i) \subset \alpha_k$, and α_k would be inconsistent. Therefore $\cup_i\alpha_i$ is consistent. Now suppose there exists a wff A not in $\cup_i\alpha_i$. Then there exists a j such that $A = w_{j+1}$. Since $\alpha_{j+1} \subset \cup_i\alpha_i$, $A \notin \alpha_{j+1}$. Hence $\alpha_j \vdash \sim A$. But then $\cup_i\alpha_i \vdash \sim A$ and $\cup_i\alpha_i$ is maximal.

We will call a set of wffs α **ω-complete** provided for every wff B, if $\exists vB \in \alpha$, there is a term t such that $\mathbf{F}^v{}_tB \in \alpha$.

CFOL-25M. $\cup_i\alpha_i$ is ω-complete.

Proof: Suppose $\exists vB \in \cup_i\alpha_i$. Then there exists a j such that $w_{j+1} = \exists vB$. But $\alpha_j \vdash \sim\exists vB$ could not be true since otherwise $\cup_i\alpha_i$ would be inconsistent. Hence $\mathbf{F}^v{}_{v\langle j\rangle}B_{j+1} \in \alpha_{j+1}$. But since $\alpha_{j+1} \subset \cup_i\alpha_i$, $\mathbf{F}^v{}_{v\langle j\rangle}B_{j+1} \in \cup_i\alpha_i$.

CFOL-26M. Let α be a consistent set of wffs of CFOL such that there are a denumerably infinite number of term variables not in α. Then there exists an ω-complete and maximally consistent set β such that $\alpha \subset \beta$. (**Lindenbaum's theorem**).

Proof: This follows by CFOL-23M through CFOL-25M.

CFOL-27M. Let β be a maximally consistent and ω-complete set of wffs of CFOL. Then the following hold:

a. β is deductively closed (i.e. $\beta \vdash A$ iff $A \in \beta$).

b. For any wff A, $A \in \beta$ or $\sim A \in \beta$.

c. $A \supset B \in \beta$ iff $A \notin \beta$ or $B \in \beta$.
d. $A \vee B \in \beta$ iff $A \in \beta$ or $B \in \beta$.
e. $A \wedge B \in \beta$ iff $A \in \beta$ and $B \in \beta$.
f. $A \equiv B \in \beta$ iff either neither or both are in β.
g. $\forall vA \in \beta$ iff for every term t free for v in A, $\mathbf{F}^{v}_{t}A \in \beta$.
h. $\exists vA \in \beta$ iff for some term t free for v in A, $\mathbf{F}^{v}_{t}A \in \beta$.

Proof: Assertion a. Let $\delta = \{B : \beta \vdash B\}$. By the closure properties of derivation, δ must be consistent and $\beta \subset \delta$. Hence since β is maximally consistent, $\beta = \delta$.

Assertion b. Assume $A \notin \beta$. Then $\beta \cup \{A\}$ is inconsistent and $\beta, A \vdash \sim A$. Hence by **CM**, $\beta \vdash \sim A$ and by a., $\sim A \in \beta$. Note that since β is consistent, this result is equivalent to $\sim A \in \beta$ iff $A \notin \beta$.

Assertion c. Assume $A \supset B \in \beta$ and also $A \in \beta$. Hence $\beta \vdash A \supset B$ and $\beta \vdash A$ and hence by **MP**, $\beta \vdash B$. Assume $A \notin \beta$. Hence, by b., $\sim A \in \beta$ and therefore $\beta \vdash \sim A$; thus, by **WIN**-4Da, $\beta \vdash A \supset B$. If, on the other hand, $B \in \beta$, $\beta \vdash B$, and by **PI1**-5D, $\beta \vdash A \supset B$. But by a., $A \supset B \in \beta$.

Assertion d. Assume $A \vee B \in \beta$. Suppose $A \notin \beta$. Then by b., $\sim A \in \beta$. Hence $\beta \vdash A \vee B$ and $\beta \vdash \sim A$. Thus by **WAN**-2D, $\beta \vdash B$, and by a., $B \in \beta$. Assume $A \in \beta$; hence $\beta \vdash A$. By **AR**, $\beta \vdash A \vee B$. The proof is analogous to that for $B \in \beta$.

Assertion e. Assume $A \wedge B \in \beta$. $\beta \vdash A \wedge B$. Hence $\beta \vdash A$ and $\beta \vdash B$, by **LS** and **RS** and by a., $A \in \beta$ and $B \in \beta$. The converse uses the same strategy with A.

Assertion f. Assume $A \equiv B \in \beta$. Then $\beta \vdash A \equiv B$. By b., one each of the pairs $(A, \sim A)$ and $(B, \sim B)$ are in β and hence are derivable from β; if one of the unnegated wffs is derivable from β, by **Bi-MP**, so is the other and hence by a., either both or neither are in β. Suppose that both A and B are in β. By **PI**-5D, $\beta \vdash A \supset B$ and $\beta \vdash B \supset A$; hence by **A**, **CINEAK**-5T and **Bi-MP**, $\beta \vdash A \equiv B$; by a., $A \equiv B \in \beta$. If neither are in β, $\sim A$ and $\sim B$ must be and the proof proceeds in the same way using **WIN**-4Da instead of **PI**-5D.

Assertion g. Assume $\forall vA \in \beta$. Then $\beta \vdash \forall vA$. By **US**, $\beta \vdash \mathbf{F}^{v}_{t}A$, for any term t free for v in A. By a., $\mathbf{F}^{v}_{t}A \in \beta$. Assume $\mathbf{F}^{v}_{t}A \in \beta$, for every t free for v in A. Suppose $\forall vA \notin \beta$. By b., $\sim\forall vA \in \beta$ and hence $\beta \vdash \sim\forall vA$. Hence by CFOL-2T, INC-6D and MN-1D, and the equivalence theorem, $\beta \vdash \exists v\sim A$. Therefore, by a., $\exists v\sim A \in \beta$ and since β is ω- complete, there is a t such that $\mathbf{F}^{v}_{t}\sim A$, which is impossible.

Assertion h. Assume $\exists vA \in \beta$. Since β is ω-complete, there is a t with $\mathbf{F}^{v}_{t}A$. Suppose there is a t such that $\mathbf{F}^{v}_{t}A \in \beta$. Then $\beta \vdash \mathbf{F}^{v}_{t}A$ and hence, by EG, $\beta \vdash \exists vA$; thus, by a., $\exists vA \in \beta$.

A wff of CFOL and similar systems which has no proper well-formed formula parts is termed **atomic**. From the characterization of CFOL, atomic wffs are either formula variables or have a predicate as principal functor (i.e. are of the form $ft_1 \cdots t_n$, where f is an n-place predicate and $t_1, \cdots, t_n$ are terms). If α is a set of wffs, the **atomic subset** of α consists of those elements of α which are atomic wffs or the negation of atomic wffs.

CFOL-28M. If β is a maximally-consistent and ω-complete set of CFOL, $\mathfrak{m}$ is a model of β iff $\mathfrak{m}$ is a model of the atomic subset of β.

Proof: For the purpose of this proof, we will introduce a special measure, closely related to the length which might be called the propositional length and which we will symbolize as L(A). Specifically, if A is atomic, $L(A) = 1$, $L(fw_1 \cdots w_n) = 1 + L(w_1) + \cdots + L(w_n)$, while $L(\forall vA) = L(\exists vA) = 1 + L(A)$. We will prove, by induction on L(A), that if $\mathfrak{m}$ is a model of the atomic subset $\mathcal{A}_\beta$ of β, then $\mathfrak{m} \Vdash A$ iff $A \in \beta$.

(α) $L(A) = 1$. Then A is atomic and $A \in \mathcal{A}_\beta$ iff $A \in \beta$. Hence if $\mathfrak{m} \Vdash A$, $A \in \mathcal{A}_\beta$ and thus $A \in \beta$. Conversely if $A \in \beta$, $A \in \mathcal{A}_\beta$ and $\mathfrak{m} \Vdash A$.

(β) Assume the assertion is true if $L(B) < k$. We will prove it for $L(A) = k$.

Case 1. $A = \sim C$. Then $L(C) = k - 1$. Hence by the hypothesis of

induction, $\mathfrak{m} \Vdash C$ iff $C \in \beta$. But $\mathfrak{m} \Vdash C$ iff not($\mathfrak{m} \Vdash A$), while $C \in \beta$ iff $A \notin \beta$. Hence $\mathfrak{m} \Vdash A$ iff $A \in \beta$.
Case 2. $A = B \supset C$. Then $\mathbf{L}(B) < k$ and $\mathbf{L}(C) < k$. Hence by the hypothesis of induction, ($\mathfrak{m} \Vdash B$ iff $B \in \beta$) and ($\mathfrak{m} \Vdash C$ iff $C \in \beta$). Assume $\mathfrak{m} \Vdash B \supset C$. Thus $\mathbf{V}_{\mathfrak{m}}(B) = 0$ or $\mathbf{V}_{\mathfrak{m}}(C) = 1$. Hence $B \notin \beta$ or $C \in \beta$. Therefore by $\mathcal{CFOL}$-27M c, $B \supset C \in \beta$. The same steps in opposite order complete the proof.
Cases 3 - 5. $A = B \vee C$, $A = B \wedge C$, or $A = B \equiv C$. The proofs are analogous to case 2, utilizing in each case the relevant clause in the definition of two-valued valuation and the relevant section of $\mathcal{CFOL}$-27M.
Case 6. $A = \forall vB$, Then $\mathbf{L}(B) = k - 1$. Hence by the hypothesis of induction, $\mathfrak{m} \Vdash B$ iff $B \in \beta$. Assume $\mathfrak{m} \Vdash \forall vB$. Hence $\mathfrak{m} \Vdash \mathbf{F}^{v}_{t}B$, for every term t free for v in B. By the hypothesis of induction, since in $\mathcal{CFOL}$ propositional length is not affected by the substitution of a term for a term variable, for every t, $\mathbf{F}^{v}_{t}B \in \beta$. Hence by $\mathcal{CFOL}$-27M, part g., $\forall vB \in \beta$. The remainder of the argument just reverses the steps.
Case 7. $A = \exists vB$. This is the same as case 6 with "$\exists vB$" substituted for "$\forall vB$", and "some" for "every" throughout.
Obviously since $\mathcal{A}_\beta \subset \beta$, every model of β is a model of $\mathcal{A}_\beta$. On the other hand, by our assertion, any model of $\mathcal{A}_\beta$ is a model of every element of β and hence of β.

We now define for any maximally-consistent ω-complete set β of wffs of $\mathcal{CFOL}$ a model structure, which is called the **Herbrand model** of β. We will symbolize it by $\mathbf{H}[\beta]$ and $\mathfrak{m}[\mathbf{H}[\beta]]$ and define it as follows: $\mathbf{H}[\beta]$ is a two-valued interpretation such that $\mathcal{I}_{\mathbf{H}[\beta]}$ is the set of all terms of $\mathcal{CFOL}$; for every operation f, $\mathbf{H}[\beta](f)$ is the function such that $(\mathbf{H}[\beta](f))(t_1,\cdots,t_n) = ft_1\cdots t_n$; and for every predicate f, $\mathbf{H}[\beta](f)$ is the function such that $(\mathbf{H}[\beta](f))(t_1,\cdots,t_n) = 1$ iff $ft_1\cdots t_n \in \beta$. Similarly $\mathfrak{m}[\mathbf{H}[\beta]]$ is the function such that if v is a term variable, then $\mathfrak{m}[\mathbf{H}[\beta]](v) = v$ and if v is a formula variable, $\mathfrak{m}[\mathbf{H}[\beta]](v) = 1$ iff $v \in \beta$. For convenience, we will from now on, if there is no danger of confusion, refer to the interpretation and the assignment of the Herbrand model respectively as $\mathbf{H}$ and $\mathfrak{m}$.

CFOL-29M. If <H,m> is the Herbrand model of a maximally consistent, ω-complete set β, then for every term t, $\mathbf{V}_{\mathfrak{m}}(t) = t$ and for every wff w, $\mathbf{V}_{\mathfrak{m}}(w) = 1$ iff $w \in \beta$.

Proof: This is trivial for terms, by the definition of the Herbrand model. Hence, again by the definition, $\mathfrak{m}$ is a model of $\mathcal{A}_\beta$ and by CFOL-28M, $\mathfrak{m}$ is a model of β. Since β is maximal, the result follows.

CFOL-30M. If α is a set of wffs of CFOL, it has a two-valued model if and only if it is consistent.

Proof: If α is inconsistent, it entails both A and ~A which is incompatible with having a model, since no assignment satisfies both A and ~A. Suppose there is a denumerably infinite set of term variables not in α; then there is a maximally consistent, ω-complete set β such that $\alpha \subset \beta$ by CFOL-26M, and since the Herbrand model of β is a model of β by CFOL-29M, it is also a model of α. If however, α contains all but a finite number of the variables, **Q**(α), as defined in CFOL-22M, does not. Obviously if α is consistent, so is **Q**(α) since all the rules are preserved under **Q**, and by our previous result, **Q**(α) has a model and then, so has α.

CFOL-31M. $\alpha \vDash_{2V} A \Rightarrow \alpha \vdash_{CFOL} A$. **(The completeness theorem)**

Proof: Suppose $\alpha \vDash_{2V} A$. Then the set $\alpha \cup \{\sim A\}$ has no models, since any model would satisfy both A and ~A. Hence $\alpha \cup \{\sim A\}$ is inconsistent, by CFOL-30 M. Hence, for some B, $\alpha, \sim A \vdash_{CFOL} B$ and $\alpha, \sim A \vdash_{CFOL} \sim B$ and by **RA**, $\alpha, \sim A \vdash_{CFOL} A$ and since $\alpha, A \vdash_{CFOL} A$, we get $\alpha \vdash_{CFOL} A$, by **NgC**.

CFOL-32M. If every finite subset of α has a (two-valued) model, α has a model. **(The compactness theorem)**

Proof: Suppose α has no models. Then α is inconsistent, by CFOL-30M. Consequently, $\alpha \vdash_{CFOL} A$ and $\alpha \vdash_{CFOL} \sim A$. Then if β is the set of wffs which occur in either derivation, we have

$\alpha \cap \beta \vdash_{\mathcal{CFOL}} A$ and $\alpha \cap \beta \vdash_{\mathcal{CFOL}} \sim A$. Since β is finite, so is $\alpha \cap \beta$. By $\mathcal{CFOL}$-21M, $\alpha \cap \beta \models_{2V} A$ and $\alpha \cap \beta \models_{2V} \sim A$. Since $\alpha \cap \beta \subset \beta$, the theorem follows.

A system closely related to $\mathcal{CFOL}$ is the one that arises if we add a special predicate which can be regarded as identity. Doing so results in a logic which, in the sense explained in chapter 12, is not a pure logic but is instead a logic of identity. We will call this system $\mathcal{CFOLI}$ (complete first-order logic with identity).

$\mathcal{CFOLI}$: A deductive first-order system, with:

Quantifiers: $\forall$, $\exists$ (both one-variable one-place)

Connectives: $\sim$ (1-place), $\vee$ (2-place), $\wedge$ (2-place), $\supset$ (2-place), $\equiv$ (2-place)

Predicate constant: = (2-place; placed between the arguments)

Axioms: $\vdash \forall v(v = v)$ where v is a term variable

Rules:

1.	$A, A \supset B \vdash B$	MP
2.	$\alpha, A \vdash B \Rightarrow \alpha \vdash A \supset B$	C
3.	$A, \sim A \vdash B$	RAA
4.	$(\alpha, A \vdash B$ and $\alpha, \sim A \vdash B) \Rightarrow \alpha \vdash B$	NgC
5.	$A \wedge B \vdash A$	LS
6.	$A \wedge B \vdash B$	RS
7.	$A, B \vdash A \wedge B$	A
8.	$A \vdash A \vee B$	AR
9.	$B \vdash A \vee B$	AL
10.	$(\alpha, A \vdash C$ and $\alpha, B \vdash C) \Rightarrow \alpha, A \vee B \vdash C$	D
11.	$A, A \equiv B \vdash B$	Bi-MP(L)
12.	$B, A \equiv B \vdash A$	Bi-MP(R)
13.	$(\alpha, A \vdash B$ and $\alpha, B \vdash A) \Rightarrow \alpha \vdash A \equiv B$	Bi-C
14.	$\forall v A \vdash \mathbf{F}^{v}{}_{t} A$	US

where v is a (term) variable and t a term free for v in A.

15.	$\alpha, \mathbf{F}^{v}{}_{v'} \cdot \beta \vdash \mathbf{F}^{v}{}_{v'} \cdot A \Rightarrow \alpha, \forall v\, \beta \vdash \forall v\, A$	UT

where (1) v and v′ are (term) variables, (2) v′ = v or else v′ is not free in any element of $\alpha \cup \beta \cup \{A\}$, (3) v is not free in any element of α and (4) v′ is free for v in every element of $\beta \cup \{A\}$.

16. $\mathbf{F}^{v}{}_{t}A \vdash \exists v\, A$ EG

where v is a (term) variable and t a term free for v in A.

17. $\alpha, \mathbf{F}^{v}{}_{v'}A \vdash \mathbf{F}^{v}{}_{v'}B \Rightarrow \alpha, \exists v\, A \vdash \exists v\, B$ ET

where (1) v and v′ are (term) variables, (2) v′ = v or else v′ is not free in any element of $\alpha \cup \{A,B\}$, (3) v is not free in any element of α and (4) v′ is free for v in both A and B.

18. $\exists vA \vdash A$ ER

where v is not free in A.

19. $t_1 = t_2, \mathbf{F}^{v}{}_{t_1}A \vdash \mathbf{F}^{v}{}_{t_2}A$ S-Id

where t_1 and t_2 are free for v in A, t_1 and t_2 are terms, and v a term variable.

You will note that CFOL1 is CFOL with the axiom and rule 19, added. Accordingly, R-inclusion as well as equivalence properties are trivial.

CFOL1-1M. Every T- and D-theorem of CFOL (as well as all systems R-included – e.g. CINEAK, WINEAK, PINEAK, ANK, WKN, INC) is a theorem of CFOL1.

CFOL1-2M. The equivalence theorem holds unrestrictedly in CFOL1 (and consequently CFOL1 is an E-logic).

Proof: This is trivial, since the corresponding results hold for CFOL by CFOL-6M and CFOL-17M and CFOL1 contains no additional connectives or quantifiers.

We turn now to a few basic properties of the "equality" predicate:

CFOL1-3D. $x = y \vdash y = x$

Proof:
1. $x = y \vdash \forall v(v = v)$ Ax
2. $x = y \vdash x = x$ 1, US
3. $x = y \vdash x = y$ Premise
4. $x = y \vdash y = x$ 2, 3, S-Id

CFOL1-4D. $x = y, y = z \vdash x = z$

Proof: 1. $x = y, y = z \vdash x = z$ S-Id

(since $\mathbf{F}^{v}{}_{y}(x = v) = [x = y]$ and $\mathbf{F}^{v}{}_{z}(x = v) = [x = z]$)

The axiom, CFOL1-3D and CFOL1-4D establish that in any interpretation, = must be interpreted as an equivalence on the set of terms. The principal purpose intended is to express identity. Note that we have not established that = must be interpreted as identity. To make the matter a bit more precise, let us recall that if we are given any set $\mathcal{I}$, every relation which is an equivalence (i.e., which is reflexive, symmetric and transitive) defines a partition of $\mathcal{I}$ such that two elements are in the same cell iff the equivalence relation holds between them. That relation which defines that partition such that each cell has exactly one member is called the **identity relation** on $\mathcal{I}$. We will call an interpretation **normal** if it assigns the identity relation to = [i.e. if **P** is a normal interpretation on a structure whose set of individuals is $\mathcal{I}$, P(=) is the identity relation on $\mathcal{I}$]. An assignment is called **normal** if it is relative to a normal interpretation, and similarly a **normal model** is a model which is a normal assignment. We will represent the set of two-valued normal models as **N2U**. We will accordingly want to show that CFOL1 is sound and complete relative to N2U.

CFOL1-5M. $\alpha \vdash_{CFOL1} A \Rightarrow \alpha \vDash_{N2U} A$ (**Soundness theorem for CFOL1**)

Proof: The proof is the same as for CFOL-21M, for the general structure and the first six cases.

Case 7. The nth step is an axiom. But if $\mathfrak{m}$ is a normal model $\mathfrak{m}(=)(x,x) = 1$, for every individual x. Thus $\mathrm{V}_{\mathfrak{m}}(v = v) = 1$, for every value that can be assigned to v and hence $\mathrm{V}_{\mathfrak{m}}(\forall v(v = v)) = 1$.

Case 8. The nth step is an application of S-Id. There exist $i < n$ and $j < n$ such that $\alpha_i = \alpha_j = \alpha_n$ and A_i is $t_1 = t_2$, $A_j = \mathbf{F}^{v}{}_{t_1}A$ and $A_n = \mathbf{F}^{v}{}_{t_2}A$. Assume $\mathfrak{m} \Vdash \alpha$. By the hypothesis of induction, $\mathfrak{m} \Vdash t_1 = t_2$ and $\mathfrak{m} \Vdash \mathbf{F}^{v}{}_{t_1}A$ and by CFOL-20M,

$\mathfrak{m} \Vdash \mathbf{F}^{v}{}_{t_2}A$, since if $\mathbf{v}_{\mathfrak{m}}(t_1 = t_2) = 1$ and $\mathfrak{m}$ is normal, then $\mathbf{v}_{\mathfrak{m}}(t_1) = \mathbf{v}_{\mathfrak{m}}(t_2)$.

As we turn to the completeness theorem, we note that substantial portions of the proofs we might use are identical to the corresponding portions of the completeness theorem for CFOL. Where this is the case or where the differences would be so small as to be obvious, we shall state the theorems without proof.

CFOL1-6M. Let $\{v_1, v_2, v_3, \cdots\}$ be the set of all term variables of CFOL1. Let $\mathbf{Q}(v_i) = v_{2i}$. For any (0-place) constant and for any formula variables x, $\mathbf{Q}(x) = x$. For any n-place functor f, $\mathbf{Q}(fx_1\cdots x_n) = f\mathbf{Q}(x_1)\cdots\mathbf{Q}(x_n)$ and $\mathbf{Q}(\forall vA) = \forall\mathbf{Q}(v)\mathbf{Q}(A)$ and $\mathbf{Q}(\exists vA) = \exists\mathbf{Q}(v)\mathbf{Q}(A)$. Finally, $\mathbf{Q}(\alpha) = \{\mathbf{Q}(A): A \in \alpha\}$. Then for any set of wffs α, α has a model iff $\mathbf{Q}(\alpha)$ has a model.

CFOL1-7M. Let α be a consistent set of wffs of CFOL1 (such that there are a denumerably infinite number of term variables not in α). Then there exists an ω-complete and maximally consistent set β such that $\alpha \subset \beta$. (**Lindenbaum's theorem**)

CFOL1-8M. Let β be a maximally consistent and ω-complete set of wffs of CFOL1. Then the following hold:

a. β is deductively closed (i.e. $\beta \vdash A$ iff $A \in \beta$).

b. For any wff A, $A \in \beta$ or $\sim A \in \beta$.

c. $A \supset B \in \beta$ iff $A \notin \beta$ or $B \in \beta$.

d. $A \vee B \in \beta$ iff $A \in \beta$ or $B \in \beta$.

e. $A \wedge B \in \beta$ iff $A \in \beta$ and $B \in \beta$.

f. $A \equiv B \in \beta$ iff either neither or both are in β.

g. $\forall vA \in \beta$ iff for every term t free for v in A, $\mathbf{F}^{v}{}_{t}A \in \beta$.

h. $\exists vA \in \beta$ iff for some term t free for v in A, $\mathbf{F}^{v}{}_{t}A \in \beta$.

CFOL1-9M. If β is a maximally-consistent and ω-complete set of CFOL1, $\mathfrak{m}$ is a model of β iff $\mathfrak{m}$ is a model of the atomic subset of β.

Despite the sameness of our strategy up to this point, we cannot, as we did with CFOL, use the Herbrand model here, because although our theorems do indeed suffice for showing that the Herbrand model of β is a model of β, it is not usually normal. Here the fact that we have established that equality is an equivalence relation comes to our rescue. We can use a variant of the technique sometimes called abstraction. Instead of choosing as our set of individuals the set of terms, we choose the partition on the set of terms determined by "equals." We accordingly define the **β-cell** of a term t_1 as the set of all terms t_2 such that the wff $t_1 = t_2$ is an element of β; we will symbolize this by $\mathbf{cell}(t_1)$. By virtue of the axiom, CFOL1-3D and CFOL1-4D, the β-cells partition the set of terms. We then define what we may call the modified Herbrand model $\mathbf{H}^*$ accordingly. The set of individuals $\mathcal{I}_{\mathbf{H}^*}$ is thus the set of β-cells. If f is an operation, $\mathbf{H}^*(f)(\mathbf{cell}(t_1),\cdots,\mathbf{cell}(t_n)) = \mathbf{cell}(ft_1\cdots t_n)$, while if f is a predicate, $\mathbf{H}^*(f)(\mathbf{cell}(t_1),\cdots,\mathbf{cell}(t_n)) = 1$ iff for every i $(1 \le i \le n)$, there exists a term t^*_i such that $t^*_i \in \mathbf{cell}(t_i)$ and $ft^*_1\cdots t^*_n \in \beta$. Let $\mathfrak{m}^*$ be the assignment such that for every term variable v, $\mathfrak{m}^*(v) = \mathbf{cell}(v)$ and if v is a formula variable, $\mathfrak{m}^*(v) = 1$ iff $v \in \beta$. It follows that the modified Herbrand model of any maximally consistent, ω-complete set of CFOL1 is normal.

CFOL1-10M. If $<\mathbf{H}^*,\mathfrak{m}^*>$ is the modified Herbrand model of a maximally consistent, ω-complete set β, then for every term t, $V_{\mathfrak{m}}(t) = \mathbf{cell}(t)$ and for every wff w, $V_{\mathfrak{m}}(w) = 1$ iff $w \in \beta$ and $<\mathbf{H}^*,\mathfrak{m}^*>$ is normal.

Proof: This is trivial for terms, by the definition of the modified Herbrand model and the fact that $\mathbf{H}^*(=)$ is an equivalence relation. Hence, again by the definition, $\mathfrak{m}^*$ is a model of $\mathcal{A}_\beta$ and by CFOL1-9M, $\mathfrak{m}^*$ is a model of β. Since β is maximal, the result follows.

CFOL1-11M. If α is a set of wffs of CFOL1, it has a two-valued normal model if and only if it is consistent.

Proof: If α is inconsistent, it entails both A and $\sim$A, which is incompatible with having a normal model, by CFOL1-5M, since no assignment satisfies both A and ~A. Suppose there is a denumerably infinite set of term variables not in α; then there is a maximally consistent, ω-complete set β such that $\alpha \subset \beta$ by CFOL1-7M, and since the modified Herbrand model of β is a normal model of β by CFOL1-10M, it is also a normal model of α. If, however, α contains all but a finite number of the variables, Q(α), as defined in CFOL1-6M, does not. Obviously if α is consistent, so is Q(α) since all the rules are preserved under Q, and by our previous result, Q(α) has a normal model, and then so has α.

CFOL1-12M. $\alpha \vDash_{N2U} A \Rightarrow \alpha \vdash_{CFOL1} A$. **(Completeness theorem)**

Proof: This is analogous to CFOL-31M.

An interesting result which follows from CFOL-30M and CFOL1-11M is the result commonly known as the **Skolem-Löwenheim theorem**.

CFOL-33M (CFOL1-13M). Every consistent set of wffs of CFOL (or CFOL1) has a model of cardinality $\aleph_0$.

Proof: By CFOL-29M and CFOL-30M (and CFOL1-9M), every consistent set of wffs has at least one Herbrand model and hence at least one model of cardinality $\aleph_0$.

CFOL1-14M. Every consistent set of wffs of CFOL1 has at least one normal model of finite or denumerably infinite cardinality.

Proof: By the same argument as the last theorem, together with CFOL1-10M and 11M, every consistent set of wffs of CFOL1 has at least one modified Herbrand model. Since the cardinality of the set of terms is $\aleph_0$, and every term is in a cell, the cardinality of the set of cells is less than or equal to that of the terms.

CFOL1-15M. There are consistent sets of CFOL1 which have no infinite normal models.

Proof: Consider the set $\{\forall x \forall y(x = y)\}$. This set is satisfied by all normal model structures that have exactly one individual and by no others. Since it has models it must be consistent, but it has no infinite normal models. Of course it will have infinite models that are not normal (including Herbrand models).

If we are willing to strengthen the amount of set theory utilized, it is possible to establish the existence of models of larger cardinality whenever a set has any infinite models. We will however not pursue this here.

Before finishing our treatment of complete first-order logic, it is worthwhile to mention that for most applications the primary interest lies in so-called closed wffs (i.e. those with no free variables); in some treatments of the model theory for first-order logic, (complete) wffs with free variables are interpreted as essentially the same as their universal closures instead of treating free variables as essentially unassigned constants as we have done. It is easy to translate from our version to the one in question, viz., if **V** is our value function, we simply define a function **V*** such that for every wff w, **V***(w) = **V**(( )w). It is interesting to see how CFOL can be altered to correspond exactly to this change in the model theory. To do this we will find it convenient to specify a system we will call CFOL1 which is equivalent to CFOL, but of somewhat simpler structure.

CFOL1: A DFOS, with a functionally complete set of connectives (as in CFOL), and including:

1. A deductively complete DZOS (e.g. CFOL rules 1-13).
2. $\vdash \exists v A \equiv \sim\forall v{\sim}A$
3. The equivalence theorem.
4. $\vdash A \Rightarrow \vdash \forall v A$
5. $\forall v A \vdash \mathbf{F}^{v}{}_{t}A$, where t is free for v in A.
6. $\forall v(A \supset B) \vdash A \supset \forall v B$, where v is not free for v in A.

CFOL1-1M. $\forall v(A \supset B) \vdash \forall v A \supset \forall v B$

Proof:

1. $\forall v(A \supset B), \forall v A \vdash A \supset B$	Rule 5
2. $\forall v(A \supset B), \forall v A \vdash A$	Rule 6
3. $\forall v(A \supset B), \forall v A \vdash B$	1, 2, MP
4. $\vdash \forall v(A \supset B) \supset (\forall v A \supset B)$	3, C(2)

5. $\vdash \forall v[\forall v(A \supset B) \supset (\forall vA \supset B)]$	4, Rule 4
6. $\vdash \forall v(A \supset B) \supset \forall v(\forall vA \supset B)$	5, Rule 6
7. $\forall v(A \supset B) \vdash \forall v(A \supset B)$	Premise
8. $\forall v(A \supset B) \vdash \forall v(\forall vA \supset B)$	6, 7, MP
9. $\forall v(A \supset B) \vdash \forall vA \supset \forall vB$	8, Rule 6.

CFOL1-2M. CFOL and CFOL1 are equivalent.

Proof: Since all of 1-6 hold in CFOL, it is clear that anything derivable in CFOL-1 is derivable in CFOL. To prove the converse we need to derive the quantificational rules **US**, **UT**, **EG**, **ET** and **ER**.

1. US is rule 5 of CFOL1.

2. Suppose $\alpha, \mathbf{F}^{v}_{x}\beta \vdash \mathbf{F}^{v}_{x}A$ where x does not occur free in α, β or A. Then there is a finite subset $\{B_1,\cdots,B_n\}$ of β and $\{A_1,\cdots,A_m\}$ of α such that $A_1,\cdots,A_m,\mathbf{F}^{v}_{x}B_1,\cdots,\mathbf{F}^{v}_{x}B_n \vdash \mathbf{F}^{v}_{x}A$. By C n + m times, $\vdash A_1 \supset (\cdots \supset (A_m \supset (\mathbf{F}^{v}_{x}B_1 \supset (\cdots \mathbf{F}^{v}_{x}B_n \supset \mathbf{F}^{v}_{x}A)\cdots)$. By rule 4, $\vdash \forall x[A_1 \supset (\cdots \supset (A_m \supset (\mathbf{F}^{v}_{x}B_1 \supset (\cdots \mathbf{F}^{v}_{x}B_n \supset \mathbf{F}^{v}_{x}A)\cdots)]$. Then by rule 5, $\vdash A_1 \supset (\cdots \supset (A_m \supset \forall v(B_1 \supset (\cdots B_n \supset A)\cdots)$ since $\mathbf{F}^{x}_{v}\mathbf{F}^{v}_{x}B_i = B_i$ and $\mathbf{F}^{x}_{v}\mathbf{F}^{v}_{x}A = A$. By MP m times, $A_1,\cdots,A_m \vdash \forall v(B_1 \supset (\cdots B_n \supset A)\cdots)$ and by CFOL1-1M, $A_1,\cdots,A_m \vdash \forall vB_1 \supset \forall v(B_2 \supset (\cdots B_n \supset A)\cdots)$. Then, by MP, $A_1,\cdots,A_m,\forall vB_1 \vdash \forall v(B_2 \supset (\cdots B_n \supset A)\cdots)$. Thus, by repeating CFOL1-1M and MP, $A_1,\cdots,A_m,\forall vB_1,\cdots\forall vB_n \vdash \forall vA$. Therefore $\alpha,\forall v\beta \vdash \forall v$.

3. By rule 5, $\forall v{\sim}A \vdash \mathbf{F}^{v}_{t}{\sim}A$. Hence $\mathbf{F}^{v}_{t}A \vdash {\sim}\forall v{\sim}A$. Then by rules 2 and 3, $\mathbf{F}^{v}_{t}A \vdash \exists vA$.

4. Suppose $\alpha, \mathbf{F}^{v}_{t}A \vdash \mathbf{F}^{v}_{t}B$, with restrictions for **ET**. By **C**, $\alpha \vdash \mathbf{F}^{v}_{t}A \supset \mathbf{F}^{v}_{t}B$. Hence $\alpha \vdash \mathbf{F}^{v}_{t}{\sim}B \supset \mathbf{F}^{v}_{t}{\sim}A$ and by the argument of part 2., $\alpha \vdash \forall v({\sim}B \supset {\sim}A)$. Thus by CFOL1-1M, $\alpha \vdash \forall v{\sim}B \supset \forall v{\sim}A)$. Then $\alpha \vdash {\sim}\forall v{\sim}A \supset {\sim}\forall v{\sim}B$ and therefore, $\alpha \vdash \exists vA \supset \exists vB$ and, by **MP**, $\alpha, \exists vA \vdash \exists vB$.

5. Let A contain no free v. ⊢ ~A ⊃ ~A, by 1. Then by 4., ⊢ ∀v(~A ⊃ ~A). By 6., ⊢ ~A ⊃ ∀v~A. Hence by 1., ~∀~A ⊢ A and thus by 2. and 3., ∃vA ⊢ A.

If we create the system CFOL1* from CFOL1 by altering 4. to 4*, A ⊢ ∀vA, we immediately get $\mathbf{Equiv}_{\mathcal{CFOL}1^*}$(A,( )A). Since that equivalence is valid in the alternative model theory we have been discussing, we conclude that CFOL1* is sound and complete relative to that model theory. The reader will note that the resulting system gives the same set of logical relations among closed wffs as CFOL and can be said to differ from it only in the interpretation given to free variables.

14
Quantification and Incomplete Logics

Just as quantifiers with rules governing them can be added to CLNEAK or any other complete logic, they can likewise be added to any of the DZOSs we have considered (as indeed to many others). To some degree, for any system which is in serious contention as a working logic, one would expect this to be done. In principle, we could go on through a systematic development like that of chapters 4 through 11, but primarily because we do not wish to extend the present volume to the extent that would require, we will not do so. However, the intrinsic desirability of giving an example of the extension of quantification to incomplete logics have impelled us to treat, if briefly, two such systems: one based on the modal system S5 and one on the intuitionist logic WLNEAK.

Before proceeding, it should perhaps be pointed out that some philosophers and logicians, notably W.V.O. Quine, appear to feel that no reasonable application can be given to a system in which modal connectives, like $\Diamond$, can appear within the scope of quantifiers. Others, like Carnap, oppose this view. It is not our purpose in this volume to argue the philosophical and semantic issues involved, but only to give a brief indication of what occurs when the kinds of methods we have applied concerning the existential and universal quantifiers, specified as they were in chapter 12, are added to a logic whose zero-order basis is one of the modal logics we have been considering.

We will accordingly define a modal first-order logic which we will call MFOL. Its primitives will be $\wedge$, $\sim$ and $\prec$ and the two quantifiers $\forall$ and $\exists$. The axiom schemata will be the 9 schemata of S1 plus axiom 11' of S5. In addition, we will adopt as rules MP, A, SHE and WFC, together with the quantificational rules US, UT, EG, ET and ER as defined in chapter 12. We will additionally use the more or less standard notational abbreviations, as follows:

Sign	For
$A \vee B$	$\sim(\sim A \wedge \sim B)$
$A \supset B$	$\sim(A \wedge \sim B)$
$A \equiv B$	$\sim(A \wedge \sim B) \wedge \sim(B \wedge \sim A)$

Sign	For
◇A	~(A ⥽ ~A)
□A	~A ⥽ A
A ⥼ B	(A ⥽ B) ∧ (B ⥽ A)

When we use any of these definitions, we will use the indication Df. In passing, the reader will note that using SHE in quantificational contexts has rather strong consequences. We will discuss some of these after our brief systematic presentation.

MFOL-1M. Every T- and D-theorem of S5 and hence NKC holds in MFOL.

Proof: Since MFOL R-includes S1*', it R-includes S4, by S4-6M. Hence MFOL R-includes S5'.

MFOL-2T (S1-31T). ⊢ □A ⥼ ~◇~A

Proof:	
1. ⊢ (~A ⥽ A) ⥽ (~A ⥽ A)	S1-4T
2. ⊢ (~A ⥽ A) ⥼ (~A ⥽ A)	1, A
3. ⊢ (~A ⥽ A) ⥼ (~A ⥽ ~~A)	2, S1-11M
4. ⊢ (~A ⥽ A) ⥼ ~~(~A ⥽ ~~A)	3, S1-11M
5. ⊢ □A ⥼ ~◇~A	4, Df

MFOL-3M. α,A $\vdash_{MFOL}$ B ⇒ α $\vdash_{MFOL}$ A ⊃ B

Proof: Let α,A $\vdash_{MFOL}$ B . Then there is a finite subset α' of α, such that α',A ⊢ B. Let C be a conjunction of all of the elements of α'. Hence by NKC, C ∧ A ⊢ A_i for every element A_i in α' and C ∧ A ⊢ A, and thus C ∧ A ⊢ B. By WFC, ⊢ (C ∧ A) ⥽ B. Then by **Ax-1**, ⊢ ~◇[(C ∧ A) ∧ ~B]. By S1'-10T ⊢ ~[(C ∧ A) ∧ ~B]. Hence by NKC, C ⊢ A ⊃ B. Therefore α ⊢ A ⊃ B.

MFOL-4T. ⊢ ∀vA ⥼ ~∃v~A

Proof:	
1. ∀vA ⊢ ~∃v~A	Theorem 12-15
2. ⊢ ∀vA ⥽ ~∃v~A	1, WFC
3. ~∃v~A, ~A ⊢ ∃v ~A	EG

4. ~∃v~A, ~A ⊢ ~∃v ~A	Premise
5. ~∃v~A, ~A ⊢ A	3, 4, NKC
6. ~∃v~A ⊢ A	5, NKC
7. ~∃v~A ⊢ ∀vA	6, UT
8. ⊢ ~∃v~A ⥽ ∀vA	7, WFC
9. ⊢ ∀vA ⥼⥽ ~∃v~A	2, 8, A, Df

MFOL-5T. ⊢ (A ⥽ B) ⥼⥽ [A ⥼⥽ (A ∧ B)]

Proof: 1. A ⥽ B ⊢ (A ∧ A) ⥽ (A ∧ B)	S3-2D
2. A ⥽ B ⊢ A ⥽ (A ∧ B)	1, S1-11M
3. A ⥽ B ⊢ (A ∧ B) ⥽ A	Ax-4
4. A ⥽ B ⊢ A ⥼⥽ (A ∧ B)	2, 3, A, Df
5. ⊢ (A ⥽ B) ⥽ [A ⥼⥽ (A ∧ B)]	4, WFC
6. A ⥼⥽ (A ∧ B) ⊢ (A ∧ B) ⥽ (A ∧ B)	S1-4T
7. A ⥼⥽ (A ∧ B) ⊢ A ⥽ (A ∧ B)	Df, NKC
8. A ⥼⥽ (A ∧ B) ⊢ (A ∧ B) ⥽ A	Df, NKC
9. A ⥼⥽ (A ∧ B) ⊢ (A ∧ B) ⥼⥽ A	7, 8, A
10. A ⥼⥽ (A ∧ B) ⊢ A ⥽ (A ∧ B)	5, 9, SHE
11. ⊢ [A ⥼⥽ (A ∧ B)] ⥽ [A ⥽ (A ∧ B)]	10, WFC
12. ⊢ (A ⥽ B) ⥼⥽ [A ⥼⥽ (A ∧ B)]	5, 11, A, Df

MFOL-6D. ∀v(A ⥽ B) ⊢ ∀vA ⥽ ∀vB

Proof: 1. A ∧ B ⊢ A	S1-1D
2. ∀v(A ∧ B) ⊢ ∀vA	1, UT
3. ⊢ ∀v(A ∧ B) ⥽ ∀vA	2, WFC
4. ∀v(A ⥽ B) ⊢ A ⥽ B	US
5. ∀v(A ⥽ B) ⊢ (A ⥽ B) ⥼⥽ [A ⥼⥽ (A ∧ B)]	MFOL-5D
6. ∀v(A ⥽ B) ⊢ A ⥼⥽ (A ∧ B)	4, 5, SHE
7. ∀v(A ⥽ B) ⊢ ∀vA ⥽ ∀vA	S1-4T
8. ∀v(A ⥽ B) ⊢ ∀vA ⥽ ∀v(A ∧ B)	6, 7, SHE
9. ∀v(A ⥽ B) ⊢ ∀vA ⥽ ∀vB	3, 8, S1-6D

MFOL-7T. If v is not free in A, ⊢ A ⥼⥽ ∃vA

Proof: 1. A ⊢ ∃vA	EG

2. $\vdash A \strictif \exists vA$	1, WFC
3. $\exists vA \vdash A$	ER
4. $\vdash \exists vA \strictif A$	3, WFC
5. $\vdash A \strictiff \exists vA$	2, 4, A, Df

MFOL-8T. If v is not free in A, $\vdash A \strictiff \forall vA$

Proof:	
1. $A \vdash \forall vA$	UT
2. $\vdash A \strictif \forall vA$	1, WFC
3. $\forall vA \vdash A$	US
4. $\vdash \forall vA \strictif A$	3, WFC
5. $\vdash A \strictiff \forall vA$	2, 4, A, Df

MFOL-9D (**S1-32D**). $\Box A \vdash A$

Proof:	
1. $\Box A \vdash (\sim A \strictif A) \strictif \sim(\sim A \wedge \sim A)$	S1-14T
2. $\Box A \vdash (\sim A \strictif A) \strictif \sim\sim A$	1, S1-11M
3. $\Box A \vdash \Box A \strictif A$	2, Df, S1-11M
4. $\Box A \vdash \Box A$	Premise
5. $\Box A \vdash A$	3, 4, MP

MFOL-10T. $\vdash \forall v\Box A \strictiff \Box\forall vA$

Proof:	
1. $\forall v A \vdash A$	US
2. $\vdash \forall v A \strictif A$	1, WFC
3. $\vdash \sim A \strictif \sim\forall vA$	2, NKC
4. $\vdash (\sim A \strictif \sim\forall vA) \supset (\sim\Diamond\sim\forall vA \strictif \sim\Diamond\sim A)$	S4-3T
5. $\vdash \sim\Diamond\sim\forall vA \strictif \sim\Diamond\sim A$	3,4, MP
6. $\vdash \Box\forall vA \strictif \Box A$	5, Df
7. $\Box\forall v A \vdash \Box\forall vA$	Premise
8. $\Box\forall v A \vdash \Box A$	6, 7, MP
9. $\Box\forall v A \vdash \forall v\Box A$	8, UT
10. $\vdash \Box\forall vA \strictif \forall v\Box A$	9, WFC
11. $\forall v\Box A \vdash \Box A$	US
12. $\forall v\Box A \vdash \sim A \strictif A$	11, Df
13. $\forall v\Box A \vdash (\sim A \wedge \sim A) \strictif (\sim A \wedge A)$	12, S1-27D
14. $\forall v\Box A \vdash \sim A \strictif (\sim A \wedge A)$	13, S1-11M

15. $\forall v\Box A \vdash (\sim A \wedge A) \strictif \sim A$	Ax-4
16. $\forall v\Box A \vdash \sim A \strictiff (\sim A \wedge A)$	14,15,A,Df
17. $\vdash \sim(\sim A \wedge A)$	NKC
18. $\vdash \forall v\sim(\sim A \wedge A)$	17, UT
19. $\sim\forall v\sim(\sim A \wedge A) \vdash \forall v\sim(\sim A \wedge A)$	18
20. $\vdash [\sim\forall v\sim(\sim A \wedge A)] \strictif [\forall v\sim(\sim A \wedge A)]$	19, WFC
21. $\vdash \Box\forall v\sim(\sim A \wedge A)$	20, Df
22. $\forall v\Box A \vdash \Box\forall v\sim(\sim A \wedge A)$	21
23. $\forall v\Box A \vdash \Box\forall v\sim\sim A$	16,22,SHE
24. $\forall v\Box A \vdash \Box\forall vA$	23,S1-11M
25. $\vdash \forall v\Box A \strictif \Box\forall vA$	24, WFC
26. $\vdash \forall v\Box A \strictiff \Box\forall vA$	25,10,A,Df

MFOL-11T. $\vdash \exists v\Diamond A \strictiff \Diamond\exists vA$

Proof: 1. $\vdash \forall v\Box\sim A \strictiff \Box\forall v\sim A$	MFOL-10T
2. $\vdash \sim\exists v\sim\Box\sim A \strictiff \Box\sim\exists v\sim\sim A$	1,MFOL-10T,SHE
3. $\vdash \sim\exists v\sim\sim\Diamond\sim\sim A \strictiff \sim\Diamond\sim\sim\exists v\sim\sim A$	2, MFOL-2T, SHE
4. $\vdash \sim\exists v\Diamond A \strictiff \sim\Diamond\exists vA$	3, S1-11M
5. $\vdash \sim A \strictif \sim A$	S1-4T
6. $\vdash \sim A \strictiff \sim A$	5, A, Df
7. $\vdash \sim\sim\exists v\Diamond A \strictiff \sim\sim\Diamond\exists vA$	4, 6, SHE
8. $\vdash \exists v\Diamond A \strictiff \Diamond\exists vA$	7, S1-11M

MFOL-12D. $\exists v\Box A \vdash \Box\exists vA$

Proof: 1. $A \vdash \exists vA$	EG
2. $\sim\exists vA \vdash \sim A$	1, NKC
3. $\vdash \sim\exists vA \strictif \sim A$	2, WFC
4. $\vdash (\sim\exists vA \strictif \sim A) \strictif (\sim\Diamond\sim A \strictif \sim\Diamond\sim\exists vA)$	S4-3T
5. $\vdash \sim\Diamond\sim A \strictif \sim\Diamond\sim\exists vA$	3, 4, MP
6. $\vdash \Box A \strictif \Box\exists vA$	5,Df
7. $\Box A \vdash \Box A$	Premise
8. $\Box A \vdash \Box\exists v$	6, 7, MP
9. $\exists v\Box A \vdash \exists v\Box\exists vA$	8, ET
10. $\exists v\Box A \vdash \Box\exists vA$	9, ER

MFOL-13D. $\Diamond\forall vA \vdash \forall v\Diamond A$

Proof:	1. $\exists v\Box{\sim}A \vdash \Box\exists v{\sim}A$	MFOL-12T
	2. $\exists v{\sim}\Diamond{\sim}{\sim}A \vdash {\sim}\Diamond{\sim}\exists v{\sim}A$	1,MFOL-2T,SHE
	3. $\Diamond{\sim}\exists v{\sim}A \vdash {\sim}\exists v{\sim}\Diamond{\sim}{\sim}A$	2,NKC
	4. $\Diamond{\sim}\exists v{\sim}A \vdash {\sim}\exists v{\sim}\Diamond A$	3,S1-11M
	5. $\Diamond\forall vA \vdash \forall v\Diamond A$	4,MFOL-5T, S1-9M,SHE

MFOL-14D. If v is not free in A, $\forall v(A ⥽ B) \vdash A ⥽ \forall vB$

Proof:	1. $\forall v(A ⥽ B) \vdash \forall vA ⥽ \forall vB$	MFOL-6D
	2. $\forall v(A ⥽ B) \vdash A ⥽ \forall vB$	1,MFOL-8T,SHE

We can summarize our main results with respect to MFOL by indicating that $\Box$ behaves in MFOL essentially like a universal quantifier on some variable other than those occurring in the wff concerned. It is, so to speak, as though there were an additional invisible term variable in every wff. A similar observation can be made about the analogy between $\Diamond$ and the existential quantifier.

When we turn to model theory, the general procedure that might be followed is fairly obvious; namely, define modal assignment sets on the basis of model structures, where each particular model structure is (so to speak, in isolation) of the kind of model structure we dealt with in chapter 13. As one might expect, some variations of the methods used in chapters 11 and 13 are applicable. There are, however, complications. The most significant one is that model structures connected by an accessibility relation may or may not have conditions which allow us to identify individuals (specific ones, or all of them). Consider the wff frequently called **the Barcan formula**: $\Diamond\exists vA \supset \exists v\Diamond A$. Now, $\Diamond\exists vA$ will be satisfied in a given model structure $\mathfrak{m}$ (assuming we construct it in the way we have indicated) provided some model structure $\mathfrak{m}'$ accessible from $\mathfrak{m}$ is such that some individual satisfies the property defined by A (i.e. that property defined on $\mathcal{I}_{\mathfrak{m}'}$ which holds is the translation of A), while $\exists v\Diamond A$ will be satisfied provided there is an element of $\mathcal{I}_{\mathfrak{m}}$ which can be identified with an element of $\mathcal{I}_{\mathfrak{m}'}$ which satisfies A. Conceivably some element of $\mathcal{I}_{\mathfrak{m}'}$ which cannot be identified with any element of $\mathcal{I}_{\mathfrak{m}}$

may satisfy A and consequently the former may be satisfied and the latter would not. The reader will note that this implies the non-soundness of MFOL in the absence of conditions sufficient to guarantee that every individual of m has an individual which can be identified with it in every model structure accessible from m. Whether one wants this condition depends of course on the intended interpretations.

This will close our very introductory glance at modal logic. We will now look, in an equally cursory fashion at a first-order logic obtained in a way similar to CFOL--that is by adding our 5 standard quantification rules, but to WINEAK instead of CINEAK. The resulting logic is equivalent to that first proposed by the Dutch intuitionist mathematician Arend Heyting. We will call it IFOL.

IFOL-1M. All T- and D-theorems of WINEAK hold in IFOL.

Proof: This is trivial, since IFOL has all rules of WINEAK.

IFOL-2M. Theorems 12-10 through 12-16 hold in IFOL.

Proof: IFOL R-includes WINEAK (and hence PINEAK, PIN, and PI) and our 5 standard quantification rules.

IFOL-3D. $\forall v(A \equiv B) \vdash \forall vA \equiv \forall vB$

Proof:

1. $\forall v(A \equiv B), A \vdash A \equiv B$	US
2. $\forall v(A \equiv B), A \vdash A$	Premise
3. $\forall v(A \equiv B), A \vdash B$	1, 2, Bi-MP
4. $\forall v(A \equiv B), \forall vA \vdash \forall vB$	3, UT
5. $\forall v(A \equiv B), B \vdash A \equiv B$	US
6. $\forall v(A \equiv B), B \vdash B$	Premise
7. $\forall v(A \equiv B), B \vdash A$	5, 6, Bi-MP
8. $\forall v(A \equiv B), \forall vB \vdash \forall vA$	7, UT
9. $\forall v(A \equiv B) \vdash \forall vA \equiv \forall vB$	4, 8, Bi-C

IFOL-4D. $\forall v(A \equiv B) \vdash \exists vA \equiv \exists vB$

Proof: We get this by the same method as IFOL-3D, using ET instead of UT.

IFOL-5M. $()A \vdash A$

Proof: This follows by a trivial induction using **US**.

IFOL-6M. The equivalence theorem (in the form stated in CFOL) holds unrestrictedly in IFOL (and IFOL is an E-logic).

Proof: Using induction on the number of connectives and quantifiers, we follow the same technique as previous equivalence theorems (see PL-14M and 2-17, utilizing PLNEAK-10M, IFOL-3D, IFOL-4D and IFOL-5M).

IFOL-7T. $\vdash \forall v{\sim}A \equiv {\sim}\exists vA$

Proof:

1. $\forall v{\sim}A, A \vdash A$	Premise
2. $\forall v{\sim}A, A \vdash {\sim}A$	US
3. $\forall v{\sim}A, A \vdash {\sim}\exists vA$	1, 2, RA
4. $\forall v{\sim}A, \exists vA \vdash \exists v{\sim}\exists vA$	3, ET
5. $\forall v{\sim}A, \exists vA \vdash {\sim}\exists vA$	4, ER
6. $\forall v{\sim}A \vdash {\sim}\exists vA$	5, CM
7. ${\sim}\exists vA, A \vdash {\sim}\exists vA$	Premise
8. ${\sim}\exists vA, A \vdash \exists vA$	EG
9. ${\sim}\exists vA, A \vdash {\sim}A$	7, 8, RA
10. ${\sim}\exists vA \vdash {\sim}A$	9, CM
11. ${\sim}\exists vA \vdash \forall v{\sim}A$	10, UT
12. $\vdash \forall v{\sim}A \equiv {\sim}\exists vA$	6, 11, Bi-C

IFOL-8D. ${\sim}{\sim}\forall vA \vdash \forall v{\sim}{\sim}A$

Proof:

1. ${\sim}{\sim}\forall vA, \exists v{\sim}A \vdash {\sim}\forall v{\sim}{\sim}A$	12-16
2. ${\sim}{\sim}\forall vA, \exists v{\sim}A, A \vdash {\sim}{\sim}A$	PLN-3D
3. ${\sim}{\sim}\forall vA, \exists v{\sim}A, \forall vA \vdash \forall v{\sim}{\sim}A$	2, UT
4. ${\sim}{\sim}\forall vA, \exists v{\sim}A \vdash \forall vA \supset \forall v{\sim}{\sim}A$	3, C
5. ${\sim}{\sim}\forall vA, \exists v{\sim}A \vdash {\sim}\forall vA$	1, 4, PLN-4Da
6. ${\sim}{\sim}\forall vA, \exists v{\sim}A \vdash {\sim}{\sim}\forall vA$	Premise
7. ${\sim}{\sim}\forall vA, \exists v{\sim}A \vdash {\sim}\exists v{\sim}A$	5, 6, RA
8. ${\sim}{\sim}\forall vA \vdash {\sim}\exists v{\sim}A$	7, CM

9. $\sim\sim\forall vA \vdash \forall v\sim\sim A \equiv \sim\exists v\sim A$	IFOL-7T
10. $\sim\sim\forall vA \vdash \forall v\sim\sim A$	8, 9, Bi-MP

IFOL-9D. $\exists v\sim\sim A \vdash \sim\sim\exists vA$

Proof: 1. $\sim\sim A, \sim\exists vA \vdash \sim\exists vA$	Premise
2. $\sim\sim A, \sim\exists vA \vdash \forall v\sim A \equiv \sim\exists vA$	IFOL-7T
3. $\sim\sim A, \sim\exists vA \vdash \forall v\sim A$	1, 2, Bi-MP
4. $\sim\sim A, \sim\exists vA \vdash \sim A$	3, US
5. $\sim\sim A, \sim\exists vA \vdash \sim\sim A$	Premise
6. $\sim\sim A, \sim\exists vA \vdash \sim\sim\exists vA$	4, 5, RA
7. $\sim\sim A \vdash \sim\sim\exists vA$	6, CM
8. $\exists v\sim\sim A \vdash \exists v\sim\sim\exists vA$	7, ET
9. $\exists v\sim\sim A \vdash \sim\sim\exists vA$	8, ER

It would not be surprising to be able to produce a variant of the modal completeness proof of WINEAK in chapter 11. We will however refrain from giving the details.

With this, we conclude our formal treatment for this book. Again, we do not wish to suggest that we have exhausted the subject, but only that we have, we hope, given a useful survey of methods. We will conclude our treatment with a brief discussion of philosophical issues related to the work we have done. To emphasize the difference between the technical treatment and the less compelling character of this discussion, we will, in the final chapter, use the first person singular ("I" rather than "we").

15
Interpretation of Formal Systems

In the preceding, I have attempted, and I trust generally succeeded, to present a body of information and technique concerning logical systems without grinding any philosophical axes (I suppose I have as many of these as anyone). In this final chapter, I shall discuss the bearing of some of the results and the significance of this type of study, and here I shall make no promises to restrain myself concerning philosophical implications.

At first sight it might seem quite reasonable to take the position that a subject as esoteric and mathematical as the formal study of logical systems probably has no philosophical implications at all, just as I suppose most people interested in philosophy would be inclined to say that the theory of partial differential equations or the theory of the multiple integral does not. Indeed, many philosophers, particularly of the so-called "ordinary language" tradition, have taken such a position with regard to formal logic. I feel that I cannot concur, for reasons which I hope will be made clear in the succeeding pages.

There are several significant aspects to the study of formal systems. While one can examine them in other ways, I shall consider them in order of decreasing formalism.

One obvious use, actually of surprisingly general importance to many logicians, is that these systems can be interesting in themselves, that is to say as an intellectually challenging game, somewhat in the way chess and multi-dimensional tic-tac-toe are. Like games of the more complex kind, it combines the possibility of results with the practical inexhaustibility of the material. Somewhat more to the point than this rather aesthetic or perhaps playful kind of purpose, is the possible use of logic in formulating concepts of mathematics more precisely: examples of this are the monumental works of Frege, Peano, and Russell. A similar project for the mathematical parts of the physical sciences form a second example, as in the work of Suppes. Likewise (though of somewhat less universal acclaim) are the attempts at clarification of philosophical issues: for example, Carnap's Logische Aufbau or Goodman's similar efforts, or

Carnap's and Reichenbach's work on probability. Generally speaking, this type of effort involves extensive use of a particular logical system, usually a complete logic like our **INC**, **ANC**, **NKC**, **CINEAK** and **CFOL** (although the weaker systems, such as **WINEAK** or **IFOL**, have been used in intuitionistic mathematics). Major emphasis must be placed on the mathematical, scientific, or philosophical problems in order for these applications to perform their intended task; as a result the consideration of alternative logical systems is secondary to them. Of course, the examination of alternative systems may be a particularly effective way of introducing various important concepts, such as various kinds of consistency and completeness, and various deductive techniques, as well as for accustoming the student to more rigorous axiomatic methods whose usefulness can then be made more manifest in other applications; indeed, the conviction that this is so constituted more than a small part of my motivation in producing this work. From this point of view features of formal systems which may have some importance in, for example, axiomatic developments of scientific theory, appear (when they do) in a particularly simple form, in systems of relatively simple structure.

Of greater interest, at least to many philosophers, are the suggestions which the results of these examinations give with respect to the nature of deductive logic and the relations between meaning phenomena in colloquial language and formal logic. Some of these issues relate to the question of whether some variety of logic, weaker than the traditional classical or intuitionist ones, might provide a more desirable model for deductive reasoning. Even where this kind of question is not at issue, one might hope for a greater insight into the features that make one choice preferable to another and for what purposes.

At this point at least one word of caution should be offered. Some philosophers identify this class of problem in a relatively simple way with the problem of determining which logic forms the basis of the use of standard logical words, such as "and," "if," "all," and the rest in colloquial, or as it is frequently expressed, "ordinary" language. I think that there are serious reasons against looking at the relations between "ordinary" and "formal" language in this way. Lack of space and the desire to avoid divergence from the principal subject of the book preclude a thorough account of the matter, but some of the reasons might become clear by pointing out a few properties of semantic phenomena in "ordinary" language. One of these has been termed **meaning shift** by the man who has up to now been most interested in these and similar phenomena, the Dutch philosopher and mathematician Gerrit Mannoury. We shall give an example relevant to logical issues without attempting even to indicate a general theory which satisfactorily accounts for it. In the variety of uses which might be called "informative" or "narrative" (and which includes a rather wide variety of what are called illocutionary acts, e.g., warning, establishing evidence at a hearing, etc.) the speaker is attempting (often, among other things) to communicate to the hearer the fact that certain things are the case. Given a certain minimum of standard conditions, the hearer, aware of this purpose, will adopt as a principle of interpretation that every portion of the act (above a certain minimum size) serves this purpose. If the speaker nevertheless utters a sentence which could not possibly do so, either because (on the expectation of the hearer), the speaker could not possibly imagine that the hearer was not already aware of this – such as "I am in the room now" or even more extremely, an obvious tautology like "students are students" the hearer, most frequently without conscious thought, reinterprets them in such a way that they express something informative. A similar thing occurs when a sentence is (in the expectation of the hearer) so obviously false that the speaker could not possibly be trying to communicate **it**. For example, the sentence, "Last week it rained so hard, it rained up through the floor," is, if uttered under appropriately casual circumstances, most frequently interpreted as if it said "last week it rained so hard, local flooding occurred and overflow water seeped up through the floor," and next most often as "last week it rained so hard, it rained through the **door**".It is even more interesting that the responses "no, that can't be so", "you couldn't mean that", "you're misusing language" or even "I don't understand" are very rare (at least when humor is not suspected). One certainly would expect such comments if the hearer interpreted the sentence as expressing the (normally) physically impossible suggestion of raindrops falling upward through the cracks or holes in the floor as they frequently do through similar defects in the roof. In addition, the interpretation given to logical words can be context dependent. That this is true with respect to "if—then" is universally conceded, but that this appears to be the case with respect to **all** logical words has perhaps not been noticed as widely. For example, "and" has often been cited as the most clearly truth-functional of the logical words. This belief, for example, apparently underlay C.I. Lewis' choice of "and" (rather than the "if—then" of Frege or the "or" of Whitehead and Russell) as his non-modal two-place connective. Indeed, prima facie, it **does** seem to be free of the kinds of special complications/ that these others have. Yet "they got married and had a child" expresses a different, and for lovers of gossip, less interesting state of affairs than "they had a child and got married" and neither is normally interpreted truth-functionally. To make matters worse "and" in: "his views became conservative and he grew rich" appears to be truth-functional, but not in "he grew rich and his views became conservative"; in the latter, but not in the former, a temporal sequence seems to be suggested or implied. To make matters even worse, "He is Jewish and a successful businessman" appears to be logically equivalent to "He is a successful businessman and Jewish" for most of us, but not for anti-Semites. Furthermore, "he became rich, grew two inches, and his views became conservative" seems to be truth-functional despite the order of reference to wealth and politics. What seems to be the common thread here is that we try to give the particle the sense of "and, as a result" if we can; if that fails we sometimes try "and, then"; if this also fails, we try the truth-functional interpretation. If this conjecture is indeed correct, it would appear to indicate that a difference in our knowledge of the facts would, at least sometimes, result in a change in our interpretation of "and." It would, for instance appear that in "he smoked heavily for forty years and died of cancer" the conjunction was truth-functional (at least if uttered by someone not in the temperance movement) if uttered in 1900, but implies causal connection or the like if uttered in America in 1980. This feature represents a more extreme divergence from popular semantic models than mere context-dependence, since the context on which the interpretation is dependent would appear to be considerably broader than the immediate linguistic context. It is perhaps even as broad as the entire knowledge (or belief) situation of the speaker and hearer (including, to a degree, their beliefs about each other). On the other hand, suppose the speaker uses "and" in a locution whose standard interpretation is non-truth-functional and subsequently contradicts the normal implications of that interpretation (e.g., by indicating perhaps that the second element preceded the first by some time). The most frequent reaction to this is not to claim or even suspect contradiction on the speaker's part, or even to correct the speaker, but rather to change one's interpretation, frequently to the truth-functional one. As I have indicated, the same phenomena can be observed with other logical words and also (as our rain example illustrates) in non-logical words as well. Nevertheless, when the particular situation is in the class of transactions we call reasoning, we find these shift phenomena receding and instead we observe a tendency to insist as far as feasible on stability of meaning, either by means of explicit assumptions or according to more or less regular patterns of inference. Exactly **which** meanings are assigned in this kind of informal or colloquial reasoning is specified only as it appears to be required in the particular case and the "rules" followed are not generally fully specified. The move to a regularized, fully specified set of rules thus constitutes a completion of this tendency, and relative to colloquial language, constitutes a sort of idealization.

Calculi as we defined them in chapter 1 are virtually as broad as games in general. Even the restriction to "logics" only regularizes the role of some concepts. But what makes this kind of system interesting, either from the standpoint of its origin in the regularization of informal reasoning or from that of its projected use as a canon by which reasoning, when challenged or questioned, may be justified, is that a certain kind of property is preserved by the rules: specifically, the property of being "true." In this context, truth is taken in the very wide and pre-metaphysical sense which assumes that what is true can justifiably be accepted, although we leave the reason for this open, and we certainly do not specify the exact account or definition of "truth." Accordingly, if a calculus is to function as a logic, the set of rules must be truth-preserving (note that this does not assume that "truth" is necessarily a truth-value, though of course it doesn't exclude it). From this viewpoint, the rules specifying derivations are most important. Those rules resulting in theses, what we have termed T-theorems in the main text, are of interest primarily in their effect on the derivations they validate. If the rules are truth (or if you prefer "truth") preserving, these simply correspond to those truths which can be known by virtue of the rules alone.

One of the consequences of this is that the most significant concept of equivalence is that of sameness of derivability. Some systems, as for example **S1** and **S1*** as defined in chapter 10, can have all theses in common, even though not all true Y-statements are in common. For example, p ⥼⥽ q ⊢ ◇p ⥽ ◇q holds in **S1*** but not in **S1**. This divergence does not however affect the provable formulae. With respect to acceptable interpretations or models, some authors have introduced the concept **strong model** for interpretations for which the rules are truth-preserving in the sense explained, and **weak model** for those that are "necessary-truth preserving."

What I have been saying above amounts to insisting that for full consideration of the character of a system, the strong, rather than the weak, models are of primary interest. For example a weak model (though in my opinion, not a particularly interesting one) of **WIN** is one in which

$\sim A$ is interpreted as $\sim\Diamond A$ and $A \supset B$ is interpreted as $\Diamond A \mathrel{-\!\!3} \Diamond B$, where the interpretations are in a (minimally) S5 modal logic. This can be seen by the fact that the axiom schemata of WIN2 are theorems of S5 (under the proposed translation) and ($\vdash A$ and $\vdash \Diamond A \mathrel{-\!\!3} \Diamond B$) implies $\vdash \Diamond B$ (since $A \vdash \Diamond A$). But since in S5, $\Diamond B$ is provable if and only if B is (this is an immediate consequence of S5-1 and D-3), all T-theorems of WIN2 and hence of WIN are provable. If however one really attempted to interpret WIN in this fashion and hired oneself out as an interpreter in a community which actually used WIN as a logic, his clients would be bewildered by the apparent insistence of the natives for concluding B from A and $\Diamond A \mathrel{-\!\!3} \Diamond B$, since B does not follow (in S5) if A is true and B false, but B is possible.

After these general observations, it is perhaps desirable to state those results which appear to have some philosophical interest and which follow from the results stated in the main work. This list is by no means intended to be complete and the reader may well find others of equal or greater interest.

1. Although the characterization of a formal system for logic must, of course, rely to some degree on a language that is understood and hence, presumably, on a natural language, the natural language elements involved are much fewer than might be imagined; these are the ability to recognize when two tokens are of the same type and when one token follows another, and in addition, the ability to follow simple instructions of the general type of transfer orders on computers; not to "understand" them except in the weak sense in which this "understanding" can be identified with following. Although these operations are epistemologically interesting in various ways, their characterization in natural languages does not involve the peculiar kinds of semantic adjustments discussed earlier in this chapter. In computer terms, the features of language which do involve those adjustments are either beyond the state-of-the-art in artificial intelligence or else involve advanced AI programs. The operations required for logic are of the kind that require only relatively simple algorithmic processes. General proofs concerning systems involve considerably more. By and large the extra underlying theory involved is mathematical; it includes substantial portions of elementary number theory and at least the recursive portions of set theory, but not any large additional portion of "ordinary" or non-mathematical language. Of course, whatever problems of a philosophical kind emerge from these theories can fairly be considered as haunting the

proofs based on them. These problems however do not affect the constructed systems themselves or, with a few exceptions, the theorems of the kinds we have referred to as T and D, or, for that matter, in most cases, the particular instances of more general theorems.

2. By far the greater number of forms of inference ordinarily accepted and which can be formulated in terms of "if--then" alone, rely on very simple properties of "if--then," specifically on the positive implication rules modus ponens and conditionalization.

3. Similarly, the greater number of forms of inference involving "implication" and "negation" (i.e. those that can be expressed with "if" and "not") depend only on positive implication rules plus the assumption that contradiction is effectively constant in meaning.

4. Despite their weakness, the specifications referred to in points 2 and 3 are sufficient to generate inference forms considered by some to be paradoxical (none of them are actual contradictions).

5. The feature of containing most of the more frequently used inferences expressible is preserved when correspondingly weak specifications of "and" and "or" are added. These include the so-called "principle of contradiction" [$\sim(A \wedge \sim A)$].

6. Despite the large number of inference forms which hold in these relatively weak systems, the ability of negation to serve as a device to guarantee rejection does not follow [even when $\sim(A \wedge \sim A)$ is provable]. The main function of the rule $A, \sim A \vdash B$ appears to be precisely to guarantee the rejectiveness of negation. Of course, the provability of $A, \sim A \vdash \sim B$ in systems like PINEAK would appear to make most of the objections difficult to sustain unless the logic were weakened further.

7. Although a plausible system of implication which satisfies intuitive notions of relevance can be defined, and can be extended to negation rather reasonably, a similar extension to normal conjunction and disjunction cannot succeed. This means that to ensure that it is weaker than PINEAK, forms of inference which we would otherwise be ill-disposed to reject, have to be given up; the most famous system of this nature rejects modus tollendo ponens (i.e., $\sim A, A \vee B \vdash B$) and restricts adjunction.

Points 2 through 7 may perhaps appear a little like a lawyer's brief for limiting our choice of reasonable working logic to the interval between intuitionistic systems (e.g., WINEAK) and classical ones (e.g., CINEAK). It should however be pointed out that it is not necessarily unreasonable to give up the (so-called syntactic) guarantee of the rejective character of negation. A view of language might guarantee or justify rejectiveness by other means, perhaps semantic or metaphysical, provided, of course, A, ~A ⊢ B really did seem more objectionable than A, ~A ⊢ ~B. Similarly, under sufficient provocation, men whom we would hesitate to consider as rash or unreasonable, have given up in other areas (e.g., foundations of mathematics, ethics, physics) principles as ancient and popularly accepted as tollendo ponens. The basic question then becomes, whether the provocation is sufficient and how hampered we are by the weakening of the system.

8. If the abstract equivalent of the derivability relation ("logical implication," or perhaps, "entailment") is a species or the whole of strict implication, the Lewis systems S1 through S3 would appear to be unjustifiably weak or else too strong. Depending on the meaning of the modalities preferred, if classical (i.e. two-valued complete) logic is acceptable for non-modal inference, the systems T, S4 and S5 have significant advantages in plausibility. There are however an infinite number of systems in the range between T and S5, and the reasons for preferring the three I mentioned are largely out of the scope of this book. Furthermore, if "logical implication" is just one species of strict implication, and the other varieties are sufficiently different, the systems between K and T may come into consideration (as they certainly would, for instance, for deontic modalities). Of course the weaker systems S1-S3 or S1*-S3* may conceivably define a meaning of the modalities which is less intimately tied to the derivability relation. In addition, we have not, in this book, even considered modal systems whose non-modal portion is weaker than classical logic.

9. Each of the standard logical operations (positive implication, normal disjunction, normal conjunction, rejective disjunction, positive equivalence) has the interesting property that there can be at most one such (non-equivalent) operation in a sufficiently well-behaved logic. One consequence of this is that, despite the fact that the differences between intuitionistic and classical implication, or disjunction, or negation, are in some sense due to their meaning, this type of meaning difference cannot be accurately represented by having both varieties occur within a single logic.

10. Other than the relatively simple mathematical character of the model theory for complete logic or attachment (or the contrary) to the equivalence between ~~A with A, there is not much on an elementary level to justify a choice of complete over intuitionistic logic or vice versa.

This would appear to be in agreement with the greater number of intuitionist authors who base this choice on the constructive character of mathematics and on doubts concerning the inference $\sim\forall vA \vdash \exists v\sim A$. The rejection of the "law of the excluded middle" would from this point of view be based in part on the absence of sufficiently strong elementary considerations favoring it, but primarily on the consequences of adopting it, particularly in set theory. These consequences, mostly revolving around the issues of impredicative definition, the "axiom of choice" and the use of non-constructive methods generally, lie outside the scope of this book.

Appendix
Historical and Bibliographical Remarks

1. Historical Notes

The purpose of this section is to satisfy the historical interests of the reader and, as far as I am able, to discharge the obligations of academic honesty.

Before entering into the details, I would like to point out that more of my ideas than I am able to trace are due to the influence of my teachers of logic: Rudolf Carnap, Evert W. Beth, Arend Heyting, and Stephen C. Kleene, to whom I must add, primarily through their writings, Alonzo Church and Alfred Tarski. The influence of these teachers on my thinking is so pervasive that the tracing of any idea of mine to one or more of them would never surprise me.

With regard to more specific indebtedness:

Chapters 1-2: The modern concept of logical calculus on which these definitions rest is primarily due to Gottlob Frege and to a lesser degree to David Hilbert, Bertrand Russell, and Charles Saunders Peirce. The formulation of structure and derivation concepts is, I believe, original in its detail, but to a considerable degree, is based on formulations by Church, Rosser, and to a lesser degree, Carnap and Gentzen.

Chapter 3: The greater portion of this chapter is based on the work of E.L. Post and J.B. Rosser.

Chapter 4: With few exceptions, the systems in chapters 4 - 9 were determined by a natural architectonic. Most of them had however been independently developed earlier and the following notes indicate the earliest source I have been able to discover.

The first formulation of a system equivalent to $\mathcal{P}1$ is in David Hilbert, Die Grundlagen der Mathematik, **Abhandlungen aus dem mathematischen Seminar der Hambürgischen Universität**, vol. 6 (1928), pp. 65-85. $\mathcal{P}2$ is due to Lukasiewicz.

An interesting formulation of **P1** first proposed by Meredith has modus ponens as the only rule and one axiom scheme:

$$\vdash [A \supset (B \supset C)] \supset [D \supset \{[B \supset (C \supset E)] \supset (B \supset E)\}],$$

in Single Axioms for the systems (C,N), (C,O) and (A,N) of the Two-valued Propositional Logic, **Journal of Computing Systems**, vol. 3, (1953), pp. 155-164.

Chapter 5: The first formulation of a system equivalent to **P1N** was by A.N. Kolmogorov in O principe tertium non datur(Russian), **Mathematitscheski Sbornik**, vol. 32 (1924-5), pp. 646-667. A system equivalent to **W1N** has been treated in A. Arnold Schmidt, **Mathematische Gesetze der Logik**, 1960.

Chapter 6: The first system equivalent to **1NC** is that of Frege's **Begriffschrift**. **1NC**-3 is due to Lukasiewicz and a variety of **1NC** (based in part on **1NC**-3) has appeared in Mates, **Elementary Logic**.

The general method used in the completeness proof is due to Leon Henkin and is frequently known in the literature as a Henkin style proof. It was first used for a slightly different purpose in Completeness of the First-order Functional Calculus, **Journal of Symbolic Logic**, vol. 14 (1949), pp. 159-166.

The first published system equivalent to **1AC** was that of Charles S. Peirce in the article On the Algebra of Logic, **American Journal of Mathematics**, vol. 7 (1885), pp. 180-202, reprinted in **Collected Works**, vol.3, pp. 210-238. An **1AC** system more closely related to the one used in this book appeared in Church, **Introduction to Mathematical Logic**, vol. I, 1956.

Chapter 7. **ANC**-3 is the first published system equivalent to **ANC**. It first appeared in Russell, Mathematical Logic based on the Theory of Types, **American Journal of Mathematics**, vol. 30 (1908), pp. 222-262, but has acquired its fame by being the propositional (i.e., zero-order) logic used in **Principia Mathematica**, 1910.

Chapter 8. The first system equivalent to **NKC** was due to Sobocinski, Aksjomatyzacja implikacyjno-konjunkcyjnej teorii dedukcji, **Prezeglad Filozoficzny**, vol. 37 (1935).

Chapter 9. Most published calculi define the bi-conditional [usually as (A ⊃ B) ∧ (B ⊃ A)], rather than use it as a primitive. As long as a standard conjunction can be defined, those systems show the same properties as those we have cited. We call such systems PINAK, WINAK and CINAK (for the systems that correspond to PINEAK, WINEAK and CINEAK, respectively).

The first system equivalent to PINAK was by Ingebrigt Johanssen, Der Minimalkalkül, ein reduzierter intuitionistischer Formalismus, **Compositio Mathematicae**, vol. 4 (1936), pp. 119 - 136. It is usually referred to as Johanssen's **Minimalkalkül**.

A system equivalent to WINAK (analogous to WINEAK2) by Arend Heyting appeared in Die formalen Regeln der intuitionistischen Logik, **Sitzungsberichte der preussischen Akademie, phys.-math. Klasse** (1930), pp. 42-56. WINAK (and hence also WINEAK) is frequently called **intuitionistic propositional logic**.

S.C.Kleene, **Introduction to Metamathematics**, Amsterdam, 1952, has a system equivalent to CINAK . The system CINAK itself was first developed by me in 1951 as a classroom example. It is however possible that it was suggested to me the year before by Beth or Kleene in conversation. CINEAK proper was introduced by me in class work sometime prior to 1970.

Chapter 10. The earliest modern systematization of a modal logic was S3, characterized by Lewis in **A Survey of Symbolic Logic**, Berkeley, 1918. S1, S2, S4, S5 are described in Lewis and Langford, **Symbolic Logic**, New York, 1932. In all of these systems, only what we have called "provability" (i.e. derivability from the null set) is defined. As a result the distinction between S1 and S1* (and S2 and S2*) cannot be expressed (since they have the same T-theorems). A system equivalent to S1' has been defined by Robert Feys in Les logiques nouvelles des modalités, **Revue Néoscholastique de Philosophie**, vol. 40 (1937), pp. 517-553, and vol. 41 (1938), pp. 217-252; another variant of it was apparently independently also introduced by von Wright in **An Essay on Modal Logic**, Amsterdam, 1951.

Chapter 11. The model theoretic methodology of this chapter is based on the notions which emerged in the late '50s and early '60s, unquestionably inspired by Carnap's **Meaning and Necessity**. The earliest well-known publication of this appears to be Kripke, Semantic Analysis of Modal Logic, **Zeitschrift für mathematische Logik und Grundlagen der Mathematik**, vol.9 (1963), pp. 67-96. Much the same group of ideas were worked out independently by, among others, Kanger (possibly the earliest), Beth, Lemmon, Hintikka, and the present author. One result of this is that the details of the construction of the theory are likely to vary a little from author to author (although with few exceptions any result is usually translatable from one presentation to the other). In a similar way, Kripke in Semantical Analysis of Intuitionistic Logic,in Crossley and Dummett (eds.), **Formal Systems and Recursive Functions**, 1965, is the first to make the relation between intuitionist and modal model theory clear, and my presentation is certainly inspired by it. The corresponding proofs for PINEAK are perhaps more original, although it is difficult to disentangle my connections with Kripke and Beth. It should be added that there are definable model theories other than those of the Kripke family for many of the weaker modal logics.

Chapters 12 - 13. The earliest systematization of first-order logic, basically the same as CFOL but having only two connectives and one quantifier was in Frege's **Begriffschrift** in 1879. The first system completely equivalent to CFOL (except for the treatment of the bi-conditional) is apparently in Kleene,**Introduction to Metamathematics**

Chapter 14. The earliest publication of a first-order modal logic was Ruth Barcan (Marcus), A Functional Calculus of First-order based on Strict Implication, **Journal of Symbolic Logic**, vol.11 (1946), pp.1-16. Barcan's system is based on S4. The earliest system equivalent to MFOL is in Carnap's Modalities and Quantification, **Journal of Symbolic Logic**, vol. 11 (1946), pp.33-46. IFOL is equivalent to the first-order logic in Heyting, Die formalen Regeln der intuitionistischen Logik, **Sitzungsberichte der preussischen Akademie, phys.-math. Klasse** (1930), pp. 42-56.

The fact that virtually all presentations of logic from 1870 to 1930, (and the majority of those after 1930) do not define derivability makes the above identifications debatable in a few cases.

2. Bibliographical notes

The main purpose of this section is to suggest further reading on logic for the interested reader. For convenience, we will list by somewhat arbitrary topics.

A. Bibliography

An extremely thorough bibliography of symbolic logic from 1666 to 1935 is given by Alonzo Church, A Bibliography of Symbolic Logic, **Journal of Symbolic Logic**, vol. 1 (1936), pp. 121 - 218. Additions and an index by subject and author are in **Journal of Symbolic Logic**, vol. 3 (1938), pp. 178 - 212.

The **Journal of Symbolic Logic** has, since its founding in 1936, maintained an amazingly complete coverage of the field in its "Reviews" section. The index to this section accordingly comprises a very thorough bibliography. Volume 26 (1961) comprises an index of the first 25 volumes. In addition a two-year index by authors is issued in number 4 of even numbered volumes and a five-year index by subject in number 4 of every fifth volume.

An interesting bibliography of philosophical issues relevant to logic and of philosophical applications of logic (with less emphasis on technical issues) is C.A.B. Peacocke and Dana Scott, **A Selective Bibliography of Philosophical Logic**, Oxford, 1978.

B. Journals

The foremost journal on the subject is without question the **Journal of Symbolic Logic**. Additional journals specializing in logic are: **Archiv für mathematische Logik und Grundlagenforschung**, **Notre Dame Journal of Formal Logic**, **Studia Logica** (Warsaw), **Zeitschrift für mathematische Logik und Grundlagen der Mathematik**, and **Journal of Philosophical Logic.** Of course, many important articles have appeared in other journals, particularly those specializing in mathematics and philosophy.

C. Elementary Textbooks

There are many, many textbooks of logic designed for the elementary level. While I don't presume to judge them all, my favorites are:

1. David Hilbert and Wilhelm Ackermann, **Principles of Mathematical Logic**, New York, 1950.
2. Donald Kalish and Richard Montague, **Logic, the Techniques of Formal Inference**, New York, 1964.
3. Benson Mates, **Elementary Logic**, New York, 1965.
4. Willard V.O. Quine, **Methods of Logic**, New York, 1950.
5. E.J. Lemmon, **Beginning Logic**, New York, 1979.
6. J.B. Rosser, **Logic for Mathematicians**, New York, 1953.
7. Stephen C. Kleene, **Mathematical Logic**, New York, 1968.

D. Classical Works

1. Gottlob Frege,**Begriffschrift,eine der arithmetischen nachgebildete Formelsprache des reinen Denkens**, Halle, 1879.
2. Gottlob Frege, **Grundgesetze der Arithmetik, begriffschriftlich abgeleitet**, vol.1, Jena, 1893.
3. Ernst Schröder, **Vorlesungen über die Algebra der Logik (Exacte Logik)**, Leipzig 1890 - 1895.
4. Alfred North Whitehead and Bertrand Russell, **Principia Mathematica**, Cambridge, 1910 - 1912.

E. **Advanced General Logic**

A number of books on logic are general in scope, but more sophisticated than those listed under C. Three interesting and well-written surveys are:

1. Alonzo Church, **Introduction to Mathematical Logic**, Princeton, vol. 1, 1956.
2. Elliott Mendelson, **Introduction to Mathematical Logic**, New York, 1964; 2nd edition 1979.
3. J.R. Schoenfeld, **Mathematical Logic**, Reading (Mass.), 1967.

Also general, but with greater emphasis on model theory ("semantics"):

4. Rudolf Carnap, **Introduction to Mathematical Logic and Applications**, New York, 1958.
5. Heinrich Scholz and G. Hasenjäger, **Grundzüge der**

mathematischen Logik, Berlin, 1961.

An interesting treatment from a constructivist viewpoint can be found in:

6. Paul Lorenzen, **Formal Logic**, Dordrecht, 1970.

For treatments emphasizing logical systems, and to a degree proof theory ("syntax"):

7. A. N. Prior, **Formal Logic**, Oxford, 1961.
8. Haskell Curry, **Foundations of Mathematical Logic**, New York, 1963.
9. H.Arnold Schmidt, **Mathematische Gesetze der Logik I: Vorlesungen über Aussagenlogik**, Berlin, 1960.

An excellent anthology of the most significant journal publications from 1878 to 1931 is:

10. Jean van Heijenoort (ed.), **From Frege to Gödel (A Source Book in Mathematical Logic)**, Cambridge (Mass), 1967.

Another fine source book:

11. Larel Burka and Lothar Kreiser, **Logik - Texte**, Berlin, 1971

Three excellent surveys, primarily of recent research results:

11. Evandri Agazzi (ed.), **Modern Logic – A Survey**, Dordrecht, 1981.
12. Jon Barwise (ed), **Handbook of Mathematical Logic**, Amsterdam, 1977.
13. D Gabbay and F.Guenther (ed), **Handbook of Philosophical Logic**, Dordrecht, 1983- . 4 vols.

F. M-Valued Logics

1. E. L. Post, Introduction to a General Theory of Elementary Propositions, **American Journal of Mathematics**, vol. 43 (1921), pp. 163 - 185.
2. E. L . Post, **The Two-Valued Iterative Systems of Mathematical Logic**, Princeton, 1941.
3. J. B. Rosser and A. T. Turquette, **Many-Valued Logics**,

Amsterdam,1952.

4. Nicholas Rescher, **Many-valued Logic**, New York, 1969.
5. D. Rine (ed.), **Computer Science and Multiple-valued Logics: Theory and Applications**, Amsterdam 1977.

H. **Modal Logic**

1. C.I. Lewis, **A Survey of Symbolic Logic**, Berkeley, 1918.
2. C.I. Lewis and C. Langford, **Symbolic Logic**, New York, 1932.
3. Rudolf Carnap, Modalities and Quantification, **Journal of Symbolic Logic**, vol. 11 (1946), pp.33 - 64.
4. Robert Feys, **Modal Logic**, Louvain, 1965.
5. Saul Kripke, Semantical Analysis of Modal Logic I, **Zeitschrift für mathematische Logik**, vol. 9 (1963), pp. 67 -96.
6. G.E. Hughes and M.J. Cresswell, **An Introduction to Modal Logic**, London, 1968.
7. G.E. Hughes and M.J. Cresswell, **A Companion to Modal Logic**, London, 1984.

I. **Some Other Varieties of Logic**

1. Haskell Curry and Robert Feys, **Combinatory Logic**, Amsterdam, 1958.
2. P.R. Halmos, **Algebraic Logic**, New York, 1962.

J. **Proof and Structure Theory of Logic ("Logical Syntax")**

Probably the most significant works in general proof theory of logic are:

1. Rudolf Carnap, **Logical Syntax of Language**, London, 1937.
2. Alfred Tarski, **Logic, Semantics, Metamathematics**, (English translation of selected papers), Oxford, 1956 (especially chapters 5, 10 and 12).
3. G. Gentzen, Untersuchungen über das logische Schliessen, **Mathematische Zeitschrift**, vol. 39 (1934) pp.176 - 210 and 405 - 431.
4. J. Porte, **Recherches sur la Théorie generale des Systèmes Formales**, Paris, 1965.
5. D.W. Barnes and J. M. Mack, **An Algebraic Introduction to Mathematical Logic**, New York, 1975.
6. Helena Rasiowa, **An Algebraic Approach to Non-classical Logic**, Amsterdam, 1974.

K. **Model Theory of Logic ("Model Theory")**

Development of the basic notions underlying model theory are largely due to:

1. Alfred Tarski, The Concept of Truth on Formalized Languages, in **Logic, Semantics, Metamathematics**, Oxford, 1956.
2. Rudolf Carnap, **Introduction to Semantics**, Cambridge (Mass.), 1942.
3. Rudolf Carnap, **Meaning and Necessity**, Chicago, 1947.

A good summary of the above is:

4. Wilhelm Stegmüller, **Das Wahrheitsproblem und die Idee der Semantik**, Vienna, 1957.

An interesting variant:

5. R. M. Martin, **Truth and Denotation**, Chicago, 1958.

Good presentation of more advanced topics:

6. J.L. Bell and A.B. Slomson, **Models and Ultraproducts**, Amsterdam, 1969.
7. C.C. Chang and H.J. Keisler, **Model Theory**, Amsterdam, 1973.

L. **Foundations of Mathematics**

The principal applications of the more sophisticated parts of logic have been in the foundations of mathematics and the two subjects are closely related. The best general surveys are:

1. E.W. Beth, **Foundations of Mathematics**, Amsterdam, 1959.
2. R.L. Wilder, **Introduction to the Foundations of Mathematics**, New York, 1952.
3. William S. Hatcher, **Foundations of Mathematics**, Philadelphia, 1968.

Some valuable works from various viewpoints:

Logicist:

4. Bertrand Russell, **Introduction to Mathematical Philosophy**, London, 1919.

5. F.P. Ramsey, **The Foundation of Mathematics**, London, 1931.

Intuitionist:

6. L.E.J. Brouwer, **Collected Works**, vol.1, Amsterdam, 1975.
7. Arend Heyting, **Intuitionism: An Introduction**, Amsterdam, 1956.
8. S.C. Kleene and R.E. Vesey, **The Foundation of Intuitionistic Mathematics**, Amsterdam, 1965.
9. Michael Dummett, **Elements of Intuitionism**, Oxford, 1977.
10. A.S.Troelstra, **Choice Sequences, A Chapter in Intuitionistic Mathematics**, Oxford, 1977.

Constructivist, near-Intuitionist:

11. Paul Lorenzen, **Metamathematik**, Mannheim, 1962.

General Survey of Constructivist Mathematics

12. Michael J. Beeson, **Foundations of Constructive Mathematics**, Berlin, 1985.

Formalist:

13. David Hilbert and Paul Bernays, **Grundlagen der Mathematik**, Berlin, 1934 - 1939.

M. **(Mathematical) Proof Theory**

The theory of **mathematical** proof

1. Kurt Gödel, **On Formally Undecidable Propositions of Principia Mathematica and Related Systems**, New York, 1962. [Reprinted from **Monatshefte der Mathematik und Physik**, vol. 37 (1931), pp. 349 - 360; also in Heijenoort, **From Frege to Gödel**.]
2. Jacques Herbrand, **Logical Writings**, Cambridge (Mass.), 1971.
3. André Mostowski, **Sentences Undecidable in Formalized Arithmetic: An Exposition of the Theory of Kurt Gödel**. Amsterdam, 1952.
4. Karl Schütte, **Proof Theory**, Berlin, 1960.

N. **Set Theory**

Generally speaking, the theory of that part of reasoning pertaining to classes and relations not representable as general first-order logic (hence as special logics, most usually logics of the element relation, in the sense defined in chapter 12). My preferred general treatments are:

1. Abraham A. Fraenkel, **Abstract Set Theory**, Amsterdam, 1953.
2. F. Hausdorff, **Set Theory**, New York, 1957 (especially for introduction to topology).
3. W. Sierpinski, **Cardinal and Ordinal Numbers**, Warsaw, 1958.
4. J.L. Krivine, **Introduction to Abstract Set Theory**, Dordrecht, 1971.

Excellent presentation of various types of set theory:

5. Abraham A. Fraenkel and Yehoshua Bar Hillel, **Foundations of Set Theory**, Amsterdam, 1958.
6. Hao Wang and Robert McNaughton, **Les Systèmes Axiomatiques de la Théorie des Ensembles**, Paris, 1953.
7. Willard V.O. Quine, **Set Theory and its Logic**, Cambridge (Mass.), 1963.

Some important special studies:

8. Kurt Gödel, **The Consistency of the Axiom of Choice and the Generalized Continuum Hypothesis**, Princeton, 1940.
9. Paul J. Cohen, **Set Theory and the Continuum Hypothesis**, New York, 1966.
10. Thomas J. Jech, **The Axiom of Choice**, Amsterdam, 1973.
11. K.J. Devlin, **The Axiom of Constructibility**, Berlin, 1977.

O. **Recursive Functions**

The theory of the computable and decidable.

1. S.C. Kleene, **Introduction to Metamathematics**, Amsterdam, 1952.
2. Rosza Péter, **Recursive Functions**, Orlando (Fla.), 1967.
3. Hans Hermes, **Enumerability, Decidability, Computability**, Berlin, 1965.
4. Harley Rogers Jr., **Theory of Recursive Functions and**

Effective Computability, New York, 1967.
5. Marvin Minsky, **Computation: Finite and Infinite**, New York,1967.
6. Anne Yasuhara, **Recursive Function Theory and Logic**, Orlando (Fla.), 1971.

An excellent source book of the most significant papers:

7. Martin Davis, **The Undecidable**, Hewlett (N.Y.), 1962.

P. **History of Logic**

1. I. Bochenski, **A History of Formal Logic**, Notre Dame, 1961.
2. W. Kneale and M. Kneale, **The Development of Logic**, Oxford, 1964.
3. I.M. Bochenski, **Ancient Formal Logic**, Amsterdam, 1951.

Q. **Series**

One cannot responsibly give even an elementary list of important works in logic without mentioning **Studies in Logic and Foundations of Mathematics**, published since 1950 by North Holland Publishing Company of Amsterdam. This series which has now exceeded 100 volumes, has firmly established itself as the senior series for advanced publications in logic and closely related fields.

Subject Index

Index of Systems

Index of Symbols